The Guide to Franchising

The Guide to Franchising

7th edition

Martin Mendelsohn

CENGAGE
Learning™

For product information and technology assistance,
contact **emea.info@cengage.com**.

For permission to use material from this text or product,
and for permission queries,
email **clsuk.permissions@cengage.com**.

British Library Cataloguing-in-Publication Data
A catalogue record for this book is available from the
British Library.

ISBN: 978-1-84480-162-6

Cengage Learning EMEA
Cheriton House, North Way, Andover, Hampshire, SP10 5BE,
United Kingdom

Cengage Learning products are represented in Canada by
Nelson Education Ltd.

For your lifelong learning solutions, visit
www.cengage.co.uk

Purchase your next print book, e-book or e-chapter at
www.CengageBrain.com

Printed by Lightning Source, UK

Contents

Foreword

If guides to particular sections of the British business community are any test, franchising is now very much a mature sector. This seventh edition of *The Guide to Franchising* is, I estimate, very nearly eight times as large as the first edition which appeared in 1970. Martin Mendelsohn, Britain's leading international authority on franchising, has picked up an immense amount of knowledge and practical experience on the way and is not one of those to keep it to himself. He is a born teacher, as this book confirms. What is more, he gets results.

As he makes clear, he entered a plea in the first edition for a trade organization for franchising. In 2002 the British Franchise Association celebrated its silver jubilee while the Queen was marking her golden jubilee. As its president for the past ten years, I do not think it is boastful to say that it has fulfilled the aims Mr Mendelsohn set for it – to raise standards in franchising, protect and inform the public and provide an authoritative voice for franchising.

The BFA is, in fact, the only representative voice of franchising in Britain and through its director general, Brian Smart, plays a highly influential role in European and international franchising circles. I often think that governments would be better advised to make membership of the BFA and the right to use its three interlocking circles symbol as a kite mark a form of quality assurance rather than automatically thinking in terms of controlling franchising by legislation. But that may be for the future.

In the meantime, Mr Mendelsohn's guides have contributed to the development of franchising as well as chronicle its growth. One of the more recent developments is the BFA's growth into a trade association with three halls, as it were. It occupies the first – Franchising House, as we might call it – as the central representative and custodial body for business format franchising. In the second, Franchisor House, it looks after the interests of franchisors, the men behind the businesses. In the third and most recent, Franchisee House, it encourages franchisees through a forum to contribute their expertise to the sector's development. As chairman of that forum I have come to recognize just how much they have to offer and how open-minded and pragmatic they are in offering it.

All this is a sign of a healthy, thriving sector of the business. So are the extensive changes which Mr Mendelsohn has felt impelled to make to this edition. If that does not confirm its dynamism, I don't know what does.

Apart from reordering the sequence logically to explain what franchising is, why you might wish to enter it and how to practise it, it has new chapters on the impact of information technology (12) and 'not for profit' franchises (13); much new information on franchising in the USA and the wider world; and more case studies.

It is a comprehensive guide and all of us in or around franchising or contemplating entering it are in Mr Mendelsohn's debt. British franchising is singularly blessed with the active, constructive support of so many different services – banks, lawyers, accountants, consultants, the franchising media etc. – and the perspective that Mr Mendelsohn brings to the sector is one of those blessings.

Sir Bernard Ingham
President, British Franchise Association

Introduction

The first edition of this book was written in 1969 and published in 1970; it comprised only 84 pages of text. It is interesting to look back at some of the issues dealt with in that edition for their relevance today. The case for pilot operations was clearly stated:

> It is essential for the franchisor to set up his own operation, invest his own money in it and test it thoroughly in practice. It may be necessary and advisable for him to test the operation in a number of different locations so that the widest possible experience under varying conditions can be obtained before a franchise is sold.

It is now accepted that would be franchisors must properly and successfully pilot before embarking on a franchise programme.

There were four case studies: Budget Rent-a-Car; Five Minute Car Wash; Wimpy; and Dyno-Rod. Budget, Wimpy and Dyno Rod are still in operation Only Five Minute Car Wash has not survived.

There was a plea for the establishment of a trade organization:

> There is a clear need in the UK for a trade organisation to be set up by the franchise companies ... This organisation is what is needed in the UK to help raise standards of franchising and to afford protection to the public. In addition to protection for the public such an organization can provide a very valuable information service for them. In addition, it will enable the industry to speak with one authoritative voice on all matters concerning the interests of the industry. Franchising in the UK is, on the whole, developing along the right lines. If the industry will properly organise itself it will undoubtedly make rapid strides toward achieving respectability in the eyes of the public.

The subsequent establishment of the British Franchise Association in 1977 has answered that plea and the functions I advocated have largely been introduced, as well as others. Certainly the Association has created not only a positive profile for franchising but also a focal point, and has established ethical standards.

By the time the fourth edition was published in 1985 the text had grown to 21 pages followed by 102 pages of appendices. Franchising developed so considerably over the 19 years from that edition to the seventh edition that it is no surprise to see that growth in size of the text has continued.

This edition, with the encouragement of Anthony Haynes, the Editorial Director of my then Publisher, Continuum International Publishing Group Ltd, has resulted in a radical reorganization of the book and the inclusion of comments on differences between the UK and US markets, as well as a chapter on the US regulatory regime.

Many of the chapters have a recognizable structure, but every chapter has been rewritten, some more than others, and new material has been introduced. Indeed, I have been surprised at the number of changes I have made to the text. Some of the material has been developed from articles which first appeared in *Franchise World* and some has been developed from the work I have done in preparing for the many lectures which I give and seminars in which I participate in many parts of the world. In addition, there are two totally new chapters. Chapter 12 deals with the issues which arise from information technology and its effect on franchising. Chapter 13 recognizes the increasing number of franchise systems which charities and 'not for profit' organizations are developing. Many of them believe that they live in a different franchising world from that inhabited by commercial franchises but there are more similarities than many would like to acknowledge.

I have in the past had the pleasure of meeting a number of franchisors and franchisees who have expressed their thanks for the guidance they obtained from previous editions of this book. I hope that this edition will prove to be equally if not more useful, not only to those who wish to learn about franchising for the first time, but also to those who are already involved, in whatever capacity. The book is based upon my practical experience in a number of roles in franchising since 1964 and there is little in it that is not backed by the experience of actual events.

There are changes to the case studies: I have revisited the Wimpy franchise which was featured in the first edition of this work some 34 years ago. I have retained the Recognition Express franchise which appeared in the previous edition because it is undergoing a radical restructuring and provides an object lesson in how to handle such changes. I am sad that this time I am not able to acknowledge the assistance from Terry Howarth, who provided me with the information I received last time.

Unfortunately, Terry passed away just as I commenced work on this edition. Terry lived to enjoy the winning by Recognition Express of the BFA Franchisor of the year 2003, which brought him great pleasure. He was Vice Chairman of the BFA and Vice President of the European Franchise Federation, and was active in the World Franchise Council. His contribution to franchising reflected his commitment and was very significant. He was deeply and affectionately respected by all with whom he came into contact. He was a great family man and above all a wonderful human being. All who knew him will miss him but, as readers will see from the case study, the good he did lives on.

I have also selected as a case study Countrywide Gardens, which has been around for some 20 years, making steady progress while keeping a low profile.

On the international front I have retained the Mothercare franchise as a good example of the success in international markets of UK retailers.

I have looked to Australia for the second international case study, which is the Pirtek System, now to be found in ten countries and still growing.

My last case study, which is the subject of Chapter 20, is the Florence Melton Adult Mini-School Corporation, which is a good example of 'not for profit franchising'.

There are many to whom I must extend my thanks for their assistance. To those who gave their time to enable me to prepare the case studies: Max Wolfenden and John Davison of Wimpy, Nigel Toplis and Adrian Waite of Recognition Express, Martin and Simon Stott of Countrywide Gardens, Andy Pollock of Pirtek, Clive Revett of Mothercare and Jonathan Mirvis of the Florence Melton Adult Mini-School. My thanks also go to the franchise managers of the banks who provided me with updated information about their activities.

I cannot omit mention of Bob Rosenberg, past President and CEO of Allied Domeq US, who first introduced franchising and me to each other so many years ago when he was President of Dunkin' Donuts, now a part of Allied Domecq. I do not believe that either of us then could have guessed what our respective futures and the future of franchising would bring. One conclusion I can reach is that we were right to take it seriously. Franchising has happily brought me many personal friendships around the world with franchisors, lawyers, consultants, accountants, journalists and business people, without which life would have been poorer. I hesitate to single any out for special mention for fear of omitting someone from what would have to be a long list.

I am very grateful to John Baer, a lawyer friend who practices in Chicago as a partner in the firm Sonnenschein Nath & Rosenthal, LLP, for his annotations throughout the book to highlight the differences between UK and US practices, as well as his splendid chapter on the US regulatory regime, which adds a fresh dimension to this book.

Brian Smart, the Director of the BFA, was most helpful in giving of his time to assist with the information relating to the BFA. I am grateful to my ever patient and tolerant wife Phyllis who has always so wonderfully supported me. I am also greatly indebted to my secretary Julie Woods for her assistance in producing the typescript and for her ability to read my handwriting so well. Julie has now suffered in helping me to write seven editions of my various books and tells me that my writing is no better and perhaps worse than when she first started working with me.

My thanks to the publishing team at Thomson Learning for their assistance and encouragement.

Lastly and certainly not least, my thanks are due to Sir Bernard Ingham, the President of the BFA, for the honour that he has bestowed upon me by the foreword which he has so kindly and graciously contributed to this edition.

Martin Mendelsohn

*To Phyllis, Paul, Sarah, David, Susan,
Rafi, Daniel, Tamar, Sophie,
Avi and Jenna*

1

The meaning of 'franchise' and 'franchising'

Franchising as a legal or marketing concept was not new when its wide use commercially started to develop in the late 1940s and 1950s, principally in the USA as well as in other countries. Nevertheless, it is a concept which remains misunderstood by many despite its widespread use. Franchising is not an industry; it is a method of marketing goods and services which knows almost no boundaries in terms of business categories. Franchising has proved over many years in the UK, as well as in the rest of the developed world and in many developing countries, that it is a viable method of distributing goods and services which can have a positive influence on economic development by its contribution to the establishment of new businesses and job creation. Indeed, it can now be found in some 140 countries worldwide. Its efficacy is strengthened by its robustness through the periods of economic downturns which occur from time to time.

The advances made by the membership of the British Franchise Association in the 27 years of its existence are quite impressive (Chapter 16). There has been a steadily growing increase in interest from many business sectors, which is gaining in momentum, resulting in a rapidly expanding use of this marketing method.

Many large UK companies, particularly retailers, use franchising as a method of expanding internationally even though they do not franchise in their domestic market. UK companies are not alone in adopting this approach.

The history of franchising is discussed below in this chapter and it will be seen that franchising evolved out of a number of business transactions, methods and practices that have been common and popularly known for many years. Among the basic features of these business transactions, methods and practices are to be found the following elements.

1. The ownership by one person of a trademark, an idea, a secret process, a patent or a specialized piece of equipment and the goodwill and know-how associated with it.
2. The grant of a licence by that person to another permitting the exploitation of the trademark, service mark, idea, process, patent or equipment and the goodwill and know-how associated with it.

3. The inclusion in the agreement, granting the licence, of regulations and controls relating to the operation of the business, in the conduct of which the licensee exploits his or her rights.

4. The payment by the licensee of a royalty or some other consideration in the nature of a continuing fee for the rights which are obtained and for any services which the licensor will provide to the licensee.

These transactions are usually referred to as *licensing* arrangements and their features, as will be seen, among others, are also found in franchise transactions.

How, then, did franchising develop into what it is now? To put franchising into its proper perspective it is helpful to consider these well known business arrangements, which have been with us for so many years, and then to compare franchising with them. It is evident, with the benefit of hindsight, that franchising has evolved as a consequence of the natural development and blending of those arrangements. If this basic point is understood at this stage it will be considerably easier to understand properly the meaning of franchising.

One of the most common of these licensing arrangements arises out of the invention of some machinery or equipment. The inventor will wish to ensure that he enjoys the fruits of his invention to the full and will, as a first step, secure his exclusive rights by obtaining a patent. He may not have the financial resources or the knowledge to achieve the maximum nationwide or, indeed, worldwide exploitation which his invention merits. He may overcome this problem by entering into agreements with others who do have the financial resources and the business acumen to take the best possible advantage of the invention. He will therefore enter into an agreement granting a licence to the other party, permitting the manufacture, sale or perhaps merely the right to use the invention in return for a capital sum, a royalty or both. This arrangement makes the maximum use of the inventor's skills and know-how, on the one hand, and the financial resources, manufacturing, marketing and other abilities of the licensee, on the other hand.

Another of these arrangements arises out of the development of a trademark in relation to certain goods. The owner of the trademark, for reasons similar to those which motivate the inventor with his patent, will grant a right to others permitting them to manufacture the goods which are identified by the trademark. A trademark licence agreement contains provisions which regulate the standards to be observed in relation to manufacture, preparation, presentation, marketing and the quality of the goods. These provisions are necessary to preserve the standards of quality and the reputation associated with the trademark. So many of the elements of a franchise transaction are found in such an agreement that many franchise agreements incorporate its elements.

On a slightly different level are those now very common arrangements whereby the use of a famous name in entertainment, sports or even a cartoon strip character is licensed. This type of arrangement is referred to as 'character merchandising'. In each of these cases, by entering into licence agreements the owners of the names and their licensees are both obtaining benefits which would otherwise not be available to either.

There are other kinds of transaction designed to benefit licensor and licensee which are worthy of mention: the appointment of a dealer by a motor-car manufacturer (this is frequently a business format franchise, which is explained below); the appointment of exclusive sales distributors; the *licensing* of the use of the name of a large oil company on a garage. In the last case everyone is familiar with the Shell, Esso or BP station, but no one would think that all garages bearing an oil company's name are necessarily owned and operated by that company.

In many cases the rights granted are commonly called franchises by business people. The oil companies are increasingly franchising their service stations; for example, Shell introduced a service station franchise; and the Esso agreement for the operation of a shop on the forecourt is very similar to a franchise agreement. Conoco introduced franchising to the shops on their service station forecourts some years ago.[1] The supermarket chains are also expanding service station and standalone convenience store operations, but not under franchise.

What, then, is new? First, there is a wider use of the name 'franchising' to describe generically 'licence-type' transactions. Second, there is the 'business format' concept, whereby a person develops a complete system for the setting up and *licensing* of a business under an identified brand, which may be a trademark, service mark or trade name, and licenses (or franchises) others to trade, utilizing the particular system and the branding associated with it.

Clearly, there are many types of transactions entered into, all described as 'franchises', each having a different application. The differences will be apparent after the main type of franchise has been defined. To avoid confusion, the main type of franchise (i.e. the total business concept) will be referred to as a 'business format' franchise, which is the name by which it is commonly known. It is the business format franchise which has been responsible for the rapid escalation in the use of the franchised marketing method and for the wider public knowledge of its existence.

In this chapter, although there is reference to formal definitions, the main purpose is to develop an understanding of what franchising is and what is involved.

The business format franchise involves not merely the exploitation of goods identified by a trademark or services identified by a service mark, but the preparation of a 'blueprint' for a successful way of carrying on a business in all its aspects. The blueprint must have been carefully prepared to minimize the risks inherent in opening any new business. Examples of the necessary preparations are given below.

- Criteria will be established by which the suitability of sites available for the positioning of the business will be judged. In the case of a mobile franchise (e.g. ServiceMaster), criteria will be established by reference to the availability of potential customers within a given marketing area.

- Facilities will have been established so that franchisees can be trained in the system and business methods which the franchisor has developed.
- The training provided will include, as may be appropriate, any special methods of manufacture, or processes to be applied to goods, or (as with fast food operations) secret recipes, methods of preparation and the manner of providing services.
- Training will also be provided in the methods of marketing and merchandising which are calculated to exploit the merits of the business to the full and, one hopes, to avoid the pitfalls.
- Following training, assistance will be given in getting the business ready to open for trading.
- The right to use the description (i.e. the brand image, which may include a trademark or service mark) by which the business is to be distinguished from other similar competing businesses will be granted, while at the same time the business is recognized by the consumer as a part of the larger organization which comprises him and his fellow franchisees. Indeed, it could be said that franchising comprises, for the customer, the benefits of a multiple network in multiple ownership, resulting in the customer dealing with the owner rather than a manager of the business.
- In order that the person who is granting the licence can be sure that the standards associated with the branding and the system can be maintained there will need to be restrictions and controls introduced into the relationship established.

The seller of the blueprint (the franchisor) will have prepared and smoothed the way for a person (the franchisee), who invariably has never previously owned or operated a business, to open up a business of his own, not only with a predetermined and established format, but with the backing of an organization which would not otherwise be available to him at a cost which makes economic sense, i.e. the backing of an organization characteristic of the head office of a large company without many of the disadvantages. For the acquisition of the franchise and the continuing services which the franchisee will obtain (see below) there will, of course, be a fee payable.

What we have then is something fairly close to the four basic features mentioned on pp. 1 and 2.

1. The ownership by one person (the franchisor) of a trademark, trade name and business system which contains confidential and other proprietary information, and the goodwill and know-how associated with them.
2. The grant of a licence (franchise) by the franchisor to another (the franchisee) permitting the exploitation of such trademark, trade name and business system which contains confidential and other proprietary information, and the goodwill and know-how associated with them.

3. The inclusion in the licence (franchise) agreement of regulations and controls relating to the operation of the business in which the franchisee exploits the rights granted.

4. The payment by the franchisee of a fee or other consideration for the rights which are obtained and the services which the franchisor will continue to provide to the franchisee.

But, in addition and fundamentally, there will always be a continuing relationship which should provide the franchisee with the full support of a comprehensive range of expert knowledge in the operation of his business in the form of the 'head office organization' of the franchisor.

One could explain the concept in the following terms:

> The business format franchise is the grant of a licence by one person (the franchisor) to another (the franchisee) which permits (and usually requires) the franchisee to carry on business (having made an investment in its establishment) under the trade mark/trade name (the brand) of the franchisor and in doing so to make use of an entire package (know-how) comprising all the elements necessary to establish a person previously inexperienced and untrained in the conduct of a business developed by the franchisor under the brand and after training to run it on a pre-determined basis with continuing assistance from its franchisor, for all of which the franchisee pays fees to the franchisor.

There have been many attempts at a definition of a franchise in the USA, the progenitor of modern franchising. Most of them seek to provide a concise expression of the elements of the transaction, which has the effect of omitting much which should be included. Definitions are usually created for a particular purpose, e.g. a legal definition seeks to describe that to which the law is intended to apply. While this book does not seek to lay down a concise definition, the definitions which have been established for various purposes must be considered. It is hoped that this book will provide a basic commercial understanding which will enable the reader to put these formal definitions into perspective.

Before reviewing the definitions which have been prepared for legal purposes we shall examine the definitions which are used by the International Franchise Association (IFA), the US franchise association, and the British Franchise Association (BFA).

First we shall consider the IFA definition, or perhaps it should more fairly be regarded as a description.

> A franchise operation is a contractual relationship between the franchisor and franchisee in which the franchisor offers or is obliged to maintain a continuing interest in the business of the franchisee in such areas as know-how and training; wherein the franchisee operates under a common trade name, format and/or procedure owned or controlled by the franchisor and in which the franchisee has or will make a substantial capital investment in his business from his own resources.

This 'description' is concise and quite comprehensive, yet at the same time it leaves many questions unanswered and omits features which should be included. To be fair to the IFA it does not promote this as a definitive description. For example, it refers to the franchisee making an investment in his own business, yet nowhere does it say that the franchisee must own his business. This point, which is a fundamental feature of a franchise, is implied rather than asserted. Another fundamental feature which is omitted is the payment of fees or other consideration by franchisee to franchisor. Excellent as the definition is, it will be far better understood by those who already have a working knowledge of the underlying commercial rationale of franchising; the definition is not for those who seek an underlying understanding.

We now examine the elements of the IFA 'description'.

1. A franchise operation is a contractual relationship ...

It should clearly be established at the outset that the franchise relationship is based upon a contract[2] and that general contract law is usually the appropriate foundation for the relationship. It is no different from any other formal contract in that the terms upon which the contract is made are expressed in the contract. Perhaps it is just that bit more important that a franchise contract contains each and every term which has been agreed, for it is a contract with which the parties are going to have to live for a very long while. Moreover, in most cases it is going to be the sole provider of bread and butter (and hopefully a little jam and maybe a dollop of cream) to the franchisee, as well as, in many cases, enabling the franchisee to pursue a dream, so that any material omission will have an impact on the course of his life.

2. ... the franchisor offers or is obliged to maintain a continuing interest in the business of the franchisee in such areas as know-how and training ...

Of course, the franchisor must maintain a continuing interest in the franchisee's business, but first, at least, get the business started. This is the first point which is omitted from the description. It is the franchisor's obligation to introduce the franchisee to and initiate him in the business which he will be acquiring. It is also the franchisor's obligation to decide responsibly whether the prospective franchisee is in fact the right sort of person for that particular type of franchise. Nothing could be more disastrous for both parties than to place a square peg in a round hole. It is the franchisor's responsibility by pre-opening training to introduce the franchisee to all the relevant areas of the franchisor's know-how which the franchisee requires for the satisfactory establishment, conduct and operation of his business.

Know-how is one of those meaningless generic terms because, until one defines what is intended to be included in the expression, it has no specific meaning. Its meaning becomes evident when one knows what it comprises and it will, of course, differ from case to case. Know-how for one fast food operation will differ from another – between hamburgers and pizza, for example. Even the know-how in one hamburger operation is likely to differ from that employed in another.

Before the franchisee opens for business, the specific know-how which is a vital part of the blueprint he is being sold, must be communicated to him. Know-how in franchising, broadly speaking, covers merchandising as applied to the particular operation, application of the principles of business management appropriate to the nature and type of business being franchised, operational methods, accounting procedures, business methods, the franchisor's secret and confidential systems, methods and in some cases formulae or recipes.[3] The franchisee must be fully trained in all these aspects before he is let loose in his own business, and when he is let loose he should have any necessary on-the-spot support to assist him in successfully opening the business.

Having reached this stage, the franchisee should have a full grasp of know-how applicable to that particular business; the franchisor should continue to maintain these services on a regular and updated basis, coupled with the provision of field support to assist the franchisee through any difficulties he encounters and promotional assistance to help to maximize the beneficial exposure of the operation to the public, to the mutual advantage of franchisor and franchisee.

> 3. … wherein the franchisee operates under a common trade name, format and/or procedure owned or controlled by the franchisor …

This brings us to the central feature around which the blueprint is developed. In all franchises there is a common trade mark, service mark or trade name: the common format is the identical nature of the business carried on by all franchisees wherever they are. Included in this format are those features which make each operational unit run by franchisees appear to be part of the same network. In a premises-based franchise one would expect to recognize the identical appearance of each unit by the presentation of common shop front, shop signs, layouts, decor, colour scheme, equipment, fixtures and fittings. If the franchise is in the service sector and the operational unit is essentially an office there will not be a shop front but the other elements are likely to be found, although in some cases that level of regimentation may not be an essential component of the business. In a van-based franchisee (i.e. where the franchisee travels to customers) one would expect to find an identical vehicle colour and livery as well as the common fitting out of each vehicle with the necessary tools of the trade or, if product sales are involved, shelving and displays of the products. The vehicles may not always be of the same manufacture if their size is adequate. The common procedure refers to the operational methods of conducting the business that is the subject of the franchise which has been developed by the franchisor.

This part of the definition refers to those matters which constitute the basic operation, and by which the public clearly identifies the individual operation as being part of a larger group of similar operations while, of course, the operation and all its counterparts have the advantage of being run on a day-to-day basis by the owner and not by a manager.

The fact that the trade name, format and procedure are owned by the franchisor and used by all franchisees in common with each other is what makes an element of control over the franchisees' business essential. Whatever the degree of control exercised by a franchisor over any franchisee it should not be regarded by that individual merely as a restriction on his ability to run his business as he thinks fit. The franchisee in reality cannot enjoy the freedom which a non-franchisee has. The franchisee in taking up a franchised business is acquiring a right to establish a business with his own resources but using someone else's name and system, and he must accept that of necessity in order to preserve the uniformity, uniqueness and effectiveness of the business. He must run his business within the framework established by the franchisor. Anyone who does not wish to do so or is not prepared to accept such a discipline should not contemplate becoming a franchisee.

A franchisee must appreciate that the franchisor and all franchisees (including himself) are dependent upon each other for success. A customer lost at one outlet can also be a customer lost to all the others. In effect, the franchisor and all the franchisees are presenting a combined operation to the consumer. As a satisfied customer whose loyalty has been gained by good quality products and/or good service moves about the country or even a region he will patronize an operation apparently part of the group which has looked after him well before, rather than that of a competitor. The disciplines and the controls which go with them are an essential part of the mechanism by which success is achieved.

4. ... and in which the franchisee has or will have a substantial capital investment in his business from his own resources.

The franchisee owns his franchised business and all the assets which are employed in or about the conduct of that business. He must also have the right to sell the equity that he has developed in the business. At this point it is well to clarify an issue which raises much confusion, namely the question of 'goodwill'. There are two types of goodwill involved in franchising.

First, there is the goodwill that attaches to the branding, i.e. the trademark, the service mark and/or the trade name and the system. Since the branding and the system belong to the franchisor the goodwill generated by the use of the branding and system accrues to the benefit of the franchisor. In the franchise agreement (as will be seen in Chapter 11) the franchisor will grant the right to the franchisee to trade using the franchisor's branding and system and to benefit from the goodwill associated with them. Franchisees will enter the franchisee system and eventually leave, and when they leave, for whatever reason, they lose the right to continue to use the branding and the system and to benefit from the goodwill.

How a franchisee leaves the system is very relevant for the consideration of the other type of goodwill. This goodwill is that which arises for accounting purposes when a sale of a business takes place at a price which exceeds the value of its net assets. The excess is called goodwill by accountants and others. If a franchisee sells the franchised business (subject to the controls normally imposed in a franchisee agreement; Chapter 11) for a sum in excess of the value of its net assets, that excess belongs to the franchisee. If that were described as the value of the franchisee's equity in his own business, which is what it is, rather than goodwill, there would be no confusion. This equity represents the value of the business as a going concern and the ability to build it is one of the motivating factors for franchisees.

The reference to the capital investment is not superfluous. It is important that a franchisee makes a capital investment that is a significant investment of his own resources – something he cannot afford to lose. This goes a long way in providing him with the necessary motivation. A person who has the money which he has invested at stake, and who can see that he has the opportunity to control the destiny and growth of his equity by his diligent attention to the correct operation of the business, will put everything he can into the business and not the lesser interest of a manager.

So far there has been no mention of payment. No franchisor is going to give anything away for nothing. If it appears that he is doing so this is something which should be investigated. No one is in business to make gifts of his products or services. Franchisors are no exception to this general rule. Payment may be made to the franchisor in any number of ways. He may ask for a franchise fee by name. He may sell a package which has the franchise fee included in the price. He may receive a fee calculated as a percentage of the franchisee's gross receipts. Whichever way the fees are to be taken by the franchisor, he will be paid both for his initial services and for the continuing service that he provides.

One other factor which must be touched upon at this stage is the issue of territorial rights, which is dealt with in more detail in Chapter 10. This is a subject on which there can be no general rule, save that franchisees will seek some assurance that where there are fixed premises the surrounding area will not be over-saturated to their detriment. Where there is a mobile franchisee the question of territorial scope becomes more significant. This issue can create many problems, for some franchised operations will thrive upon a massive saturation of an urban area while others will, by their nature, require a carefully defined and protected area of operation. Apart from the business considerations there are legal implications which arise from the application of competition laws. These considerations and implications are dealt with in detail later in this book.

We now examine the BFA definition and contrast it with the IFA description which has just been considered.

A contractual licence granted by one person (the franchisor) to another (franchisee) which:

(a) permits or requires the franchisee to carry on during the period of the franchise a particular business under or using a specified name belonging to or associated with the franchisor;

(b) entitles the franchisor to exercise continuing control during the period of the franchise over the manner in which the franchisee carries on the business which is the subject of the franchise;

(c) obliges the franchisor to provide the franchisee with assistance in carrying on the business which is the subject of the franchise (in relation to the organization of the franchisee's business, the training of staff, merchandising, management or otherwise);

(d) requires the franchisees periodically during the period of the franchisee to pay to the franchisor sums of money in consideration for the franchisee or for goods or services provided by the franchisor to the franchisee; and

(e) which is not a transaction between a holding company and its subsidiary (as defined in Section 154 of the Companies Act 1948) or between subsidiaries of the same holding company or between an individual and a company controlled by him.

Apart from paragraph (e), which clearly has a technical basis, and is calculated to exclude in-house arrangements, the definition embodies much of the IFA definition which has been analysed above. The following points of comparison will be of interest.

The definition:

(i) confirms the contractual nature of the relationship;

(ii) confirms that there is a right or licence granted to the franchisee to carry on the business. The definition, however, does not:

(a) provide that the franchisee must own his own business;

(b) state that the franchisee must provide for his investment out of his own resources; and

(c) confirm that the franchisor will be obliged to provide initial training;

(iii) deals with the question of control by the franchisor over the manner in which the franchisee carries on the business;

(iv) confirms the obligation of the franchisor to provide the continuing assistance which is so essential; and

(v) deals with the question of the payment of franchisee fees.

Like all definitions, it has been coined for a particular purpose, and no doubt it was the intention of the BFA to frame its definition on such a basis that membership will be available to companies whose franchise, while not strictly a 'business format' franchise, is still a franchise of a more limited nature (see Chapter 2 for a discussion on other types of franchises). Membership of the BFA carries with it responsibilities, and it is clearly in its interests and in the interest of members of the public that, as long as the business to be conducted is what may be reasonably described as a franchise within the generic sense in which the term is understood in business circles, such a franchisor should have the ability to join the BFA. The BFA is dealt with in detail in Chapter 16.

It is significant that the definition omits reference to the initial training setting up the business, and it is also significant that the definition omits the requirement that the franchisee should have made a substantial capital investment out of his own resources in the business he would operate, but the omission of these factors does not prevent this definition from having its intended meaning.

The parallels between the two definitions are quite clear, and from these definitions and this discussion emerge the following basic features which should be present in a 'business format' franchise.

1. A franchise relationship is founded upon a contract, which should contain all the terms agreed upon.
2. The franchisor must first develop a successful business format (the system) which is identified with a brand name, which may be a trademark, service mark and/or trade name.
3. The franchisor must initiate and train the franchisee in all aspects of the system prior to the opening of the business so that the franchisee is equipped to run the business effectively and successfully and assist in the opening.
4. After the business is opened the franchisor must maintain a continuing business relationship with the franchisee in the course of which it provides the franchisee with support in all aspects of the operation of the business.
5. The franchisee is permitted under the control of the franchisor to operate under the branding format (trademark, service mark, trade name) the business systems developed and owned by the franchisor and to benefit from the goodwill associated therewith.
6. The franchisee must make a substantial capital investment from his own resources.
7. The franchisee must own his business.
8. The franchisee will pay the franchisor in one way or another for the rights which he acquires and for the continuing services with which he will be provided.

Having looked in outline at the commercial arrangement which lies behind the franchise method of marketing and the definitions used by two major franchisee associations, we now examine the approach adopted by those who have established legal definitions of franchising. Before we do so it is important to understand that legal definitions do not seek to explain; they seek to establish a method of identifying a particular business practice with which it is proposed to deal in the legislation in which the definition appears. There are four legal definitions which will be considered.

First, there is a definition of franchising in Section 75 of the Financial Services Act 1986:

> franchise arrangements, that is to say, arrangements under which a person earns profits or income by exploiting a right conferred by the arrangements to use a trade name or design or other intellectual property or the goodwill attached to it.

This definition is scarcely helpful for understanding and is flawed: what is intended to be meant by income which is earned as distinct from profits, and why the use of 'or' when detailing the intellectual property element and goodwill when 'and' would be more appropriate? Since the definition of franchise arrangements is intended to exclude them from the definition of 'a collective investment scheme', which definition clearly does not include franchising, the worthlessness of the definition, to put it at its most charitable, for the purpose of the discussion is clear.

The next definition is that which appeared in the Block Exemption Regulation for Franchise Agreements, which was adopted by the European Commission on 30 November 1988. This Regulation provided exemption from the competition (anti-trust) laws of the European Community for those agreements which complied with its terms. This Regulation expired on 31 December 1999 and was replaced by a new Regulation (Block Exception Regulation for Vertical Agreements; see Chapter 10). Although the 1998 Regulation is no longer in force, its definition, which is not used in the new Regulation, is worth consideration.

> 'franchise' means a package of industrial or intellectual property rights relating to trade marks, trade names, shop signs, utility models, designs, copyrights, know-how or patents, to be exploited for the resale of goods or the provision of services to end users.

This definition is limited and technical but clearly recognizes the role of branding and know-how (the system). However, it is confined to franchises where the franchisee is selling goods or providing services to an end user (i.e. the ultimate consumer). The definition is deliberately limited since the European Commission made it plain in the preamble to the Regulation that industrial franchisees (i.e. those which concern the manufacturing of goods) were not intended to be governed by the Regulation, since they consist of manufacturing licences based upon patents and/or technical know-how, combined with trademark licences. The definition also excludes franchises involving the sale of goods at wholesale level, since the Commission lacked experience of such franchises, without which it did not feel able to legislate.

The Commission definition did not stop at the treatment of the word 'franchise'; it defined a 'franchise agreement' and it is in this definition that many of the business features which we have discussed emerge.

The expression 'franchise agreement' means an agreement whereby one undertaking, the franchisor, grants the other, the franchisee, in exchange for direct or indirect financial consideration, the right to exploit a franchise for the purposes of marketing specified types of goods and/or services. It includes at least obligations relating to:

- the use of a common name or shop sign and a uniform presentation of contact premises and/or means of transport;
- the communication by the franchisor to the franchisee of know-how;
- the continuing provision by the franchisor to the franchisee of commercial or technical assistance during the life of the agreement.

Some of the words contained in this definition were themselves defined:

'contact premises' means the premises used for the exploitation of the franchisee or, when the franchise is exploited outside those premises, the base from which the franchisee operates the means of transport used for the exploitation of the franchise (contract means of transport).

'know-how' means a package of non-patented practical information resulting from experience and testing by the franchisor which is secret, substantial and identified.

The expressions 'secret', 'substantial' and 'identified' were also defined but for the purpose of this discussion they are not relevant.

These two definitions of 'franchise' and 'franchise agreement' should for our purpose be read together. They blend the definitions of what franchising is with some of the techniques which are used in structuring franchise arrangements. However, if we review these definitions against the basic features listed on pp 1 and 2 we find the following elements present.

1. There must be a contract (see definition of franchise agreement).
2. There must be a system developed (see definition of know-how).
3. There must be training (i.e. communication of know-how).
4. There must be continuing support (i.e. the continuing provision of services).
5. There must be the grant of the right to operate the business using the system and branding (i.e. one party grants to the other the right to exploit a franchisee and 'the use of a common name or shop sign').
6. These are barely implied in the definition but since the Regulation is conditional upon the franchisee indicating its status as an independent undertaking it seems the Commission takes these features for granted. Certainly the status of a franchisee as an independent business is recognized in the preamble to the Regulation.
7. There must be payment for the rights (i.e. 'in exchange for direct or indirect financial consideration').

As well as providing a legal definition for the purposes of the Regulation it will be seen that the Commission has also incorporated a number of the commercial features which form part of the overall description of a franchise, as well as the techniques for implementing a franchise programme which are discussed in this book.

The final definitions to which reference should be made are those which are to be found in the USA, where there is much legislation in which franchising is defined. There are two definitions to which reference will be made. The first is that which appears in the state of California legislation, which was the first franchise legislation when introduced in 1970 and effective 1 January 1971.

'Franchise' means a contract or agreement, either express or implied, whether oral or written, between two or more persons by which:

(1) a franchisee is granted the right to engage in the business of offering, selling or distributing goods or services under a marketing plan or system prescribed in substantial part by a franchisor;

(2) the operation of the franchisee's business pursuant to such plan or system is substantially associated with the franchisor's trademark, service mark, trade name, logo type, advertising or other commercial symbol designating the franchisor or its affiliate; and

(3) the franchisee is required to pay, directly or indirectly, a franchisee fee.

The definition is extended to include contracts involving petroleum dealers and there are also definitions of franchisor, franchisee and franchise fee.

This definition of 'franchise' is less extensive than the European Commission's definition and is typical of those which have been adopted in statutes in those states in the USA which have laws which directly focus on franchising.[4]

The second US definition at which we shall look is that which appears in the Federal Trade Commission Franchise Rule. This rule became effective in 1979 and has the following definitions.

(a) The term 'franchise' means any continuing commercial relationship created by any arrangement or arrangements whereby:

(1)(i)(A) A person (hereinafter 'franchisee') offers, sells, or distributes to any person other than a 'franchisor' (as hereinafter defined) goods, commodities, or services which are:

(1) identified by a trademark, service mark, trade name, advertising or other commercial symbol designating another person (hereinafter 'franchisor'); or

(2) indirectly or directly required or advised to meet the quality standards prescribed by another person (hereinafter 'franchisor') where the franchisee operates under a name using the trademark, service mark, trade name, advertising or other commercial symbol designating the franchisor; and

(B) (1) The franchisor exerts or has authority to exert a significant degree of control over the franchisee's method of operation, including but not limited to the franchisee's business organization promotional activities management, marketing plan or business affairs; or

(2) The franchisor gives significant assistance to the franchisee in the latter's method of operation, including, but not limited to, the franchisee's business organization, management, marketing plan, promotional activities or business affairs; provided however that assistance in the franchisee's promotional activities shall not, in the absence of assistance in other areas of the franchisee's method of operation constitute significant assistance; or

(ii)(A) A person (hereinafter 'franchisee') offers sells or distributes to any person other than a 'franchisor' (as hereinafter defined) goods, commodities or services which are:[5]

(1) Supplied by another person (hereinafter 'franchisor') or

(2) Supplied by a third person (e.g. supplier) with whom the franchisee is directly

or indirectly advised to do business by another person (hereinafter 'franchisor') where such person is affiliated with the franchisor; and

(B) The franchisor:

   1) Secures for the franchisee retail outlets or accounts for said goods, commodities or services; or

   (2) Secures for the franchisee locations or sites for vending machines, rack displays, or any other product sales display used by the franchisee in the offering, sale, or distribution of such goods, commodities or services; or

   (3) Provides to the franchisee the services of a person able to secure the retail outlets, accounts, sites or locations referred to in paragraph (a)(1)(ii)(B)(1) and (2) above; and

(2) The franchisee is required as a condition of obtaining or commencing the franchise operation to make a payment or a commitment to pay to the franchisor or to a person affiliated with the franchisor.

The terms 'franchisor' and 'franchisee' are broadly defined:

The term franchisor means any person who participates in a franchise relationship as a franchisor as denoted in paragraph (a) or this section [i.e. the paragraph defining 'franchisor'].

The term franchisee means any person (1) who participates in a franchise relationship as a franchisee as denoted in paragraph (a) of this section or (2) to whom an interest in a franchise is sold.

There are exemptions or exclusions, which briefly include:

- oral contracts, where there is no writing which evidences any material term or aspect of the relationship or arrangement;
- 'fractional franchises' where the franchisee has another related business and the franchised business does not represent more than 20% of the dollar sales volume of the franchisee;
- the total of payments to the franchisor or person affiliated to the franchisor are less than US$500 during the first 6 months of operations;
- employment relationship;
- partnership relationship;
- membership of a bona fide co-operative association; or
- a bare trademark licence.

It will be appreciated that while the first part of the definition relates to business format and product distribution franchises, the second part relates to the wider business opportunities field. Good examples of the sort of business opportunities which the definition includes are rack jobbing and vending machine routes.[6] Some of these opportunities can be structured as business format franchises.

The US definitions are limited to the 'nuts and bolts' and do not add to the basic elements what might be described as the methods of implementing a franchise in practice which the commercial and European definitions all contain.

The basic elements in these US definitions, however, do include many of the eight features listed above.

1. There must be a contract (but except for the FTC Franchise Rule, it need not be in writing to be caught by the US statutes).
2. There must be a system.
3. There must be a branding, i.e. trademark, service mark, trade name etc.
4. There must be a grant of rights.
5. There must be payment of money.

How all the elements are combined together, and the techniques which are employed to enable a franchise to be established and operated, are discussed in the chapters which follow.

Early history of franchising

It is possible to search through history and find examples of trading practices which have a resemblance to franchising. The guild system which was introduced in the City of London in the twelfth century is one such example. Many quote the tied public house system as an example of franchising, although it is merely an exclusive purchasing arrangement lacking many of the features of a franchise. In strict legal terms the word 'franchise' means a grant of rights from the crown and in some countries, e.g. the USA and Australia, it has been held by the courts that the word 'franchise' means a grant by a governmental authority. To this day there exist in the UK ancient franchises to hold fairs or markets and to provide ferries, bridges and fords across rivers and streams on the terms in which they were established, which still hold good.

The technique of franchising with which this book is concerned is generally believed to have started in the USA when, following the Civil War, the Singer Sewing Machine Company established a dealer network.

Whatever claims may be made by franchising communities in various parts of the world one must credit the United States business community with the ingenuity which has led to such a widespread use of the technique which is described in this book.

The technique of franchising did not derive from one moment of inventiveness by an imaginative individual. It evolved from the solutions developed by businessmen in response to the problems with which they were confronted in their business operations. It may be said that at the beginning of the twentieth century driving and drink (but not alcoholic) and drug stores were the catalysts for franchising activity, followed by a trickle of developments until the 1930s, when Howard Johnson started his famous restaurant chain in the USA, and the 1940s and 1950s, which saw the birth of so many of the modern giants of the world franchising community.

Categories of franchise

During these distinct phases different categories of franchising emerged and involved all levels in the chain from manufacturer to consumer. Thus we find franchisee arrangements between:

- manufacturer and retailer;
- manufacturer and wholesaler;
- wholesaler and retailer; and (lastly but certainly not the least)
- retailer and retailer.

The way in which each of these categories has benefited from its use of franchising is explained in some detail in Chapter 2.

The growth of franchising

In examining the growth of franchising one must start in the USA as not only is it the cradle of modern franchise development, but also it is the largest market place for franchising systems and until recently provided the best statistics. It is undoubtedly the largest exporter of franchising systems despite the great advances which have been made in other countries, notably Canada, Japan, Australia, France, Germany and the UK. Franchising in some form exists in over 140 countries and that number will continue to grow, although in many cases the number of franchise systems will be very small.

When one bears in mind that it was only in the 1950s that franchise systems began to develop in large numbers, the growth rate in the USA has been impressive. According to *Franchising in the Economy* (1988), whose publication by the US Department of Commerce has now been discontinued:

> Franchising sales of goods and services in more than 509,000 outlets were expected to reach $640 billion in 1988, about 7% higher than a year earlier and about 91% over the level of sales at the start of the 1980s. Employment in franchising, including part time workers, will probably reach 7.3 million by the end of 1988.

Product and trade name franchising, which typically include automobile and truck dealers, petrol filling stations and soft drink bottles, have achieved a growth in sales despite the reduction in the number of outlets. Almost the whole of the reduction is attributed to the closure of petrol filling stations. The publication shows sales of £72 billion in 1972 from

262,100 establishments compared with sales of £281 billion in 1988 from 140,820 establishments.

Business format franchising has been responsible for much of the growth of franchising in the USA since 1950. The publication shows sales of £17.9 billion in 1972 from 189,640 establishments compared with £118.8 billion in 1988 from 368,458 establishments – a rise of 6.62 times in sales and 1.94 in establishments. Although the figures which represent the position in 1988 (the last year for which such comprehensive figures were available) are themselves impressive, one must question whether the increases over a 16-year period fully justify the tremendous 'hype' which in the USA is attached to the growth rate of franchising. The number of business format franchisors offering their products and/or services to prospective franchisees also rose steadily from 909 franchisors in 1972 to 2177 franchisors in 1986.[7]

That the numbers involved are growing is undoubted but many of the increasing number are small and there are many whose lifespan in the statistics for whatever reason is quite short. It is also probable that there are more franchisors than the figures suggest, bearing in mind the difficulties in identifying and locating those who are involved in franchising.

The impact of franchising in the USA was (and probably still is) due in no small measure to large franchisors, those with 1000 or more units each, who dominate business format franchising, with 56 companies accounting for 48% of all sales and 49% of all establishments in 1986, the last date for which these figures are available. From the author's observations it is reasonable to suggest that this same pattern exists in many countries. It is no bad thing because these giants give franchising the favourable exposure which it needs to encourage the ambitious and to maintain its progress.

Notwithstanding the great increase in volumes of sales and numbers of outlets, the percentage of total retail sales by franchise outlets in the USA remained remarkably constant for many years but has recently regained an upward surge.

According to a survey prepared for the International Franchisee Association it was projected that this figure would rise to 50% by the end of the twentieth century but it did not achieve that target.

According to a survey of franchise associations conducted by Arthur Anderson in 1995 there were then 3000 franchisors in the USA, with 250,000 franchisees (but see page 19 for the current figures). There were no figures for the numbers of outlets and many franchisees own more than one outlet and some own a considerable number in one or more systems. It is not possible to compare this survey with the previously available information as the information gathering approaches were different.

The USA and Australia are the main countries in which government-sponsored statistics have been available but there are statistics available from other countries, which vary from the professionally prepared in, for example, Canada and the UK, to best estimates made by franchise associations, derived principally from information supplied by their members and obtained from other market sources. There are other surveys but many of them seem to draw their information in the main from other published sources (including franchise associations) rather than from independent research. The information shown in Table 1.1 appears to be the best available and indicates the level of franchising activities in some of the major economic markets.

Table 1.1

This table comprises the most recent information available

Country	Number of Franchisors	Number of Franchisees	Annual Sales (billions US$)	Number of Jobs
Argentina	300	8,000	n.a.	40,000
Australia	708	52,000	46.7	700,000
Austria	320	4,525	2.5	n.a.
Belgium	170	3,500	3.4	n.a.
Brazil	600	53,000	7.1	350,000
Canada	1,327	63,642	90.0	n.a.
Chile	60	300	0.150	50,000
China	1,900	87,000	2.9	110,000
Colombia	80	600	n.a.	9,800
Denmark	134	3,746	n.a.	15,000
Dominican Republic	80	600	n.a.	n.a.
Finland	164	3,100	3.5	22,000
France	719	33,268	33.0	350,000
Germany	810	3,900	22.3	330,000
Greece	30	n.a.	n.a.	n.a.
Hong Kong	90	2,320	n.a.	n.a.
Hungary	250	5,000	n.a.	100,000
Indonesia	261	2,000	n.a.	n.a.
Ireland	113	864	0.084	7,453
Italy	536	22,000	12.8	50,000
Japan	1,000	200,000	145.0	n.a.
Korea (South)	1,300	100,000	0.840	500,000
Malaysia	187	6,000	5.0	80,000
Mexico	600	n.a.	n.a.	n.a.
Netherlands	360	14,150	10.6	129,000
Norway	60	400	n.a.	n.a.
Peru	59	440	0.375	3,250
Philippines	700	4,000	1.7	100,000
Poland	122	10,213		108,000
Portugal	357	2,000	1.1	35,000
Singapore	350	2,300	n.a.	n.a.
South Africa	393	20,899	9.1	310,000
Spain	865	40,484	7.5	100,000
Switzerland	150	n.a.	n.a.	n.a.
Thailand	150	n.a.	n.a.	n.a.
United Kingdom	677	34,400	15.6	326,000
United States	1,400	350,000	1,000.0	9,000,000
Uruguay	140	350	0.360	3,600
Total	15,397	1,050,101	1,416	12,388,803

Source: The information in this table has been provided by the International Franchise Association between 2001 and 2003, compiled from information supplied to it by the franchise associations in the countries mentioned, except Poland, for which information was provided by Profit System, the United Kingdom where the information is obtained from the NatWest/BFA 2003 United Kingdom Franchise Survey, and China where the information was provided by the Chain Store and Franchise Association.

The regular production of reliable statistics in countries other than the USA and the UK has been slow to develop. Whichever method of preparing statistics is employed it is certain that no one succeeds in identifying all franchise systems in any market place, and that some companies included in the statistics are either not franchisors, or are, for one reason or another, only transient.

The figures provided in Table 1.1 are in some respects puzzling. The figure of 810 franchisors for Germany is startlingly high, particularly when one considers the development of franchising there. In 1991 they claimed 265 franchisors; the rate of growth suggested needs independent verification. On the other hand, the figure for the Unites States seems to understate the position. In 1991 there were reported to be in excess of 2500 systems with 542,496 franchised outlets. One doubts whether in reality there has been over a 10% decline in the numbers of franchisors and a loss of 142,496 franchised outlets, although there has been a decline in the number of petrol stations.

In the absence of properly made independent professional surveys it is difficult to rely on the accuracy of the figures provided. Even with such studies it is impossible to identify all franchise systems. From studies which are available the turnover in systems is quite high as some systems exit franchising while new ones join. The turnover level can be as high as 10-20%.[8] The figures provided can therefore only be indicators rather than a complete and accurate statement of the reality.

One should also bear in mind that the table contains only 38 countries, yet there is franchising in at least 140 countries. The likelihood is that these figures could be doubled to reach a more realistic idea of the impact which franchising has had throughout the world.

Crossborder franchising has been developing since the early days and in the vast majority of countries in the world where franchising is found, systems have been imported or exported or both. Chapters 14 and 15 deal with international franchising.

Comments on the UK market

It is perhaps a sobering thought for us in the UK to appreciate that McDonald's and Kentucky Fried Chicken, the two largest franchise operations worldwide, have between them more outlets than the entire franchise community in the UK. Indeed, it is probable that the 20-25 largest franchisors have between them more outlets than are to be found in the entire European Union - sobering perhaps but not surprising in the light of the earlier reference to the market share which large franchisors have in franchising in the USA.

This potential presents opportunities for UK franchisors since there is no European Union member state which can be said to be over-franchised given this perspective. So far as we in Britain are concerned we must accept that the franchisor and outlet numbers are well below our potential and that this provides opportunities to others to take up the challenge. If one applies the same proportionate exercise to the UK only in population terms then the UK will need to increase franchisor numbers by 110 and outlets by 105,000 in order to catch up with the US size of market penetration. This is based on the figures published in the Arthur Anderson survey referred to above.

The 2003 NatWest/BFA Franchise Survey revealed that the year to January 2003 was a year of consolidation. The number of franchise systems in the UK increased by just over 1%. The number of franchised units rose by 1% to 30,800, while sales rose by 3% to an estimated £9.5 billion. Those directly employed in franchising numbered 326,000; it will be appreciated that there will be many, working in companies which supply products and services to franchised businesses, who owe their employment to franchising. Appendix A gives a summary of the NatWest/BFA 2003 Franchise Survey results.

Elsewhere

A summary of the Australian government survey issued in May 1989 by the Bureau of Industry Economics provides a wide range of statistical information making some interesting comparisons with the US market. For example, the number of franchisors per million of population was 13.9 in Australia compared with 8.4 in the USA; and the number of outlets per million population was 671 in Australia and 1456 in the USA. The figures given in Table 1.1 indicate that there are 708 franchisors in Australia, and 52,000 outlets. However in a survey conducted in 1998 by Colin McCosker and Lovelle Frazer at the University of Southern Queensland, 730 franchisors and 50,100 outlets were identified in Australia.

The growth of franchising internationally has spread throughout all continents and regional zones with varying degrees of activity. The different levels of growth reflect business climates, availability of spending power, legal and political problems. The former East–West political divide has been penetrated by increasing numbers of franchisors establishing a presence in China, Hungary, Poland, the Czech Republic, Romania, Russia and many other managed or formerly managed economies. Growth in some of those countries has not been as rapid as many were hoping for but demographic, logistic and bureaucratic hurdles, as well as a lack of financial resources and distribution facilities, have all combined to slow down progress. Despite that, some franchisors report exceptional sales in outlets in some of these markets, with some reporting top selling stores, e.g. Moscow. In addition to these countries, the Middle East and Asia have shown substantial increases in numbers.

Franchising is being considered as a method of marketing goods and services by an ever increasing number of companies and is likely to grow at a considerable pace not only in the UK and the European Union but elsewhere in the developed and developing world.

Notes

1. In the USA, it is quite common to see food marts and convenience stores operated on the same property as a service station. These are usually separate franchise arrangements with the operator of the service station.
2. Under most state definitions used in the USA, a 'franchise' may be either oral or written, although under the Federal Trade Commission Franchise Rule, only written contracts are covered.
3. None of the USA definitions of 'franchise' use the term 'know-how'.
4. The USA has both franchise disclosure/regulation laws and relationship laws. While most of the definitions follow this approach, there are some significant variations. The disclosure document is most often called an 'offering circular'.
5. This part of the FTC Franchise Rule covers what is commonly known in the USA as a 'business opportunity'.
6. Twenty-four states in the USA regulate business opportunities separately from franchises, while one state regulates them in its franchise law.
7. The number of franchising companies in the USA is currently estimated to be between 2500 and 3000 companies.
8. In a study conducted for the IFA by FRANDATA found that in 1996 there were 1156 registered franchising companies in 12 US states studied and 1178 registered companies in 1997 in those same states. The study also found that 321 franchise systems registered in 1996 were 'missing' in 1997 and had been replaced by 339 'new ones'. There may be many reasons for this disparity, but it suggests that a lot of smaller franchisors may offer franchises for only a short period of time.

2 What can be franchised?

This book is concerned to a large extent with the business format franchise which is described and analysed in Chapter 1. It has already been explained that there are other types of franchises. Franchise arrangements, in the widest commercial use of the word, are those transactions in which one person grants rights to another to exploit an intellectual property right involving, perhaps, trade names, patents, trademarks, equipment distribution, a fictitious character or a famous name, but not amounting to the conduct of a discrete business comprising an entire package, and a business blueprint, which are essential features of the business format franchise.

There are franchises involving transactions between:

- manufacturers and wholesalers;
- manufacturers and retailers;
- wholesalers and retailers;
- retailers and retailers.

In order to illustrate the four categories of transaction there follow examples of the types of arrangement involved in each case.

Manufacturers and wholesalers

This first category came into existence when soft drink manufacturers established the practice of franchising their bottling facilities. Briefly, what they did (and indeed some still do) was to grant the right within a defined area to make up and bottle (or now, canning) the drink using a concentrate of syrup manufactured by and obtained from the manufacturer in accordance with the manufacturer's requirements, and to distribute the resulting products. There are also arrangements for the supply of syrups and dispensers which are now commonly used in bars, cafés, restaurants and public houses. Prime examples of this category are Coca-Cola and Pepsi-Cola.

Manufacturers and retailers

This category is involved with what are frequently described as 'first generation franchises' and includes some of the oldest of this type of franchise arrangement. It developed out of the arrangements made by the automobile industry in the early years of its existence. The problems with which they were confronted resulted in the establishment of franchised dealer networks.

There are also the arrangements made between petrol companies and their filling station proprietors. So many of the elements of the business format franchise are present in these arrangements that they may appear to be quite close to achieving that status. Indeed, many motor manufacturers' 'main dealer' arrangements are business format franchises. There are, within the scope of the petrol companies' arrangements with filling station proprietors, different types of transaction ranging from a licensee or tenant of premises owned by the petrol company to a sales agreement with the owner of the filling station, which may or may not be exclusive. In recent years many of the petrol companies have added convenience stores to the forecourts of their filling stations and in some cases have varied their arrangements with licensees to something much closer to a business format franchise. There is a distinct trend now for the supermarket chains which have moved into petrol sales to establish their own convenience stores on their forecourts.

There have also been arrangements made between convenience store operators (whether or not franchised) and petrol station owners for the establishment of convenience stores on the petrol station forecourts.

Wholesalers and retailers

This category is not clearly identifiable, at a glance, as being distinctly different from the manufacturers and retailers category. There can really be no commercial reason to differentiate between them except that the franchisor is a wholesaler rather than a manufacturer. The types of business which come within this category include hardware stores, chemist's shops, supermarkets and automobile aftercare businesses.

Retailers and retailers

For this category, one need only look as far as the traditional well known business format franchises. It is not necessary to look to the USA for examples; there are some well known UK franchises which illustrate this type of growth. Prontaprint is a good example. This was started as a pilot operation which was expanded to three stores and then, as was the intention from the outset, the concept thus developed was franchised. The vast majority of 'high street' franchises have developed in this way:

franchising has been chosen by the franchisor who had established outlets at the retail level as the marketing method most suited to the expansion of the business.

The above categories do not amount to some of the traditional methods or practices described in Chapter 1 as being the business methods from which the business format franchise evolved, namely agencies, distributorships, licensing and know-how agreements. We shall therefore briefly examine the nature of these arrangements and compare them with franchising.

First, we shall consider agency. An agent is a person with either expressly given authority to act on behalf of another person or one who, by the nature of his relationship with that other person, is implicitly authorized to act on his behalf. The authority given may be a special authority which is limited to doing one or two specific acts or it may be a general authority giving the agent unrestricted power to act. Fundamentally, an agent does not act on his own behalf and he is not a buyer and seller of his principal's products. The agent usually receives a commission on sales. He acts on behalf of and in the name of his principal. There is no separation of principal from agent in the eyes of third parties dealing with them. Whatever the agent says or does is completely and effectively binding upon his principal. Between the agent and the principal, there are duties which each owes the other, but the third party is not usually concerned with whatever these private arrangements may be.

In all franchise arrangements the parties usually go to great lengths to ensure that no agency relationship arises. Indeed, invariably in franchise agreements there is a specific provision to establish that the franchisee is not the franchisor's agent or partner and has no power to represent himself as the franchisor's agent or as being empowered to bind the franchisor. Agreements should require the franchisee prominently to draw the attention of third parties to the fact that he is a franchisee or licensee of the franchisor so that the consumer or others who deal with the franchisee are in no doubt as to the identity of the person with whom they are doing business.

The expression 'agency', like the expression 'franchise', is used quite often in the wrong context. It is, in fact, often used in the context of distribution arrangements. A distributor is, in essence, usually a wholly independently owned and financed wholesale operation which is granted certain distribution rights in relation to a product.

The real relationship between the parties is that of seller and buyer. The distributor is a completely independent businessman. Unlike the agent, in his dealings he does not bind the person by whom he has been granted the distribution rights. He may carry a range of products in respect of which he has a distribution agreement, and he may have competing or conflicting lines.

The business he conducts is his own business and he will conduct it according to his own methods and under his own name. He is no doubt motivated purely by commercial considerations in deciding whether or not to accept any restrictions which may be imposed upon him in a distribution agreement. The distributor buys for his own account and takes the full risk of whether or not he will be able to resell at a sufficient profit. The vendor is remunerated by whatever mark-up is reflected in the price. The buyer and seller relationship may also be present in a franchise agreement, but in most cases it should only be a feature and not the whole substance of the arrangement.

Licensing and know-how agreements are members of the same family. A licence is descriptive of the nature of a transaction by which one party authorizes another to carry out or perform certain activities without which his conduct would be an infringement of the rights of the authorizing party. A know-how agreement is a particular type of licence agreement and is most widely to be found in relation to manufacturing processes. These types of arrangement largely arise out of patent or trademark exploitation and will usually authorize the manufacture of a product or a piece of equipment. This is not necessarily the only business carried on by the licensee: he may well be combining his activities under the licence or know-how agreement with many other activities. It is quite likely that he will be selected to be a licensee because of his existing relevant skills. It may be that the product which is being manufactured under licence is complementary to, or an accessory of, something else that he does or makes. Alternatively, it may just make a useful addition to his existing range. Again, like the distributor, he is an independent businessman. He runs his own business according to his own methods and under his own name. He does not act by or on behalf of the person who granted him the rights. He will pay fees for the exercise of the authorized activities, usually in the form of royalties. This type of transaction is the closest analogy there is to a business format type of franchisee and differs from it in at least the sense that there is no obligation upon such a licensee to adopt the trading name and comply with the business format and system imposed by another.

How does franchising differ in practice? Let us take as a simple example a company which manufactures meat products and introduces a hamburger as one of its new lines. Experience shows that the hamburgers sell well and are very popular. A bright young man in the marketing division suggests that the company opens up its own restaurant to sell the hamburgers – which it does.

The company could, at that point in time, have decided to obtain a wider distribution for its product by entering into a licensing agreement with other meat manufacturers for the hamburger to be manufactured according to the same recipe in various parts of the country or territory with which we are concerned, or indeed other countries and territories. It may do this in any event. It may have a distribution network of its own or it may distribute through meat wholesalers under distribution agreements. It may also consider using its existing sales force or appointing one.

In this case, however, the company has decided, in addition or as an alternative to using these traditional methods, to open up a retail outlet, and it develops a limited menu fast food operation built around its hamburger. It has thereby provided an additional method of exploitation of its product and secured retail outlets for the sale of the hamburgers. It has gone directly into the retail market but it does not have sufficient capital, or does not wish to commit the necessary large amount of capital, to open rapidly a chain of what could prove to be very successful hamburger bars. Accordingly, it decides to exploit the distribution of the product at retail level by granting franchises or licences to others who will run identical hamburger bars modelled on exactly the same basis as the 'pilot operation' which the manufacturer has set up. The franchisees will trade under the same name which has become established by the franchisor, using the same format and the same procedures, and they will sell the same product. A consumer should feel on entering each store that it is part of the same organization and that the service and product are identical in each store. In other words the company establishes a business format franchise.

The manufacturer has expanded its distribution network; it has secured additional selling points; at the same time it is utilizing the staff and facilities of its head office by providing a back-up to the franchisees in various stores. It is therefore making a far more economic use of the amount of expertise available in its organization. Rapid growth of the retail outlets can be achieved without the franchisor having to make available a considerable amount of capital resources or to stretch its manpower resources, which, perhaps, it can ill afford or it is reluctant to do.

What is the franchisee's position? He is certainly not an agent. He is not acting on behalf of the franchisor and he is not binding or committing the franchisor. He owns his business, as an independent businessman who has put the necessary capital into the business, and he runs it and manages it. He is not a distributor in the ordinary sense, although he is part of the franchisor's distribution network. His position is not incompatible with a distributorship for he is certainly buying a product and selling it, but he is applying a process to the product before resale and provides a range of complementary products and services within a business format. He performs his activities as a principal. He does not have other lines; he is not running any other business independent of this franchised business. He is trading under a name owned by the franchisor and is using the franchisor's business system. So although there is a contrast with a distributorship, both franchisee and distributor are part of the chain in the supply of products to the consumer, except that the franchisee operates at retail level while the distributor operates at wholesale level. He will pay the franchisor for products at a price which may or may not include a mark-up and he may also pay fees based on turnover or a combination of both mark-up and fees.

How does a franchise compare with licensing and know-how agreements? In fact the same sort of contrast can be found as exists with the distributorship, although licensing and know-how agreements are even closer relations of franchise transactions than a distributorship. One is inclined to the view that the business format type franchise is directly analogous to the know-how and licensing arrangement. Let us therefore take another look at the franchise arrangement which has been described.

There is a licence granted permitting the franchisees to trade under the trade name and using the particular format. There is certainly a know-how agreement. Know-how is imparted in all aspects of the franchised business. Before he is established in business the franchisee will need to be trained in the basic business skills relevant and limited to this particular type of business and in the operational requirements. He will also expect assistance in site selection, design and remodelling of the store, equipment, marketing and promotion. The franchisee will also expect a continuing interest to be taken in him by the franchisor providing guidance when needed, promotional activities, innovation and so on.

What makes the franchisee's position different from the other arrangements is that uniquely the franchisee operates under the trade name of the franchisor and uses the franchisor's business system. With traditional arrangements the agent, the distributor or the licensee has his skills and experience which he is making available with the framework of the agency distributorship or know-how agreement. In the franchise arrangement the other party (i.e. the franchisee) does not have the skills, or experience, so he is to be given them and then sustained to the extent that he needs it.

One element which is missing from the equation is the agency element, 'agency' being used in the strict sense. No franchisor would want to enter into a franchise arrangement in which the formal relationship between him and the franchisee was that of principal and agent. If that were the case, with all the inherent risks, he might just as well operate his own branch and employ a manager.[1]

Franchising, therefore, is not merely an alternative, it is in reality another weapon in the armoury of the manufacturer, wholesaler or retailer which can be utilized to expand his business in addition to the other methods available to him. It will therefore be appreciated that there is very little that cannot be franchised. Any business which is capable of being run under management is, on the face of it, capable of being franchised. This does not mean that every such business will franchise successfully. The successful franchises are usually built round novel concepts, business systems and trade marks with associated goodwill. They are introducing what are invariably novel approaches within an existing business category and, indeed, the food industry demonstrates this factor more readily than most. The financial implications also need to be taken into account particularly where there are low margins, when the cost of franchisor services may make it difficult for the business to be structured viably as a franchise.

A restaurant or a café is a class of business which has existed for many years, yet, when Wimpy emerged on the market in the UK in the 1950s, the new type of approach (the limited menu concentrating on doing a little but well) brought immediate success. A further illustration of this point is that in the USA there are countless different types of food operations under franchise, particularly with the now ready acceptance of a range of ethnic foods and cuisines.

The proposed franchise system should aim to fill the gap in the market by providing a service or product which is not readily available or available at all. Its introduction should also be timed correctly, for there is no point in introducing a franchised scheme for a service or product which the public have outgrown and do not want or which is on the wane. Temporarily fashionable ideas should also be avoided; they may not have staying power. The clearest idea that can be obtained of what can be franchised is to examine the experience of others. Over the years many lists and classifications of business under franchisee in the USA have been published. The following list appeared in the first edition of this work in 1970 and remains valid as an indication of the nature and extent of businesses which are capable of being franchised.

1. Accounting/tax services. This embraces tax preparation, computerized accounting systems for specialized professions, small business and traders.
2. Agribusiness.
3. Art galleries.
4. Auto diagnostic centres.
5. Auto rentals/leasing.
6. Auto supply stores.
7. Auto transmission repair centres.
8. Auto washes/products/equipment.
9. Automotive products/services.
10. Beauty and slendering salons.
11. Building and construction.
12. Business aids/services.
13. Campgrounds.
14. Catalogue sales.
15. Chemical maintenance products.
16. Children's products/services.
17. Cleaning/maintenance/sanitation services.
18. Cosmetics.
19. Credit/collection services.
20. Dance studios.
21. Dispensing equipment (food and beverages).
22. Domestic services.
23. Employment and temporary help services.
24. Entertainment.
25. Food operations. This category is broken down into 19 types of operation:

    Barbecue

    Cantonese

Chicken

Donuts

Fast foods

Full menu

Hamburgers/frankfurters

Italian

Mexican

Mobile units

Pancakes/waffles

Pizza

Roast beef

Sandwiches

Seafood

Smorgasbord

Speciality

Steaks

Miscellaneous food operations (e.g. bakery routes)

26. Fund raising.
27. Glass tinting.
28. Health aids/services.
29. Health clubs.
30. Hearing aids.
31. Home improvement.
32. Industrial supplies/services.
33. Lawn and garden care.
34. Marketing sales promotion.
35. Motels.
36. Nursing homes.
37. Office machines/systems.
38. Paint/chemical coatings.
39. Paint stripping.
40. Pest control.
41. Pet shops and services.
42. Physical conditioning equipment.
43. Printing/duplicating services.
44. Publishing.
45. Rack merchandising.
46. Rentals and leasing (general equipment).
47. Safety systems.

48. Sales training.
49. Schools/instruction.
50. Scientific social introductions.
51. Sewer cleaning.
52. Signs.
53. Sport/recreation.
54. Stores (retail). These include such stores as: dry cleaners; shoe and heel bars; ice-cream; bridal salons; jewellers; gift shops; and coin-op laundries.
55. Swimming pools.
56. Telecopy systems.
57. Television systems.
58. Travel agencies.
59. Tree services.
60. Vending operations.
61. Vinyl/plastic repair.
62. Water conditioning systems.
63. Weight control.
64. Wigs/hairpieces.
65. Miscellaneous products and services.

The British Franchisee Association's membership covers the following 73 business classifications with an additional 49 subclassifications:

1. Motor vehicle services.
   (a) Fast fit of clutches gearboxes and brakes;
   (b) Commercial vehicle power washing.
   (c) Replacement and repair of windscreens and sunroofs.
   (d) Automobile paint repairs.
2. Drain and pipe cleaning and repairs.
3. Print shops.
4. Fast food.
   (a) Fried chicken.
   (b) Hamburgers.
   (c) Sandwich bars.
   (d) Coffee bars/cafés and restaurants.
   (e) Pizza.
   (f) Baked potatoes.
   (g) Chicken and ribs.
5. Home improvements.
   (a) Gas and electrical safety inspections.

(b) Renovating and upgrading windows.

(c) Building preservation services.

(d) Refurbishing and remodelling kitchens and bathrooms

(e) Lock fitting and security installation.

(f) Window blinds.

(g) Internal decoration.

(h) Building care and maintenance.

(i) Domestic and light commercial electrical installation and repair.

(j) Furniture care and spot stain removal.

(k) Refurbishing flat roofs.

(l) Domestic lawn treatment.

(m) Fitted bedroom furniture.

6. Parcels delivery services.

7. Hairdressing.

(a) Ladies.

(b) Gentlemens.

8. Retail.

(a) Off licences.

(b) Greetings cards.

(c) Pine furniture

(d) Post office.

(e) New and second-hand goods retailer, cash provider and cheque changer

(f) Home delivery of frozen goods.

(g) Shoes.

(h) Pet foods.

(i) Chocolate and confectionery.

(j) Nursery goods and toys.

(k) Television and hi-fi.

(l) Fireplace and fire retailers.

(m) Direct sales of aromatherapy and natural bodycare.

(n) National school wear centres.

(o) Electrical.

(p) Snacks.

(q) Cosmetics.

(r) Conservatories, windows and doors.

(s) Video games, consoles and accessories.

(t) Dancewear.

9. Hydraulic and industrial hoses.
10. Maintenance services for soft furnishing and disaster restoration.
11. Employment agency (executive search).
    (a) blue collar supply of temporary workers.
12. Industrial cleaning and hygiene services.
13. Domestic cleaning services
14. Carpet and upholstery cleaning.
15. Sign makers.
16. Estate agency.
    (a) Property management and residential letting.
17. Wheeled bin cleaning.
18. Commercial vehicle power washing.
19. Convenience stores.
20. Business postal and communications services.
21. Removal and storage facilities.
22. Industrial chemicals.
23. Landscape and grounds maintenance services.
    (a) Weed control.
24. Music and singing classes (pre-school).
25. Office and industrial cleaning.
26. Maids services.
27. Pre-school physical play.
28. Theatre schools for children.
29. Repointing service for brick and stone buildings.
30. Healthcare recruitment.
31. Hair and beauty supplies.
32. Video rental and sales.
33. Private investigation bureau.
34. Workshop consumables and maintenance for industrial users.
35. Milk and dairy produce distribution.
36. Landscape gardening.
37. Manufacture and sale of name badge signage, trophies, awards, promotional products.
38. Distribution and automotive hand tools.
39. One-hour film developing and printing.
40. Insurance brokers.
41. Vinyl coverings repair and restoration.
42. Careers IT and office skills training centres.

43. Laundromats.
44. Executive and management training.
45. Diet and fitness clubs.
46. Suppliers of office products.
47. Travel agencies.
48. Nursing and care service provider.
49. Private home meals delivery service to the elderly and infirm.
50. Cost management consultants.
51. Office printer supplies and printer repairs.
52. Domiciliary care services
53. Lock fitting and security installations.
54. Dairy products.
55. Short-term rental of personal computers.
56. Music and singing club for pre-school children.
57. Education (after-school programme).
58. Hydraulic and industrial hoses.
59. Sale and hire of wedding and bridesmaid dresses and mens' formal wear.
60. Taxation and accountancy services.
61. Cleaning computer equipment.
62. Franchise consultancy.
63. Estate agency board contractors.
64. Wedding and portrait photography.
65. Refill printer cartridges.
66. Banking and legal agents.
67. Flavour sealed beverage capsules and dispensing equipment.
68. Further purification of cooking oils in catering.
69. Preservation of flowers.
70. Marketing of educational toys, games and books.
71. Mortgage advice.
72. Tree stump grinding specialists.
73. Home delivery rentals of DVD, VHS or computer games.

In assessing whether a business may be franchised the following criteria should be considered.

1. The concept including the products and services must be proved in practice to be successful (e.g. there must be adequate pilot operations).
2. It should be distinctive both in its public image and in its system and methods.

3. The system and methods must be capable of being passed on successfully to others within an economically sensible time frame.
4. The financial returns from the operation of the franchised unit must be sufficient to enable:
   - the franchisee to obtain a reasonable return on the assets employed in the business;
   - the franchisee to earn a reasonable if not good reward for his labours; and
   - the franchisee to make payment to the franchisor of a reasonable fee for the services which he will continue to supply to the franchisee.
5. The income generated by the franchisor from the operation of the franchisee must be sufficient to cover the franchisor's overheads and to earn a reasonable profit.

A word of caution, however: a prospective franchisee must decide whether he is being offered a franchise at all. A franchise scheme must contain the elements of a franchise as described in Chapter 1 to qualify as a business format franchisee.

A number of business opportunities offered in good faith are often loosely described as 'franchise opportunities'. A number of business opportunities are not offered in good faith and are deliberately mis-described and/or disguised as 'franchise opportunities' in an attempt to cash in on the good reputation of franchising. Examination of the elements of the transaction by reference to the principles contained in Chapter 1 will assist in reaching a conclusion as to whether or not it is a franchise. The types of business which are likely to be within this category are distributorships, sales agencies or sales representatives and dealerships as described earlier in this chapter. These have certain elements of a franchise, but usually a vital element, such as the continuing relationship as well as a business format and system, is almost completely lacking. While these other types of business do not amount to a business format franchise they are frequently conceived and developed by the application of the principles upon which such a franchise is based.

New schemes amending and adopting these principles will arise from time to time. This is only natural. It is, however, important that any prospective franchisees should recognize the extent of the services and facilities being offered to him. The fact that a particular business on offer does not amount to a business format franchise does not of itself mean that it is not worthwhile.

The ingenuity of businessmen has fully demonstrated the versatility of franchising as a business method. Unfortunately, however, the ingenuity of the modern businessman has not been limited to the pursuit of legitimate, ethical franchising. Indeed, franchising offers scope for the fraudulent as the transaction involves a continuing relationship. If, therefore, the initial franchisee fee is set too high, allegedly to cover some of the continuing services which are never intended to be provided, the scope for fraud is obvious.

There developed what has become known as a 'pyramid selling' scheme, which is also sometimes described as a multi-level marketing scheme or more recently network marketing.[2] Such schemes involve the sale of distributorships to purchasers who may divide and subdivide them and sell them on to those whom they recruit as sub-distributors. Expansion of these enterprises takes place on the chain-letter principle. The ostensible object is to build up a sales force which will sell the company's products or services from door to door. In fact, selling the goods or services is difficult, they are usually expensive and areas are often saturated with other distributors. Selling distributorships is much more lucrative and becomes, effectively, the company's business, and that of participants in the scheme or system.

There is a very good description of a pyramid selling scheme in a 1972 case in the UK in which the then Secretary of State for Trade and Industry brought proceedings to wind up two companies which were engaged in a pyramid selling scheme. The case was heard by Mr Justice Megarry (as he then was), who described the scheme in the following terms:

> The sale of cosmetics is conducted through a hierarchy of individuals. At the lowest level there are 'Beauty Advisors', who sell the company's products direct to members of the public. Above them there are the 'Supervisors', who not only themselves sell to members of the public, but also each recruits and supervises a team of beauty advisers. Above the supervisors are the 'Distributors', who constitute the top rung outside the company, and may have a team of supervisors under them. As I have indicated, the rights that go with the position of distributor or supervisor are embraced by the term 'franchisee'. The company allows a discount of 60 per cent on its products, and when a beauty adviser makes a sale, he or she receives half that discount, and the other half is shared equally between the supervisor and distributor above the beauty adviser in the chain. On direct sales by a supervisor, the supervisor receives a commission of 45 per cent, and a commission of 15 per cent goes to his distributor. On direct sales by the distributor, the full 60 per cent commission goes to the distributor.
>
> In addition to any profit that the company makes on the sale of cosmetics, the company has the other source of income that I have mentioned. A distributor has to pay £1,500 to the company for his position. If he has been recruited by another distributor, that distributor receives a commission of £795 from the company, the company keeping the balance of £705. On the other hand, the supervisor pays the company £700 for his position, and for his recruitment the company pays a commission of £245 keeping the balance of £455. If the new supervisor has been recruited by a distributor the distributor keeps the whole of the commission. If the new supervisor has been recruited by another supervisor, the commission is in effect split between the supervisor and his distributor, the supervisor receiving £140 and the distributor the remaining £105.
>
> After a supervisor has been appointed, he may secure his promotion to distributor on paying a further £800 to the company, this sum bringing his initial £700 up to the requisite £1,500. On such a promotion occurring, the distributor who originally recruited the new distributor, or whose superior recruited him, receives a commission of £550, the company keeping the remaining £250 out of the additional £800.

The financial incentive to recruit distributors or other participants in the scheme is self-evident. The lack of incentive to sell products was reflected in the evidence, from which it emerged that average sales of products during the period July 1971 to January 1972 reached a peak of between £8 and £9 per week per participant. On the other hand, one distributor had received £5625 for the sale of rights to participate.

The main emphasis by the companies in marketing the scheme was placed upon the money which could be earned by the recruitment of distributors and supervisors. The rewards could be considerable. If a distributor could each month promote one supervisor to be a distributor and the supervisor appoint another to take his place the distributor would earn £10,800 in a year. The company, of course, would have been paid £13,920. There is no mention of the income to be generated by sale of products.

Evidence was given by the Government Actuary that if each distributor achieved the targets indicated in the manual after two years there would be over 16 million distributors. If on the other hand each distributor achieved as encouraged in the manual, double the rate, there would be 16 million distributors after one year, over 66 million after 13 months and over 280 billion in two years. The judge concluded that the projected figures in the manual were 'utterly devoid of reality'.

The fundamental difference between franchising and pyramid selling lies in the objective of the participant which, when fulfilled, will earn him profit; the franchisee intends to and can only make his profit from conducting his fast food restaurant, mobile service or other business. The pyramid participant gets his main profits from recruiting equal or lower status participants. Supplying goods or services to consumers is incidental and may be of so little advantage that the participant does not bother with it. A franchisee, on the other hand, gets nothing from recruiting others.[3] A pyramid participant (except at the lowest level) gets practically nothing from anything else.

These pyramid schemes have been recognized as containing elements which are dishonest and, accordingly, when the Fair Trading Act 1973 was introduced it contained provisions which define pyramid-type schemes.

The provisions of the Fair Trading Act 1973 were amended by the Trading Schemes Act 1996, which is a legislative overkill, affecting as it does many respectable trading relationships which have never subjected prospective parties to the abusive and fraudulent behaviour which is an inherent feature of pyramid selling schemes. As far as franchising is concerned the Act clearly applies but there are regulations which grant exemptions for what are defined as

- single tier schemes, i.e. those cases where there is a franchisor at the one level and its franchisees at the next level down and there are no other levels; or
- those schemes in which all the parties in the system network trading in the UK are registered for Value Added Tax.

The Act and the regulations are highly technical and all franchisors and prospective franchisees should take professional advice as to their applicability. The regulations seek to introduce safeguards for would-be participants.

It is vitally important to be able to recognize involvement with a pyramid type scheme because the dishonest often ignore the law and the money may have gone before any action can be taken. Obviously before signing a contract or parting with money one should take proper professional advice. It is a matter for suspicion if one is offered or told that there will be a reward (i.e. payment, supply of cheaper products or any other disguised benefit) for doing something totally unrelated to the sale of the basic product or service with which the scheme is involved. For example, one may be offered a percentage payment of any sum paid to the promoter of the scheme for recruiting another participant, or for persuading such a participant to purchase a higher position in the scheme. Other rewards could include a profit or commission on sales, or the provision of services or training to other participants in the scheme, or a commission on sales effected by other participants in the scheme. Attendance at sales meetings should be avoided but if one is tempted to join such a meeting the temptation to sign up on the spot must be resisted so that appropriate professional advice can be taken. If one is not permitted to remove the documents, as often happens, one should never sign and should not pursue the proposition further.

Pyramid selling schemes have cost some unsuspecting people a great deal of money; there are many legitimate franchises in which to invest without becoming involved in pyramid schemes. No legitimate franchise system will do what the pyramid schemes do and that is to promise rich rewards quickly and without hard work. Whatever is being franchised legitimately will offer reasonable prospects of good rewards in return for the hard work and application which is the lot of all successful self-employed businessmen.

There are six situations in which existing established businesses have particularly become involved in the franchise method of marketing. These do not take into account international expansion through franchising and other applications mentioned elsewhere in this book.

1. The expansion of an established retail chain by:
   - adding new franchised stores, thus reducing the need for additional capital and manpower;
   - a combination of franchising existing stores and franchising additions to the chain.
2. The turning over to franchising of marginally profitable or unprofitable stores in a retail chain. By removing from the profit and loss expense items such as the cost of employment of staff, including holiday and sickness cover and head office overheads, and replacing them with a franchisee working for himself and paying a franchise fee, the performance of the store can be dramatically and favourably transformed.

3. By the sale of selected operations coupled with the grant of a franchise to the purchaser a business can raise capital either to enable it to reduce borrowings or to enable it to diversify its business interests.

4. A company with underused wholesale storage and distribution facilities can establish a franchise providing additional outlets for the products in which it deals, thus enabling it to make more economic use of its facilities.

5. A manufacturer can establish a franchise in order to secure outlets for its products.

6. From a prospective franchisee's point of view there are those franchised businesses which can conveniently be added on to an existing business with which it is compatible. A good example of this sort of 'marriage' would be the establishment of a car hire business on the forecourt of a motor dealer. This sort of add-on business is often described as a 'fractional franchisee'.

Undoubtedly further applications will be developed. One must avoid approaching franchising as a rigid, closely defined business method. It is quite the reverse: it is a flexible marketing method from which many lessons may be learned and applications developed.

Notes

1. In the USA, franchisors may have vicarious liability for the acts of their franchisees if there is found to be a principal–agent relationship.
2. In the USA, pyramid schemes (as opposed to legitimate multilevel marketing businesses) are illegal in all states and at the federal level.
3. In the USA, some franchisors will pay referral fees to franchisees who recruit new prospects.

3 Why franchise your business?

There are two fundamental advantages to a businessman who decides to franchise his business. Both flow from the fact that it is a feature of franchising that the growth of the network is achieved by using the resources of the franchisees.

The first franchisee's resource of which use is made is financial. Each franchised outlet which opens does so with capital provided by the franchisee. It could not really be otherwise since it is the franchisee who will own the assets to be employed in that outlet. The opening of each outlet does not therefore require the provision by the franchisor of capital. This does not mean that a franchisor does not need to find capital for its own business (see Chapter 7), but the capital requirements for its own business will not extend to the cost of establishing each outlet in its network. The provision by the franchisee of the capital required to open each outlet enables the franchisor to achieve a rapid growth rate of the system without the normal constraints imposed upon a business which has to generate sufficient surplus profits, raise capital or borrow to fund its development.

There are broader advantages available since financial institutions find it more attractive to lend where the risk is spread. Franchising helps them achieve this objective. Since each outlet opened by a franchisee to whom financial assistance is given represents a separate loan backed by the resources of the individual there is a spread of risk compared with lending to one business to assist it in opening a number of outlets. (The approach of banks to financing franchisees is discussed in Chapter 7.)

The second franchisee's resource of which use is made is the manpower resource which the franchisee represents. The franchisee will have responsibility for the day-to-day conduct of the business. The franchisee will provide the local controls and will operate the franchisor's system with the interest and concern of an owner of the business. He will recruit, train, motivate and supervise his staff. He will bring his skills and whatever entrepreneurial abilities he has to bear upon his business and, it is hoped, maximize the opportunities with which the franchisor's name and system provide him. His will be the concern of an owner and not an employed manager, and the result should be a well run and more profitable outlet.

From these two fundamental resources flow a number of other

benefits. In addition, there are benefits which flow from adopting the franchise method of marketing. These may be summarized as follows.

1. The number of staff which a franchisor needs to run a franchise network is invariably far fewer than a business needs to run a network of company owned outlets. For example, a franchisor does not need to provide relief managers or other staff to cover holidays or illness. In franchising the franchisor provides essentially what can be described as a range of advisory and support services with a focused and specialist team concerned with the business. This enables franchisees to benefit from the cumulative experience of the whole network.

2. The franchisor's capital requirements will be lower because the franchisees provide the capital to establish each outlet. In addition, the franchisee will often be paying the franchisor initial franchise fees as each outlet opens.

3. The franchisor will not be involved in the day-to-day running of each franchised outlet.

4. The franchise network can grow as quickly as the franchisor can recruit and train those suitable to be franchisees, acquire premises (unless the franchisees operate from vehicles) and most importantly develop its infrastructure to cope with the expanding size of the network.

5. The franchisor will find it easier to exploit territorial areas which are not already within the scope of his organization as franchisees with local interests, community involvement and knowledge can be recruited.

6. The introduction of a franchisee to an existing branch in a multiple chain can convert a loss-making, or marginally profitable, outlet into a profitable outlet, thus enabling a business presence to be maintained when otherwise it might have to be closed down. This outcome is achieved by removing from the profit and loss account for the outlet such expense items as the cost of employment of the manager and staff, including the cost of holiday and sickness staff cover, as well as the proportion of head office overheads which will normally be allocated to the outlet. Although a franchise fee will be payable it will be a considerably smaller charge on the income of the outlet than the normal head office overheads and the other costs referred to.

7. A franchisor has fewer staff problems with which to cope as he is not involved in the employment of the staff or the staff problems of each individual outlet.

8. It is a commonly held belief that the local management of each franchised outlet should on the whole be keen, well motivated and extremely alert to minimize costs and to maximize sales – much more so than would be the case with a manager. While this is undoubtedly true, it does not always mirror experience. There is

anecdotal evidence that in cases where managed outlets have been converted into franchised outlets there have been significant increases in turnover. However, some franchisees reach a comfort level which satisfies their needs and have no ambition to do better – this is a challenge to which the franchisor has to find an answer (see also below).

9. A manufacturer can secure outlets for its products by establishing a franchise at wholesale or retail level which deals in those products.

10. A wholesaler which has under-utilized storage and distribution facilities can establish a retail franchise dealing in the products which it distributes, thus providing additional outlets for those products and enabling it to make more economic use of its facilities. There can be some legal problems for wholesalers who embark upon this course in the light of competition law. These problems are discussed in Chapter 10.

11. An existing business with multiple outlets can raise capital to enable it to reduce borrowing or to diversify its business interests by selling off some or all those outlets and simultaneously entering into a franchise agreement for the future operation of those outlets. This will require the proper establishment of a franchise system as well as the overcoming of a number of problems which are discussed elsewhere in this chapter.

12. Franchising offers the scope to an existing single owner of a multiple chain to develop its future outlets by a franchise system rather than expanding its company-owned outlets, thus reducing the calls upon its capital and manpower resources.

13. Certain types of franchise schemes are able to benefit from the development of national accounts. There are many large industrial concerns having a number of factories, offices and depots throughout the country which require the services offered by some franchise networks. Franchisors are able to negotiate with them for each franchisee to service the requirements of the local branches within his franchised area. None of the franchisees would have the ability or the capacity to negotiate or service arrangements of this nature on his own, yet the group as a whole has the capacity to do it. Each franchisee by the quality service which he provides to the franchisor's customer ensures that the group as a whole retains the business of the large national multiple outlet company. This sort of benefit would not be available at all to an independent trader.

A word of caution: franchising is not a panacea for the ills of an ailing business or a business operating in a declining market. The success of franchising is built on the successful operation of franchised businesses by franchisees using proven successful formats and systems. Franchisees do not need a franchisor to lead them into failure. No one needs a franchisor to achieve that.

There is of course a downside as with so many things in life. We have seen that there are two fundamental advantages to a business in adopting a franchise but there is one area which causes more difficulties to franchisors than any other: it is the franchisees themselves. This may seem to be a strange statement but most of the problems with which a franchisor will be confronted will arise from its dealings with the franchisees as 'people'. Indeed, one could go as far as to say that the relationship between a franchisor and a franchisee is founded on conflicts of interest. The first area of conflict is that the franchisor is offering to prospective franchisees the notion that they are setting themselves up in their own business. That, of course, is correct. The franchisee firmly believes that he is his own boss in his own business – both statements are correct but they tell only part of the story. What is happening in reality is that the franchisee is being permitted for a finite term to operate a business using the franchisor's name and system. He therefore operates within a structured and defined framework. Someone else can make decisions by which he will be affected and those decisions could have an outcome more favourable to the franchisor than the franchisee. Ideas which the franchisor has for driving up gross sales may be at the expense of profit margins. That results in higher fees for the franchisor and lower profits or proportionately lower profits for the franchisee. In practice, no franchisor whose emphasis is on how much better we can do at his franchisee's expense will last for long. This regime does not prevent franchisees from bringing their personal skills to bear to improve their position – many do so successfully but as one delves further into the issues and techniques the tensions which are inherent in the relationship become more apparent. Those franchisors and franchisees who recognize the conflicts and the tensions which exist and handle them properly do best. The subject of franchisor and franchisee relations is so important that two chapters in this book (Chapters 8 and 9) are devoted to it. The personal relationship between franchisor and franchisee, and the way in which it is managed, are crucial to the success or failure of the franchisee and ultimately the franchise system.

This relationship is constantly and repeatedly put under strain. Many of the symptoms are clearly and regularly experienced by many franchisors, and include the following.

1. A franchisee may develop a feeling of independence: he is successful; his business is running well; and he is earning what he expected to earn or perhaps even more. He tends to wonder why he needs the franchisor at all. He becomes convinced that the reason for his success is that he is running his business well on his own initiative. This presents a challenge for the franchisor. After all, the franchisor may be doing his job well and helping his franchisee to achieve success only to find that the franchisee now thinks that he is the person who was responsible for his own success and that the franchisor is superfluous to his requirements. This attitude can develop into a desire by the franchisee to break away from the franchise and go it alone. This is a matter which calls for a correct

response and a skilful exercise in franchisor/franchisee relations. Ultimately there will be contractual sanctions but they must be looked upon as a last resort.

2. A franchisor has to ensure that standards of quality, of services and of goods are maintained throughout the franchised chain. Its field support staff will act as supervisors of these standards as well as providing support to the franchisee. The franchisor's staff who deal with franchisees must be aware of the problems involved in dealing with franchisees, who will often see nothing wrong in trying to cut corners and in adapting the disciplines of the system to suit their own convenience and perceived cost savings. Firm, close direction may well be needed in some cases and one must always be conscious that a small unchallenged deviation from the system today can become a larger problem tomorrow and much more difficult to cope with as the franchisee's confidence at having 'got away with it' grows. There is also the risk that other franchisees who become aware that the franchisor has not enforced system compliance on a defaulting franchisee will themselves believe that they can take liberties.

3. Despite the belief that franchising produces well motivated franchisees there are some franchisees who are not alive to the opportunities which their business presents them. This problem could be symptomatic of more than one underlying cause:

- The franchisee may not really be suitable for self-employment and may not be able to cope.
- The franchisor may have made a mistake in his selection of the franchisee and the franchisor may have compounded that mistake by not employing the right selection procedures. For example, the franchisor's business may require the franchisee to be a good salesman and the franchisee may not possess the necessary personality, inclination or determination to engage in sales activities.
- The franchisee may have reached a level of satisfaction with his lot in life: he is earning more than ever before and can afford all he needs; he does not see the point in working harder to achieve more. What he fails to appreciate is that no business can stand exactly still where one would like it to be; it can only get better or decline.
- The franchisee may not be operating the system properly.

Each of these causes will require a different approach to be adopted and each will require a different solution. Above all the franchisor must never forget that the franchisee does own his business. The franchisee has to be educated and coaxed into accepting that the franchisor's suggestions in response to the problem do amount to sound advice. It is not the same thing as saying to the manager of a business 'it is now company policy that 'so and so' should be done and therefore you must do it'. A franchisee can never be treated in this way. If the franchisor's reasoning, explanations and example are good it should be possible for it to make the franchisee see how much more sensible he would be to do what he is advised by the franchisor to do. Some systems which become large tend to overlook this need for the proper handling of such situations or their staff develop the attitude that because they are so large and successful they are in a better position to dictate. That is a big mistake. If reasoned explanations and example do not work before resorting to the contract and its remedies the franchisor should re-examine the problem, analyse its approach and consider whether a different approach may be better.

4. A breakdown of trust can develop between the franchisor and franchisee. Mutual trust is a fundamental ingredient of the relationship which the parties should be developing. This breakdown may be caused by many factors but it is most likely to arise from misunderstandings and flawed communications. In addition there may be incompatibility between the franchisee and the individual within the franchisor's organization with whom the franchisee has to deal. Another cause of mistrust can be the discovery by the franchisee that the franchisor is receiving 'kickbacks' from suppliers about which the franchisee had not been told.

5. A franchisor may well believe, with some justification, that in training a franchisee he is preparing a possible future competitor.

6. The franchisor must be sure that the person selected as a franchisee for the franchise is suitable for the particular type of franchise and has the capacity to accept the responsibility of owning his own business. The franchisor owes it to prospective franchisees and to the growth of his own business to ensure as far as is possible that no one who is unsuitable is allowed to take up a franchise. It is not always easy to overcome this hurdle since experience shows that even the best managed franchisors can suffer from this problem as unexpected and unforeseeable problems do arise.

7. There is often difficulty in obtaining the cooperation of franchisees in investing in the decoration and renovation of their premises and upgrading of equipment so that the consumer is always given service in the manner stipulated in the franchise agreement and in a manner consistent with the franchisor's system brand image and the reputation of the franchised network. No business can survive without changing to reflect a dynamic market place in which consumers have increasing demands and choice. The franchisor must make sense of its proposed innovations and be able to explain how they are calculated to meet market expectations and prove cost effective.

8. There are some franchises where the franchised business forms part of a larger business which is carried on by the franchisee. An example of this sort of business would be a car hire franchise

owned by a motor dealer and run from the same premises as its main business. (Such a franchise is often referred to as a fractional franchise, i.e. the franchised business is a small fraction of the franchisee's total business.) The franchisee could find a negative interaction conflict and varying expectations between the staff working in the two types of business which may operate to the detriment of either or both.

9. Efficient communications play a great part in effective system and franchisee management. Chapters 8 and 9 deal with this issue in detail.

10. The amount of profit in cash terms which will flow to the franchisor from a franchised outlet will be less than the profit potential of the company-owned outlet. As a return on capital the franchised outlet will produce a better result. This should not be a surprise since the profit centres are different – the profit from a company-owned outlet will reflect the effort and overhead costs (including head office costs) as well as the capital investment. The franchisor in establishing its franchise system makes its capital investment which it expects to recoup out of franchise sales and the income generated by the system, which will also pay the day-to-day cost of running its organization and supporting its franchises. The two levels of income as a percentage of the cost of setting up the franchisee will be far higher than that derived from company-owned outlets.

11. Where (as is usually the case) the franchisee pays fees calculated as a percentage of gross income, there is a risk that the franchisee may not be fully disclosing his gross income (this issue is dealt with in Chapter 10).

12. There may be difficulties in the recruitment of an adequate flow of suitable persons as franchisees and/or in a premises based business, in being able to secure sufficient numbers of premises for outlets.

In summing up the disadvantages with which a franchisor is faced, it will be appreciated that most of them arise from dealing with the franchisee as an individual and the personalities involved. People problems would also confront a non-franchisor businessman. However, there is a vital and subtle distinction between running one's own business and running a franchised business, in that the franchisee owns his business and he will resent the franchisor trying to impose the same regime on him as if his business were merely a branch of the franchisor's company. Each party must appreciate how essential are cooperation and mutual dependence and a tolerance and understanding of the way in which the other thinks.

4

Why take up a franchise?

In Chapter 6 there is a detailed review of the considerations which a prospective franchisee should bear in mind when deciding upon whether or not to become involved in self-employment and how to 'check out' a particular franchise and franchisor. A prospective franchisee will have to become a businessman capable of making decisions, and before embarking upon his venture he has to make three vital decisions: whether or not to embark upon a business venture:

- Does he want to run his own business?
- Does he want to consider whether to become a franchisee?
- Which particular business and franchisor he should select?

If he decides after considering all relevant factors and taking advice that he wants to run his own business he does not need to consider the second and third options unless he wants to discover what franchising has to offer before making a final decision. That would be a wise step to take.

This will involve an assessment of the advantages and disadvantages of franchising from the franchisee's point of view so that the prospective business person can compare becoming involved in franchising as a franchisee with establishing his own non-franchised business. It is helpful to review the pros and cons of franchising and in particular the restrictions and risks which a franchisee has to accept and which will exist throughout the franchise relationship.

When a new business is established the owner may or may not have had previous experience of running his own business or of running a particular type of business which may represent the dream that motivates him to prove that his own ideas work. Such a person will invariably have to discover by trial and error the most cost-effective way of running the business, including the investment of capital. The question to be resolved is whether the owner will succeed in achieving sufficient profitability before his financial resources are used up. If he does he will not join the sad statistic of 25% of new business ventures which fail in the first two years; if he continues to do well he will not join the 40% of new business ventures which fail in the first five years.

The person may consider buying an existing business but this also involves risks, for the business may turn out to be very different from what that person thought he was buying. Further, that purchase will not provide training for one who needs it or the strength of belonging to a larger group with the advantages described in this chapter.

Franchising provides the prospective franchisee with a business opportunity which has been through this high-risk phase of development; the cost and risk of establishing the business as a viable business in the market place which is capable of being successfully franchised should have been borne by the franchisor who has developed it. This type of exercise by the franchisor will be based upon a pilot operation and its scope and purpose is detailed in Chapter 5. What the franchisee is buying into is the research, development and investment of the franchisor, thus reducing the high risk inherent in establishing a new business. While the risk level is considerably reduced, this does not mean that there is no risk. Franchised businesses fail for a variety of reasons which are discussed in Chapters 5 and 6, but the failure rate for new franchised businesses for whatever reason is, as far as one can ascertain, from anecdotal evidence somewhere between one-sixth and one-eighth of the failure rate for non-franchised new businesses. This opportunity to lock into the benefit of the system developed and established by the franchisor using the concept of franchising provides a number of advantages from which a franchisee can benefit.

1. The franchisee's lack of basic business or specialized knowledge and experience is overcome by the training programme of the franchisor.

2. The franchisee has the incentive of owning his own business with the additional benefit of continuing assistance from the franchisor. The franchisee is an independent businessman operating within the framework of the franchise system. This provides the opportunity to the franchisee through hard work and effort to maximize the return from his business and the value of his investment.

3. In many cases the franchisee's business benefits from operating with the benefit of a name and reputation (a brand image) and goodwill which are already well established in the mind and eye of the consumer. Of course there are emerging franchise systems whose names and reputations are not so well known – this is a factor for the prospective franchisee to evaluate. In all franchise networks there are three basic levels of performance despite the fact that all franchisees are provided with the same raw material. This should come as no surprise since each one of us is different.

   - There are the high flyers who do extremely well, having the right attitude and approach, as well as some entrepreneurial skills which enable them to make the most of their opportunities.
   - Then there are the average performers who operate the system and basically achieve the anticipated performance levels. Their attitude and approach is sound but they lack the flair of the

high flyers. They will earn a decent living more or less in line with their expectations.

- Finally, there are those whose performance levels are low.

  (a) They joined the franchise system with the best of intentions but they now do not display the will or the aptitude or have reached their comfort level.

  (b) They will have changed their mind and want to get out of the franchise. They clearly made a mistake in believing they could cope with self-employment perhaps because they believed the franchisor would remove all the risk for them.

  (c) It may not be their fault at all; there may have been a misjudgement of the quality of the location or the location may have become less good because of local road (and pedestrian) traffic changes.

  (d) The development of their business may have been slower than anticipated and they feel disillusioned and let down.

4. The franchisee will invariably need less capital than he would if he was setting up a business independently because the franchisor, through the experience gained from pilot and other operations, should be able to advise on the most cost-effective use of resources. There should not be the need to replace equipment bought in ignorance by a non-franchised business person.

5. The franchisor should provide the franchisee with a range of services which are calculated to ensure, as far as is practicably possible, that the franchisee will enjoy the same degree of success as the franchisor has achieved in its company owned operations, or a greater one. These services will include:

   - the application of developed criteria for the selection and identification of trading locations, or if the franchisee is based upon mobile operations, the area of such operations;

   - guidance to the franchisee to assist in obtaining occupation rights to the trading location, complying with planning (zoning) laws, preparation of plans for layouts, shop fitting and refurbishment and general assistance in calculating the correct level and mix of stock (inventory) and in the opening launch of the business;

   - the training of the franchisees and staff in the operation of the business format and the provision of an operational manual with detailed instructions;

   - the training of the franchisee and staff in any methods of manufacture or preparation which may be appropriate;

   - the training of the franchisee in methods of accounting, business controls, marketing, promotion and merchandising;

   - the purchase of equipment;

- obtaining finance for the establishment of the franchisee's business; and
- getting the newly franchised business ready for trading and opened.

6. The franchisee invariably receives the benefit, on a national scale (if appropriate), of the franchisor's advertising and promotional activities. It is usual for each franchisee to make a contribution towards the funds which are expended for this purpose. There are many and varied approaches to dealing with these advertising and promotional activities (see Chapters 5 and 7).

7. The franchisee may receive the benefit of the bulk purchasing power and negotiating capacity which are available to the franchisor by reason of the existence and size of the franchised network. There may be competition (anti-trust) laws which can impact on such arrangements.

8. The franchisee has at his disposal the specialized knowledge and experience of the franchisor's 'head office' type organization while remaining self-employed in his business.

9. The franchisee's business risk is greatly reduced. However, no franchisee should be under any illusion that he is not going to be exposed to any risk at all. All business undertakings involve risk, and a franchised business is no exception because it is under the umbrella of the franchisor. To be successful, the franchisee will have to work hard, perhaps harder than ever before. The franchisor will never be able to promise great rewards for little effort. The blueprint for a way in which to carry on business successfully and profitably can rarely be the blueprint for a way of carrying on business successfully without working or without risk.

10. Most franchisors provide support to assist the franchisee with problems which may arise from time to time in the course of running his business. The ways in which this support has been and is provided here varied over the years as systems have evolved and methods of communication become more sophisticated. The support can include:
    - field staff
    - head office staff who may be communicated with by
      (a) mobile (cell) phones
      (b) fixed line phones
      (c) e-mails
      (d) intranet
      (e) extranet
      (f) face to face meetings
      (g) at regional franchise meetings

11. The franchisee has the benefit of the use of the franchisor's patents (rarely), trademarks, service marks, trade names, copyright

material, trade secrets, know-how and any secret processes or formulae.

12. The franchisee has the benefit of the franchisor's continuous research and development programmes designed to improve the business and its range of products and/or services, to keep it up to date and competitive.

13. The franchisor obtains the maximum amount of market information and experience from the network which becomes available to be shared by all the franchisees in the network. This should provide the franchisee with access to a breadth of information which would not otherwise be available to him if he were not a member of the franchised network.

14. There are sometimes some territorial guarantees in appropriate cases which protect the franchisee from competition from the franchisor and other franchisees of the franchisor within a defined area around the franchisee's business address or in the case of a mobile franchise a defined area of operation. This will invariably involve legal issues under competition (anti-trust) law which are dealt with in Chapter 10. Franchisees may consider themselves as under threat from franchisors who place franchisees too close to each other, causing cannibalization of sales making it more difficult for the franchisees to be successful. These are areas where legal advice is essential.

15. The recognition by the banks of the advantages of franchisee financing (Chapter 7) have made lending sources and terms available to franchisees which are more attractive than those offered to non-franchised new businesses.

Against these advantages, there are disadvantages or costs to the franchisee which have to be considered.

1. Inevitably, the relationship between the franchisor and franchisee will involve the imposition of controls. These controls will regulate the quality of the service or goods to be provided or sold by the franchisee to consumers. It has been mentioned previously that the franchisee will own his business. However, the business which he owns is one which he is licensed to carry on in accordance with the terms of his contract, which will require compliance with the franchisor's business system. He must accept that for the advantages enjoyed by him, by virtue of his association with the franchisor and all the other franchisees, control of quality and standards is essential.

2. The franchisee will have to pay the franchisor for the services provided and for the use of the business system through initial and continuing franchisee fees, although there are many ways in which a franchisor may obtain income from the activities of the network (Chapter 7).

3. Each bad franchisee has an adverse effect not only on his own business, but indirectly on the whole franchised chain of businesses and all other franchisees. The franchisor will therefore need to impose standards, and demand that they are maintained so that the maximum benefit is derived by the franchisee and indirectly by the whole franchised chain from the operation of the franchisee's business. That is what makes it necessary for a franchise agreement to have a one-sided look to it.

4. This is not to say that the franchisee will not be able to make any contribution or to impose his own personality on his business. Many franchisors encourage their franchisees to make the contribution to the development of the business of the franchised network which their individual talent and qualities permit.

5. A prospective franchisee may find it difficult to assess the quality of the franchisor. This factor must be weighed up very carefully by the prospective franchisee for it can affect the franchisee in two vital areas.

   • the franchisor's offer of a business format package may well not amount to what it appears to be on the surface;

   • the franchisor may be unable to maintain the continuing services which the franchisee is likely to need in order to sustain his business.

   This aspect is dealt with in detail in Chapter 6.

6. The franchise contract will contain some restrictions against the sale or transfer of the franchised business. This is a clear inhibition on the franchisee's ability to deal with his own business but, as with most of the restrictions, there is a reason for it. The reason is that the franchisor will have already been most meticulous in his choice of the franchisee as his original franchisee for the particular outlet. Why then should he be any less meticulous in his approval of a replacement? Naturally he will wish to be satisfied that any successor of the franchisee is equally suitable for that purpose. In practice there is normally very little difficulty in the achievement of successful sales or transfers of a franchised business (this is discussed in detail in Chapter 11). Some agreements provide for the payment of fees to the franchisor to cover the cost of dealing with applications and training the new replacement franchise. If the franchisor introduces the purchaser there can be a fee to be paid for the introduction.

7. The franchisee may find himself becoming too dependent upon the franchisor and fail to produce the personal drive which is necessary to build up a successful business and to take full advantage of the foundations for business development which the franchisor's business format provides. Some franchisees lose their perspective. They delude themselves into believing that the franchisor has a duty to be so concerned about their particular business that he should ensure that the franchisee has a flow of

customers and provide a degree of day-to-day involvement, both of which are inconsistent with franchising as a concept.

8. The franchisor's policies may affect the franchisee's profitability. For example, the franchisor may wish to see his franchisee build up a higher turnover (on which his continuing franchise fee is based), while the franchisee may be more concerned with increasing his profitability, which does not necessarily flow from increased turnover.

9. The franchisor may make mistakes of policy; he may arrive at decisions relating to innovations in the business which are unsuccessful and operate to the detriment of the franchisee. This is why franchisors are always urged to market test innovations thoroughly before their introduction and to be able to demonstrate to franchisees the cost-effectiveness of the introduction of new ideas.

10. The good name of the franchised business or its brand may become less reputable for reasons beyond the franchisee's control.

These are the advantages and disadvantages which every franchisee must weigh up and consider before making the decision on whether or not he wishes to enter into a franchised business. In Chapter 6 there is detailed guidance on evaluating a franchise opportunity. The advantages and disadvantages listed here must be taken into account when considering the factors mentioned in that chapter.

5 How to become a franchisor

There are seven basic elements involved in creating and developing a franchised business.[1]

1. The basic business concept.
2. Pilot operation.
3. Developing the franchise package.
4. Developing the operational manual.
5. Marketing the franchise package.
6. Selecting franchisees.
7. Developing the franchisor's organization.

Although these elements are listed in a sequence there are many areas of overlap and some of the elements will be developing in parallel with others. A good example of this overlap is provided by element 7, since the franchisor's organization clearly will be developing throughout the whole process. We shall consider each element in turn, when the way in which they interact will be evident.

The basic business concept

The establishment of a franchise system invariably arises in one of two ways. The first is when a business person decides to expand an existing business by use of the franchise method of marketing. The decision to do so may be reached for various reasons. The business may, for example, have the potential for a more rapid expansion than the proprietor's resources in terms of capital and staff would permit. Organic growth will be too slow; the cost of borrowing to finance growth may not appeal to the proprietor; the prospect of increasing staff numbers with the swathe of regulations and rising social security costs is unattractive.

There have been many instances where the proprietor has decided to expand using the franchise method of marketing by responding to approaches made by customers of his business who ask for a franchise because the business appeals to them. There are also many businesses which do not franchise in their domestic market but which do so in their international expansion.

The second is where a business is established with a view to franchising from day one. The latter case is not to be recommended for the beginner although there are an increasing number trying to do so. An experienced franchisor may be able to proceed in this way, although significantly few have tried or succeeded.

It should be understood that franchising is not a path to salvation for an ailing business. It will not produce, if ethically and soundly run, an immediate positive cashflow and profits. On the contrary, the underlying business which is to be franchised will need to be developed in the same way as any other business. Capital and manpower resources will have to be devoted to the development of the concept, its marketing and sustenance. For the business to be franchised successfully it will have to be financially successful.

As will be seen in Chapter 7, it may be some years before profits and positive cashflow can be expected from franchising activities. Franchising must, therefore, be developed from a sound financial and business base, which will support and not drain the resources which will have to be devoted to the franchising activities. The franchisor will need to have sufficient capital resources to sustain its franchising activities until the moment when profits are being earned, which will depend on the healthy and sustainable growth rate which can be achieved.

It is essential to keep the business which is to be franchised simple. Others will have to be taught to operate it as successfully as the innovator, and the more complex it is, the more difficult it will be to recruit, train and support franchisees. So, basically, the scope must deliberately be limited to a framework which is manageable by others. It is also important that the business is easy to set up in terms of installation and equipment. It is no accident that most franchised businesses concentrate on providing a limited range of products or services to a high standard.

Consider a fast food operation as an example. The simpler the design and layout of the kitchen and preparation areas, the more standardized the decor, design and layout of the take-out and/or restaurant area, the easier it will be to adapt premises to the design and the more rapidly can one cope with the establishment of each operation. Shopfitters can prepare modules which make it easier, quicker and more economic to prepare the premises for the business.

There is also the paramount need to keep the menu simple, so as to reduce the inventory requirements and make it possible to keep the preparation and serving of the food simple, quick and efficient and at the same time to keep portion control at an effective level. One is more likely, with a simple and restricted menu, to limit the amount of equipment to be employed and thus reduce the requirements of the business in terms of space, levels of investment and maintenance.

Retail outlets provide another example of the activities which the franchisor must try to keep simple. Apart from the design, decor and layout, which are all vital, there is the question of the stock inventory. The more extensive it is, the broader the range, the more complex is the task of all who have to deal with it, and the greater the likelihood of financial loss through poor stock choice, control and mismanagement.

A franchise system growing in size can also make arrangements for frequent supplies of stock to avoid franchisees holding large stocks. The use of EPOS systems greatly assists in putting such arrangements into practical use. The overall aim should be to simplify control, reduce paperwork and make the system as foolproof as possible. On the whole, these basic principles will apply whatever the business being franchised.

Another objective must be to provide franchisees with a support service and information which no single trader in business with competitors (increasingly highly aggressive and low margin operators) could ever hope or expect to match. Thus, we see that the development of the concept requires meticulous planning and anticipation of needs.

It is also important that one defines clearly the market at which the business is aimed. There is little point in having a good idea and a great business in prospect if, for example, as can be the case, one is dependent for referrals upon others in the particular trade, who do not see the need to deal with one's business, or who are already coping with the aspect of the business in which one is interested and will see no benefit to themselves by dealing with another business providing a similar service or product. Such a situation might arise, for example, in a franchise which is providing a service to the automotive after-market and is relying on local garages to feed it with work.

The dangers inherent in aiming oneself at the ultimate consumer, if that consumer is likely to go to the established trade first, must be considered. This could arise if one is intending to provide a specialist service which is catered for by existing, more comprehensive business services. In such a case, there will probably be a heavy promotional cost to deliver the right message to the market place before the business becomes accepted in its own right. That is a burden which falls on the franchisor, and its cost and likely effectiveness will be a factor in his decision taking.

There are five other factors to consider.

1. Franchisees with finance: will one be able to attract franchisees with, or able to acquire, sufficient financial resources to enable them to become established with those who have availability of an adequate level of capital (including working capital)?

2. Franchisee skills: will one be able to attract franchisees with the necessary basic ability to enable them to acquire the skills required in the operation of the franchised business and to teach those skills to their staff?

3. Premises: can a sufficient flow of suitable premises be found at rental levels which will enable franchisees to trade profitably?

4. Consumer demand: has the franchisor demonstrated that there is sufficient market demand or can it afford to devote adequate resources to establish a sufficient market demand before it invites franchisees to invest in the business?

5. Market sector: is the business sector healthy or in decline; is the product a temporary fad or a flash in the pan? Does it have staying power?

One should aim to make the business distinctive in its total image. Each franchised business which is successful has its own distinctive branding and an innovative concept, which sets it apart from other businesses of the same type. This is what makes consumers choose to patronize that business as well as, or instead of, others in the same business sector. The existence of competitors can often be very healthy. It can help to develop the overall market and act as a stimulant to both franchisor and franchisees.

Do not simply copy or imitate others. In the long run this is not a profitable course to adopt. They may have legal sanctions which they can apply, but even if they have not, they are probably already working out how to update and improve upon what they are presently doing. They will no doubt, through the development of their business and their experience, always keep one step ahead. It should also be understood that the copier does not have the benefit of laying the foundations of his knowledge through experience and that a shallow base makes his business vulnerable.

In order properly to protect the exclusive recognition of the business image it is best if at all possible to base it upon a trademark registration for goods and/or services. Most people who select a name try to use one which is descriptive. This may seem a good marketing idea but it will be doomed to failure as a trade mark since descriptive marks are not permitted. The reason for this is that a registered trade mark gives the monopoly right to use it. If it describes the business or what the business does it would prevent others with similar businesses from being able to describe their business or what they do.

The following factors should be considered when choosing a trade mark:

1. It should be easily pronounceable, catchy and brief.
2. Bearing in mind the possibility of global expansion one should take care that when translated (if it needs to be) it will not be offensive.
3. Invented words are likely to be more readily registrable as trademarks.

Remember above all that the franchisee's business will not only have to provide sufficient profits to enable the franchisee to obtain an acceptable return on capital and a reasonable income from his work, it must also provide sufficient revenue to enable the franchisee to pay a fee to the franchisor for the provision of all the continuing services which will be available. Unless the business can generate sufficient revenue for these purposes it probably is not capable of being established as a franchise.

Many successful franchises are businesses where a high degree of personal service to the customer is important (e.g. retailing, fast food, quick printing) and they require the personal presence and commitment of the franchisee at the point of sale. Regular features of such businesses are long hours, coupled with fast, reliable and friendly service. The length of hours to be worked by the franchisee will not necessarily be confined to the hours during which the business is open to the consumer. There will always be work to do, administrative, accounting, marketing and promotion, as well as the need to provide for 'thinking time'.

As mentioned in Chapter 2, the following criteria should be considered when judging the franchiseability of a business:

1. The concept must be proved by practical experience to be demonstrably successful.
2. The business should be distinctive in its brand image and in its system and method.
3. The system and method must be capable of being passed on successfully to others within an economically sensible time frame.
4. The financial returns from the operation of the franchised business must be sufficient to enable:
    (a) the franchisee to obtain a reasonable return on the capital employed in his business;
    (b) the franchisee to earn if not good, reward for his labours; and
    (c) the franchisee to make payment to the franchisor of a reasonable fee for the services which the franchisor will continue to supply to the franchisee.
5. The franchisor must be able to make a sufficient ongoing profit from fees received from franchisees.

The pilot operation

Having developed a business concept, it is essential that at least one pilot operation, and in many cases a number of pilot operations, should be established. How many pilot units are required will depend upon how representative of the planned outlets in the network are the locations of the pilot operations. It may be that before the franchisor can be sure it is ready to demonstrate the viability of its franchise piloting should take place in different locations which are similar to or representative of the locations in which it is anticipated that franchisees will operate. It may also be necessary to keep the pilot operation running for extended periods generally in excess of 12 months, particularly where seasonal factors have to be taken into account. A franchisor with an established business may be able to benefit from experience gained from the operation of existing outlets but even if they exist he should still operate at least one pilot operation under the same conditions as are intended to be applied to the proposed franchise system to ensure that the system works in practice. It will be prudent to run more than one pilot unit so as to eliminate any distortions arising from the results of one unit through the close attention it receives or the uniqueness of its location.

It has been suggested to the author that a pilot operation is not always possible or relevant, and that the franchisor can guarantee the operation on a money-back basis. In the author's view, this is a dangerous attitude and one which negates the fundamentals upon which business format franchising is established.

Fundamentally and essentially, the franchisor should be selling access to a sophisticated package of proven know-how. If the franchisor has not proved his ability to operate his package with success and put his own money at risk he has no right to market the franchise. Nor, indeed, will he have established the goodwill, reputation and identity of the brand which is associated with his package. It is irresponsible to seek to establish a franchise by trial and error, and at the expense and risk of the initial franchisees. Initial franchisees do not have as their function the operation of pilot units and the risks entailed in order to test the market for the franchisor.

A guarantee of money back is no substitute for a lost business, a lost opportunity or in some cases a lost dream. In any event, how, with an untried and untested concept, does one ensure that the franchisor will be there with adequate money to pay back those who claim? Even if the franchisor and the money are there, inevitably there will be disputes about whether the failure was that of the franchisor's concept, or of the franchisee in not complying with the franchisor's guidelines.

The great responsibility which a franchisor has to its franchisees cannot be emphasized too strongly. Franchisees will be invited to part with what are for them substantial sums of money (which may often represent their life savings and/or a mortgage on their home), change their whole way of life and become to a great extent dependent upon the franchisor's concept and the franchisor's system for the welfare of themselves and their families.

Apart from these justifications for the pilot operation, it will fulfil the following functions.

1. As it will put the brand name before the public the viability of the concept in practice will be developed and become established as acceptable and exclusively associated with the brand in the mind of the consumer, at least, initially in the area surrounding the location of the pilot.

2. It will identify problem areas and enable the franchisor to provide solutions in relation to:
   (a) marketing;
   (b) acceptability and availability of the product or service;
   (c) methods of marketing, promotion and merchandising.

3. What are the requirements of and how to comply with:
   (a) local by-laws;
   (b) building regulations;
   (c) fire regulations;
   (d) health and safety at work;

(e) disability legislation;

(f) employment laws;

(g) anti-discrimination laws;

(h) planning and zoning requirements which may be relevant to the particular type of business;

4. The franchisor should also concentrate on other factors which it needs to know for the benefit of its future franchisees.

(a) streamlining of shopfitting methods;

(b) staff availability and training requirements;

(c) taxation, including VAT (sales tax) and customs and excise duties (if any);

(d) other factors of a legal and business nature relevant to the particular type of business.

5. It will enable the franchisor to experiment with layouts (see later comments) and to discover the best combination of equipment as well as the cost-effectiveness of resources necessary for the conduct of the business. Alternative presentations of the decor and design of the interior and exterior of the premises can be tried out so that the most effective can be used.

6. The potential of and actual trading experience of different types of location can be obtained. This will include experimenting with opening hours to discover what are the optimum hours during which the business should be operating. It should be borne in mind that a decision will have to be made about opening hours, that staffing requirements will vary according to the time of day and week and seasonal factors, and that the franchisee will need guidance on staff scheduling to avoid incurring ongoing costs with staff which are unnecessary and uneconomic. On the other hand, trade may sometimes only develop slowly at certain 'non-traditional' times (e.g. late at night or on Sundays). It may not develop sufficiently at all unless a commitment is made to be open at those times for at least a period of several months so that customers are aware that the business is open.

7. It will be appreciated that as training in the operational side of the business is necessary, so too is training in business management and accounting techniques. In developing the pilot operation, particular attention should be paid to the introduction of simple and effective systems of accounting, stocktaking and controls (e.g. in a food operation, portion and quality controls).

8. The franchisor will need an operations manual (see below). The pilot operation will 0provide the basic information from which the operations manual will be prepared and the franchisor must be careful to record the lessons learned so that they are effectively employed for the benefit of the franchisees.

The layout of the premises will obviously differ from case to case. Some businesses are very dependent upon the way in which goods are merchandised, while others will not be (some need work and preparation areas).

Taking a fast food business as an example, the layout will have to be carefully planned so that the preparation progresses by logical steps without the need, as far as possible, for staff to retrace their steps. The whole operation of preparation will in all probability be timed and if the layout is such that a few unnecessary seconds per operation are inevitably required this could add up to the need for an additional employee. The availability within easy reach of what is required is essential if staff are not continually to be getting in each other's way. This is essentially the practical application of basic work study techniques. Portion control and size will have to be established to ensure customer satisfaction and to enable guidance on pricing policies to be established. If these factors are not properly resolved they could reduce the profitability of the operation, and the cumulative effect of failure to pay attention to such details could make the difference between a scheme which could be franchised and one which could not.

Even when the viability of the concept has been proved with the pilot operation this does not mean that the need for continuous 'pilot' operations ceases. The need, in fact, is greater, except that from being called 'pilot operations' they become what are called company-owned units.

The franchisor has to remain ahead of the game. It must continually be experimenting and developing, and by being in the field at the sharp end in the market place it will be able to put its experiments and developments into practice in its own outlets. It will be able to demonstrate to the franchisee that what it suggests is proved and tested in the field. It is just as important that the continuing developments are proved and tested as it was to prove and test the initial concept by the establishment of the pilot operation.

A franchisee may at some time need to be persuaded that his unit needs refurbishment; that equipment should be replaced; and that he must update the appearance of his unit. If the franchisor makes the investment in its own units and can achieve a cost-effective result the franchisor has the persuasive power of demonstrated successful achievement available to it. This approach can extend to the product and/or services innovation and in other areas of the business. What better way is there to persuade a franchisee than to be able to demonstrate by the performance of the company-owned units what can be achieved? 'Do what I have done and you should achieve the positive benefits my trialling has produced' is infinitely better than 'do what I say'.

Developing the operational manual

The need for an operational manual (or manuals) has already been pointed out. Indeed, it is stating the obvious.

The manual will contain in written form the complete systems and methods for conducting the franchised business.[2] It will invariably have the benefit of copyright protection which an oral explanation could not have. It thus forms an essential part of the legal methods by which the franchisor protects its ideas, know-how and trade secrets. It will, therefore, be appreciated that the manual should be comprehensive and cover in detail all aspects of the day-to-day running of the franchised business.

In practice, the franchisee will first have contact with the manual when he attends for his training, when it will be the basic training course textbook, and then it will be provided to him on loan to be available as a continuing guide to the conduct of his business.

It is difficult in any publication to cover all types of franchised operations. This chapter will deal with what might be regarded as the sort of provisions one might expect to find in every manual, and then provide some specific ideas which may be appropriate for particular types of franchised businesses.

Introduction

Each manual should contain some introductory remarks explaining the basic nature of the operation and the business philosophy which the franchisor wants all franchisees to embrace. The introduction should spell out in broad terms what the franchisee can expect from the franchisor, and what the franchisor will expect from the franchisee.

Operational system

There should then follow a detailed description of the operational system which explains how the operation is set up, and how and why the various constituent elements fit in with each other.

Equipment

A section in the manual should deal with the equipment which is required for the operation of the business. It should give a detailed explanation of what the equipment is, its function and how to operate it. Guidance should also be given on how to troubleshoot basic and common faults which are likely to develop. There should be a directory of telephone numbers in the manual and this will include the telephone numbers of supply and service centres for the equipment (see below).

Operating instructions

This section will probably be broken down into a number of subsections. The following are suggested.

1. Opening hours/days.

2. Trading patterns.

3. Staff schedules and rotas.

4. Use of standard forms and procedures.

5. Requirements as to staff appearance (e.g. uniforms).

6. Staff training procedures.

7. Procedures for employing staff and compliance with statutory obligations. This is an area which is becoming more complex as the law is rapidly changing. There are also many anti-discrimination laws, e.g. racial and disabilities, of which franchisees need to be aware in running their businesses.

8. Procedures for disciplining and dismissing staff and the statutory obligations imposed on the franchisees as an employer. This is also an area which already is a legal minefield.

9. Pricing policies. It is likely that it will be illegal for the franchisor to seek to impose prices on the franchisees. This will not prevent the franchisor from issuing a recommended price list or from establishing maximum prices, but the recommendations must not be enforced.

10. Purchasing policies (these can be affected by legal considerations; see Chapter 10), ordering procedures and delivery arrangements.

11. Product standards (quality and quantity).

12. Service standards.

13. Customer complaint procedure.

14. Staff duties: a detailed job description for each member of the staff should be included which sets out not merely the nature and extent of the duties, but also the methods and procedures to be adopted in performing them.

15. Reporting requirements and how to comply with them (see also point 22 below).

16. Payment of franchisee fees: the detailed procedure for calculating and accounting for fees with specimens of the appropriate forms.

17. Accountancy: the specified accounting methods to be employed by the franchisee and the flow of information required to be provided to the franchisor to assist him in the provision of guidance to the franchisee. Advice on VAT requirements and PAYE and how to complete the necessary paperwork should also be given.

18. Cash control and banking procedures, including procedures for dealing with cheques, switch cards, cheque cards and credit cards.

19. Advertising and marketing: basic guidance on standard point-of-sale advertising, marketing and selling techniques, with a list of do's and don'ts.

20. Requirements in regard to the presentation of the franchisor's house style and the way in which the franchisor's trademark should be used.

21. Insurance: details of cover recommended and any schemes offered by or through the franchisor. Alternatively, guidance on how to go about getting the cover required. Many franchise agreements contain a requirement for minimum insurance cover to be obtained by the franchisee.

22. Stock control procedures. The existence of electronic point of sale systems can assist not only in stock control but also in obtaining the basic reporting and accounting information which can be downloaded by the franchisor on a daily basis.

23. The franchisee will need advice about the increasing volume of laws which affect the way in which he conducts his business. Anti-discrimination (whether sexual or racial) laws as well as disabilities legislation, referred to above, are examples. Where a business has more than 5 employees there is a requirement to provide access to pensions opportunities.

24. Any additional information which is necessary to explain how the business system is to be run.

Standard forms

There should be a section devoted to standard forms which will include all those already referred to above. Additionally, there could be the following.

1. Contracts of employment which comply with current legal requirements.

2. Agreements with managers or staff requiring them to keep the franchisor's trade secrets, methods etc. secret and confidential and not to use or disclose them for any purpose except for the discharge of their responsibilities as employees.

3. Contract forms to be used in dealings with customers in the course of the conduct of the franchised business.

Technical supplement

This is to be found in businesses where equipment has a vital role in preparing the end product for the consumer. This would contain more detailed technical information about equipment than is contained in the section dealing with detailed operational methods. It is not uncommon to see manufacturers' explanatory literature supplemented by material prepared by the technical staff the franchisor's organization.

Franchisor's directory

A directory of who's who in the franchisor's organization, and whom to contact for any particular aspect of the franchised business.

Telephone and e-mail directory

A directory of all useful telephone numbers and e-mail addresses, such as service centres and suppliers.

These are the core provisions which one would expect to find in most manuals, with such variations from business to business as are needed to reflect the difference in their nature and/or in the way the franchisor has organized the business system. In appropriate cases (two are now offered as examples) one would expect to find further sections, as well as some consequential variation of the sections previously mentioned.

Fast food

- Recipes
- Menu content and variation according to time or day
- Methods of preparation of food
- Kitchen procedures, including kitchen layout
- Times for preparation, cooking, holding and serving of each menu item
- Portion quantities, including how many portions should be produced from a given quantity of ingredients
- Stock requirements (range as well as quantities)
- Display and merchandising techniques
- Local advertising, promotion and public relations
- Where to obtain approved ingredients for menu items and their preparation and shelf life.
- Supplier arrangements/purchasing sources and procedures.
- Customer complaints procedures
- Special industry applicable legal requirements, e.g. health, safety and hygiene
- Planning:
  - by-laws
  - disposal of litter
  - night operations
  - noise
  - parking
  - work permits for foreign staff
- Cleaning routines

Retail outlet

- Stock inventory requirements, quality, quantities, range and shelf-life of products
- Supplier arrangements/purchasing sources and procedures

- Store layouts
- Display and merchandising techniques
- Customer relations
- Issuing guarantees and dealing with claims
- Customer complaints procedures

The list could be almost endless as one looks at the variety of franchise offers: Hotels, car rentals, print shops are but a few diverse examples. The specific manual requirements of each will differ both in nature and scope.

All franchisors should be conscious of the need constantly to keep their methods under review and to introduce changes and variety so that their operation is competitive in the market place. Such changes and variations should be reflected in supplements and amendments to the manual or manuals so that the franchisee is always kept informed and up to date.

This is likely to apply particularly to the marketing, advertising and promotion section of the manual. For this reason the marketing section is often produced as a separate volume in order more readily to facilitate the updating process.

It is also not necessarily good enough just to send franchisees details of changes and amendments. Many franchisees may not read the material sent, or if they do it will not register in their minds and the supplements or amendments may not find their way into the operational manual. The franchisor has to ensure that franchisees do assimilate the material and do act upon it. Increasingly, franchisors are looking to use the Internet or to create an intranet to communicate with franchisees. Quite apart from the need to institute legal safeguards before using these methods of communication, the risk of franchisees not responding to them is at least as great as it is with written material. Field support visits, franchisee meetings and additional training may well continue to provide the best methods of getting the message accepted. Modern technology has its advantages but it may not provide solutions without a realistic evaluation of its limitations.

Developing the franchise package

The successful running of the pilot operation is essential to the preparation of the franchise package. The experience obtained in setting up and running the pilot operation will provide the basis upon which the elements in the package are structured. The package involves bringing together the elements of the business, reflecting the accumulation of the franchisor's total operational experience in a transmittable form.

It might be appropriate at this stage to consider employing the services of a consultant. Assuming that one wishes to employ the services of a franchise consultant, what are the criteria by which he should be judged and what safeguards are there? There are four general headings:

1. Ethical standards.
2. Experience in franchising.
3. Verification of reputation.
4. Terms and scope of employment (including charges).

Ethical standards

Any person who is offering consultancy services must be able to approach the client in an objective way. He must place the client's interests first and that means that if necessary he should advise a client not to proceed with what he proposes, even when it means that the consultant will thereby lose business. He must avoid obvious conflicts of interest between clients and his own duties. In the author's view it is unethical for a franchise consultant who is assisting franchisors in setting up their business to hold himself out as being able objectively to advise franchisees who wish to have assistance in evaluating a franchise. The strong temptation exists to direct such a person from his area of interest to a client of the consultant, especially if the consultant is part of his client's sales force.

The question also arises as to how far the consultant should properly become involved in the selling of franchises for a client.[3] There are a number of considerations to be taken into account, and those which apply to an employee and are dealt with below should be reviewed, since they apply equally to the use of an outside consultant. While a consultant may be able to give the franchisor advice on franchise marketing and on selection of a franchise, he should not be employed to sell franchises; nor should he be paid by reference to the number of franchises sold or upon a sale taking place.

He should be paid for the advice given and not because he has persuaded someone to sign up. The decision about whether or not to accept a prospective franchisee must rest with the franchisor and no one else, and it must be a decision taken based solely upon the suitability or otherwise of the applicant.

In advising clients, all ethical consultants should bear in mind the code of ethics of the BFA. Although not every franchisor will wish to join the BFA, the Code of Ethics is a guide to proper conduct by franchisors to which no bona fide reputable franchisor should object. Indeed, if a consultant were to set himself as a target the eventual qualification for membership of the BFA by all his clients, the standards of franchising would undoubtedly benefit.

Experience in franchising

If a person wishes to offer himself as an adviser on franchising to others, based upon the experience he has in the field, the quality of that experience is important. Ideally he should have been involved in an actual franchise operation and at a sufficiently high level of management to have had responsibility for important decisions concerning the operation of the franchise. Someone who is employed in a franchise company at a supervised low level of management is not likely to be able to justify the requisite experience of franchising. After all, if the consultant is holding himself out as competent and able to advise how to go about setting up marketing and operating a franchise, it is best if he can demonstrate that he has a level of achievement which justifies his claims. There are a few questions which can be posed under this heading:

1. What is the consultant's experience in the field of franchising?
2. Is it general, or is it limited to a specific aspect?
3. Does he have experience in the particular aspect on which advice is required? (e.g. marketing image, design, retailing, distribution, fast food, practical field experience, the contents of manuals).
4. Has he actually worked in a franchisor company other than in a consultancy capacity? What was his job? What were his responsibilities? To what extent was he under supervision or direction?
5. Is he a member of any professional body? What are his qualifications?

Verification of reputation

It is advisable to verify that the consultant has actually held the position which he represents that he has held. If a consultant or anyone is dishonest, that dishonesty is usually not confined to limited areas; it will be broader. One should therefore check up on the consultant as much as possible. No reputable franchise consultant with a good track record of experience will object; on the contrary, he will be pleased and proud to demonstrate the quality of his track record. He will also be pleased that one is taking such care, since if everyone did, the business opportunities for the incompetent and less reputable consultants would diminish rapidly. Additionally, the following questions should be asked:

1. Can the consultant provide you with references? You should specify the classes of persons from whom you would like to see references (e.g. bankers, accountants or solicitors) concerning his financial position and reputation. Other references could come from persons known and established in franchising who know of his reputation and background by personal contact. If he is relying on his past experience from his involvement in franchising then references should be sought from those for or with whom he worked.
2. Can, and will, the consultant make arrangements for you to select from his past and present client list and speak to your own selection about their experiences with the consultant?
3. If he offers his services as a salesman of franchises (and you wish to employ him for that purpose despite the views expressed in this

book), can arrangements be made for you to speak to franchisees, of your choice, to whom he has sold franchises and also to their franchisors so you can consider the quality of the outcome?

Terms and scope of employment (including charges)

It is the prospective franchisor who must decide upon the role which it wishes the consultant to play. The fact that one employs a consultant does not mean that the consultant is able to run the business or advise on every aspect of the business. It is the adaptation of the business to the franchise method of distribution about which advice is being given. The range of services which the consultant offers should be explained by him and a decision has to be made by the franchisor about the extent of the involvement of the consultant it requires. It would be sensible to have exploratory meetings with the consultant and agree on terms of reference for his role. Indeed, one should not employ a consultant unless and until those terms are clearly defined in writing. Agreement should also be reached over amounts and the method of calculating fees to be charged. A lump sum for a specific task may be offered and one must be certain that the amount involved is fair to both parties. It may be better to be charged an agreed hourly rate when it is easier to control the expenditure and assess the value of the work if the franchisor closely monitors what is being done and the time taken on each of the elements. It may be sensible initially to set a specific task for the consultant and either develop the relationship further or terminate it if not satisfied.

The elements in the package

The franchisor will have to know the right location for an outlet and the criteria by which the site or the scope of a territory can be judged. Clearly, the factors which are dealt with in this chapter will not necessarily apply in all cases. Some franchise operations are dependent upon the foot traffic passing the specific location from which trading is to be carried out, some may depend upon advertising and marketing, followed by telephone contact. Retail and fast food franchisees are typically in the former category, although some of these types of businesses could be the intended destination of the consumer, while such franchisees as Dyno-Rod, Chemical Express (Chemex) and ServiceMaster are in the latter. Furthermore, experience with the pilot operation should have indicated when custom is likely to arise and what time of day or week is likely to produce the peaks of business activity.

It is suggested that the following considerations should be taken into account in assessing the degree of business activity a particular site may be capable of generating. The requirements will differ in some cases and so may the conclusions to be drawn from the information revealed by enquiries.

It may be thought that these criteria would apply to every business whether or not it is franchised. That is so, as there is no reason why these aspects should differ. What is different is that the franchisee is expecting to benefit from the franchisor's know-how and experience while in the non-franchised sector the individual has to work it out for himself. Since the franchisor is offering to provide know-how to others, the franchisor's research must be done thoroughly to ensure that the franchise sold and the advice given are soundly based.

1. **Type of street**
   (a) Dual carriageway. Is there a centre barrier which prevents the motorist from crossing to the other side of the road?
   (b) Local road or trunk road.
   (c) The availability of motorway or just off motorway services sites is restricted.
   (d) Is off street car parking available? What restrictions are there on parking in the streets in the vicinity of the location.
   (e) Roadside locations which were once difficult to secure are growing in numbers but do not suit all types of business.

2. **The environment**

   Environmental factors are increasingly important in assessing the suitability of sites and the appropriateness of the type of business. There is and will in the future be much legal regulation involving environmental considerations; this will be ignored at considerable peril.

3. **Foot and/or road traffic volumes**

   The volume of traffic must not be permitted to mislead. For example, road traffic may not be able to stop if the flow is travelling too quickly, if there is too much congestion, risk of congestion or no parking readily available. Similarly, foot traffic can be quite large, but uninterested for various reasons, such as commuter foot traffic to and from a railway station. Those who commute are invariably in a great hurry and may only stop for a quick purchase or may not stop in the numbers sufficient to justify the establishment of the proposed business. One should not ignore the fact that many railway stations or travel facilities now include shopping areas as a feature which also attract non-travelling shoppers but which may draw customers away from other businesses in the area surrounding such travel facilities. One should not be misled by the proximity of a pedestrian crossing. Crossings take people away from as well as bring them towards a location. If the crossing is leading to a town centre, or shopping area, it could place the location just outside the main flow of the pedestrian traffic.

4. **The degree of identification to which the premises are exposed**

   This will depend for its importance on the nature of the particular business. Most businesses will benefit from the best exposure. There are some which are the intended destination of the consumer to whom that factor may not be so vital.

5. **Landmarks which may generate a potential for business**
   (a) Museums
   (b) Schools
   (c) Cinemas, pubs, discos, nightclubs
   (d) Proximity to the leading multiple and department stores in a high street or shopping malls or centres
   (e) Office blocks
   (f) Sports facilities (which may provide evening and weekend business)
   (g) Travel facilities, e.g. railway stations (subject to the above comments), tube stations (in London), coach depots, car parks
   (h) Tourist attractions

In the case of a mobile franchise, where the franchisee visits the customer, careful evaluation has to be made of catchment areas and an assessment of what are realistic territorial allocations. Experience will have to be obtained of the different considerations which apply to urban and non-urban areas.

Having decided that the particular location is acceptable by the relevant criteria, one also has to assess the premises for their suitability for the purposes of the specific business. This would be the case, of course, regardless of the fact that there will be a franchisee involved. The factors to be considered, and the effect they may have on the business, would include the following.

1. The size of the premises and whether one can fit into them all the necessary fixtures, fittings and equipment (if any) while still providing sufficient selling space or space for providing any on-site services.
2. The suitability or otherwise of the premises for conversion into the required end product. This must take into account such factors as the need to provide adequate ventilation and to comply with health and safety requirements as far as may be appropriate to the type of business and to accommodate disabled staff and customers.
3. The availability of the essential public utility services at the premises.
4. The amount of any premium which may have to be paid to acquire the premises, and the amount of rent and business rates.
5. The terms upon which the lease will be granted.
6. An assessment of the cost and the likelihood of obtaining the following, drawing upon the experience gained in running the pilot operation:
   (a) planning consents;
   (b) building by-law consents and fire certificates;

(c) complying with any of the statutory or local authority by-law requirements which apply in the particular area; and

(d) landlord's permission to carry out any works and the assignment of the lease.

In the case of a mobile franchise it is the assessment and selection of the area of operations which is important; the location of trading premises is a secondary factor and in many cases, certainly in the early stages, the franchisee may be able to run the business from his home. The need to be visible and uniform in appearance is achieved by the use by each franchisee of the same type of vehicle, which is decorated in a distinctive livery so that each operational unit is a moving advertisement for the franchise system and the franchisee's business.

Marketing of these sorts of operation is calculated to ensure that potential customers are aware of the service being offered so that when they require that type of service they will think of the franchisor's brand: use by consumers of these services is invariably on an occasional 'as-the-need-arises' basis and the most frequent point of contact is the telephone. These schemes tend therefore to be marketed by the use of their telephone numbers in association with their name and to be heavy users of Yellow Pages and other telephone directories and guides. One cannot also ignore the possibility of using the Internet or other electronic sources of information and promotion. In some cases the franchisor will provide a toll-free centralized number through which consumers can make contact with the network. In cases where the franchisees market their own phone numbers the control by the franchisor of the telephone numbers associated with the trade name is essential and the franchisor will tend either to become the subscriber or to require that on termination of the franchise agreement the franchisees will surrender the use of the number, preferably by transfer to the franchisor.

The experience gained in running the pilot operation will enable the franchisor to prepare standardized plans, specifications, packages of equipment and/or shopfitting (which may be modular) which can be varied and amended so as to fit in with the requirements of particular premises. The basic needs in terms of fixtures, fittings and equipment will have been established, as will the correct layout for the particular premises. The franchisor will also have to be able to give advice on the decor of the store so that it reflects the established brand image. It should also be possible with the information available to the franchisor to streamline the preparation of any applications that are necessary for planning and by-law requirements. These applications can often be supported with brochures which explain and illustrate what is proposed.

The franchisor may make arrangements with suppliers of the basic materials or products in which the franchised business deals for their sale to franchisees at competitive prices. These arrangements may extend to suppliers of any bags, boxes or other materials which are utilised at the point of sale. It may also usually be arranged that these materials will bear the franchisor's trademark or trade name. Arrangements will have to be made with equipment suppliers so that supplies are available in quantities sufficient to meet the franchisee's demand for equipment and spare parts and for their repair and servicing.

Systems of work will have to be put into written form. Job descriptions will have to be prepared explaining the scope and all the facets of each employee's activities so as to fit in with the overall scheme. Promotional literature, including point-of-sale material, will have to be created, as will any common format literature and notepaper.

The franchisor will have to set up training schedules and training facilities for franchisees and their staff. The importance of a properly structured training programme cannot be over-emphasised. This is not something which can be relegated to the category of 'I will work something out when we have our first franchisee'. The training requirements for the franchisee and his staff should be identified, the length of the course and how it will be presented must be carefully structured. The contact between franchisor and franchisee in the initial training phase will have a considerable bearing on the quality of the relationship. The training course will have to cover all facets of the conduct of the franchisor's business system so that the franchisee is, on its completion, capable of running the business and complying with his contractual obligations. However, while standards must be high the course must not be so long that the franchisee cannot afford to attend it and remain financially viable.

The franchisor should prepare simple accounting procedures and business systems which are to be operated by the franchisee. The training course would include tuition in the use of these systems.

The accounting procedures and business systems will fulfil two purposes. The first is to ensure that the franchisee has the correct flow of information available to enable him to see where his operation is going wrong or, if it is going right, that it is, in fact, proceeding according to plan or better. The second is to provide the franchisor with the information to enable it to provide continuing advisory and follow-up services as well as forming part of its control mechanisms. The franchisor will also have crucial financial information available which can be used in dealings with prospective franchisees.

The franchisor will develop the necessary information to enable it to give advice to the franchisee about the leasing of premises or equipment, and other contracts into which the franchisee may have to enter with suppliers and with those who provide maintenance services for the equipment which is used in the franchised business.

There is an increasing emphasis on the use of computer technology with requirements for the installation of hardware by franchisees with modem links to the franchisor. The ownership of the software rights have to be dealt with and software licences obtained from the software houses which create the software.

The franchisor will need to explore the availability of financial facilities for his franchisees. In doing so he will learn whether he has prepared his franchisee proposition sufficiently well to convince the sources of such facilities that it is acceptable. The banks have established an influential role in franchisee development as a result of expertise which they have acquired (Chapter 7).

All these factors are finally brought together into what is called the franchise package. This is the basic 'product' which the franchisor is offering to sell to its prospective franchisees. Having done this the franchisor has to market the package to potential franchisees.

The franchisor will have to be satisfied that a market for franchisees exist. It will need a supply of people who have the qualities and skills which the franchised business requires and they must have the financial resources.

The franchisor will also have to establish that the property market will provide a flow adequate to match the available prospective franchisees at rents which make sense.

None of this will help if despite the success of the pilot operations the market sector in which the franchised business is to operate is not healthy with good prospects. A new and bright idea with a limited life span and popularity will also not work.

Marketing the franchise package

The best way for a franchisor to market a franchise package is based upon its ability to demonstrate its success. No matter how impressive the franchise package looks it is the quality of the underlying business which is all important. For the newly established franchise system, the track record to date will be crucial. If there is only one pilot its performance will have to be very convincing to satisfy the franchise market place that it is worth an investment. Even if the franchisor has been able to develop more than the one pilot prospective franchisees will consider whether the franchisor has the financial resources to sustain its business until it reaches critical mass and is earning profits.

Some franchisors maintain a low profile in the marketing of the initial few franchisees. Many are more aggressive. It can be very tempting to respond to many requests (as often happens) for franchises from prospective franchisees in the early days when the franchisor has spent a considerable amount of money in developing the franchise system and is anxious to generate a positive flow of income. Franchisors often suffer a great deal of difficulty with early franchisees whose recruitment was premature and whose credentials were not as thoroughly assessed as they should have been because the franchisor was more interested in rapid sales, or under financial pressure, to respond to the short-term need for cash flow without recognizing the risks which this approach may bring. Careful and considered development are crucial if one is to avoid laying the foundations for later difficulties.

In marketing franchises, many have found that editorial comment in local and national newspapers is an effective method of attracting enquiries. This can only be achieved if the franchise, or someone connected with it, provides newsworthy material. There is also luck to be taken into account, since even newsworthy items may be dropped if something better turns up. One could employ public relations consultants, but doing so might involve a greater expense than most franchisors could afford at such an early stage. However, since this approach can be effective it should be investigated thoroughly before being dismissed.

Most franchisors make contact with their franchisees in one of the following five ways.

1. A customer of a non-franchised (but similar) business may ask the franchisor to grant a franchise to him.
2. A customer of one of the pilot operations may ask to become a franchisee.
3. The prospective franchisee is attracted to the opportunity by a friend who has taken up a franchise, or by talking to an existing franchisee.[4]
4. The prospective franchisee responds to a news item or feature in a newspaper or magazine mentioning the franchise.
5. The prospective franchisee has seen an advertisement in such media as *Franchise World* or the business opportunities sections of the various daily or Sunday papers. The *Daily Express* and the *Daily Mail* have regular features on franchising.[5]
6. The prospective franchisee meets the franchisor at a franchise exhibition.
7. By visits to the website of the franchisor or the British Franchise Association which has links to members' websites.

A grand opening of one or more of the pilot operations can create a public event at a relatively modest cost, which could attract media attention at the local level. Attention to detail is essential, for little credit will be given to a spectacular launch where the arrangements go wrong. Suppliers may be persuaded to provide products at special discounted prices and/or to take advertising space in a special feature in a local newspaper but the franchisor may need persuasive arguments to obtain such support.

Having achieved some measure of public awareness through the visible success of the pilot operations, the franchisor will then need to make some similar public display to mark the decision to expand using the franchisee method of marketing. It is crucial that the early franchisees, and their locations or territories, are carefully chosen. At all costs, the franchising operation must avoid a false start. Successful early franchisees are a very effective demonstration of what their successors may hope to achieve. By contrast, if the early franchisees experience difficulties, whatever the reason, it will be more difficult for the franchisor to attract new franchisees.

The financial terms (i.e. initial franchise fee, plus ongoing turnover-based fees, or mark-up on supplies or other sources of the franchisor's income) must be structured to ensure that the franchisee will obtain a proper and attractive return on his capital and income for his labours.

The opening of the first franchised unit may be approached in the same 'grand opening' manner as the pilot operation. It is useful to provide the press, particularly the local press, with a thumbnail sketch of the franchisee involved so that human interest and personal finance/ investment stories can be written, together with appropriate career details of the franchisor and results to date. The establishment of new small business with job creation opportunities will be of interest.

All the facts and data provided must be truthful and accurate, and presented in a direct, positive manner which can be easily assimilated. It is likely that a well organized grand opening event will be so hectic and well attended that there will be little time for lengthy explanations with complex details. This means that the written material made available is important. It will invariably form the basis of any editorial comments which may subsequently appear in the press.

The aggressive approach does not appeal to all, nor indeed is it necessarily the right approach in each case. Some may take the view that they do not want significant publicity at such an early stage of development. Such people consider a quiet build-up of the network to be more important; more extensive publicity can follow when the franchise is soundly established and ready to move forward at a quicker pace.

However, one factor which is undoubtedly essential is that the franchisor must be patient at this crucial stage. It must not try to expand more quickly than its capacity to attract well qualified franchisees and to service them allows, as otherwise its infrastructure will not be able to cope with the needs of the network.

The franchised business will be advertising for customers for its products/services and the side-effect of such advertisements may well be to generate enquiries from prospective franchisees.

Having gained publicity or obtained a lead for a prospective franchisee, the franchisor must not produce, in response to enquiries, a brochure or other literature which does not do the franchisor justice. There are many franchisors who let themselves down by the poor quality of their printed material. It must never be forgotten that the material supplied in response to enquiries will be part of the franchisor's 'shop window'.

It is sensible to prepare an attractive set of literature. This should explain who are the people involved in the franchise system and their experience, and it should give the history of the business and a description of the franchisor's services. It is always a good idea to include some pictures of the business premises and/or vehicles and of the people involved in the business. By this stage, the franchisor should have a business of which he is proud and will be pleased to promote its virtues to prospective franchisees.[6]

Many franchisors follow a set procedure when marketing the franchise. It should be appreciated that out of every 100 enquiries, 80 will probably never get beyond the initial communication, ten will on submission of personal details be unsuitable, fewer than ten may be worth meeting and discussing the proposition with, and two or three at most may be suitable and finally buy a franchise. This means that it will be all too easy for a franchisor to waste a lot of money on expensively produced marketing material. There are three ways to cope with this. One is to be very careful about what to spend on the material, another is to be careful about handing it out so that less is wasted and the third is to be careful about both.

Marketing the franchise requires considerable patience (no apology for repetition – it is important). No franchisee worth having should be waiting with pen poised to sign the contract.

The franchisor must consider the suitability of the prospective franchisee. This involves consideration of a wide range of factors which are considered below, but consideration should also be given to factors which are calculated to ensure that the prospective franchisee has considered his position very carefully and that certain basic elements are present. These include the following.

1. Is the prospective franchisee suited to the rigours of self-employment with the stress involved?
2. Is he fully committed to and capable of undertaking all that is involved in running the franchise?
3. Will he fit in and get on with the franchisor's head office and field team?
4. What is the prospective franchisee's past history?
5. Does he have adequate financial resources?
6. Is his commitment supported by his family?

The franchisor should bear in mind that not only is it in his own interests to ensure that his franchise system and self-employment are right for the prospective franchisee, but also it is in the prospective franchisee's and all other franchisees' interests.

The franchisor will also have the task of explaining the contract and the reasoning behind its provisions, which will call for thoroughness and a great deal of patience. It must be remembered that, for the franchisee, this can be the biggest commercial decision in his life. There will be disappointments for the franchisor because some prospective franchisees whom the franchisor would consider ideal will decide against buying the franchise.

What then is the procedure? It is very important to get this right. First impressions always count a lot and the written presentation will tell a lot about the franchisor and just how businesslike is his operation.

1. The franchisor may receive a letter or phone call from the prospective franchisee. The initial contact may be made at a franchise exhibition when such preliminary discussions can take place.[7] No franchisor should ever 'sign up' a franchisee at the exhibition at which the first meeting has taken place. All normal investigations and procedures must still be followed, particularly in a case where the prospective franchisee may have been influenced by the euphoria of the event. The franchisor will usually respond by sending out or handing over an illustrated presentation describing

the franchise company and its success story. (Many franchisors are careful with handout material at exhibitions to save the expense of handing over costly material which is destined for the bin when the recipient arrives home.) Sometimes this material presented in a question and answer form. Some companies explain briefly what franchising is. The franchisor may find it convenient at some stage to send prospective franchisees a copy of *How to Evaluate a Franchise* (published by *Franchise World*) or to encourage them to purchase the *British Franchise Association* franchisee information pack. Franchisors find that this guide and pack put franchising into perspective for potential franchisees and their professional advisers, who may never have previously had contact with a franchise transaction.

2. The presentation is often accompanied by an explanation of what the franchisor does for its franchisees in terms of setting them up and in continuing to service their needs and requirements thereafter.

3. Some financial information is also usually despatched with the initial material.[8] This must never be presented to franchisees as a suggestion of what one will achieve. Rather, it will illustrate a profit performance which may be achieved if certain levels of sales are reached. These figures must be prepared with care and contain a proper explanation of what they do represent so that the prospective franchisee is not misled and so that the franchisor is not creating possible problems for himself later on if things go wrong. Any such information which is presented to prospective franchises must be based on verifiable actual performance achieved by the franchisor or franchisees.

4. The franchisee should also be invited to complete an application form to provide the franchisor with details about the franchisee to enable the franchisor to find out whether the franchisee has the financial resources and is a suitable person with whom to proceed further.

5. After the application form is received and evaluated the franchisor will have to decide whether or not to arrange an interview with his prospective franchisee. A franchisor should understand that many of the requests he receives will not be from serious enquirers and may be from other franchisors or prospective franchisors who wish to see what it is offering.

6. There should be a series of meetings before a final decision is made about whether or not to proceed to signing a contract.

It is to be emphasized that considerable time and effort will be involved in finalizing the first few franchise contracts and getting the new franchisee open for business and trading. The process will be even longer when suitable property has to be acquired and converted. The franchisor should not rush its fences, or expect rapid results in the initial stage of its franchise sales programme. In particular a franchisor should never allow itself to get into the position where it does not feel comfortable about saying 'no' to a prospective franchisee if it does not believe that the relationship will work, even if it is under financial pressure.

Selecting franchisees

The selection of franchisees is not an easy subject on which to give advice, particularly as it is of crucial importance. It is one of the ironies of life that one has to learn by one's mistakes in order to gain experience. Franchising is no different, and the skill of choosing the right franchisee is, of necessity, developed with experience.

It is not uncommon to find that a franchisor will have more problems from among the first ten franchisees than from those who subsequently join the network. It is also not unknown for some of those early unsatisfactory franchisees to poison the atmosphere later on by stirring up the network because of their dissatisfaction with their underachievement. This may have arisen because they were not suited to the role as a franchisee and they are angry. They feel they have something to settle with the franchisor.

One of the most common mistakes which is made by new franchisors is to be too ready and willing to establish initial franchisees and to give them special deals. This is quite understandable, since at that point the franchisor has spent a great deal of time and money on establishing his franchise system and in running his pilot operation. He wants to expand quickly and see a return on his investment as soon as possible. He is at the point of maximum vulnerability just when he requires the strongest nerve. It is a great mistake to accept as a franchisee someone who is willing to buy the franchise unless he matches up to the franchisor's requirements in every respect. That is just as important with the first as it is with the hundred-and-first franchisee. Standards of selection must never be relaxed or compromised. In the early days in particular the franchisor must be patient and have the ability and resolution to turn down applicants if he is not absolutely certain that they will be good franchisees.

There are many franchisors who, having become established, express the wish that they could be rid of some of their earlier franchisees who were accepted because they were available, and not because they matched up to the franchisor's requirements. These franchisees would not qualify for acceptance at the present stage because the franchisor is now established and can afford to be more selective and patient. Would one set up a pilot operation in a totally wrong location merely because it was available, or would one wait patiently for the right site? One would, of course, wait for the right site. So with the initial franchisees it is essential to be patient. Wait for the right person. It will pay in the long run.

There are franchisors who give special deals to initial franchisees to lure them in, again as a means of starting up quickly. This is also a mistake and, as experience shows, on the whole builds up problems later on when one has to exercise control over such franchisees, who still rate themselves as 'special cases' and feel that they are always entitled to 'special treatment'. Additionally, franchisees do talk to each other, and special deals cause ill feelings, with attendant difficulties for the franchisor as the later entrants to the network discover that they have different less beneficial terms, which they will resent. This creates resentment which can escalate into real difficulties.

Many franchisors develop what they call a franchisee profile as the number of their franchisees increases. This reflects the pattern of qualities and qualifications of the franchisees which they have set up in business. As an example, a franchisor may be able to say that his franchisee is most likely to be a family man, aged 39–45 years, with two children and the following attributes and attitudes: he has had a successful career in middle management, is fed up with the lack of prospects and stifled by company policies, is keen and anxious to be his own boss, is supported by his family in his ambitions, has no previous experience in the type of franchised business on offer and has adequate finance backed by a fairly good equity in his house on which he can borrow.

It is important that the prospective franchisee has enough money to get started, but possibly not much more, although a 'rainy day' fund can be a useful resource to have available.[9] While the franchisee may have to borrow some of the funds, say up to 50%, or even as much as 70% (which some banks are prepared to offer), the rest should be his own cash. Any borrowing should be arranged with an ethical source of funds (e.g. a reputable bank, finance house or insurance company) and over a sufficient length of time to enable the business to generate adequate profits to enable payment of the borrowed funds, and the interest thereon, to be made while leaving sufficient for the franchisee's reasonable living expenses. Five- to ten-year loans should be satisfactory for most purposes.

It is as well to remember that if the franchisee has not put in any funds of his own or alternatively is too rich, he may be tempted to walk away from the franchised operation if difficulties are encountered, rather than work his way through them. A financial commitment the loss of which would be felt by the franchisee is a considerable incentive and is usually regarded as an essential feature of a franchise transaction.

An ambitious, committed individual is an ideal prospect likely to prove to be a successful franchisee but one must be certain that his ambition will not lead him to become creative as far as the franchisor's system is concerned. No matter how ambitious, the franchisee must accept that he is operating someone else's system and not his own.

In some cases large companies have become good franchisees, and there are some very successful multiple franchisees, notably in hotel, fast food and retail businesses. The large corporate franchisees, by contrast with the small proprietorial corporate franchisees, can present problems for a franchisor. It is more difficult in such a case to control and restrict the spread of the franchisor's know-how, and secret and confidential information. An economically strong franchisee, who may be more financially powerful than the franchisor, would be a considerable opponent in the event of any disputes. Further, the large company may find the constraints imposed upon it by franchising too restrictive and may gradually introduce what it thinks are improvements to the system. Such a situation is challenging since the large company may consider that its experience in its own operations equips it better than the franchisor. For these reasons it may be sensible for most franchisors not to deal with large companies as franchisees, certainly not until the network is strong enough for the franchisor to be able to withstand the pressures to which it could be subjected.

However, the more common type of relationship is basically one between the franchisor and the individual franchisee (who may form a company) and is a very personal one. The success of the personal relationship is indeed the key to the successful growth of the whole operation.

Franchisors will look for many qualities in their franchisees. An individual franchisee must be healthy and able to withstand the stresses and strains of being self-employed with no regular salary, unlike in the past, and facing up to the prospect of losing all can impose considerable stress.

The franchisor should have at least one meeting with the prospective franchisee and family in their own home. Seeing them together, and the way in which they live, and keep and maintain their home, can tell a lot about them. Those who live in a sloppy manner are likely to run their business in the same sloppy way. Do not find out too late when a simple additional procedure can provide the information required. Meeting them together will also enable the franchisor to judge just how committed the family is to the proposed venture and how likely they may be to interfere. Such interference does occur from time to time and can only put the franchisor/franchisee relationship at risk.

Most franchisors do not require their franchisees to have prior experience of their particular trade, as full training will normally be provided. Indeed, some franchisors believe that the person with experience of their type of business will be more difficult to train in the franchisor's particular methods. It can be difficult effectively to 'untrain' someone and retrain him so that in the future he will not ignore the system or think he knows better than the franchisor what should be done. On the other hand, there can be some businesses where a background knowledge of the trade or technical know-how is essential and since it cannot be taught within an economically viable time frame the prospective franchisee must have the requisite basic knowledge. In such a case, the franchisor's training will have to be very thorough and so will the continuing supervision of operations.

Age is relatively unimportant in many cases as long as the prospective franchisee's health is good, although advanced age may render people unsuitable for some particular kinds of business. In some franchises, a husband and wife (partner) team is an ideal combination with both partners active in the business. Even where this is not appropriate, it is important that the prospective franchisee has the total support of his or her spouse (or partner). There may be telephone messages to be taken and relayed at unsocial hours of the day and night, normal mealtimes will often be missed and there may be widespread disruption of the normal pattern of social and domestic life. Divorce and other breakdowns in the relationship, particularly if there is a partnership agreement relating to the franchised business, can be destructive as the franchised business and the franchisor can find itself in the middle of bitter conflict.

The prospective franchisee must be independent enough to be able to manage a business on his own. However, he must be dependent enough to want to work within the rules of the franchise system and not continually to be challenging the franchisor and the system and seeking an excuse to break away.

It is essential in view of the relationship which exists in a franchise for the franchisor and franchisee to have mutual trust and respect. The franchisee must be someone whom the franchisor can trust with his name and goodwill. Will he be honest in his financial returns on which the management services fee income will depend? Will he give his staff and customers honest and fair treatment? On the other hand, can the franchisee trust the franchisor, and does the franchisor deserve that trust? The franchisor must demonstrate a successful record of ethical business practice.

Can the prospective franchisee, with the franchisor's help, cope with running his own business, probably for the first time? The first couple of meetings should provide clues on this score. The franchisor should be able to tell if the prospective franchisee is serious in his approach by the way he asks questions about the operation and also the effort which he puts into visiting outlets and generally vetting the franchise proposition. The prospective franchisee should be encouraged to ask questions and to talk about himself and his aspirations.

Will the franchisee be receptive to the training and guidance which he will be given? Does the franchisor feel that the franchisee will have the capacity to cope with the assimilation of information and be able to apply it in practice?

Finally, the franchisor will have to decide whether he likes the applicant. Since both parties will doubtless see (and hear) a lot of one another and are mutually dependent, it is most important that they get on well with one another and have mutual respect. The 'chemistry' must be right. After all, both parties will be working considerable hours for the same end – the success of the franchisee. The franchisor does need the franchisee to be successful. The success of both the franchisor's and the franchisee's businesses will be inextricably interwoven.

Assuming the prospective franchisee is keen to proceed, the ultimate decision must be made by the franchisor. This is a decision which has long-term consequences for both parties, who must be happy with the arrangement.

If the franchisor chooses to make use of the services of a consultant when considering recruitment, the two must work very closely with each other. The reputable consultant will know that it is the franchisor who should finally select franchisees and he will want the franchisor to be interested and involved. An ethical consultant may help the franchisor in acquiring the skills involved in selecting the right franchisees, but the consultant should never sell franchises. The consultant should be paid a professional fee for services actually rendered and never a commission on sales.

In summary, the franchisor should select his franchisees deliberately and cautiously, and allot sufficient time to do the job properly. Remember, it is a crucial decision for both parties. The franchisee will often have at stake his whole life savings and life-style. The franchisor for its part will have at stake the reputation of its business, its future income and its credibility in selling further franchises.

Developing the franchisor's organization

As in any business, it is sensible for the franchisor to set up and expand its organization gradually in line with the development of its business. It would not be financially sensible to take on too many staff initially when there are as yet no franchisees. On the other hand, it is essential that all the franchisees (especially the early ones) are fully serviced so the franchisor must have properly trained staff available to deal with the requirements of the network and may not leave the hiring of the requisite staff until after franchising commences. It is a matter of timing and judgement on the part of the franchisor to ensure that it has sufficient staff resources and skills to provide for the franchisee's needs. It can make a lot of sense for the franchisor to recruit its managers of pilot operations with a view to their broader involvement in the network's development.

There will undoubtedly be expenses incurred in establishing the franchisor's organization to accommodate the development of franchisee recruitment before there is any income. It is very likely – indeed it is invariably the case – that the franchisor will suffer net losses in the first years. How many years it will be before profits are made will vary from case to case and will be affected by the growth rate of the business, but the time span can be as much as three to five years. There will be unavoidable expenses of trade mark and/or service mark registration, brochure production, staff salaries, office overheads and expenditure, travel, advertising, promotion, legal and accountancy advice etc. before and while the franchisees become established and the fees on turnover, or mark-up on the supply of goods, begin to flow to the franchisor. It is neither a solution nor good practice to charge unrealistically high initial franchise fees. The franchisor must plan to receive the majority of his income from the successful operation of the business by the franchisees. The initial franchise fee should be a relatively modest sum of money and represent the 'entrance fee to the club', covering in some degree the value of membership of the network and providing a contribution towards the establishment expenses incurred by the franchisor, including site and franchisee evaluation training and supervision (see Chapter 7).

Continuing franchise fees

There is often great difficulty in assessing the right level at which to fix continuing franchise fees. There is no such thing as the 'norm'. The fees will vary depending on many factors, the most major of which are the nature and extent of services to be provided by the franchisor and their value to the franchisee. (There is a full discussion of franchise fees in Chapter 7.)

The franchisor is faced with expenses in the early stages which its income from the franchisees will not cover. However, it should not despair as its income should grow faster than its expenses. The staff required to cope with five franchisees may well be able to cope with 25. Each new franchisee who commences operations represents additional income for the franchisor and, as the turnover of each franchisee increases, the franchisor's income will also increase (see Chapter 7).

Source of income

Each franchisee should represent a secure and growing source of income to the franchisor, provided that the franchise is a good viable system, and is kept that way by the sensible management of the franchisor. Furthermore, successful existing franchisees will provide a source of additional expansion for the franchise network as they seek to reinvest their profits by opening further units. It is not uncommon to find that existing franchisees are a significant source of recruits for new outlets.

The relatively long-term nature of the franchise contract with its continuing obligations is a major advantage over the normal sales operation, where, say, individual items have to be sold to the same retailer every few weeks in competition with other suppliers. The latter type of operation needs a large sales force and heavy continuous advertising, and there is always the fear that the customer will choose to buy a competitive product or even the same brand from another supplier.

These factors have an important impact on the type of organization which the franchisor should develop in the early stages. Basically, it will need few, but competent, people who have a broad knowledge and are hard-working. 'Hard-working' is not lightly said, since the franchisees will in many cases be working long hours, sometimes seven days a week, and, having invested their life savings in the franchisor's idea, will generally expect to be able to make contact with the franchisor whenever they feel the need. Running a franchise involves a great deal of unsocial hours, working time and effort.

Breadth of knowledge is also important, as the franchisee will want answers on all sorts of subjects and will prefer to cover them all in one conversation with the particular person to whom he is talking, or with whom he is accustomed to deal. The functions most franchisors need to emphasize are finance (accounting), franchisee sales, marketing and operations (including innovations). Each of these is examined in turn.

Finance (accounting)

For the new franchisor, the financial aspects should be capable of being dealt with by the staff who deal with its own company operations. They should be able to devise and develop a simple accounting system for the franchise network and be capable of giving financial advice to franchisees and in relation to the operation of the accounting system. Regular returns and accounts will be required from franchisees and it is vital that each franchisee understands from the outset exactly what is required in this respect. This understanding should be instilled in franchisees during training. The availability of many software programs may well enable the franchisor to find the system which best provides for its needs. The use of electronic point of sale systems and hardware can provide all the information which both franchisor and franchisee need.

The information which is required should fulfil two objectives.

1. It should enable the franchisor to monitor each franchisee's performance as well as provide the basis for calculating the fees to be paid.
2. It should enable the franchisee to see for himself how his performance compares with his business projections and with the objectives which he and the franchisor have set, and with the other franchisees in the network.

The procedure for providing the information should be made as simple as possible, but that does not mean that essential steps should be avoided. The information required will be in three categories:

1. Gross revenues.
2. Profit and loss statements.
3. Capital expenditure.

There will be provisions in the franchise contract requiring the franchisees to submit the various categories of information at stated intervals.

Gross revenues

Information relating to gross revenues will be required by the franchisor at the same intervals as the franchise fees are required to be paid, although some franchisors require more frequent provision of this information. The period fixed for payment of fees should be as short as possible, weekly if feasible, so that the franchisee will be required to discipline himself to attend to his financial records each week and to write out a cheque for fees each week. If his finances are shaky and fees are delayed, the problem is then discovered sooner rather than later so that remedial action can be taken. The disciplines of attending to financial records each week will ensure that up-to-date financial management information will be available to him and the franchisor. The franchisor should require the franchisee to provide him with a copy of the relevant information.

A simple form for weekly reporting might look as follows. It is assumed that the week finishes at the close of business on a Saturday.

Weekly gross revenues-fee remittance form/tax invoice

Address of store/operation . . . . Store no. . . . .

Accounting reference no . . . . Week ending . . . .

Franchisee's name and address . . . . Franchisee's VAT no. . . . . . .

	1 Total gross revenues	2 Less VAT	3 Total for fee calculation	4 Number of customers	5 Average value per customer
Sunday					
Monday					
Tuesday					
Wednesday					
Thursday					
Friday					
Saturday					

Fee calculation

Total revenue (per column 3)   £ . . . .

Management services fee . . . % thereof   £ . . . .

Advertising contribution . . . % thereof   £ . . . .

Total   £ . . . .

VAT at 17.5% thereon   £ . . . .

Total remitted by cheque herewith   £ . . . .

I certify that the figures set out above are true, correct and complete.

Signed . . . .   Name in full . . . .

Franchisee . . . .   Date. . . . .

Profit and loss statement

A profit and loss statement will identify whether margins have gone astray and can help to identify existing or developing problems. Again, the more frequently the information is available, the better. If possible a profit and loss account should be prepared weekly. In most businesses, the five most important factors to check are sales, gross margins, stock, cash and wages. They are the chief variables. It is important that all should be checked on a weekly basis. If the level and range of stock are such that weekly checks are impracticable a monthly check should be carried out. Any longer period results in inadequate financial information being available to franchisees and to the franchisor. The lack of such information prevents the franchisor from providing supporting monitoring advice to the franchisee and hinders the franchisee in the management of his business.

The sales should be checked frequently, with takings being reconciled between cash register and amounts banked at least every day. If the business operates a shift system, the takings should be physically counted and agreed at the end of each shift before those responsible for the shift which is ending leave the premises. Some operations require hourly till readings to develop information to assist in the anticipation of the business flow.

Where credit is given, great care must be exercised to ensure regular payment of receivables, as cash flow is as important as sales. There is no point in achieving high sales if the money is not available to be used by the franchisee. A lack of positive cash flow could destroy what could otherwise be a successful business. The higher the level of receivables the more capital the franchisee must have available to finance his business.

If the business involves product sales, a system must be devised for checking the stock of products at regular intervals. The longer the interval the less valuable the information available. Without this information, there is no check on shortages, theft or gross profitability. Proper ordering is difficult if the franchisee does not know what he has. The advent of computerized cash registers (electronic point of sale) which can record stock movements can assist but cannot replace actually checking physically to ensure that what the machine says is what is really there.

A typical profit and loss statement is as follows:

Profit and loss statement

Gross revenues	£..........
Less VAT	£..........
Total revenues	£..........
Less cost of sales	£..........
Gross profit	£..........

It should be noted that there may be differences in the breakdown of these items. In a fast food operation, there could be a breakdown between the cost of food and cost of packaging. Where there are separate elements involved it may be wise to break them down to assist in the monitoring of performance and controls. Additionally, if the operation involves the carrying of stock, the opening and closing stock figures have to be taken and netted off to provide an accurate gross profit figure.

Other deductions need to be made before the net profit figure can be calculated:

<u>Less:</u> **Operating expenses**
    Salaries/wages
    Rent, rates, service charges
    Management services (franchise) fee
    Advertising fee
    Any additional local advertising
    Insurance
    Telephone
    Electricity
    Gas
    Repairs and renewals
    Travel expenses
    Sundry expenses
    Bank charges and interest

Allowance will have to be made for depreciation before the net profit is accurately stated. Upon receipt of the profit and loss statement, the franchisor should check the figures to see whether they reveal any departure from the performance criteria which he has established.

In order to facilitate the rapid production of the required information, the franchisor should provide simplified profit and loss statement forms. The variable items of revenue, cost of sales, gross profit, wages and franchisee fees are entered every week with standard amounts entered for the other items, e.g. rents, rates. This method enables useful information to be produced within a day or two of the end of the week so that the franchisee himself and the franchisor are both rapidly aware of any problems and how the business is developing in general. The standing amounts can be updated as they vary. The increasing use of accounting software packages and accounting monitoring services (which can be outsourced) can reduce the workloads and the need for paper transfers, with e-mail and downloading readily available.

A useful check is for the franchisor to make available the key performance criteria of the network e.g. revenues, cost of sales, wage percentage, spend per customer etc. of all units (franchised and company-owned), on a weekly basis, accompanied by a brief commentary on any significant features. The figures will be of interest to franchisees and can often create competition between franchisees to become the best performers in the network.

Capital expenditure

Capital expenditures are more difficult to control. The danger is that a franchisee does not appreciate that his expenses have to be deducted from his gross revenues before he has any profit for himself, as well as setting aside the VAT received and allowing for the tax payments which he will have to make. There is a tendency to spend prematurely on the good things in life. It is wise to call for a balance sheet at periodic intervals so that some indication of the financial health of the business is available.

It is useful to have full accounts reviewed every quarter (or at least every six months) by external accountants and audited accounts on an annual basis.

The franchisor's existing financial and administrative staff can provide advice and a brief guide to matters such as the payment of wages, employment regulations and VAT returns.

In time, it may be necessary to have additional accounting staff for the franchised side of the business, but certainly not initially. Indeed, there is much to gain from using the existing staff. They will be able to advise from a basis of knowledge and experience of the business and also they will doubtless deepen their own understanding of the company's business in the process.

Some franchise companies with in-house computer capacity provide an accounting service to franchisees, which in turn provides a greater ability, both to the franchisor and franchisee, to monitor and control the franchisee's business.

Franchisee sales

On the sales side, the proprietor of the business will initially have to do the selling himself; indeed, there is a considerable case for him to continue to do that. Selling, used in its normal sense, is not necessarily an appropriate word.

It is more a case of explaining the proposition, the services offered, the contractual basis and terms. The proprietor of the business is the appropriate person anyway, as he should understand the motivation and concerns of the prospective franchisee about to go into business on his own, probably for the first time.

Recruiting a specialist salesman from outside is potentially dangerous at any time but is particularly so in these delicate early stages; such a person would not know the business and the franchisor would not know him well enough to rely utterly on his judgement and his ethics when it comes effectively to parting people from their life savings. The use of outside consultants for the sale of franchises is not recommended. Indeed, the provisions of the Trading Schemes Act 1996 (See Chapter 2) may affect such an arrangement.[10]

When extra help is required on the sales side, those to be involved should be taken on one at a time, with impeccable references from previous employers, very carefully screened and thoroughly trained. They must also understand the ethics of franchising and they must become experts at the 'soft sell'. Hard selling has no place in franchising. Alternatively, the franchisor could consider transferring someone from his own operational organization to assist on the sales side. The advantage of recruiting from existing staff is that they will understand the business goals of the system, they have the systems knowledge and their integrity is known.

These comments concerning the proprietor carrying out the sales function are made on the assumption that the franchisor is a proprietorial company. Where this is not the case (e.g. where the operation to be franchised is part of a large organization), then the head of that division – the director in charge, or the managing director of the subsidiary company – should similarly devote himself personally to the selling effort.

Any individual specializing in sales activity should be paid a good salary, with regular reviews and good conditions of service, plus perhaps a performance bonus.[11] The aim should be to attract and retain a career-minded individual with a view to a long service career, who will produce a steady flow of high-quality results. He will provide an essential future link with franchisees, who will often consult him as an 'uncle figure' when problems arise. Ethical franchising is not a foot in the door, immediate performance, high bonus or 'you're out' type of selling operation. Therefore, the financial incentives used to attract that type of salesman are totally inappropriate in franchising.

Marketing the product or service

In the early days of franchising activity it is unlikely that the franchisor will need any specialist additional marketing staff. If the franchisor already has a marketing capability for company operations, it should be used. If the franchisor employs an advertising agency, they should also be briefed on the franchising plans. If the franchisor does not have an advertising agency it is recommended that one be appointed. If the franchisor is too small at this stage for an agency to be interested the franchisor should obtain experienced assistance.

Expenses must be carefully watched, especially in the early stages when little can be afforded. However, good design work to establish the image will be needed. Some of this may already exist, but in switching to a franchise it may be wise to take another look at existing material and perhaps ensure greater distinctiveness. There are specialist design firms who offer such a service.

There will be advertisements to place, and public relations events and press releases to be handled. All these items should be carefully considered and it is best to start with a modest programme and ensure that the money spent is wisely invested. At this stage, more than any other, it is vital to obtain full value for money.

Although specialist agencies exist, as the franchisor's organization grows so too will the capacity to do a great deal of promotional, marketing and design work in-house. In time, when size and income justify it, the franchisor should have staff who specialize in promotion, marketing and design work. They will need to liaise with specialist agencies and with the franchisees in the field. Considerable advantage will be gained from discussions with franchisees about various marketing and promotional ideas. Point-of-sale material is often worth trying in company-owned outlets and then with selected franchisees before its introduction throughout the network.

A continuous and positive approach to marketing and promotion from within the franchisor's organization is also good for the morale of franchisees; it preserves continuity and will assist in demonstrating in practice the franchisor's concern with the success of the franchisee's businesses.

Operations (including innovations)

The franchisor will undoubtedly need sufficient staff to provide franchisees with the detailed help they require to prepare and launch their new venture. The franchisor has the obligation to continue to monitor and advise the franchisee and if necessary control him after the launch.

The obvious source for a candidate will be one of the existing operational staff from a company operation. At first only one person will be required, someone who is an experienced all-rounder, particularly good at operations in practice. He must be able personally to perform all the tasks necessary and be prepared to roll up his sleeves and actually work alongside the franchisees in the early days.

The preparation of the operations manual should also be the responsibility of the person chosen to be in charge of operations.

In the early days, training is likely to be carried out at company-owned operations by one of the franchisor's experienced managers, using the manual which has been written. If the company already has a training officer, well and good, but most new franchisors will not be so well blessed and will need to maximize the use which can be made of their existing operational staff and facilities. It should be recognized that franchising is different from employment and the person engaged in training will have to adjust his thinking to the different discipline which is required in dealing with franchisees.

As the franchise network develops the franchisor will be able to provide a classroom with a mock-up of an operational unit.[12] This may be sited conveniently on the floor above, or in space behind, an existing company operation. The staff involved in operations will expand with the growth of the business and the operational support side of the franchised business will develop along a number of paths.

1. There will be the initial training of new franchisees and staff.
2. There will be the continuing retraining of franchisees and staff. Much of this can be done at the franchisees' premises. Its main purpose will be to work out operational flaws, to eliminate bad habits developed by the franchisees and to introduce new methods.
3. There will be a team in the field offering on-the-spot operational advice and able to train franchisees in new techniques and systems.
4. There will be those dealing with product or service innovations and experimental ideas. These should always initially be tried out in the franchisor's company operations.

The quality of the franchisors' field support and monitoring services is important. The franchisor, even in the early stages of his development, has to contemplate that there will be difficulties. It must be ready to cope.

The franchisor should also consult with its bankers, accountants and solicitors. The franchising project should be fully explained to them at an early stage, as it is possible that they may not know too much about the subject. The bankers may be helpful in providing finance for franchisees and may be able to introduce the franchisor to their franchisee managers and franchise team for investigation and guidance. It is not generally sensible for the company to be involved in financing franchisees themselves, either by lending funds or by providing guarantees.[13] The function of the franchisor should be limited to introducing the franchisees to the sources of finance which are available and providing any necessary information which the source reasonably requires.

The accountants can be asked to advise on methods of monitoring the franchisees' financial performance. Solicitors will advise the franchisor about the protection of its rights; they will prepare the contractual documentation and review any franchisee sales literature.

In summary, the initial organizational requirements for the new franchisor with limited resources are the following.

- **Franchisee sales**. Proprietor or managing director, plus a good secretary.
- **Marketing of the product or service**. Proprietor or managing director himself, plus a good secretary, plus advice from outside designers and an advertising agency.
- **Operations**. One person transferred from one of the franchisor's existing operations, who may be a manager originally recruited with this role in mind.
- **Shopfitting and equipment**. The operations person, plus outside suppliers/shopfitters.
- **Training**. A manager of one of the franchisor's own operations which can be used as a training centre.
- **Finance and administration**. Existing company personnel, plus help from the franchisor's bankers, accountants and solicitors.

There remain three important considerations to remember.

1. The owner or managing director of the franchisee must be fully involved personally since he must be prepared to demonstrate his faith in his business and in franchising.
2. The maximum use should be made of existing company staff for reasons not only of economy, but also knowledge, experience and dependability. The choice of initial supporting and managerial staff is, therefore, vital and should be made with an eye to the future and their potential to extend their scope.
3. There can be no franchise activity unless and until a successful and sufficiently profitable pilot operation is first established.

Services

The franchise relationship invariably involves the provision of a wide range of services by the franchisor to its franchisees. The first service provided is to establish the business which is operated and which will be franchised and to prove that it is successful in operation. This service involves the franchisor in risking its own resources in opening and running a new business (or in adapting an existing business) so that the process of discovering and remedying difficulties can be thoroughly explored and executed in order that successive franchisees will be insulated from the development risks inherent in opening a new business. The successful and skilful performance of this project by the franchisor will lay the foundations for the development of the franchised businesses. If this part of the franchisor's job is not properly performed the achievement of success by the network will be more difficult.

In addition there will be the considerable risk that the way in which the franchise system is structured may be flawed, reflecting the failure to learn the necessary lessons and correctly to apply them.

Assuming that this task has been carried out effectively (see above for a more detailed discussion of development of concept and pilot operations), the services provided by a franchisor will be of two distinct types:

- those services provided in the selection and training of franchisees and assisting them in opening for business; and
- the ongoing services which are provided to franchisees during the lifetime of the franchise relationship.

Each of these types of service is important; the initial services result in the conversion of a prospective franchisee with perhaps no previous business experience into a business person equipped to run the franchised business; the ongoing services should be designed to enable the franchisee to be sustained in his business successfully and with the benefit of the updating of relevant technical and business know-how, marketing, promotion, advertising, research and development so that the market place is properly exploited for the benefit of the network in order that the business can cope with developing competitive pressures. We shall consider each of the two types of service.

Initial services

Although few consider it to be the case, these services commence (as mentioned above) with the development stage and continue with recruitment and all that follows up to the actual day of opening of the franchisee's business and sometimes for a few days beyond that day.[14]

Recruitment

This may not usually be regarded as a service provided by a franchisor to its franchisees. However, it should be, since although the franchisor, in recruiting franchisees, is serving its own ends because it needs franchisees to expand the network it also needs to be selective. The selection process should include the franchisor assisting the franchisee in making an objective balanced judgement about whether self-employment is right for the franchisee; whether the franchised business matches the franchisee's skills and aptitudes; whether the franchisor is right for the franchisee and vice versa. If a franchisor provides this service to its franchisees the franchisor will have a better chance of entering into agreements with well motivated, committed and well suited franchisees, which should assist the network to achieve a healthy growth rate.

A franchisor who can say 'no' when all is not completely to its satisfaction will enhance its prospects of success as well as succeeding in building a network of higher quality franchisees. This is particularly important in the early days and months of the development of the system, when ineffective franchisee selection can act as a barrier to growth.

Training

Training should cover two aspects. First, the franchisee must be trained in basic business skills. These will include accounting, reporting methods and systems, staff selection, staff management and control, business procedures, documentary systems necessary for the purposes of controlling the operation and elementary business training which will enable the franchisee to do a basic analysis of whether or not his business has developed or is developing problems and what to do about them. This training will not be so detailed that the franchisor will, in effect, be running a business management college. The training provided by a franchisor will be limited in its application and scope to providing the franchisee with the basic skills necessary for the purpose of conducting the particular business which he is being franchised to operate.

The accounting system which the franchisor should set up should be so arranged as to provide the minimum of work and effort for the franchisee consistent with the provision of the maximum vital information for effective management. The system should be geared to produce the vital flow of financial management information which is necessary for the franchisee to see where he stands at all times. The value of up-to-date meaningful financial information cannot be over-emphasized. Without it the franchisee will not be able accurately to know how his business is performing. The information should show trends, stresses and strains which, if correctly interpreted, will enable appropriate action to be taken in relation to the management of the business at the earliest possible moment.

This information will also be provided to the franchisor, who should be able to interpret what it reveals about the franchisee's business and his conduct of that business and to provide guidance, although not all franchisors are able to provide this sort of service.

The staff selection and staff management and control training the franchisee will receive should provide him with the basic skills he requires for interviewing staff, assessing their capabilities and training them in the work they will have to do. Handling people is largely a matter of experience, but there are nevertheless guidelines which can be given to help the inexperienced. The franchisee will, when he combines the practical experience he will obtain with the procedures which have been laid down for him, find that he is achieving far more than he would otherwise have been able to. This training should also provide the franchisee with an understanding of the legal requirements imposed upon an employer and how they should be complied with.

The franchisor will invariably design and prepare certain forms which the franchisee will have to complete as part of his reporting requirements. These forms will be designed to show the performance of the operation and demonstrate to the franchisor and franchisee the areas in which the franchisee needs to improve his performance. There should be a sound reason for any forms which the franchisee is compelled by the franchisor to complete. It is not the franchisee's function to operate as a source of useless information; nor should a franchisor want to clog up its own administration with unnecessary paperwork.

The franchisee should be trained so that he can develop the ability to detect problems as they arise in his business and thus be in a position to take remedial action without waiting for the franchisor's field support staff to call upon him or respond to a call for help and diagnose that avoidable trouble is brewing or has already taken its toll on the business.

The franchisee must also be trained in the operational aspects of the business. In a food franchise, for example, the franchisee will be taught portion control, quality control, preparation methods, any particular recipes and any particular processes which will have to be applied to the food before it is sold to the consumer. The franchisee will invariably be required to attend a training school to be trained in these aspects.

Above all, whether or not there is a training school, the franchisee must, after he completes his training, be capable of stepping into his own business and opening and running it without pausing to scratch his head and wonder from where his next piece of inspiration will come.

Premises

Many franchisors assist the franchisee in acquiring suitable premises and then preparing them for use as a franchised outlet. This will involve a number of stages:

- site selection criteria;
- planning and by-law compliance;
- lease negotiation;
- design and remodelling of premises.

We shall consider each in turn.

Site selection criteria

The franchisor will, with the criteria for site selection which he has established, investigate and evaluate sites for the franchisee.[15] In some cases the franchisee may himself search for premises for consideration and approval by the franchisor. The franchisor should advise whether or not the sites come within its established criteria, which will include not only the quality of the trading position but whether the franchise operation can physically be accommodated in the space available. A franchise company would not be unreasonable in instructing its site finders that unless the site which they are considering is one into which they would invest every last penny they themselves possess they should not recommend it for the purpose of a franchisee's business. This may seem to be an extreme position but it is certainly a sound principle upon which to operate. No franchisor should expect a franchisee to invest his money in something in which the franchisor would not itself invest. The franchisee should appreciate that in approving a site a franchisor is not infallible. The franchisor is exercising a judgement based on experience but it cannot guarantee that its judgement is correct. For the franchisee blindly to accept the franchisor's opinion without question can be dangerous. The franchisee should closely question the franchisor, particularly if he has doubts about the site. He can of course take advice himself. If his doubts cannot be resolved he should not proceed.

Planning and by-law compliance

There will be cases where the premises which have been found do not have existing planning use which enables them to be used for the business of the franchise system. In such a case planning permission will be necessary and the franchisor will usually be able to give assistance to the franchisee in obtaining any necessary consents under the planning legislation. There are a number of ways in which the franchisor can assist, particularly as it is likely to be a problem which can be anticipated. The franchisor will in all probability have had to obtain planning permission before in other cases and will have an adviser available to assist. In cases where the concept is new the planning authorities will need to have the concept and proposed use explained. An illustrated brochure can often assist in explaining the proposed business. Such a brochure can also be used to explain the business to estate agents representing landlords of proposed premises. In the shopfitting or other conversion of the premises the appropriate building by-law regulations have to be complied with; the franchisor's architect, surveyor or design team may well be able to assist, as well the contractor.

Lease negotiations

A further service which many franchisors offer to franchisees is assistance in negotiating a lease of the premises with the landlords or their agents.[16] As explained above, with a new concept there may be the need for an explanatory document to assist. The franchisor's involvement in the negotiations could benefit the franchisee and assist him in obtaining premises for which he as an individual may not have been acceptable. The franchisor may find that in order to obtain the best sites he has to become involved as a tenant of the premises and sublet to franchisees or find some other way to enable a letting to be achieved. Becoming a landlord is not without risk and a discussion to become involved in this way needs to be considered with care. There are legal as well as business risk issues to be considered, such as the liability for the franchisor to enable further payment of rent after a franchisee sub-tenant fails.

Design and remodelling of premises

The franchisor should assist the franchisee in the designing and remodelling of the premises, which will have to be prepared in conformity with the franchisor's requirements. The franchisor will usually have standard plans and specifications prepared which can be adapted for the particular premises which have been obtained. In some cases the franchisor will prepare amended plans. In others he will require the franchisee to employ an architect or surveyor to prepare the plans and to pay for them. In other cases the shopfitter may prepare amended plans; this is a service which many shopfitters offer.

The franchisor may offer a complete plan preparation and shopfitting service. Alternatively the franchisor may give the franchisee assistance in deciding which particular shopfitter's estimate to accept. The franchisor may also give the franchisee support in the supervision of the shopfitters while they carry out their work. Most franchisors, although they offer such assistance, will not be prepared to accept the responsibility which the franchisee's own surveyor, for example, would accept. Specialized professional advice is the responsibility of the franchisee and should be obtained.

Equipment requirements

The franchisor will, if standardized equipment is not already part of the package which he has sold to the franchisee, give advice and assistance in the selection of the correct equipment at the right prices. The franchisor should have the relevant information readily available and some franchisors provide a list of equipment with brand names and model numbers and locations so that the franchisee can try to obtain a better deal elsewhere.

Opening stock

The franchisor in appropriate cases will provide the franchises with an opening stock inventory list, and will make arrangements for the franchisee to purchase this stock from its own purchasing department or from suppliers who are nominated or approved for the purpose.

The acquisition of stock and its delivery to the outlet on time is crucial to the success of the opening. The franchisee's training should have included guidelines on marketing and promotion as well as the techniques of merchandising products. The franchisor will in appropriate cases provide assistance with merchandising (perhaps with planograms) so that the products are correctly displayed; in some cases assistance with merchandising may be provided on an ongoing basis.

Business launch

Many franchisors provide the franchisee with on-the-spot assistance in the final preparatory arrangements for the store opening. Franchisors typically provide opening assistance by having a team which could comprise as many as two or three people in the location to assist the franchisee in getting the business off the ground. Initially they may have to cope with a heavy volume of work as the public try out the business. The franchisor's opening crew will seek to ensure that the franchisee is properly putting into practice the lessons which he learned during training. The opening crew should remain with the franchisee until they are satisfied that he is into the swing of things and is coping well enough to be left on his own.

It is only when he is left alone after the initial shock that the franchisee will have the opportunity to begin to develop his true potential. At this stage, it is important to emphasize again that the franchisee must realize that no franchisor can guarantee to him success, least of all success without work. A franchise is not a passage to wealth without effort. Most franchises will require long hours of solid work on the part of the franchisee in order to achieve success. What the franchisor is offering is a ready-made formula for carrying on business which in similar circumstances has proved to be successful. It will give to the franchisee whatever assistance it can in an endeavour to ensure that the franchisee will achieve a similar degree of success. This cannot be guaranteed, and any franchisor who offers firm guarantees of success to franchisees should be viewed with caution by prospective franchisees.

Ongoing services

The range of ongoing services which a franchisor provides to his franchisees should give the franchisee the proper level of support in the operation of his business.[17] In addition the franchisor should be creating a climate in which good franchisor–franchisee relations are developed and maintained. This will of course require the franchisee to play his part and look to the future with research, development and market testing capabilities in place. The range of ongoing services may include some or all of the following:

- monitoring and support;
- training;
- 'head office' organization;
- research and development;
- market research;
- advertising and promotion;
- communications.

We shall examine each in turn.

Monitoring and support

The franchise system and contract should have built into them a reporting and monitoring system which will not only ensure that the franchisor has a method of checking that the correct fees are paid but will also provide the franchisor with the information it needs to monitor the franchisee's performance so that it is in a position to detect trends in the franchisee's business and perhaps notice any warning signs. Not all franchisors offer a monitoring service in view of the heavy demands which it can make on specialized and limited resources.

The operation of such a monitoring system can be a valuable tool for both franchisor and franchisee. For the franchisee there will be the discipline of preparing meaningful information which will provide him with vital data concerning his own business and its financial performance. For the franchisor there is a record of network performances against which individual and all franchisees' performances can be reviewed and put into a global perspective.

Information, no matter how detailed, by itself is not enough; there needs to be personal contact with someone who knows the franchisee and his operation and to whom the information provided will mean something. The franchisee should always know who will be available for guidance if he has problems or difficulties. The franchisor should therefore ensure that the franchisee is familiar with the franchisor's 'head office' team and that he knows who deals with what. There will often be a specific point of contact with a member of the franchisor's field support team who should be in touch with the franchisee regularly both by phone, e-mail and by personal visits to the franchised outlet. The franchisor's field support staff should be available at short notice if the franchisee has a real problem.

The field support staff may find on a regular routine visit to the franchisee's business that all is not well because, perhaps, the franchisee is not following the system correctly. Retraining may be necessary where, for example, bad habits have developed or the franchisee has not adopted notified improvements to the system. In such a case the support staff member could remain or arrange to return shortly to the premises while he retrains the franchisee (and staff if necessary) and puts him on the right lines. The franchisee must not rely too heavily on field support; he must learn to solve his own problems; he should look to the franchisor as a shoulder upon which to lean and as a source of assistance to him when things get a bit too much or when he is confronted with something outside his normal experience.

The franchisor's field support team should be available at all times to the franchisee when required. The words 'when required' are used advisedly. The franchisor cannot be expected to know by some telepathic process that the franchisee expects help from him at any particular time. Communication is an essential feature of the relationship and the franchisee has a responsibility in this respect as well as the franchisor. The franchisee must keep in touch with the franchisor and must let the franchisor know when he has difficulties. The franchisee must not delude himself, he must face up to difficulties as they arise and not try to pretend they do not exist.

The franchisee should telephone his field support contact from time to time if he has not been visited, and have a chat with him, for out of these discussions much good can come. He must also read very carefully all literature and circulars which reach him from or through the franchisor, for by this means, if the franchisor is performing his functions correctly, the franchisee will be supplied with valuable operational information. Nothing could be more annoying than for the franchisee to call in assistance when the answer to his problems is contained in the literature which has been circulated to him and which he has just not bothered to read.

The franchisee must appreciate that the franchisor's field support staff want to work with him to help him but that he must also help himself. He cannot expect the franchisor to run his business for him and provide support on call – that is not the franchisor's function. The franchisee must adjust mentally to the fact that he is a businessman in his own right and behave as one.

Whatever the benefits of franchising, the elimination of risk is not one of them. While risk is reduced and failures are lower than is the case with non-franchised new businesses, there are and always will be failures. It is important for the franchisor to understand why there has been a failure and to investigate to see whether it could have been avoided so that the lesson learned can be used to good advantage in the future. Much media treatment of franchisee failure is one-sided; it is meat and drink to the media to be able to describe the failures but they do not find it such good news (or should one say bad news) to learn that the failure was more attributable to the omissions, deeds and misdeeds of the franchisee than those of the franchisor. Perspective is important and there is no doubt that franchisees have failed:

- because the franchisor had not properly tested the concept before franchising;
- because the franchisor was under-capitalized;
- because the franchisor took bad decisions;
- because the franchisor was dishonest;
- because what was involved was not a franchise but some other fraudulent scheme described wrongly as a franchise; and
- because the franchisor failed to provide the continuing services properly or at all.

So, clearly, the reasons which may lead to the failure of the franchisor may equally well bring down the franchisee. Unless the franchisee has the financial and business resources to seek his own salvation by continuing to trade he will also fail. On the other hand, there have been franchisees who have failed despite their franchisor's support and assistance while other franchisees in the same network have succeeded. Short of a fatal misjudgement of the quality of the location all franchisees are provided with the same 'DIY' kit so in theory they should all do equally well. As in all walks of life there will be those who perform in an average way, there will be high flyers and there will be those who under-perform.

Whatever the reason for the failure of the franchisee the symptoms will probably first show themselves as a shortage of cash, with the franchisee failing to pay franchise fees. This cash shortage (insolvency) does not happen overnight unless of course the franchisee spends the night at the races and loses all his money in one evening.

Invariably, insolvency is a developing problem and the benefit of the field support system and the franchisor's monitoring of franchisee performance should reveal the warning signs so that efforts can be made to avoid the problems which will follow. There will always be many warning signs before the franchisee reaches insolvency: for example, he will be slow in paying; he will be slow in doing a lot of things which he should be doing to keep his business and his staff on their toes. He may also reduce stock purchases so his inventory is not as good as it needs to be. The franchisor should be aware of the developing insolvency a long time before the point of no return is actually reached.

Ascertaining the reason why the franchisee is sliding into insolvency is important:

- it could be that he does not follow the system;
- it could be that he will not take advice from the franchisor (which quite often happens);
- he may not be suited to the business;

- he may be under-capitalized;
- he may be spending too much on non-essentials; or
- he may not work hard enough.

However hard one may try in selecting a franchisee it is a value judgement and one may or may not be right. With experience one is more often right than wrong, but even so, some franchisees will be selected who are not capable of running the business.

Some franchisees who are not familiar with business assume that every pound which passes into their till is theirs to spend as they wish. They forget that they have bills, overheads and taxes to pay, and consequently their drawings out of the business are much heavier than they should be: the level of drawings is not justified by the net profitability of the business. It is very difficult to tell a franchisee how much money he should draw out for himself and to seek to control his level of drawings.

There could well be other reasons which are contributory, but it is important to know why the franchisee is sliding into insolvency, because without properly identifying the reason it is not possible to prescribe a cure. Therefore the franchisor should ensure that those in his organization with the right skills are brought into the picture as soon as the danger signs become evident.

It may well be that the circumstances are such that the franchisor will decide that he will terminate the contract, long before a bankruptcy situation is reached, because however much he tries, he is not able to get the franchisee to comply with the contract or the directions given to him. If the franchisor decides not to terminate, he may well think, 'I made a mistake, this is not the right man for the franchise, he's not capable of running the franchise as well as I thought he was.' The franchisor has a duty to try to help a franchisee who is running into difficulties to recover as much of his loss as possible. He would also be well advised to provide help to the franchisee to try to help him to achieve success. This may require promotional support, retraining or additional hands-on support or assistance in rearranging finance or a combination of some or all of these. Ultimately, if the franchisee is unsuitable, the franchisor could try to assist him in finding a purchaser of the business on a basis which will recover for him as much as possible of his capital investment. Sometimes a franchisee will not respond, but experience shows that franchisees (with rare exceptions), if properly handled, usually do respond, and are quite relieved that someone is prepared to assist them and help them out of their difficulties.

Training

The franchisor will find that there will always be a need for training. Franchisees who do not operate the system properly may need retraining. The franchisee may need help in training his staff and in how to do it for himself. There will also be a need to train franchisees in the introduction of innovations which the franchisor may develop from time to time. These may involve system changes or the use of new equipment, or perhaps new applications and uses of existing systems and equipment which promise to be more cost effective for the franchisee in practical use.

'Head office' organization

At the apex of this activity there is, of course, the 'head office' organization of the franchisor. The organization would normally contain specialists in each of the fields in which the franchisee is likely to require assistance. There should be specialists in the management and accountancy aspects of the business; specialists in advertising, marketing, public relations; specialists in product quality control, equipment quality and control; specialists in all the other various aspects of the business with which the franchised chain is concerned.

Under these circumstances the franchisee is better off than the manager of a local branch within a national chain. In a national chain the accent will be on ensuring that the manager runs his branch in accordance with the policy of the company. While to some extent this would apply to a franchised organization, there is not the same rigidity. Each franchisee must be treated as an individual. His problems must be treated as those of an individual, and the approach of the team at the highest management level cannot be to dictate to the franchisee what he should do and what company policy is, but rather to try to train him and to instil in him the interest which an individual should have in running and managing his own business, albeit within the established framework. The franchisee must be persuaded to see the sense of what is expected of him.

The franchisor's interest is in seeking to achieve for the franchisee the success of which his business is capable and to bring the best out of him as an individual. The franchisor should certainly not resort to dictating to the franchisee unless the franchisee insists on breaking his contract or fails properly to operate the system.

If the franchisee wishes to sell his business the franchisor may also be able to assist in obtaining a prospective purchaser for his business. Whether things are going well or not for the franchisee it is quite likely that the franchisor will have contact with many prospective franchisees who may be interested in taking over a business of this sort. The franchisee can often obtain valuable assistance from a franchisor when he does decide, for whatever reason, that the time has come to dispose of his business.

Research and development (including market research)

The franchisor should have research and development facilities in relation to the products, the services or the system and the market image projected. He should constantly be seeking to innovate and introduce ideas and methods for improving the business of the franchised network and the operational systems. A franchisor which does not try to improve its system is likely to have to deal with discontented franchisees who may wonder why they are continuing to pay franchise fees after they receive their initial training.

The franchisor should be experimenting with new product lines and/ or the introduction of new or improved services. These products and services must be compatible with the existing business and should be thoroughly market tested before they are adopted as part of the franchisor's system. A franchisor with company-owned operations can do his market research by offering the products and/or services in those operations to test the efficacy of their introduction. The franchisor may also involve some selected franchisees in market testing through their operations.[18] All changes, whether to system products or services, should be as carefully evaluated as the original operation which was the basis upon which the franchise was started, so that the franchisor can demonstrate to franchisees the likely benefit which should result from their introduction.

The research and development activities can extend to exploring new sources of supply of good quality materials, supplies or products for the franchisees so that costs are kept to the most economic level possible. As the network grows its bulk purchasing requirements will also grow, resulting in considerable accounts with manufacturers and suppliers. This should produce valuable savings for each individual franchisee, since bulk purchasing can reduce prices and retrospective volume rebates can also be available. Manufacturers of supplies also promote products and provide marketing support which the size of the network's account may justify. Benefits and savings can thus be obtained for franchisees which would not be available to them outside the franchise network when they would only have their own individual resources with which to bargain.

Advertising and promotion

In most cases the franchisor will undertake responsibility for advertising, promotion and public relations for the network. The cost is invariably borne by the franchisees (Chapter 7) through the contributions they make to the franchisor for this purpose. The franchisor's advertising and promotional schemes should exploit to the full the national corporate image of the franchised network as the provider of goods and/or services. Many franchisors involve franchisees in the development of advertising and promotional schemes through wide consultation or through discussions with franchisee associations. In some countries franchisors involve franchisees in cooperative type structures to develop such advertising and promotional schemes.

In structuring the advertising arrangements the franchisor will have to bear in mind a number of factors.[19]

1. First and foremost will be the need to establish and maintain a strong branding for the network which is favourably received by the

consumer. The franchisor will need to be in control of the way in which this branding is projected. Since integrity of the branding by which the network is known is so vital the franchisor will either generate all the advertising output or subject any which a franchisee wishes to conduct to an approval system.

2. Consideration must be given to what will be the most effective method of reaching the consumer market for the network's products or services. Will national advertising suffice? Will regional advertising be appropriate? Will local advertising and promotion by each franchisee be the most effective? The answers to these questions will have an influence on the franchisor's decision.

3. The franchisor will also need to consider whether to generate the materials required 'in-house' or to use outside services.

4. Will the franchisor assist franchisees with the provision of point-of-sale material out of the advertising contributions or will a separate charge be made? How will in-store or point-of-sale promotions by manufacturers and suppliers be dealt with?

5. Will the franchisor provide franchisees who wish to advertise locally with blocks, bromides or camera-ready copy which they can utilize for that purpose? This could not only result in the cost-effective use of resources but also provide the franchisor with the ability to control the way in which the advertisements display the branding.

6. What degree of consultation does the franchisor intend to have with franchisees? (There is more about this issue more generally in Chapters 8 and 9).

The franchisor will undoubtedly need to have someone in his organization to deal with advertising and promotion as well as public relations.

Promotion does not stop with advertising, marketing and public relations. The franchisor can also exploit the development of national accounts whose local business can be transacted with franchisees so that each franchisee benefits from obtaining business to which it would not have had access but for its membership of the franchise network.

Communications

Good communications in franchising are fundamental to a franchisor's success. The role of communications is dealt with in detail in Chapters 8 and 9.

Notes

1. In the USA, other matters will also need attention (See Chapter 17)
2. In the USA, it is becoming increasingly common for the operations manual to be provided electronically to the franchisees through a secure Internet website link.
3. In the USA, a consultant involved in the selling of franchises becomes a 'franchise broker' for the franchisor. He will have to be disclosed in the offering circular and registered in two states.
4. In the USA, the offering circular will contain a list of all franchisees or the closest 100 franchisees.
5. In the USA, eight of the franchise registration states require that an advertisement offering franchises for sale be filed with the state and be subject to review before being used to sell franchises in the state. There are certain exceptions for interstate and Internet advertising.
6. In the USA, an increasing number of franchisors market through their Internet websites. These website ads may be subject to review by the eight states that review advertising, although most of them will not review the websites if they are not specifically directed at prospects in their states and the franchisor complies with the state's procedures for exempting that advertising.
7. In the USA, franchisors (whether or not they are US franchisors) exhibiting at a trade show must have available offering circulars for prospective franchisees unless in the case of non-USA franchisors they are not intending to sell franchises to be operated in the USA..
8. In the USA, information given to a prospective franchisee from which a specific level or range of actual or potential sales, costs, income or profit from franchised or non-franchised units may be ascertained is an 'earnings claim'. Earnings claims have to be included in the offering circular and must be substantiated.
9. In the USA, the offering circular must disclose the franchisee's estimated initial investment in the franchised business. The final category in this disclosure are the additional funds required by the franchisee before operations begin and during the initial phase of the franchise, which must be at least three months or a reasonable time period for the industry.
10. As noted above, an outside consultant who wants to sell franchises would be considered to be a 'franchise broker' in the USA.
11. In the USA, employees of the franchisor or its affiliates who engage in franchise sales have to file sales agent disclosure forms with most of the franchise registration states.
12. In the USA, the training programme (including the names of the instructors and their backgrounds) must be disclosed in the offering circular.
13. In the USA, if a franchisor offers or provides financing to its franchisees, the terms and conditions of the financing arrangement have to be disclosed in the offering circular.
14. In the USA, franchisors must disclose in their offering circulars the obligations they will perform before the franchised business opens.
15. In the USA, the franchisor must disclose in its offering circular the methods it will use to select the location of the franchisee's business.
16. Some franchisors in the USA own or lease premises which they in turn lease or sublease to their franchisees.
17. In the USA, franchisors must disclose in their offering circulars the obligations to be met by the franchisor during the operation of the franchised business.
18. McDonald's executives often observe publicly that many of the best ideas to improve their system came from their franchisees.
19. In the USA, details of the franchisor's advertising programme must be disclosed in the offering circular.

6 How to become a franchisee

How being a franchisee differs from running your own non-franchised business

Buying a franchise is just like buying a business, but with a difference. What is that difference? In the case of a conventional business, the seller is asked questions and provides answers and, it is hoped, a proper set of accounts. The buyer makes up his mind whether he would like to buy. There are 'going market rates' for various types of business, and after perhaps some haggling over the price a deal is struck. The buyer takes over the business and will run it in whatever way he thinks best.

In the case of franchising, there are a number of other very important factors to consider. A franchisee will be entering into a long-term relationship with the franchisor in which he will have to rely on the franchisor to a large extent for the success of his own business. The franchisee will not be allowed to run his business in whatever way he thinks fit. He will have the obligation to run it precisely in accordance with the franchisor's system.

One will find that there are four primary factors affecting the business which would not be there if one were trading independently outside the franchise system. These factors are:

1. The existence of the franchisor.
2. The obligation to use its name and systems, and submit to its control.
3. The risk of events occurring which are detrimental to the business without the franchisee being in the position to exert any influence over them (e.g. the business failure of the franchisor, actions by other franchisees which bring the business into disrepute).
4. The ability of the franchisor to continue to provide services of a standard which makes them worthwhile and valuable to the success of the franchisee's business.

A franchisee can find he is vulnerable to one or more of these factors and must, therefore, be aware of the risks in order to be able to ask the right questions and make a sound judgement when assessing a franchisor. In this context, it is useful to review the most common causes of failure by franchisors.

1. **Inadequate pilot tests.** With a new concept, there is a danger that the franchisor has not pilot-tested his system sufficiently well to have proved its viability in the market place. The problem is that it is difficult to judge what represents sufficient pilot-testing. However, if there can be any general rule, it is that the testing should be for as long as is necessary for the franchisor to prove the viability of his system in a variety of locations and market conditions which as closely as possible are similar to those where the franchisee wishes to operate. One must also ensure, for example, that seasonal factors have been recognized and allowed for by the franchisor. In reality, it can take a new franchisor two years to develop its system to the point at which it is ready to market the franchise. In assessing a franchise, one should take great care to ensure that the pilot-testing has been fully and thoroughly carried out. As interest increases in franchising, there are likely to be more franchises on offer where proper piloting has not been done. Without being able to prove that there is a fully tested and successful system, one could probably question whether, in fact, there is a franchise to sell.

2. **Poor franchisee selection.** It is a common tendency in the early days of a franchise for the franchisor to accept, as franchisees, those who are readily available but may be unsuitable. This occurs because a franchisor can be under a great deal of pressure to make some quick sales, or because it has not at that stage been able to identify properly the characteristics and qualities which its franchise calls for in a franchisee. Poor selection inevitably brings problems which slow growth and divert the management resources of the franchisor away from other vital tasks. Unhappy franchisees are not a good advertisement for the franchise system.

3. **The franchise may be badly structured.** This can be the result of inadequate pilot-testing, the inability to anticipate likely problems and/or the failure to draw the right conclusions from the experience gained during pilot testing. Structural problems lead to operational difficulties, and these in turn to financial problems and difficulties in developing and managing a network of franchisees.

4. **The under-capitalization of the franchisor.** Many franchisors fail to recognize that it can take three to five years after commencing franchising to reach a point at which they achieve some profitability. More capital may be required if the franchisor supplies the products, as this may tie up capital in large inventories. Franchising is not a solution to its problems for a company which is in financial difficulty and it would be foolish to become involved with a franchisor whose business has such problems.[1]

5. **The franchisor may run its business badly.** The fact that a business operates as a franchisor does not insulate it from business error, even though the franchise may have a basically sound

structure. As a prospective franchisee, one must, therefore, prepare a different set of questions from those which would be asked when buying a conventional independent business. It must also be understood that just because someone is a franchisor it does not mean that his business cannot fail, nor does it mean that franchisees are protected from failure. However, a well tested and structured franchise offered by a properly capitalized franchisor does provide the franchisee with a better prospect of success than he would have if he were to go into business independently.

It should also be appreciated that taking a franchise is not a substitute for hard work. To succeed as a franchisee, as in any worthwhile business venture, it will take a lot of hard work, complete commitment to the business, and the patience to allow time for the business to become established. There is no such thing in franchising as work-free overnight riches or success.

In assessing a franchise opportunity, one must consider the following factors, which are all of prime importance.

- Examine the franchisor's financial position in great detail.[2] An accountant will be able to help. It should be evident that the franchisor has spent money on proving that his concept works in practice, and that he is adequately capitalized and financed to run the business in the future.
- Check how thoroughly the franchisor has market tested the business.
- Assess how well the system works in practice. Are the existing franchisees (if any) pleased with their businesses and the performance of the franchisor?[3]
- Does the business have staying power, or is it based on something which is temporarily fashionable? Here today and maybe gone tomorrow is not a sound investment.
- No one should buy a franchise from anyone other than the franchisor. Do not finalize a deal with franchise brokers. They tend only to be interested in making sales and are not around later when problems may arise.
- Ask a solicitor to check the franchise agreement, preferably one who has experience in the field. (The British Franchise Association has a list of affiliate lawyer members with experience in the field. A personal recommendation from a satisfied client will also be worth following up.). A franchisor needs to have controls in the agreement to ensure the uniformity of the system and the quality of its products and/or services. The agreement should be fair to the franchisee and the franchisor, and it should cover the services which you have been told you will get from him. However, by nature the contract will be one-sided.
- It must be understood that there is always the risk that a franchisee might not be successful in the business, despite the success of others.

He may not perhaps be suited to the stresses and strains of being his own boss. His family may find that the strain is difficult to live with, and put him under more pressure. He must sure that he and they can cope.

Self-examination

Everyone who decides that he would like to have his own business should subject himself to a detailed self-examination of his attitudes, capabilities and long-term goals. Some factors in any such examination apply whether or not the business is a franchise, while some are specific to franchising. There are factors which are fundamental to the assessment.

Every prospective franchisee must:

- engage in this self-examination exercise;
- be completely frank with himself; and
- not delude himself into pursuing his original desires, regardless of what he knows to be the correct answers to the questions which he must ask himself.

Consideration should also be given to a factor to which no attention appears to be paid when franchisee failure is reported in the media. Franchisees can be the cause of their own downfall. It should be borne in mind that at least 50% of franchisees who experience failure are themselves responsible for their plight. The provision by the franchisor of his know-how, system and business format does not guarantee success. The franchisor provides a basic DIY business kit, but the success of the practical operation of this 'kit' depends greatly upon the franchisee's skill and ability in maximizing the opportunity which it presents.

This factor sometimes makes it difficult to ascertain the reason for failure, although there is now enough experience available to identify the characteristics which give rise to self-induced failure by franchisees.

Any potential franchisee who engages in critical self-examination should be aware of these characteristics in case he recognizes that he himself possesses one or more of them. What are these characteristics? They include the following. (The examples quoted have actually occurred and are not figments of the author's imagination.)

1. **The franchisee who has previously been in business for himself, and possibly in the same type of business as the franchise system.** Such a person may have entrenched ideas of his own and thus be less receptive to the ideas of the franchisor and the disciplines of the system. It is for this reason that many franchisors will not accept as franchisees those who have previous experience in their type of business. Life being what it is, there are exceptions, and there are cases where previous market knowledge and experience

are essential, since they cannot be learned in an economically sensible time frame. However, the acceptance by the franchisee of the disciplines of the franchise system is fundamental. If he feels that the franchisor has little to offer that he believes he does not already know he should forget franchising.

2. **Franchisee complacency.** No franchisee can afford to be complacent. There have been cases in which franchisees have failed to make the necessary effort because, as they put it, 'I am now a boss and bosses don't work.' The boss syndrome can be quite dangerous. Franchisees who have this problem behave in the way they think bosses should behave, which they usually believe means spending without working and earning. No one can succeed on that basis. If the prospective franchisee's expectations of business life as his own boss are along these lines he should avoid self-employment because if he puts this attitude into practice he will be doomed to failure.

3. **The franchisee who loses his nerve.** This takes two forms.

   (a) The franchisee who simply loses his nerve when, after opening, the responsibilities and magnitude of the task of being a self-employed businessman dawn upon him.

   (b) The franchisee who cannot live with the losses which many businesses make in the early days before they become established. This loss of nerve occurs even in cases where the franchisees have been warned that it will happen and have been advised to arrange their finance on such a basis that they have the working capital to sustain them during the start-up period. A strong nerve is necessary to be able to cope with trading losses while building a business.

4. **The franchisee who does not follow the system.** This is more likely to occur after the franchisee has been in business for a period of time and has become successful. He begins to believe that he and not the franchisor is the reason for his prosperity. In part, he will, of course, be contributing to his own success. Some franchisees are better than others and some are more prosperous than others because of their diligence and hard work. The danger arises when this leads to an arrogant belief by the franchisee that he knows best and where this in turn leads to a rejection of the franchisor's system or a desire to impose his will and effect changes without authority.

5. **Interference from other family members, or well intentioned but busy-body friends.** It is important that the franchisee should have the support of his family (particularly his or her partner), but support is one thing and interference is another. It can be appreciated that a partner will have the welfare of his (or her) partner at heart, but the partner should not usurp the franchisor's function, or take on the franchisor on behalf of his (or her) partner. That is a recipe for disaster. Many franchisors will wish to interview both partners, even when only one is applying for a franchise, in order to make an assessment of the degree of support which is likely

to be forthcoming, as well as the degree of interference. Busy-body friends should be avoided like the plague. They should be politely kept apart from the business, especially those who profess to have an expertise which they consider to be of vital benefit to their friend the franchisee. A person who is easily led and finds it difficult to reach decisions independently will find self-employment a dangerous undertaking.

6. **The franchisee who expects too much to be done for him.** Some franchisees feel that the franchisor should be doing more for them on a day-to-day basis than is the case in a franchise system. The franchisee who previously had a job with a salary will have to accept that he is now dependent upon his own performance for his take-home pay. He cannot if the going gets tough expect the franchisor financially to bale him out. A franchisor does, of course, provide fall back assistance (not financial) to a franchisee with problems. It cannot be expected to offer a day-to-day presence, or the local involvement and initiative necessary to develop the business. That is the franchisee's contribution, and no prospective franchisee should enter into a franchise relationship if he believes that the franchisor should be involved on a day-to-day operational basis in the business. The only exceptions are those franchise systems which specifically provide such involvement. (Examples would be where the franchisor operates a central booking or ordering facility, or accounting system.).

7. **The franchisee who does not have the right aptitude.** This type of franchisee falls into two categories. In the first category are those who are so blinded by the attractiveness of the franchise opportunity that they do not recognize their own inabilities and deficiencies or indeed those of the franchisor. A franchisor can never know as much about the franchisee as the franchisee knows about himself. The franchisee must be honest with himself and the franchisor. If, for example, the franchise system needs the franchisee to be an active salesman and he knows that this is something he would find difficult he should hesitate to become involved. On the other hand, a franchisee who likes meeting people and who feels that the franchise of his liking will involve him in stifling administrative duties should think again. In the second category are those who have perhaps been in employment at a senior management level and are not accustomed to rolling up their sleeves and working hard at the basics and at the sharp end of a business. The subsequent sale of a franchised business which has been taken over by a franchisee with the right attitude often proves how wrong was the predecessor's attitude.

These, then, are the characteristics which signal problems for the prospective franchisee. Those who are counselling the franchisee, including the franchisor, should assist him in questioning whether he will fall within one or more of these categories. The characteristics should be kept in mind as a general background against which to proceed with the evaluation process.

Let us now consider a widely voiced statement: 'Franchising is safer than independently setting up in business on your own account.' This, broadly speaking, is correct, and it is certainly so in the USA, where it is claimed to be borne out by statistics. In the UK the experience of members of the BFA as a whole, of reputable franchise companies and of the banks involved in franchise finance bears out this claim. The annual BFA survey sponsored by the National Westminster Bank (see Appendix A) also supports this claim.

It is popularly claimed that while 90% of all new businesses fail within a five-year period, the comparable percentage in the case of franchisees is not more than 10%. This popular claim is a step in the right direction, but it is a misleading statement of the position. The sum of the evidence which is available, particularly the experience of the banks, supports the view that franchising is a safer method of entry into a new business than going it alone. The likelihood of a new franchised business failure is approximately somewhere between one-sixth to one-eighth of the risk with new non-franchised businesses.

However, there are dangers in making claims about the high levels of success in franchising. The prospective franchisee may:

- drop his guard when evaluating a franchise because he has heard such claims and come to trust the system as a whole, regardless of what may be the position in the particular franchise which he is considering;
- be lulled into the false belief that all he needs to do to make a lot of easy money is to sign a franchise agreement; and
- ignore the fact that it is still necessary to select the right franchisor who has properly prepared the franchise for the market place and the franchisor who is right for the franchisee.

The lessons to be drawn are that each franchise offering must be considered on its own merits in the light (at the very least) of the guidance offered in this book and in the certainty that franchising is not the easy way to quick riches. In life, nothing comes easily, and this is certainly true of franchising. Most successful franchisees have worked very hard to achieve their success.

Franchising should, however, reduce the risks inherent in opening a new business. This is because one of its main attractions is that the franchisor is selling the benefit of the experience he has gained in running his own business (or his pilot operation) and has detected and solved the problems with which any new business is always faced. The franchisor has carried the development cost, which often the individual cannot afford to bear or risk. Franchising should, therefore, provide the franchisee with a business which has a proven record of success upon which he can build. No franchise should ever be offered, or be considered, as a work-free way of making money. If it is offered in this way, the prospective franchisee should be suspicious, and if he regards the opportunity in this way, he should stop being greedy and come to his senses.

It is surprising that there are a significant number of prospective franchisees who seek proper advice before entering into a franchise contract but who fail to heed that advice because it was not what they wanted to hear. In other words, they have already made up their minds when they take advice and what they are told makes no difference. This particularly applies with new franchise systems where the tendency is to believe that however badly structured and inadequately tested it is, getting in early is desirable because those in first make most. This attitude is really only a manifestation of greed which prevents rational thought. While those 'in early' in a well structured and properly piloted franchise system may do extremely well, the risks are higher, as will be seen below, and the prospective franchisee must be prepared to take a deep breath, reconsider his position and say 'no', however much he is enamoured of the proposition, unless objective investigation coupled with sound independent advice confirm the necessary quality of the franchisor and its proof, by having spent its own money and run the development risk, that it indeed has a well tried, tested and successful business format.

The factors discussed are all important in the process through which all prospective self-employed businessmen should go before taking the plunge. Indeed, the prospective franchisee must not lose sight of the fact that in deciding whether or not to go into a franchise he is also deciding to go into business on his own account, albeit in a particular type of business which has been structured in a certain type of way.

The following questions should be asked and answered honestly and put into the perspective of the franchised business in which the franchisee is interested.

1. Do I understand franchising and what is involved?
2. Am I qualified physically and temperamentally for self-employment?
3. Will my age/health permit me to run the business long enough to recover my initial investment and to make the effort worthwhile? Conversely, am I too young to have the maturity to run my own business, and employ and direct people?
4. Do I possess sufficient financial resources to enable me to start a business, and survive while it is struggling to become established?
5. Do I have the nerve and force of will to survive expected losses while building up my business and to cope with any unexpected set-backs?
6. What are my natural aptitudes and skills? Do I have the skills relevant for this system, e.g. manual dexterity, organizational skills, selling and marketing skills? Does this franchise opportunity provide me with the right platform for me to exploit and maximize my strengths?

7. Am I at my best with mental or physical tasks?

8. Are my strengths to be found in sales or organization?

9. Do I mix well with people?

10. Will I be able to handle staff?

11. Do I have the ability and commitment to work hard?

12. Am I prepared to work unsocial hours?

13. How will my family be affected by my decision and the calls which the business will make upon my time?

14. Do my family wholeheartedly support my proposed venture?

15. Will any of my family be able, available and happy to help me?

16. Am I prepared to put whatever assets I now possess at risk? Can my family and I stand the stress which may follow taking such a risk?

17. Will I be able to raise sufficient finance?

18. What am I looking for, and can I achieve it:

    (a) job satisfaction?

    (b) a challenge?

    (c) status?

    (d) improving ones standard of living?

    (e) capital gain?

    (f) lots of money? (Is this a wise attitude?)

    (g) an investment (absentee owner)?

19. Will the business be sufficiently challenging for me over a period of time?

20. Can I accept the disciplines of a franchise system?

21. Will I resent the franchisor's authority?

22. Do I possess sufficient ability to exercise initiative and to capitalize on the opportunities presented to me? Do I possess the requisite levels of motivation, drive and ambition? Will I relax when I reach a certain level of success or will my ambition not have boundaries?

23. Would I be better off if I enter the ranks of the self-employed other than through the franchise route?

24. Finally, what do I want to achieve in life?

It is vital for the prospective franchisee to subject himself and his attitudes to the closest possible scrutiny. He should be sure he knows himself and knows what it is that he is looking for. He should ensure in carrying out the self-assessment procedures which are recommended that his particular strengths and weaknesses are relevant to and will be effective if put to use in the particular proposition which he is considering and the demands it will make.

Type of business

The position of the franchise system in the market in which it trades is a vital consideration. Not only should the particular franchised business be examined in relation to its own activities, but an assessment should also be made of the prospects for the overall industry or trade sector of which it forms a part. The franchise will be dealing in goods or products, the provision of services or a mix of both. Table 6.1 contains a comparison of the various considerations which should help in making an assessment.

Table 6.1		*Goods or products*	*Services*
Comparison of considerations	1.	Are the products new? Have they distinctive advantages over their competitors?	Is the service to be provided a new one? Has it a distinctive advantage over competitors' services?
	2.	Has the franchised business been thoroughly proven in practice to be successful?	Same
	3.	Is this a product distributorship, or agency, which is not really a franchise but one which is promoted as a business format franchise and thus suspect?	Does this service have a novel or distinctive element about it which clearly distinguishes it from other similar and competitive businesses, and is it clearly a franchise and not some other type of arrangement?
	4.	Does it have staying power?	Same
	5.	Is it in a market area which is in decline?	Same
	6.	Is it in a growth market?	Same
	7.	Is it exploiting a fad or a current fashion which is likely to be transient and short-lived?	Same
	8.	How competitive is the market for the particular products?	How competitive is the market for the provision of these services?
	9.	How competitive is the price of the products?	How competitive is the price at which the services are to be offered?
	10.	Can this competitiveness be maintained?	Same
	11.	What is the source of supply of the goods or products?	Not applicable
	12.	How certain is it that the source will be available for the future?	Not applicable
	13.	Are alternative sources of products of comparable quality and price available?	Not applicable

14.	Are the products protected by a trade mark? If a celebrity name is used, remember that celebrities and their reputations come and go, and so too can any related franchise.	Is there a strong, distinctive trade name or trade mark associated with the provision of the services? If a celebrity name is used, remember that celebrities and their reputations come and go, and so too can any related franchise.
15.	Are the products produced by a patented invention? Does the franchisor have the long-term right to benefit from the patent?	Not strictly applicable, although it is possible for a patented product to be featured in a service business so this could still be relevant. Is the service based on an exclusive process?
16.	Does the franchisor have his lines of supply properly tied up?	Not applicable
17.	Is there adequate back-up in terms of guarantees and service facilities?	Not applicable
18.	Could the manufacturer or supplier easily by-pass the franchisor and you, and set up his own competitive franchise?	Not applicable
19.	What is the reputation of the goods and products?	What is the reputation of the service, or process?
20.	What is the reputation of the supplier?	Not applicable
21.	If it is a successful franchise newly imported from another country will it hold a similar appeal in the UK market? Has it been market tested in the UK by careful and thorough pilot-testing as if it were a UK-originated system?	Same

Do not underestimate the importance of the questions in Table 6.1. Make sure that the proposition has been well enough tested and for a long enough period of time for one to be satisfied that the market really exists and has long-term prospects.

Please do remember, and there is no apology for the repetition, that one must not enter into self-employment and franchising if one is not prepared to risk losing all! No prospective franchisee should delude himself into believing that any franchisor guarantees his success and that he will underwrite a franchisee's failure. The business risk the franchisee runs is his. That risk must be fully understood and appreciated.

Assessing the franchisor

The assessment of the franchisor is a very important part of the process of making up one's mind about whether or not to take up a franchise and if so which to choose.

Do not assume that just because someone calls himself a franchisor, it means that it really is one. Many who perpetrate frauds will often try to lull the unsuspecting into believing that what they offer is a franchise when it is not. One should not allow oneself to be misled, particularly by these promoters of spurious schemes who suggest that disproportionately high rewards will follow. Remember that in calling a proposition a franchise when it is not is the first stage in the marketing of fraudulent so-called opportunities (see references to pyramid selling and other schemes in Chapter 2). Get rich quick offers should also be ignored – these fraudsters are playing on the greed which some people have.

It is quite common for a person with a business to be approached by someone who feels that he would like to become a franchisee of that business. This is very often the first time that the owner of the business has heard of franchising and in such a situation he is totally unprepared and quite incapable of offering a viable franchise. Frequently, the response by the owner of the business is to rush out and ask his solicitor for a franchise contract.

There is, of course, more to franchising than a contract. That, in a sense, comes last after the commercial viability of the business as a franchise has been properly structured and established. So do not make the mistake of trying to rush the owner of an existing but non-franchised business into selling a franchise. There have been cases where an approach from a prospective franchisee has acted as catalyst for the creation of a new franchise. But from the planting of an idea to the establishment of a viable franchise can take a considerable amount of time. Indeed, very few properly structured and piloted franchised systems can be ready for marketing in less than one or two years from the time the idea is first conceived depending on the degree of piloting which is necessary.

If one, as a prospective franchisee, believes that the business is attractive, patience is essential and one must wait until the owner has had the opportunity to develop a proper franchise system in which it would be safe for a franchisee to invest. Otherwise, one may well be contributing to one's own downfall.

Most of the franchise systems on the market are likely to be at different stages in the development and maturity of their franchise. The more franchisees there are, the easier will be the task of assessment because there will be many franchisees to talk to about what the franchise and the franchisor have done for them.

In situations where the franchisor is just getting off the ground, greater care is needed in making a choice, but this does not mean that one should not take up such a franchise. New franchises can and do provide splendid opportunities for those who take the trouble to investigate them properly and choose wisely. Table 6.2 illustrates the different stages in the development of a franchise system and the problems which can arise at each stage.

	Number of franchisees	Comments
Table 6.2 Stages of development	1–10	The franchisor at this stage is still feeling its way. This is when it will be discovering whether it has been sufficiently thorough in pilot-testing its concept. Has its pilot-testing been wide enough, or conducted over a sufficiently long period?
		It is very vulnerable at this stage to its inexperience in selecting franchisees. It will also be feeling impatient because it has invested its resources in preparing to market its franchise and it will want to get on with selling its franchises as rapidly as possible in order to develop some cash flow.
	11–40	The franchisor has now overcome its first hurdle, but it may be facing the problem of having among its first ten franchisees four or five who are unsatisfactory (the reasons for this are explained in Chapter 5). The unsatisfactory nature of these franchisees may not yet be apparent, but they could already be taking up a disproportionate amount of the franchisor's time. At this stage, if the franchise has not been properly structured, various stresses and strains will begin to emerge.
		There should be good feedback from existing franchisees which should help the prospective franchisee.
		The franchisor should at this point be developing its organizational infrastructure to cope with a hoped-for increasing number of franchisees and the growth of its business. Care must be taken to ensure that the growth rate does not outstrip the infrastructural resources and capacity of the franchisor.
	41–100	By now the franchise is relatively mature. The franchisor should be well organized and enjoying a reasonable return from its activities. It will now be turning its attention to laying the foundations for substantial expansion. It will also be at the phase at which it will need to evaluate what is happening within the franchise. Does it need a fresh approach? Does it fulfil its function?
		Certainly, it will be a very different franchisor from the one at stage 1–10. It should now be possible to see how capable the franchisor is at adapting to progress and change and how well he has serviced his franchisees. As is the case with the 11–40 franchisees the existing franchisees will be able to provide some indication to a prospective franchisee of how satisfied they are and what they may not like about the way the franchisor services and deals with them.
	Over 100	The franchisor will now have reached maturity and all the relevant information with which to assess the franchise should be readily available. The existing franchisees will provide a valuable source of information about the quality of the franchisor as well as the franchise system and the relationship which exists between them. The ability of the franchisor successfully to adapt to change and respond to developments and opportunities in the market place should also be apparent.

Fundamental questions

What qualifies the franchisor to be a franchisor? What is its background? How well has it prepared its scheme? What is there to suggest that it is able to deliver on its promises and obligations?

To answer these important questions, the franchisor should be asked to provide the following information:[4]

1. What is your business background and experience and that of your directors and principal shareholders (or partners)?

2. A detailed history of the development of the business to date.

3. What steps have you taken to prepare your business for franchising? (This and questions 4–8 are particularly appropriate for a franchise which is in the early stages of development and will become less relevant as the size of the franchisor's network grows.) There is little point in asking a franchisor which has over 15 or so franchisees how well it piloted its ideas. The franchisees in the system will provide much more valuable information on this aspect of the operation.

4. What knowledge or experience do you have of franchising and how did you acquire it?

5. How many pilot franchise operations did you establish before you began to offer franchises for sale?

6. How much of your own cash did you invest in establishing that your business was franchisable?

7. How can I be sure that you have adequately investigated the market place and that you have acquired sufficient knowledge so that I can be satisfied that I am investing in a thoroughly tested business which has had the experience of confronting and solving the daily problems which arise? Please provide details of the performance achieved by pilot operations. Please explain why you consider that the number of pilot operations which you conducted was sufficient in numbers and range of locations or area of operations to prove that the concept works and that you are justified in commencing franchising operations.

8. Why did you decide to franchise rather than develop your business by the expansion of your own operations?

9. What is the growth rate you are planning over the next five years?

10. What is your corporate structure? How well can it cope with the growth of your franchise network and what plans do you have for the expansion of your support staff and the development of your infrastructure?

11. Who are the senior executives who will be influencing and planning the growth and development of the franchise network and dealing with the franchisees?

12. Can you confirm that none of these senior executives has ever been:
    (a) involved as principal, shareholder or executive in a company which has gone into receivership or liquidation, or had an administrative receiver appointed or an administration order made against it?
    (b) bankrupt or made an arrangement with his creditors?
    (c) involved in a franchise company which has experienced business failure?
    (d) unsuccessfully involved in business as a franchisee?
    (c) convicted of a criminal offence (other than a motoring offence not involving imprisonment)?
13. Please provide details of the following.
    (a) How many franchisees do you presently have? May I have their names and addresses?
    (b) How many franchisees did you have 12 months ago?
    (c) How many franchisees, within the past two years, have:
        (i) had their contracts terminated by you?
        (ii) terminated their contract with you?
        (iii) mutually agreed with you to terminate their contract?
        Please explain the circumstances.
14. How selective are you in choosing franchisees? Please explain your approach.
15. Please provide a copy of your latest audited accounts.
16. Can you confirm that there has not been any deterioration in your financial position since such accounts were prepared? If confirmation cannot be given, please explain why not.
17. Please confirm that you have made arrangements adequately to finance your activities during at least the ensuing year.
18. Are you a member of the BFA? If so, which category of membership?
19. Have you applied for membership of the BFA and been refused?
20. Who are your bankers? May I take up a reference from the bank for at least the level of my proposed investment?
21. Do you have any arrangement with any of the banks which offer franchisee finance? If so, with which and may I have details?
22. Please provide at least two financial and business references, other than your bankers.

The views of existing franchisees and the experience they have had with their franchisor are always very important. However, and particularly (but not exclusively) in the case of early franchisees, beware of any franchisees who may have caused, or largely contributed to, the problems of which they complain. This possibility has been referred to above.

Advice should be taken from a solicitor and accountant and they will help you to place the replies you receive in perspective. But whatever the replies and advice you receive, you must satisfy yourself that the franchisor whose system you decide to join is one which will provide you with a long-term business relationship and that the franchisor is one on whose judgement you feel that you can rely.

Assessing the business proposition

The business of the franchisor has to be investigated. This investigation should be concerned with securing answers to the following issues.

1. How is the business structured?
2. What will the franchisor do to assist the franchisee into business?
3. What are the operational factors which are relevant and have to be considered?
4. What are the detailed procedures for getting a franchisee established in the business and what services will be provided to achieve that?
5. What ongoing services will be provided and how will they be delivered?

At this point of the investigation the franchisee should be trying to ascertain the 'nuts and bolts' of the franchisor's operational system and its methods of working.

In most cases, the franchisor will provide the franchises with the services mentioned in Chapter 16 in order to assist the franchisee in obtaining his premises and preparing them for the opening. However, there can be cases in which the franchisor offers what is called a 'turnkey' operation. This means that the franchisor obtains the site and fully refurbishes, shopfits and stocks the store before handing the franchisee the 'key' against payment of the cost. In a turnkey operation, the franchisee, who will receive his training while his shop is being prepared, does not get involved in any way in the construction and fitting out work, although the franchisor will keep in close contact with him during construction and will keep him in the picture and consult with him about what is being done. The franchisee will, of course, be responsible for the cost of fitting out, equipping and stocking the business.

The following questions should be asked.[5]

1. What is the total cost of establishing a business under your franchise?
2. What does this cost include?
3. What capital or other costs will be incurred by me in addition to the cost of establishing the business?

4. Do I have to pay a deposit? If so, on what terms? Are there any circumstances in which, if I do not proceed, I will lose my deposit, or any part of it? If so, please explain.

5. What initial franchise fee do I have to pay? What is it for?

6. How much working capital do I need? What is the basis for your calculation of this requirement?

7. How long will it take to set up the business from the time we sign a contract to when we actually open?

8. What training facilities are there and where do you provide them? How long will the training last and what will it include?

9. Who pays for the training? Who pays the expenses I incur in attending the training, including fares and hotel accommodation?

10. Do you provide training facilities for my staff? If so, on what terms? if not, who trains them, and if I have to do so how am I provided with the means to do so?

11. What level of gross profit margin should I expect to achieve? Please itemize the expenses which I shall expect to incur. What level of turnover do I need to achieve to break even and how long should it take to reach that level?

12. May I see actual accounts which confirm, or fail to confirm, any projections with which you provide me? Can they be relied upon? Or are they merely illustrations (see below)?

13. What financing arrangements are available and what terms for repayment will there be? What rate of interest will be required and will the bank or finance company want security?

(Note: the questions which relate to financial performance will probably be answered in a qualified way. Very few franchisors will be prepared to make representations or give warranties of what financial performance will be achieved. Any franchisor who is prepared to give firm representations or warranties in regard to likely financial performance should be viewed with suspicion. A franchisor should be prepared to disclose actual figures which have been achieved, although he should not identify any franchisee who achieved the figures without that franchisee's consent. No franchisee should ever rely upon the financial projections as being a guarantee that they will be achieved. There can be many reasons why they are not achieved, including market trends and economic factors affecting business as a whole, as well as the franchisee's own performance capability and deficiencies.) [6]

14. Is the business seasonal? In the case of a relatively new franchise involving a seasonal business, particular attention should be paid to whether the pilot-testing was of a sufficiently long-term nature to be certain that seasonal factors have been taken into account. In the case of a longer-established franchise, the position should be more clear.

15. What opening support staff do you provide?

16. Do you organize an opening launch of the business? If so, what does it consist of and what will it cost me if not included in any initial fees?

17. How do you make your money?

18. Do you charge ongoing franchise fees? What are they and how are they calculated?

19. Do you make a mark-up on product sales to your franchisees? Is that instead of or in addition to the ongoing franchisee fees?

20. If you make a mark-up on products, how much and what sort of protection do I have against unfair and unjustified increases?

21. Do you take any commission from suppliers of goods or materials to franchisees? If so, please provide details.

22. Do you receive any other income or commissions from any other source based upon that source's business dealings with your franchisees? If so, please provide details.

23. Will I be obliged to maintain a minimum continuing franchise fee, purchase a minimum amount of goods or impose other performance targets? What happens if I fail to meet such a commitment? How do you calculate these minimum commitments so they are fair to both of us?

24. What advertising and promotional support do you provide?

25. Do I have to contribute to advertising and promotional expenditure which you incur? If so, how much? Do you provide an auditor's certificate or other proof that the sums you receive for advertising and promotional expenditure have been spent for those purposes?

26. What point-of-sale and promotional literature do you supply, and what do I have to pay for it?

27. What help will I receive in local advertising and promotions? What will it cost me?

28. Will I be able to obtain and motivate a sufficient number of competent staff? Will they require specialist skills and are such people readily available?

29. Which of the following continuing services will you provide after the business has commenced:

    (a) research and development;

    (b) market testing;

    (c) negotiation of bulk purchasing terms for the benefit of franchisees;

    (d) field support;

    (e) performance monitoring;

    (f) general business advice;

    (g) advertising, marketing and promotion?

30. Are there any other continuing services provided by you? If so, please provide details.
31. Which of your field support staff will be my link with you after I have opened the business?
32. Can I meet him or her?
33. Can I meet some of your other field support staff?
34. Can I meet your head office team?
35. How long have they each been with you and do they have a service contract which will ensure continuity?
36. Please explain the procedure which you will adopt to get me ready to open your business.
37. Will you find me a site, or do I have to find it myself?
38. What will be the opening hours of my business and are these likely to be varied?
39. Will I own the equipment necessary to operate the business?
40. How soon and often will I have to spend money on replacing equipment or remodelling my premises?
41. How many times in the past at what intervals and at what expense to franchisees have you required re-equipping or remodelling to take place?
42. What systems do you have for keeping franchisees in touch with you and each other?
43. Do you publish a newsletter?
44. Do you hold regular franchise meetings?
45. Is there a franchisee association within your network?
46. How will I cope with my accounting and record keeping?
47. What restrictions will there be on what products I can sell?
48. Do you provide instructional and operational manuals?
49. What will you do if by a clear mistake you misjudge my site, and it does not produce the anticipated figures, resulting in a loss?
50. What would happen if I ran into operational problems which I was unable to solve? What help would I get?
51. How can I be sure you will do what you promise?

What happens if the franchisor fails?

Fortunately, there are not many examples in practice of a franchisor becoming bankrupt or going into liquidation. None the less, the subject is important since there have been failures (particularly in recessionary times) and there certainly will be more in the future. In making a decision to take up a franchise the possibility must be borne in mind as well as the consequences. The fact that someone sets himself up as a franchisor does not mean that he is thereby invested with an aura of invincibility and cannot fall.

A franchisor may fall for a number of different reasons.

1. There may have been a deliberate fraud.
2. There may have been a badly structured franchise.
3. The business which is being franchised may not have been sufficiently well market tested.
4. The franchisor may be under-capitalized, particularly in crucial early years.
5. There may be a good franchise system but the franchisor runs his end of the business badly.
6. The franchisor may make bad policy decisions.
7. The franchise scheme may fall foul of the law. Remember laws can change.
8. The franchisor may be bad at selecting of franchisees.
9. There may be over-rapid expansion leading to lack of adequate infrastructural support for franchisees.
10. There may be a lack of management ability or just plain incompetence in the franchisor's organization.

In some of these cases the collapse of the franchisor may cause irretrievable loss, and in this connection one has in mind those losses referred to in (1), (2), (3) and (7), the first three having been avoidable and the last perhaps avoidable or perhaps unforeseeable. In such cases the franchisee will probably be left with little except a financial loss and a large headache. He may have some sort of business still left which, with imagination and hard work, he can work up sufficiently to reduce or even eliminate his losses. It may be that what he is left with cannot be worked upon at all and he has to cut his losses and close up as soon as possible. It could also be that the franchisee has so little past experience and training that he is not capable of continuing without a franchisor's support. The possibility of joining another or a competitor's franchise system should be considered in such a case.

It is of little comfort to one who finds himself in that position to be told that he should not have gone into the franchise at all, since the weaknesses would have been apparent had proper enquiries been made. In one respect a potential franchisee is now far better placed to judge the good, the bad and the fraudulent than he ever was in the past. A higher level of expertise has been developed in the legal and accountancy professions, and the government business advisory services and centres are a useful source of advice. The banks involved in franchising provide an additional source of informed advice which should not be ignored. The BFA runs educational programmes and sells a franchisee information pack to prospective franchisees. The implications of BFA membership are dealt with in Chapter 16.

However, all may not be lost for the franchisee, since there are other possibilities to be taken into account. The franchisor will be the proprietor of:

- the system under which the franchised business is operated;
- the know-how associated with it;
- trade secrets;
- trade marks and/or trade names with associated goodwill; and
- copyright material.

None of these will disappear with the franchisor's business failure. They will be assets of the business with which a liquidator or receiver will have to deal, but subject to the rights granted in respect thereof to the franchisees.

The liquidator or receiver will be seeking to obtain whatever is the market price for these assets but, since the rights granted will also be subject to the provision of a franchisor's services, it may not be easy to dispose of them. The value which the liquidator receiver will be seeking to dispose will be enhanced by the potential income from the franchisees under the franchise agreements. The liquidator may also consider whether the contracts should be brought to an end but it is likely that the franchisor's business would be more attractive to a prospective purchaser with an established network of franchisees in position.

There are two potential purchasers of these assets. The first is a competitor of the franchisor that may or may not already be a franchisor itself. If it is a franchisor it may have reservations about whether the former competitor's disgruntled franchisees could fit in. It also has to consider whether too many of the franchisees' locations are too close to his franchisees to make integration difficult or impossible. It may consider whether the two brands could be run in competition with each other. The risks for it would be very high. Undoubtedly it would insist on meeting all the franchisees to see whether a working relationship would have any prospect of success. If it is not yet a franchisor the opportunity presented to it may have the effect of triggering its entry into the field with a ready-made network. It would, however, have to be very sure of its own franchising ideas and ability to develop the right sort of relationship with the franchisees, who may resent the intrusion presented by new ideas. The franchisees may well not be manageable after what they have suffered.

The second potential purchasers are the franchisees themselves. It is unlikely that the franchisor will have become bankrupt or gone into liquidation without some warning signs having been apparent for some time. The warning signs should not be ignored.

The franchisor will usually have contractual obligations to:

- provide management back-up;
- provide advertising;
- maintain standards;
- provide continuing development;

- supply and/or arrange the supply of products etc.;
- provide field support;
- provide the other services described in Chapter 00 and above in this chapter.

As financial resources become stretched its ability to finance the provision of these services will be impaired. Its franchisees should notice the deterioration of or decline in the provision of services and undoubtedly will be complaining. Some franchisees may add to the franchisor's cash-flow problems by stopping the payment of franchise fees in retaliation for the failure to provide services. This could be a dangerous course for the franchisees to follow since it would probably ensure that they are in breach of their contractual obligations and weaken their position. It is essential for the franchisees to take legal advice before committing any breach of their contracts.

Additionally, some franchisees may take steps to terminate the franchise agreement for the breach of its provisions by the franchisor and make damages claims. These claims will probably be worth little in view of the franchisor's lack of financial resources. The consequence for a franchisee who terminates or whose agreement is terminated for his breach of contract will, in all probability, mean that he is prohibited thereafter from using the franchisor's:

- system;
- know-how;
- trade secrets;
- trade mark/trade name and goodwill;
- copyright material.

He will also be limited in his future activities by a restrictive covenant although where the franchisor is in breach such covenants may not be enforceable. Termination may not be the best step to take. It should also be borne in mind that there may be some bargaining power available to a franchisee who does not terminate and is in a position to make a claim in dealing with a liquidator or receiver.

Depending upon the maturity of the franchise system there may exist a Franchisee Advisory Committee or some informal liaison between franchisees. In any event it is quite likely, with the franchisor labouring noticeably under the strain of a lack of cash, that the franchisees will get together to discuss their common problem with a common approach to the franchisor.[7] In the author's view, this is the best course for franchisees to take in these circumstances. Again, there may be different views on what to do and on the degree of involvement which some wish to have. However, the best prospect they have is that the franchise system is kept in existence and the best way for them to achieve that, if it is what they want, is to pool their resources to enable them to take advice.

In most franchise chains franchisees have varying degrees of ability and the most able may well have been involved for a sufficiently long time to be capable of providing many of the franchisor's services and of organizing the employment or involvement of others with the requisite specialized skills. The franchisees in this predicament should therefore organize themselves, or such of them as wish to be involved, so that they can negotiate to acquire the assets, which can be taken into a joint company which those concerned can own. Some thought will have to be given to the structure in that company and the rights to dispose of shares. The company will then have to be organized – it may be that one of the more able and successful franchisees could successfully take over this responsibility. Such a group would be able to deal with suppliers of goods and products who may be disenchanted by having been let down by the franchisor but who may be persuaded by the number of franchisees involved and their determined attitude to continue supplying on a favourable basis.

If it is not possible to negotiate such a purchase of the assets the franchisees may wish to go their separate ways using different trading names. Some may wish to do this even if the assets can be acquired. Others may be nervous about breaking free. It may be possible to compromise any claim for damages which franchisees may have against the franchisor by acquiring the right, for a significant period, to continue using the trade marks/trade names, goodwill and system for a nominal charge free from post-termination restrictions until the franchisee can reorganize his business or the franchisor's business is restructured and perhaps able successfully to re-establish its former activities. The franchisees will have a role to play and should consider whether their most prudent course would be to embark upon a programme of constructive cooperation with the franchisor or to follow one of the other alternatives described above.

If the franchisees are able to continue to use the trade marks, trade names and system there will be merit in cooperative effort, at least to ensure the pooling of advertising and promotional resources and the bargaining power which gives advantage to a group compared with a number of individuals.

Final steps

The prospective franchisee must weigh up and consider the advantages and disadvantages of franchising described in this book, as well as the replies to the questions suggested, before making the decision on whether or not to enter into any specific franchised business venture. A decision must also be made as to whether the advantages, such as the established business format, training and support provided by the franchisor, are worth having in return for surrendering some independence and submitting to the degree of outside control which is inherent in a franchise transaction.

The prospective franchisee must decide whether the particular franchisor is the right person with whom to do business. He must also decide whether he is personally and temperamentally suitable for this type of relationship. The prospective franchisee may also consider the advice of a businessman friend whose judgement he respects, as well as a solicitor and accountant with specialist franchise experience. He should certainly discuss the matter with his immediate family.

When all these relevant factors have been weighed up, the legal issues and the franchise contract considered (Chapter 00) and proper professional advice taken, then the prospective franchisee has to make his final decision. If he is not able to make his decision with confidence, after having heard all his advisers have to say, he should consider whether he is indeed capable of running his own business, whether franchising is right for him, whether the particular franchisor is right for him and whether the particular business is the right one for him.

Summing-up

To sum up, a prospective franchisee must pay close attention to the following factors:

1. Weigh the advantages and disadvantages.
2. Assess yourself.
3. Assess the business.
4. Assess the franchisor.
5. Assess the franchise package.
6. Speak to existing franchisees.
7. Don't become so 'besotted' with the franchise opportunity that you lose all objectivity.
8. Consider and put into perspective the advice of others, who are qualified to give it.
9. Do not dismiss advice which is given because you do not like it or it is not what you want to hear.
10. Consider and consult your family.
11. Make up your own mind.

The following are danger signals, which either (as in the case of pyramid schemes) rule out the proposition or indicate that you need to make a very deep and careful scrutiny of the particular franchise you are considering. So beware of:

1. Heavy initial franchise fees.
2. Pyramid-type schemes. (Note: they may not be called by this name, they may be called multi-level distribution or network marketing or even by some other name. It is the way they are structured and what they offer which is crucial, not the label used – see Chapter 2.)

3. Franchisors whose initial fees are very high and whose continuing fee income is too low to support the services with which they should provide to their franchisees.
4. Contracts which do not match promises in the marketing literature and are vague and lacking in detail.
5. The hard sell.
6. Franchises which are based on passing fads or fashions which may not have staying power.
7. A franchise consultant purporting to offer independent, objective advice, but who is, in reality, offering a franchise for sale on a commission basis. There is an obvious conflict of interest.
8. Get rich quick offers.
9. Franchisors who have not invested in pilot operations.
10. Fee arrangements where a minimum fixed cash sum has to be paid regardless of whether or not there is sufficient business.
11. Franchisors who have a significant number of franchisees who are not happy with the quality of their services.

Notes

1. In the USA, many of the registration states will scrutinize the capitalization of the franchisor. If the franchisor is too thinly capitalized and does not have what the regulators view as sufficient net worth or operating capital, the states may require that initial franchise fees be escrowed or collections deferred until the franchised business opens, or a bond posted. In rare cases, registration may even be denied.
2. In the USA, the franchisor's audited financial statements for the past three years must be attached to the offering circular as an exhibit.
3. In the USA, a list of all the franchisees or the closest 100 must be disclosed. In addition, the names and addresses or franchisees who have been terminated or ceased doing business in the franchisor's most recent fiscal year have to be listed.
4. In the USA, most (but not all) of this information may be disclosed in the offering circular.
5. In the USA, most (but not all) of this information should be disclosed in the offering circular. See Chapter 17
6. In the USA, this type of information would be viewed as an 'earnings claim' which has to be disclosed in the offering circular.
7. In the USA, although terminology varies, a franchise advisory committee is typically set up and controlled by the franchisor, while a franchisee association is an independent body formed by the franchisees themselves.

7 The financial aspects of franchising

In franchising the franchisee earns his revenue from the operation of the individual unit. The franchisor earns his revenue from the income which he can generate principally from selling franchise packages, from continuing franchise fees and/or mark-up on product sales. As will be seen below, there are other potential sources of revenue for the franchisor. The franchisor cannot expect to generate a flow of revenue which is not justified by the quality and range of the services which it provides to franchisees. The franchisee will be expecting value for money – a range of services and perhaps products which would otherwise not be available to him and at a price which he can afford and which makes sense to him. It must be remembered that the basic business which the franchisee is running must generate sufficient profits to enable the franchisee to:

- obtain a return on his investment;
- earn a reward for his labours;
- make the contracted payments to the franchisor.

If the franchisee's business cannot achieve that there must be a question mark about the viability of the proposition as a franchise. In addition, the franchisor must be able to generate a sufficient flow of revenue to enable him to cover his overheads and make a profit on his operations as franchisor.

The franchisor should have established by the operation of its pilot operation how profitable the franchisee's business is likely to be. This knowledge is essential to enable the franchisor to assess the level of revenue which a franchised business is capable of generating and affording so that an informed decision may be made about the financial viability for both franchisee and franchisor.

Establishing franchise fees is not done by guesswork; it is a matter of proper calculation. If fees are established at a wrong, low level the franchisor may not be able to trade profitably. If fees are established at an excessively high level the franchisees may not be able to trade at a sufficient level of profitability.

Establishing fees for the supply or provision of services is not as easy as establishing the price for goods. In the case of goods the direct and indirect cost of production and distribution can be calculated with some degree of accuracy. The cost of provision of services is more difficult to ascertain. The franchisor in many cases will be providing services and will find it difficult to know how to calculate the proper level of fees, particularly as that calculation will have to survive the growth and development of the network. Where there is a supply of products by the franchisor on which the franchisor is obtaining a mark-up, whether or not there is a requirement for the franchisee to make a payment of continuing franchise fees, there is a risk that the franchisee will be vulnerable to overcharging by an adjustment of the product mark-up. While in practice there is little that a franchisee can do to negotiate a franchise fee he must be aware of the sources of revenue for the franchisor arising out of the activities of the franchisees in the network:

- The franchisee must know how franchise fees are calculated so that he can judge whether they are fair.
- The franchisee must be able to relate the level of fees to the range and quality of services which he receives. If he does not receive, in return for those fees, services of an added value in excess of the amount of the fees, the involvement of the franchisor may be difficult to justify. Even if the franchisee initially accepts a level of fees which do not satisfy that criterion the franchisor should not congratulate itself on a fine deal but should be aware that the franchisee will later on in the relationship probably be discontented when he has a fuller appreciation of the situation.
- The franchisee should examine the franchisor's approach to franchise fees; this will provide an insight into the franchisor's attitude.
- if the franchisor is the supplier of the product the method of adjusting prices will be important.

Figure 7.1 shows the sort of trend one might expect to find in the development of a franchise network. The initial fee income is shown as providing the main sources of income in the early stages and then being caught up and overtaken by continuing franchise fees. The figure illustrates the way in which the expense of running the franchisor's

Costs and incomes over time in the development of a franchise network.

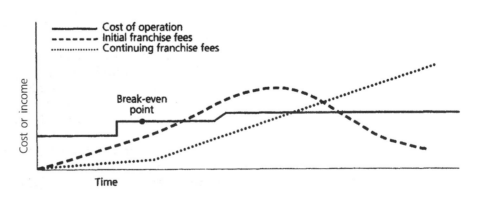

organization grows in steps (there may well be more steps than shown in the figure). Each step prepares it to cope with the expansion which follows to the point where the organization is developed and the rising continuing fees result in an increasing profitability because the organization has reached its optimum level in its domestic market (at which point it may consider international development, see Chapter 14). The staff required to cope with five franchisees may well be able to cope with 25 franchisees and those who cope with 35 may well be able to cope with up to 50 and so on. The figure makes clear the need in the early stages for the franchisor to provide adequate working capital to finance the initial deficits; indeed, the time span before the break-even point is achieved can be as much as three to five years depending upon the ratio of growth. Franchisors pushing for rapid growth sometimes ignore the need to finance and establish the infrastructure to accommodate that growth – it is a mistake to do this. The figure ignores any profitability from pilot or company-owned store outlets.

We shall now review the various potential sources of revenue for a franchisor and comment upon each.

Initial franchise fee

In most cases the franchisee will be charged an initial franchise fee. How this will be identified will depend upon how the franchisor structures his franchise package. In its simplest form the franchisor will provide a range of services to help the franchisee to establish his operational unit and will charge a fee. The fee will cover the provision of these services as well as training and may include an element which is attributable to the value of joining the franchised network, represented by the strength of the name and the goodwill associated with it. As the strength of the name increases so may this element.

In a more complex arrangement the franchisor may well acquire and fully equip the trading premises for the franchisee and upon completion of the franchisee's training hand over the 'key' to the franchisee. This approach is called a 'turnkey operation' and the franchisor will probably charge an initial franchise fee by way of a mark-up on the cost of the elements contained in the package, including training. The fee charged in a turnkey operation would probably also include the element attributable to joining the franchised network (see below).

In another approach the franchisor may in addition to the provision of a range of services sell to the franchisee an equipment package comprising all the initial equipment requirements of the franchisee's business. The sale price will include an initial franchise fee by way of mark-up on the cost of the equipment to include the elements referred to above.

There are some who express the view that the franchisor should set the initial franchise fee as low as possible so as to reduce the franchisee's cost of setting up to a minimum level. Others do not share that view and will charge a full initial franchise fee which takes into account all the cost factors as well as a mark-up. These cost factors will reflect the total cost of recruiting, evaluating, training and establishing the franchisee in business, including legal, accounting and site finding fees. In the case of some franchise systems the element which will be included for the cost of joining the network will vary depending upon the level of maturity of the network and the value of the name and of membership of the network.

In the early stages of the franchisor's development the income from initial franchise fees will be an important source of revenue for the franchisor and the build-up of other sources will be slower depending upon the build-up of the network and of the franchisees' businesses (Figure 7.1). Of course if there is a product mark-up the ongoing revenue flow will build up more rapidly.

The franchisor will have to accept that initially while its flow of franchisees is being developed its income will be far less than its cost of operations; as mentioned, it could well be three to five years before the franchisor achieves the break-even point in its franchising activities. This factor means that the franchisor must face up to a requirement to have adequate capital resources to enable it to sustain its operations until break-even is reached. In this sense the franchisor's needs and requirements are no different from any other new business which will take time to develop a level of profitability. There are those who believe that setting up a franchise will produce immediate positive cash flow and profitability and thus solve the problems with which a business, which is experiencing difficulties, is confronted. That is a fallacy, as is the belief that a business in difficulty is a good base upon which to build a franchise system.

It is also unrealistic for the franchisor to seek to shorten the period which it will take to reach the break-even point by charging high initial franchise fees, for, quite apart from the issues referred to above, the higher the cost of entering the fewer prospective franchisees who can afford it and the greater the return from the franchisees' operations will have to be to justify the outlay.

According to the NatWest/BFA Survey dated February 2003, 96% of franchisors charge an initial fee and the mean amount is £22,100, which seems on the high side. The authors of the survey point out that this represents an increase of 50% on the previous year, so it must be treated with a degree of caution, or possibly it results from packaging the fees in a different way. In previous editions it was suggested that the initial fees would fall within a range of 5–10% of the total cost of the franchise package. Given the increasing maturity of the franchise community it would appear that the range may now be 10–15% of the total cost of the franchise package.

It is clear not only that it is possible to raise the initial franchise fee in the course of time to reflect the growing strength and success of the franchise but also that it has happened over the course of time. In some cases membership of the network in itself is of great value. It is prudent to review the fee in any event from time to time to reflect inflationary pressures on overhead expenses. The franchisor would do well to remember that its success will, in the long run, be dependent upon its ability to help the franchisee make the most of his money. This objective can be assisted by keeping the initial investment level as modest as possible; there are more potential franchisees with £25,000 to invest than there are with £50,000 or more.

It would be very unusual for the initial franchise fee to be the only fee the franchisor will ever receive, as otherwise he would have no capacity to finance the continuing relationship. While such a fee is invariably charged it is usually tied to one or other of the fees which are described below.

Sale of the franchise package

The franchisor can structure the sale of the franchise package in a number of ways.

Turnkey

This approach involves the franchisor in acquiring the necessary premises, shopfitting and equipping them so that they are ready for occupation by the franchises and for the commencement of business. In such a case the franchisor would contract with the franchisees to provide these services and the franchisees would undertake to pay for them. Such payment would in all probability be made in stages during the period while the work is proceeding. The price which the franchisor will charge will invariably include a mark-up on the cost to him of the services. That mark-up may also include the initial franchise fee or the franchisor may still separately charge the initial franchise fee. In any event, the franchisor will have the opportunity to earn a gross margin by the mark-up which he charges.

This does not provide the franchisor with a blank cheque to charge as it pleases. The charges made should fairly represent the added value represented by the franchisor's contribution in organizing the acquisition of the premises and carrying out the appropriate works. If the franchisor loads the cost of the initial package unrealistically it runs the risk that:

- the price will be a deterrent to a prospective franchisee, particularly when compared with the price of entry to competing networks;
- the financial structure will not permit the franchisee to obtain a reasonable return on his investment;
- a bank or other lending institution from which the franchisee seeks financial assistance could well conclude that the figures do not justify their involvement;
- the long-term prospects for the growth and development of the franchise system will be harmed.

These factors apply not only to the 'front-end' charges which a franchisor may make but also to all sources of income of which the franchisor takes advantage. Quite apart from the franchisor seeking too many sources of income it should be a fundamental principle that the franchisor should never make a secret profit at the expense of franchisees. Not only will this invariably involve unfairly reducing the franchisee's margins, it may also prevent franchisees from obtaining the benefits of the negotiating power of the network. In addition, the discovery by franchisees of the existence of a secret profit will at worst destroy the trust and confidence which franchisees should have in their franchisor or at least seriously undermine the relationship.

Equipment package

The franchisor may, by contrast, provide the franchisee with specifications and plans so that the franchisee can, after acquiring the premises, organize the requisite shopfitting. The franchisor may offer to sell to the franchisee an equipment package which will comprise all the equipment required to be installed in the premises for the purposes of the franchised business. The franchisor will, no doubt, have bought in the equipment from suppliers (including manufacturers) at a discount below the market price. The franchisor could charge a mark-up to cover the cost to it of putting the package together and to make a contribution to its general overheads.

Equipment purchasing

In another type of approach the franchisor may, as in the case of the equipment package, provide the franchisee with specifications and plans so that the franchisee can, after acquiring the premises, organize the required shopfitting. As far as equipment is concerned the franchisor will provide the franchisee with a list of branded or otherwise specifically described equipment which is approved by the franchisor and which the franchisee is free to obtain from any supplier of such equipment.

Generally

Whichever of the approaches is adopted (other than the turnkey), the franchisor will wish to be satisfied that the shopfitting works comply with its requirements, specifications and plans.

Leasing the equipment

Some franchisors arrange for the leasing of equipment to the franchisee rather than a sale, so as to reduce the cost of the initial package. The franchisor may receive a commission from the leasing company.[1] Alternatively, but less frequently, the franchisor will lease the equipment direct to the franchisee and take a profit on that transaction as, since he is providing the financing, he is entitled to charge for it. Indeed, in some cases where the franchisor's system involves the use of specialized patented equipment, it is only possible for a franchisee to arrange to lease that equipment, the franchisor being reluctant to sell it. With the increasing cost of financing the establishment of a new business, finance packages which are prepared will often include leases of equipment. Rental of equipment can also often be arranged with suppliers.

What the franchisee must know is the extent to which the franchisor can add to its capital cost and the cost of running its business by receiving commissions from suppliers or lessors of equipment who are approved or nominated by the franchisor.

Specialized equipment

In some cases there may be an obligation imposed upon the franchisee to purchase future supplies of novel or essential equipment from the franchisor. Such sales will undoubtedly include a profit element for the franchisor. In a franchise which is dependent upon a specialized piece of equipment the obligation may extend to the purchase and use of later and improved versions of the equipment. In such a case the franchisee should be satisfied about two aspects: first, that new equipment cannot be imposed upon him when the existing item of equipment is doing the job perfectly well, whatever refinements the newer equipment may have; second, that the franchisor cannot over-charge the franchisee by unreasonably increasing the mark-up. Any change of equipment for a later model which the franchisor wishes the franchisee to purchase should be justified in terms of increased efficiency and output, resulting in a cost-effective alternative.

Leasing of premises

Leasing of premises is a complex aspect of franchising, with problems which arise not only from the legal implications but also from the attitudes, practices and balances of negotiating power which are prevalent in the property market at the relevant time.

1. Sometimes the franchisor will be able to negotiate terms for leasing a suitable site on extremely good terms in view of the value of the covenant which the franchisor is able to offer the landlord. The franchisor may decide to sublet these premises to the franchisee at a higher rent, thus earning a profit rental for himself. Whether or not the franchisor becomes involved in the leasing of premises will be a structural decision to be made when the franchise package is brought together (Chapter 5). If the franchisor has decided not to be involved in the ownership of the premises it may nevertheless find that, owing to pressure from landlords or their estate agents, it must become involved, in order to secure the best locations. That

involvement may be by provision of a guarantee but franchisors should only enter into guarantees sparingly and with a full appreciation of the downside in terms of exposure to risk. There is no inherent reason why a franchisor should not be involved in property; there are many significant franchisors (e.g. McDonald's) who have property involvement as a fundamental policy.[2]

2. The franchisor may, in some cases, own or acquire the freehold of the premises from which the franchisee is to trade and grant a lease to the franchisee.

3. In both the above cases the franchisee should take care to ensure that the terms contained in the lease are those which prevail in the market, allowance being made for the risks taken and the support given by the franchisor. Care must also be taken to ensure that the franchisor does not use the lease to impose unreasonable conditions which he would not be able to impose in the franchise contract.

Generally

Where the franchisor provides the financial resources for the provision of any of the above arrangements the franchisor must consider whether he wants to risk the franchise relationship because there is a financial problem between franchisor and franchisee. The franchisor should also appreciate that a disgruntled franchisee will, justifiably or not, tend to blame the franchisor for his problems. It may not make sense to provide him with the ability financially to embarrass the franchisor by withholding payment. It is advisable to involve an outside provider of financial facilities.

Continuing fees

Management services fees (royalties)

In order to finance the provision of continuing services to franchisees the franchisor has to secure a regular flow of income. This is normally achieved by charging continuing franchise fees, which are often called management services fees or royalties and sometimes (in the case of a product distribution franchise) coupled with a mark-up on the supply of products, or there may be a mark upon the products (see Chapter 10 for an explanation of the legal problems which may be involved in the supply of products).

There is no easy formula to assist in fixing the level of continuing franchise fees. Given the general difficulty which there is in fixing fees for the provision of services the answer is not readily apparent. In seeking to establish the level of fees to be charged the franchisor has to take a medium- to long-term view. It will take time for the network to reach the size which will produce economic viability. As explained above, this can take three to five years. The franchisor must initially prepare a five-year business plan with realistic projections of growth and calculate what level of continuing franchise fees will enable it to achieve a healthy financial structure for its business. In doing this the same exercise will have to be undertaken in respect of the projected number of franchised businesses during the five-year period so that the right foundations have been laid for the franchisor's business plan. Furthermore, the franchisee's business will have to be judged on the basis of a level of continuing franchise fees which can be afforded, bearing in mind the principles discussed in this book, and be competitive with other franchise systems. The overall average amount of continuing franchise fees is in the region of 7.2% of gross revenues of the franchisees. This does not include advertising contributions (see below), which overall average 1.6% of such gross revenues. (The figures quoted are taken from the 2003 NatWest/ BFA Franchise Survey; see Appendix A.)

The survey identifies other charges made by franchisors for an IT support fee of 2% and other charges of 4.1% without saying what for. The advertising contribution is stated to be charged by only 45% of franchisors and continuing franchise fees are charged by only 70% of franchisors, both of which levels seem very low, although it appears that 71% of franchisors supply stock to franchisees, of whom over two-thirds do not charge a mark-up.

While most franchisors charge a continuing franchisee fee as a straight percentage fee based upon the gross revenues of the franchisee, it is possible, although not as common, for the franchisor to establish a fixed fee or to require payment of a minimum level of fees. The British Franchise Association Guide to its Code of Ethics provides that if a franchisor wishes to establish performance criteria it should not exceed 70% of the bona fide gross sales based upon the average of the franchise network. It should not be necessary to establish fixed minimum fees since a well motivated franchisee should not need such targets to be set. A franchisee should be only too anxious to maximize the opportunities which the franchised business provides him. Fixed fees can benefit a franchisee if their level is not too high but adjustments need to be made at regular intervals and it is not easy to produce a fair way of making such adjustments without the franchisees being vulnerable. From the franchisor's point of view the fixed fee basis may be superficially attractive but it does not take care of inflation or reflect growth and could inhibit or prevent it from developing properly the business and the range of services available to franchisees through lack of resources.

There are those who consider that the percentage fee is the best way, as the franchisee knows precisely how much he has to pay; he knows precisely how to calculate it; and he knows that the franchisor will not be taking fees in any other way. The franchisor also knows where he stands and benefits from the inflationary increase in gross revenues and from the growth in the business to which his efforts as a franchisor will have contributed, including his investment in developing and sustaining the franchise system.

The other view held by many is that this is not a good way to charge a franchise fee. The view is that psychologically the franchisee will not like parting with his money to somebody else. In the early days while the franchisee's business is becoming established and is not yet achieving profits, the franchisee will not be too happy paying fees to the franchisor despite the fact that they are to pay for services which are being provided. Even when the franchise is profitable it can be painful for the franchisee visibly and frequently to part with a slice of hard-earned cash. Furthermore, as the franchisee feels a degree of independence from the franchisor, which is a stage through which many successful franchisees go, he will become more aware of the drain from his pocket and more reluctant to pay the franchise fee.

There are many good franchises which operate on the percentage fee basis and there are some good franchises which operate on a different basis although they are in the minority. Certainly, from the franchisor's point of view the percentage fee basis is a safer and more reliable method. It is easier to administer and more satisfactory from the competition law point of view. In the case of a franchise where the franchisor is the product supplier, very often there is a combination of the percentage fee and product mark-up.

One common error is to apply the misnomer of 'royalty' to continuing franchise fees. The error usually arises because franchise fees are invariably calculated as a percentage of the gross income of the franchisee rather in the same way as one calculates royalties. Royalties are what is called passive income, i.e. income arising from the use of an asset rather than an income earned in exchange for services or goods. The common examples are royalties for the exploitation of a patent or for the use and publication of copyright material. Franchise fees are a payment by the franchisee in return for the continuing services which the franchisor will provide to the franchisee. It cannot be denied that some part of the fee represents a charge for the use of the trademarks and business system of the franchisor. What proportion of the fee that part will be is difficult to judge unless it is specified but, for it to be significant, the continuing franchise fee would have to be much larger than the services supplied would justify. In practice this is rarely the case.

Sale of products

In some franchises, particularly those where the franchisor is a manufacturer or wholesaler or where trademarked goods are involved, the agreement will compel the franchisees to buy goods from the franchisor or a nominated supplier of the franchisor. The franchisor obtains a return by marking up the goods. This mark-up may be all he receives, so that it is, in fact, a franchise fee as well as a gross profit on the sale of the goods. Where a nominated supplier is used the franchisor can obtain income by receiving a rebate from the supplier. Rebates on supplies which reflect the bulk purchasing power of the network arguably should be made available for the benefit of franchisees. Some suppliers will provide retrospective rebates, which reflect sales during the relevant period, and some will provide advertising allowances which are to be spent by the network. There are some franchisors who distribute rebates to franchisees.[3] There are some who have structured their franchise fees at a level which reflects their expectation of income from this source. Advertising allowances can be applied for the benefit of the network's advertising and promotional activities (see below, advertising funds).

One of the difficulties which can arise with charging franchise fees by product mark-up is that the franchisee can be at the mercy of an unscrupulous franchisor. There are undoubtedly many companies which operate this system fairly and properly, often delaying price increases to the last possible moment. It is, nevertheless, a method of payment of a franchise fee which should be carefully scrutinized by the franchisee. The franchisee should satisfy himself that the franchisor is not taking and cannot take unfair advantage of him and that there are forms of protection upon which he can rely. If there are no proper safeguards in the contract the franchisee should question whether he should sign it.

It is essential for the franchisor to consider the alternatives available. Invariably it is fairer for both parties to have the percentage fee payable rather than the mark-up on goods. If the franchisor contrasts his income calculated as a mark-up on the goods with his income calculated as a reasonable percentage of the franchisee's gross revenue, he will often find that he is no worse off. The franchisee can look at a relatively modest percentage fee in the confident knowledge that the franchisor will not be able unreasonably to increase the margin for himself at the franchisee's expense. A franchisor which is a manufacturer or which has its products manufactured for it would still expect to make the same margins on the sale of those products as it would when selling to third parties. In making its decision about how to structure the payments it will undoubtedly have regard to this consideration. Indeed, if too much is charged, whichever approach is adopted, the franchisee cannot succeed and that lack of success will not help the franchisor to develop his business.

Two factors clearly emerge from the above, First, as far as the franchisor is concerned, he must make a policy decision at the very earliest moment on the manner in which he will charge franchise fees. He must budget to ensure that the flow of fees which he receives from the various sources are sufficient to show him the return which he needs to cover his overheads and to make a reasonable profit within a sensible time frame, bearing in mind his growth prospects. Second, as far as the franchisee is concerned he must ascertain the sources of the franchisor's income. He must satisfy himself that the franchisor will not be in a position unfairly to take advantage of him.

Advertising funds

Most franchise schemes provide for expenditure on advertising and promotion by either or both franchisor and franchisee.[4] Where the franchisor undertakes the obligation to advertise and promote there are three alternative methods of approach when dealing with the cost.

1. The franchisor makes a charge to the franchisee of a sum calculated as a percentage of the franchisee's gross income rather in the same way that the continuing franchise fee (management services fee) is calculated. The sums received by the franchisor from the franchisees are spent by the franchisor on advertising and promotion. Most franchisors will want to have complete control over the advertising and promotional activities upon which the sums in the fund are spent.

2. The franchisor includes the advertising and promotional expense within the continuing franchise fee and undertakes to spend not less than a minimum percentage of such fees on advertising and promotion. Again, most franchisors will wish to have the same degree of control over advertising and promotional activities.

3. The franchisor undertakes to conduct advertising and promotional activities to the extent that it thinks fit without collecting a contribution or allocating a fixed sum for the purpose. This approach could be adopted when the franchisor is a manufacturer who is already a substantial advertiser on its own account and the franchisees will inevitably benefit.

Apart from these approaches there are franchise operations in which it is considered better to concentrate on local or regional advertising and promotion rather than on a national basis. In such a case the franchisor will probably require the franchisees to spend a fixed percentage of gross income each year for this purpose.

In all cases, national, regional and local, the franchisor will insist on control of the form and content of all advertisements and promotional material, since it is his name and system which are being advertised.

The role of the banks

As franchising is an inherently safer way of establishing a new business it is not surprising that the banking community has appreciated the advantages of lending money to franchisees. This is not only the case in the UK; banks in many countries have also become heavily involved in franchisee financing, including the Republic of Ireland, France, Spain, the Netherlands, Australia, South Africa and Canada. In the USA, because of restrictive banking laws, franchisee bank financing did not develop to the extent that it has in some other countries and although the situation has improved the market is probably so different there that it will continue to develop in its own way.

In June 1981 the National Westminster Bank as it was (now NatWest Bank) became the first to establish a franchise finance department. It was quickly followed in August 1981 by Barclays Bank. Since then the other banks have followed these initiatives, and the Royal Bank of Scotland, the Midland Bank (now HSBC), Lloyds Bank (now Lloyds Bank TSB), the Bank of Scotland and in Northern Ireland the Ulster Bank and the Bank of Ireland have all from time to time established franchise departments. Not all have remained visibly active in the market. The banks currently prominently active are NatWest, Royal Bank of Scotland, HSBC, Lloyds TSB and the Bank of Scotland, which recently re-emerged after a long absence. Many of the banks have sponsored franchising activities. NatWest sponsors the annual franchising survey commissioned by the BFA (see Appendix A). The Royal Bank of Scotland has sponsored training activities by the BFA and research in connection with the establishment by the BFA of the Franchisee Forum. HSBC sponsors the Franchisor of the Year and the Franchisee of the Year awards, respectively presented at a gala lunch and gala dinner, which have become the major features of the franchise year. Lloyds TSB sponsors the BFA franchisor and franchisee guides. The banks have also demonstrated their wish to have a continuing association with and involvement in franchising by joining the BFA as affiliate members.

The reason why banks entered the field of franchising is that they recognized that franchising is a safer way of establishing a new business. Furthermore, with the proven concept and the 'umbrella' of the franchisor's organization, the ability of the business to generate sufficient profit to enable the franchisees to repay their obligations and to live comfortably is more readily recognizable. This enables the banks to consider lending a greater proportion of the franchisee's set-up costs than would normally be considered appropriate.

Each of the banks which entered the market initially adopted the same approach: the appointment of a franchise manager at the centre, around whom the department could be developed. Barclays abandoned this approach in 1992 and has now ceased to be visibly active in the market place. There have been refinements made by each of the banks, while they have ensured the continuation of the basic structure which preserved the Banks' know-how. The alternative would be to educate the whole branch network in franchising and in how to evaluate a proposition. This would result in an inconsistency of approach which could be damaging and confusing and ensure that the corporate know-how of franchising was spread so thinly as to be incapable of being put to good use.

The specialist manager at the centre, with a developing team around him, enables the bank to acquire and develop its know-how in relation to franchising and pass it on to those who join the department. There is a skilled application of the knowledge acquired, which enables rapid evaluation of propositions and the establishment of a consistent attitude towards each franchise system. The local manager faced with the prospective franchisee borrower can be provided with a brief not only about franchising in general, but also about the specific franchise proposition into which his customer wishes to enter and which he is being asked to consider, although, as will be seen below, the Royal Bank of Scotland and the Bank of Scotland have developed a different approach.

The specialist franchise group can guide lending colleagues about whether or not to be involved in lending to any particular franchise system making use of the requisite knowledge and experience. Apart from the two Scottish banks a bank's decision on whether to lend to a particular individual is taken by the local manager, who will interview and evaluate him, supported by all the relevant information about the franchise system and the franchisor which has been supplied by the bank's franchise department.[5]

It is interesting to see how the banks have fine tuned and adapted their approach in the light of experiences while remaining highly competitive and not losing sight of their original purpose.

Although a bank may well be identified with a particular franchise by a franchisor promoting the provision of loans to its franchisees by a particular bank, the banks cannot warrant the viability of the franchise or its suitability for any person. It must be emphasized that a prospective franchisee should make a detailed evaluation of the franchise before making his decision about whether or not to proceed to take up any proposition. The fact that a bank has made loans to franchisees in any system should not form any part of the franchisee's decision.

We shall examine the approach of the main UK banks providing specialist financial services to the franchise community.

NatWest

NatWest has been taken over by the Royal Bank of Scotland but continues as a separate and competing brand. The NatWest franchise section is led by a national franchise manager supported by a team of four, including two other franchise managers.

The NatWest franchise section has three main objectives.

1. To provide the bank's network of over 1500 branches, business centres and regional offices with a general understanding of franchising and a specific knowledge of any franchise opportunity at the time when the local manager is discussing the financial needs of a potential franchisee.

2. To inform customers and the general public on the intricacies of business format franchising and to give general guidance to prospective franchisors on the needs of the industry and to discuss with them their proposals for franchise development.

3. To assist with the provision of finance to franchisees through a network of area franchise managers. Close contact is maintained with established franchisors who are able to benefit from the ready source of finance available to their franchisees.

The bank is aware that with a properly structured business format franchise, the risk of failure is reduced and the level of finance provided to franchisees may be up to 70% of the total investment cost, which is greater than would generally be available in a normal 'start-up' situation.

The franchise managers supplement the local knowledge of the branch manager with detailed information briefs on all franchise systems as back-up support to the manager when he is considering the financial needs of any prospective franchisee.

Although the bank does not warrant or recommend any particular franchise operation, it is able to provide prospective franchisees with a general information pack. This includes the bank's checklist for choosing a franchise, which assists in the evaluation of a franchise opportunity, and articles which discuss the requirements of both franchisor and franchisee.

The bank franchise section and its team of managers have also been involved in a number of activities including:

- video guide for prospective franchisors and franchisees;
- seminar presentations, including those with the Franchise Alliance from 2000 to the present date;
- the sponsorship of
  - (a) the NatWest/BFA Franchise Survey 1984 to the present date
  - (b) the European Franchise Federation/NatWest Survey 1997–1998.

The bank's UK franchise section has been active in the international arena and has cooperation agreements for franchising with banks in the leading European countries. The franchise section has been supportive of the franchise community in some 35 countries by providing speakers at seminars on the subject of franchising and the provision of training for bankers in the developing countries.

In short, the bank's involvement goes far beyond the provision of finance and is supportive of franchise development on a very broad basis.

The Royal Bank of Scotland

Following the acquisition of NatWest by the Royal Bank of Scotland the combined banking group took the strategic decision to align its franchise functions with the relevant brands in the high street and its corporate finance functions. The two retail franchise departments of NatWest and Royal Bank of Scotland stayed within the business bank area of each bank and focus very much on franchisee transactions. They compete with each other in exactly the same way as the branch network of each bank on the high street.

In order to service the funding requirements of the franchisors in the corporate market the Royal Bank Group formed a corporate and commercial franchise department with the specific remit of working with franchisors and larger multi-unit franchisees. This structure does not exist in any other clearing bank and has the unique feature of being dual branded by being able to offer funding solutions for franchisors using either Royal Bank of Scotland or NatWest depending upon the customer's preference. This franchise function concentrating on franchisor issues has enabled the Royal Bank to develop a new range of financial products involving a number of corporate banking areas covering both debt and equity options, which may be suitable for management buy–outs and buy-ins and structured finance deals which enable directors of existing successful businesses to realize some of their equity.

The corporate and commercial franchise department also has responsibility for international franchise development in line with the Royal Bank's overall international strategy. Linking up with strategic banking partners throughout the world, the Royal Bank is able to assist franchisors who are looking to expand overseas and also put in place structured funding packages for international franchisors looking to expand in the UK.

The bank's franchise group is organized nationally, with the national franchise manager based in Edinburgh and supported by seven regional managers. The regions currently are Scotland, North of England, Midlands, East Anglia, Greater London, South East and South West. In practice a flexible approach is adopted if necessary, ignoring boundary lines so that resources are provided where customer demand requires.

The bank continues to support franchising by making its contribution to the BFA, supporting its educational activities, speaking at seminars, exhibiting at franchise exhibitions and in various other supporting roles including such institutions as local enterprise boards and Scottish Enterprise. The regional managers are called specialist franchise development managers. They are appointed for a minimum period of three years to provide continuing support and stability in the relationships which they have developed with customers. These managers are given sector-specific training and build tailored financial packages to suit the customer's needs, whether franchisee or franchisor. With their training they are able to assist customers on their understanding of the advantages and disadvantages of franchising.

The bank has loans available up to 70% of the total project cost, including the initial fee, equipment, vehicles (if appropriate) and shopfitting costs (if appropriate). Working capital repayments are usually geared to the initial terms of the franchise agreement but the bank is prepared in appropriate cases to consider whether renewal provisions provisions can be taken into account. The bank also introduced the possibility of the use of the Small Firms Loan Guarantee scheme.

The bank offers its customer a free business planning software CD with 12 months' free usage of *My Business Essentials* accounting software.

Having established the finance package and the customer's accounts, the franchise development manager introduces the customer to a dedicated business relationship manager to deal with the day-to-day running of the customer's account. The managers liaise with each other.

HSBC

When Midland Bank became a member of the HSBC Group, the latter inherited the specialist franchise unit which Midland Bank had established many years ago. The unit is run by a national franchise manager with supporting managers and staff.

The franchise unit supports the bank's branch network, its customers and franchising in a number of ways.

Internally

- Providing advice and guidance to enable the bank's relationship managers to support existing business customers looking to expand their business via franchising.
- Maintaining detailed profiles of specific franchise opportunities to provide the relationship manager with a greater understanding of the relevant franchise operation when discussing the financial requirements with a potential franchisee.

Externally

- Providing advice and guidance to prospective franchisors looking to expand their business via franchising.
- Providing advice and guidance to prospective franchisees.
- Publication of franchisor and franchisee guides which are available to customers and non-customers alike, providing guidance about buying a franchise, or expansion through franchising, as well as guidance on setting up a new business and how to go about borrowing money.
- Maintaining relationships with existing franchisors, visiting as many as possible on a regular basis, discussing how the bank can support the financial requirements of their franchisees and keep up to date with any changes and development within their business.

Franchise sector

- Maintaining relationships with franchise sector professionals, accountants, lawyers, consultants and the British Franchise Association.
- Continued sponsorship of the BFA Franchisor and Franchisee of the Year awards. Over the past 15 years, HSBC has awarded over £150,000 in prize money alone, and the press coverage giving positive success stories about franchising has been extensive.
- Participating in and supporting the BFA during National Franchise Week, helping to raise the profile of franchising and hosting a launch event at the bank's headquarters.
- In 2003, HSBC sponsored the BFA video/DVD, provided to prospective franchisors and franchisees with the BFA's information pack.
- Sponsorship of an edition of *How to Franchise Internationally* by Martin Mendelsohn.

- HSBC sponsors the Horwath training initiative, the diploma in franchise management. The diploma programme has been formally accredited by Middlesex University Business School and will provide academic credits towards an MA (franchising) degree.
- Continued sponsorship support, together with the other banks involved in franchising, for the BFA's website.
- Supporting the BFA and franchise community by providing speakers at seminars on the subject of franchising.
- Publication of articles in key franchising publications.

HSBC's activity in the franchise sector is calculated to help its franchise team to understand the current issues faced by the sector, and to build and maintain strong relationships with members of the BFA (franchisors, franchisees and professional advisors) to enable it to maintain a high profile and high level of customer service.

With over 9500 offices in 79 countries and territories, HSBC is well placed to expand its franchise financing expertise to its global network.

Lloyds TSB

Lloyds TSB considers that a franchisee of a well developed and structured proven business should have a better chance of success when compared with someone starting a business in their own right. To reflect this the bank established a separate franchise unit in 1982. This unit currently has a manager and two assistant managers. The carries out regular personal and telephone contact with most franchisors operating in the UK. This enables the bank to build and maintain a comprehensive database of information:

- to support franchisees with their research into their chosen system;
- to support business managers with their decision-making when lending to a franchisee.

The unit also provides an ongoing internal education programme to keep business managers up to date with developments in the sector
The unit aims:

- To provide initial guidance to existing business customers who are considering franchising as a growth strategy. This helps them to understand fully the implications and processes they need to follow to achieve this successfully and the resources they will need to have available. This will include emphasizing the importance of taking the right professional advice to develop their franchise.
- To build and maintain relationships with fellow professional advisors to the sector, and the British Franchise Association, to support the ethical standards set and maintained by the association.
- To introduce prospective franchisees to the Lloyds TSB business manager network so these customers can benefit from the support

structure which Lloyds TSB has in place to support its customers' chances of succeeding in business.

- to support the drive to increase awareness of franchising among the public by regularly taking part in seminars and lectures on the subject, and producing brochures to help increase understanding.

The bank considers that the UK franchising community's strong position is greatly assisted by the way in which its banking community supports franchising. Looking at many other countries, banks typically make no differentiation between their lending policies for franchisees and their policies for small business start-ups in general. The tangible support provided by the bank to franchising includes:

- a dedicated team specifically trained in all aspects of the sector;
- sponsorship of the British Franchise Association information guides;
- regularly speaking at British Franchise Association and Scottish Enterprise educational seminars;
- exhibiting at franchise exhibitions;
- dedicated pages on the bank's Internet portal, which help the public and potential franchisees to research franchising further;
- dedicated pages on the bank's internal intranet site, providing detailed information accessible to all business managers, ensuring that consistent information about the sector is available to them;
- provision of a comprehensive series of solution guides to help franchisees and franchisors to develop their businesses;
- regular contribution of articles to the national and regional press, and industry journals;
- promotion of franchising within the bank, including at director level, which allows a specific overall lending policy to the sector to be agreed, so enabling franchisees to secure preferential funding terms.

Bank of Scotland

The Bank of Scotland has made a welcome return to the franchising scene after an absence of some years.

The franchise team has at its head the bank's UK director of franchising and start-ups, and is led on a day-to-day basis by the director of national franchising, supported by three franchise managers and an administrator. Not surprisingly, the bank concentrates primarily on funding franchises of long-established franchises with a successful track record.

Prospective franchisees meet the bank's franchise manager, who makes the lending decisions in each case from a full range of loan products, including overdrafts, asset financing and factoring and the benefit of the small firm's loan guarantee scheme. Having set up the loan arrangements the franchise manager hands the franchisee over to a relationship manager, who will be the franchisee's bank contact.

The bank endorses the view that franchising has benefits which setting up a business independently does not achieve. The bank does not endorse or warrant any franchise. It requires the preparation by a prospective franchisee of a full and detailed business plan.

The bank highlights the issues to be considered by prospective franchisees when buying a franchise and assists with the preparation of the business plan. Their prime objective is to match the financial package to the franchisees' individual circumstances.

Notes

1. In the USA, a franchisor in its offering circular would have to disclose the precise basis on which it or its affiliates may derive revenue or other material consideration as a result of required purchases or leases.
2. In the early days of franchising in the USA, the three most important characteristics of a franchise were 'location, location, location'. Even today, if you see a McDonald's restaurant, a Burger King or another hamburger chain may be right around the corner.
3. In the USA, franchisors must disclose in their offering circulars any rebates they receive from third parties as a result of franchisee purchases. A few state laws require that such funds be used for the benefit of the franchisees.
4. In the USA, the franchisor's advertising programme must be disclosed in the offering circular.
5. In the USA banks often want to take a lien on the franchise agreement so that if the franchisee defaults on the bank loan, the bank can step in and run the franchised business. Such bank liens are often heavily negotiated with the franchisor, who may want the bank to employ a qualified manager to manage the business or may want the bank to find a qualified purchaser within a set time, such as one year.

8 Franchisor–franchisee relations

The foundations

In this chapter we examine the relationship between the franchisor and franchisee from the moment of first contact through to the development of a mature network. As will be seen, the relationship changes as the franchisee moves from a state of ignorance about the way in which to conduct the franchised business and almost total dependence, to being a confident, successful operator of that business with a growing feeling of independence. In some cases the franchisee may not be successful but may experience difficulties for various reasons, which may include:

- factors outside the control of both parties, e.g. general economic conditions;
- some deficiencies in the franchisor, its system or its support services;
- some deficiencies in the franchisee's attitude or execution of the lessons learned from the franchisor.

Many of the issues which are identified in this chapter as having a bearing on franchisor–franchisee relations are dealt with elsewhere in this book in the appropriate chapters. The relationship between franchisor and franchisee is a very special one and is different from most business relationships.

There is an analogy to be drawn between parent–child relations on the one hand and franchisor–franchisee relations on the other.[1] In the early stages of the franchise relationship the franchisee, like a child with a parent, is dependent upon the franchisor for his sources of information and the understanding of how to apply the knowledge acquired. As the franchisee gains practical experience he becomes less dependent, and in some cases positively independent to the point that he no longer sees the value in his association with the franchisor, or at best a diminished role for the franchisor. He regards himself as being totally responsible for his success and he resents the payments he is making to the franchisor and the controls to which he is subjected. Furthermore, he may see no need to continue to be supplied with any products or services by the franchisor.

This is similar to the developing parent–child relationship - as the child grows older so it becomes less dependent and more fiercely independent. The child has its own ideas, cannot see the need for parental control and rejects parental influence. So both the franchisor and parent face a similar problem. It is the recognition of and response to the changing and evolving nature of the relationship which is an essential element in the skill of both franchisor and parent. Those who deal with this problem best are the most successful in practice.

There is also a vital difference, for when the child becomes an adult it is free to do whatever it wants to do. Respect for parental feelings and guidance may or may not be considered, but even so it is the child's final choice of career and the country in which it wishes to pursue that career which dictates events.

The franchisee, however, is locked into the franchise relationship throughout the term of the contract (and any renewals) or until he sells his business. That he is a mature franchisee with years in the business behind him will give him no greater freedom to run his business than the newest recruit to the system. That is fundamental to the franchise method. The fact that the intelligent, ambitious, entrepreneurial franchisee does well and applies himself diligently to the development of the franchised business has to be recognized. His input should be encouraged and he should be treated with respect, as should the ideas which he can contribute. However, the franchisor cannot allow the franchisees to the control of the franchise system and its development. The fundamentals remain true at whatever stage one finds oneself. The franchisees operate the franchisor's system using the franchisor's names and trade marks and the franchisor must have the final word on what can and cannot be permitted. Indeed, without centralized control the franchise system and network could rapidly lose its corporate identity, uniformity of branding and range of products and services provided.

It may be said that franchising involves the development of a multiple chain of outlets in multiple ownership. What it does not involve is multiple ownership of a multiplicity of subtly different outlets. It is for such a reason that the controls which appear in a franchise agreement to be rigid cannot be qualified as so many franchisees would like by the insertion of the word 'reasonable'. The prospect, that in a mature network of say more than 50 franchisees, that a franchisor may have to cope with 'reasonable' but different requests from each franchisee is not only difficult to cope with but is incompatible with the maintenance of uniformity. Uniformity cannot be maintained if a 'reasonableness test' has to be applied to each request by a franchisee to initiate change or vary existing procedures. The recording of what is or is not permitted in each individual case will become a burden and create endless opportunities for conflict. Furthermore, the task of field support staff in educating themselves in the differences will be considerable, as will the opportunities for misunderstandings and disputes.

Lastly, and not least in significance, it will become impossible to know what is the franchisor's system and know-how. This will make the protection of the vital property rights of the franchisor very difficult, with adverse repercussions for both franchisor and the network of franchisees.

In addition, the provisions of the European Community Block Exemption Regulation for Vertical Agreements may not be complied with, since it may not be possible for the franchisor's know-how to come within the definition contained in the regulation (see Chapter 10).

From these issues we learn that there must be:

- respect by both franchisor and franchisee for the basic principles upon which the franchise system of marketing is based, which are the foundations of its success;
- respect by the franchisee for the achievements and guidance which the franchisor provides, not respect so blind that the franchisee does not see when the franchisor should be questioned and challenged, but respect for the ownership of the name, system know-how and practical experience upon which the franchise is based and all that such ownership implies;
- respect by the franchisor for the achievements of the franchisee and the contribution to the system which each franchisee can make, gained from his experience in running an operational unit.

This assumes that all is well with the system, and between franchisor and franchisee, and that all the plans, hopes and expectations fall into place. Even if this Utopian state of affairs could exist it would not last for long if all parties did not put a great deal of effort into the maintenance of the franchisor–franchisee relationship. The relationship does not end with the signing of the contract any more than a parent's duties and obligations end with the birth of the child. The vagaries of the relationship, the strains and the stresses all combine to provide the parties with great challenges in an endeavour to ensure success.

There are many areas which can give rise to stress in the relationship.

1. The franchisee is not suited to self-employment.
2. The franchisee does not have the right aptitude for the particular franchise operation.[2]
3. The franchisee may feel let down by what he expected not being matched by the reality.
4. The franchise is in an early stage of development and the franchisee does not consider that the franchisor has conducted sufficiently comprehensive pilot testing of the operations.
5. The franchisor may feel that the franchisee is not putting in the right level of effort.
6. The franchisee is dissatisfied with the up-front franchisor services.
7. The franchisee fails to make payments and/or reports on time.
8. The franchisee fails to maintain operating standards.
9. The franchisee seeks to break away from the system.
10. There are problems with the quality (or lack of quality) of the location.

11. Difficulties arise over the sale of the franchisee's business.
12. There are personality clashes between the franchisor's staff and the franchisee.
13. There are failures of communication.
14. The franchisor behaves too autocratically.
15. The franchisees resist change and improvement.
16. The franchisees are dissatisfied with the franchisor's promotional and advertising activities.
17. The franchisee's business is not as successful as the franchisee thinks it should be.
18. The franchisee's business is not as successful as the franchisor thinks it should be.
19. The franchisor does not provide the right level of back-up with field support staff.
20. The franchisee takes niggling liberties in his operation of the system.
21. The franchisor is not understood and seen by franchisees to be implementing research and development programmes to maintain and/or improve the franchise network's competitiveness in the market place.

The parties' responsibilities

The franchise relationship will come into existence as a result of the efforts of the franchisor to recruit franchisees and the interest of the franchisee in becoming a franchisee. Before either of them reach that stage of their development the franchisor will have prepared its franchise system for the market place or may have been established for some period of time. The franchisee will have concluded that he wishes to own and operate his own business.

As emphasized in other chapters of this book, the franchisor should have done its homework properly, as should the franchisee. There is always and quite properly a great emphasis placed upon the franchisor's obligations to a franchisee.

1. Properly to pilot-test and prove that the business is profitable.
2. Honestly to present the facts to the franchisee to enable the franchisee to make an informed decision.
3. To provide an effective and efficient range of initial services to assist the franchisee in establishing his business.
4. To establish the skilled range of continuing support services, which will include:

    (a) operational back-up;

(b) updating of the operational manual;

(c) marketing and promotional support;

(d) advertising on a national or regional basis with funds contributed by franchisees;

(e) standards and performance monitoring;

(f) research and development; and

(g) the benefits of the bulk purchasing power which the network commands.

The franchisor is also regarded as having a responsibility to exercise care in its choice of franchisees. He should not accept as a franchisee anyone who merely applies and has the money. There is much more to making a choice than that. The British Franchise Association Code of Ethics deals with the issue in the following terms:

> A franchisor shall select and accept only those franchisees who, upon reasonable investigation, possess the basic skills, education, personal qualities and adequate capital to succeed. There shall be no discrimination based on rank, colour, religion, national origin or sex.

By becoming a member of the BFA a franchisor accepts the obligation to work within the framework established by the Code of Ethics.

There does not exist any similar framework within which franchisees should operate. The process of franchisee selection by a franchisor is not the one-sided exercise which perhaps some franchisors would suggest it is. The entry into the contract and the establishment of the franchise relationship is very much a combined effort. Both parties have to be right for each other, and in addition the franchisee has to be able to:

- cope with the stress and strain of self-employment; and
- demonstrate the qualities which the business which is franchised requires of those who run outlets.

The franchisee, although he owns the business, has to accept the constraints which franchising will impose upon him and the restrictions on his freedom to do exactly what he pleases.

One would suggest that the prospective franchisee has the obligation to be open and frank with the franchisor. What is being created is a two-way relationship. The prospective franchisee must accept the responsibility to be open and frank with the franchisor. The prospective franchisee should not risk jeopardizing the future relationship by not accepting that he owes it to the franchisor (and to himself) to reveal all that is relevant for the franchisor to make an informed decision. It is as important for the prospective franchisee to be told by the franchisor that it does not consider the prospective franchisee to be right for the franchise system as it is to be told that he or she is suitable.

1. He must be honest with himself over the issue of whether he has the qualities which equip him to cope with self-employment; is he and

are his family prepared to live with the disruption to life which self-employment can bring with it? Searching self-examination is very necessary at this stage.

2. He must, whatever the temptations, be totally objective in his evaluation of the franchise opportunities which interest him. There are far too many franchisees who become so 'taken' with a proposition that all normal danger signals are ignored. Advice is not listened to because it does not confirm what the franchisee wanted to hear. Thus one finds a significant number of people signing up to become franchisees where the franchisor has not properly market tested his operations, where the franchisor's financial situation is clearly unsatisfactory, and where the franchisor's contractual arrangements place the franchisee at a severe disadvantage in relation to such matters as product supply and price, terms of transfer of business and renewal rights which are easy to defeat and/or which cost unreasonable sums to exercise. Any would-be franchisee who cannot be totally objective and who ignores obvious danger signals will find that not only will franchisor–franchisee relations be poor but the franchisor may not survive. Another danger is that even if the franchisor is a good franchisor with a well developed system, the franchisee may, by lacking in objectivity, take on a franchise which does not suit him and his capabilities.

3. The franchisee should not allow anyone else to sort out a 'short list' of prospective franchise opportunities for him, although there are some who offer this sort of 'matching' service and claim it is successful. He should personally meet and discuss the opportunities available with as many franchisors as will be prepared to meet him. Both parties will benefit enormously from this, particularly the franchisee. Both parties will be making a very important decision; the more prospective franchisees a franchisor can interview the more experience obtained and the better will be the quality of those who enter into the franchise; the more franchisors the prospective franchisee can meet the more he will learn about franchisors and the opportunities on offer. The greater the franchisee's experience in meeting and discussing opportunities with franchisors the more likely he is to make the right choice when exercising an objective judgement. These meetings and particularly those with the franchisor with whom the franchisee will enter into an agreement will be laying the foundations of the future franchisor–franchisee relationship.

4. The franchisee must be completely honest and open in his dealings with the franchisor. This is the approach he expects of the franchisor, so he must divulge all that is relevant to enable the franchisor to reach an informed conclusion about the franchisee. A franchisee who feels let down when he discovers that what the franchisor told him was not the whole or the right story should understand that a franchisor will feel let down if the franchisee withholds material information from him. Either way, the trust

which each must have in the other is damaged or even destroyed and the relationship will at best be difficult if not impossible.

It must therefore be appreciated by both franchisor and franchisee that their pre-contract meetings and discussions are laying the foundations for a possible long-term future relationship. It is in the interests of both parties that the ground rules for the relationship are clearly explained and established.

The main areas which give rise to stress in the relationship are listed above; some of these can be taken into account at this early stage of discussion. If each of the parties is aware of these potential problem areas they can and should feature in the pre-contract discussions so that each can judge the other's reaction and take a view about the future.

At this stage in the discussions the franchisor should reveal to the franchisee all sources of income which the franchisor derives from the operation of the franchised network. No franchisor should have any source of income which the franchisees do not know about and the franchisor must not make any secret profits. The relationship will suffer considerably in terms of loss of trust or respect if franchisees find that the franchisor is profiting at their expense from a source of which they are not aware.

It is also important that the franchisor does not do 'special deals' with any individual franchisee. Special deals create problems in the relationship:

1. The franchisee who is given a special deal always regards himself as a special case and will always expect privileges.
2. Other franchisees who do not have such special deals will resent those who do and the franchisor for not having given them the same deal.

The franchisor should ensure that the franchisee understands what the franchising method of marketing is and how it works in practice. It is crucial that the franchisee understands the nature and scope of the relationship and what is expected of a franchisor and a franchisee. The franchisee must be made aware of what will later be:

- provided to him by the franchisor as continuing services and how these services will be provided; and
- expected of him in terms of standards, operating procedures and likely expenditures on keeping the image fresh and the business up to date.

The quality of the franchisor's training is a key factor in ensuring that these foundations for the future are properly explained and will provide the introduction to the franchisor's operational manuals and the day-to-day operation of the franchised business. The franchisor should be capable of explaining and indeed should explain to the franchisee the reasons for the operational requirements and the individual provisions in the franchise agreement. A franchisee who can be given a proper perspective and understanding of the way in which the operational and legal obligations are brought together will find it easier to come to terms with the one-sided nature of the arrangement, which is essential if the franchisor is to be capable of maintaining the standards and the integrity of his name, goodwill and operating system. These requirements place the art of communications high on the list of skills which the franchisor must possess. Whatever he promises and demands should not only be in the contract and manual but should be represented by daily reality in his dealings with franchisees. These early dealings between franchisor and franchisee are crucial, as they set the tone for what will follow; what follows must involve the delivery by both the franchisor and franchisee to each other of what is expected, undertaken and promised.

Above all, both parties must appreciate that they are laying the foundation for what needs to be a harmonious positive 'partnership' (not in the legal sense) for their mutual advantage. What they should not be doing is laying down the foundations for conflict within a legal arena. Once any of the parties reaches for the contract the relationship has failed. If both parties can always bear in mind that they are better off if they perform their obligations and conduct their relations with each other on the basis that the contract should never be looked at after it is signed until it needs to be renewed, that will be a good start. Good franchisor–franchisee relations do not just happen; they have to be worked at.

The continuing relationship

We now move on to the stage in the relationship when the franchisee has signed his contract and undergone training. The franchisor should now be delivering the services to the franchisee which should result in a successful opening of the franchisee's business. This will be at a time when the relationship between the parties should not be tainted by any ill feelings; instead there should prevail a spirit of willing cooperation. That is not to say that this will always be the case for, even at this early stage in the relationship, there is no guarantee that some franchisees will not be testing the franchisor's resolve by attempting to cut corners and save money by seeking to get by with a lower level of specification than the franchisor requires. Such an attitude on the part of an individual franchisee could be an indication that there may be long-term problems with that particular individual. This attitude at such an early stage may be a warning that if not brought under control this franchisee will always challenge the franchisor's system, methods and authority.

In the early stages of the development of a franchise network the franchisor is far more likely to take on, as franchisees, persons who are unsuitable. There are two reasons for this. First, the franchisor is inexperienced at the task of assessing and evaluating the suitability of prospective franchisees and has not yet developed the art of knowing and recognizing the relevant qualities which a franchisee of his network should possess. Second, the franchisor will be anxious to embark upon his programme of selling franchises so that his initial investment in pilot operations and the establishment of a franchising infrastructure of his business can be rewarded. This anxiety is often translated into a loss of objectivity coupled with impatience, which results in the recruitment of franchisees who apparently have the requisite basic qualities but who may be temperamentally and by nature unsuited for the relationship with the particular franchisor or unable to bring the right skills to the network's operations. For example, the franchisee may lack ability as a salesman when sales ability is a crucial feature of the franchise system.

These two factors combine to provide the foundation for problems which may not be capable of resolution by even the best possible franchisor–franchisee relation programme of the franchisor. It is common to many franchise networks that of the first 12 or so franchisees there will be more difficulties to contend with than with those who subsequently join the network. Apart from the fact that the existence of these 'difficult' franchisees will make disproportionate demands upon the franchisor's resources there will also be difficulties in recruitment, as well as resentment of the problems by other franchisees which can affect the network as a whole. Normally a good franchise will sell itself, but no matter how good the franchise, bad news from early entrants, whatever the cause, can only inhibit growth as prospective franchisees are deterred by their contact with those franchisees. It is also a feature found in mature networks that some of the early 'difficult' franchisees later become active organizers of franchisee dissent, causing disruption to a network and a diversion of franchisor's and franchisee's financial and manpower resources from their normal business activities.

Franchisors should recognize that it is vitally important to ensure the correct selection of all franchisees to the system but particularly the first 12 in order to avoid the potential future problems which can arise. Patience and the ability to say 'no' when advisable are essential. Great care should be taken to ensure that franchisees have the requisite skills and are not likely to find the day-to-day requirements of their business alien to their nature.

These factors are to be emphasized, since if the foundation, which comprises the initial franchisees, is not sound the task of fostering and maintaining good franchisor–franchisee relations becomes that much more difficult.

The responsibility for good franchisor–franchisee relations is shared by franchisor and franchisee but undoubtedly it is the franchisor who must take the initiative in establishing their tone and quality. The franchisor and franchisee must not take each other for granted. If they do the franchisor will be neglecting his responsibilities and the franchisee will be failing to develop as an independent businessman to the full extent of his entrepreneurial abilities. The franchisor should be seeking to create a climate in which the franchisee feels that he is being encouraged to develop his business and apply his entrepreneurial skills. He should be made to feel a member of the 'family' and be encouraged to provide his input, based upon his experience, for the good of the network of which he is a member. Many innovations in franchised networks are prompted by suggestions which originate with franchisees.

Good franchisor–franchisee relations do not occur spontaneously, they flow from a conscious effort on the part of both parties to work at enhancing the relationship. It can be easy for a franchisor to take advantage of his franchisees. Many franchisees join systems because they have a strong belief in the basic business and their prospects for success. Their first feelings if the franchisor is, to their mind, under-performing are of disappointment and frustration coupled with a strong wish to try to get the franchisor properly to perform his obligations. Apart from the fact that no franchisor should allow any franchisees to be able to claim under-performance, the perception (even if unjustified) that the franchisor is under-performing is a clear indication that the franchisor is failing properly to communicate with his franchisees and is not concentrating his efforts sufficiently well on the franchisor–franchisee relationship. In seeking to maintain the relationship at the right level the franchisor should understand that the franchisees' perception of his role and performance are very important and channels of communication must be kept wide open and thoughtfully used to ensure that the franchisees' perception of the franchisor's abilities are consistent with reality. Before dealing with channels of communication there are a few other points worthy of consideration.

The franchisee's contribution to good relations with the franchisor requires that the franchisee should work at doing his job properly and wholeheartedly. The operational standards must be complied with. The franchisee should work hard to make a success of his business – no clock watching!; reporting requirements and financial obligations should promptly be met – nothing could be calculated to do more harm than failure to provide what the franchisor will regard as vital information and to pay monies due. The franchisee should participate in events organized by the franchisor, e.g. annual regional franchise meetings, contributions to franchise network newsletters.

For his part the franchisor must concentrate on maintaining and improving the quality of his services. In short, the franchisor should deliver what he promised he would. The ongoing back-up, demonstrating an interest in the franchisees and the development of their business, is important. Also important is the maintenance for research and development and the processing and evaluation of new ideas. Demonstration by the franchisor of its ability and will to introduce new ideas, adapt the system, modernize the image and introduce new product lines or services so that the business remains competitive will provide welcome comfort to a franchisee and enhance the relationship.

The franchisor should ensure that not only does he give the franchisee value for money in the provision of continuing services but the franchisee perceives that he is getting value for money. The franchisee should feel that he is getting more in value than the fee payments (however structured) cost him. This requires the introduction and maintenance of excellent means of communication between franchisor and franchisee.

The franchisor should take trouble to ensure that written communications are not only received but read, assimilated and acted upon. The role of field support staff in ensuring that this occurs is very important. Field support staff are the eyes and ears of the franchisor; they must be receptive and not hostile to what the franchisees have to say. Field support staff should be trained to look out for the early warning signs that something is amiss. Any such signs should be acted upon, for even if there is no logical or apparently justified ground for complaint, the fact that the franchisee is unhappy should be sufficient to raise the alarm that something needs to be done.

The franchisor must have a system for dealing with the stresses and strains which will always arise in any network no matter how well it is run. In the final analysis the managing director and/or chairman of the franchisor company must be prepared to become involved to ensure that the right outcome is achieved.

It is suggested that the franchisor should ensure that all his staff understand the importance of the highest possible quality of franchisor–franchisee relations. Staff training should ensure that the emphasis is placed upon the quality of good relations and how they can be achieved and maintained. The franchisor should appoint a senior member of staff backed by and reporting to the chairman or managing director to have responsibility for ensuring that these policies are effectively maintained.

Notes

1. In the early days of franchising in the USA, many franchisors liked to talk about their 'partnerships' (non-legal) with franchisees. Some still use that or a similar term to describe their relationship with their franchisees.
2. In the USA, this is a mandated disclosure using the offering circular.

9 Channels of communication: franchisee advisory associations

None of the efforts which franchisor and franchisee make to enhance their relationship will be effective unless there is a programme in place to ensure good and effective channels of communication between them. It will be appreciated from Chapter 8 that communications are a two-way process. The franchisee cannot respond to the franchisor unless the franchisor has made its point clearly and effectively and the franchisor cannot know what concerns the franchisee unless the franchisee opens up frankly and honestly to the franchisor. Whatever frustrations either party may feel about the actions or non-actions of the other, communications must not be conducted on a background of hostility; they must always be approached in a constructive way with a view to resolving problems to the mutual advantage of franchisor and franchisee. Hostile action tends to bring hostile reaction and a deterioration in relations which will inevitably be counter-productive and result in a situation which helps no one. Hostility should not be a feature at any stage of the working relationship.

One may summarize the areas on which efforts should be concentrated in order to enhance good relations.

Personal contact

Personal contact is an important feature of the relationship and must never be neglected. Even successful franchisees require personal contact with the franchisor; their success should not result in their neglect by the franchisor. They may not need as much personal contact or attention as the unsuccessful nor will they need the same level of input. Dialogue with successful franchisees not only keeps high their level of awareness that they belong to the network, it also assists in the perpetuation of their belief that membership of the network is worthwhile and that they are getting value for money. Their very success, of which they will be proud, has to be recognized and encouraged. They may well also prove capable of providing the franchisor with a valuable input which can assist in developing ideas and product or service lines.

Personal contact will be provided in most cases by specialist staff at the franchisor's office and the franchisor's field support staff. However the franchisor organizes his resources he should ensure that all his staff recognize that each franchisee is special to the franchisor and respond to each of them on a personal basis. Each franchisee must be dealt with on the basis that his role and importance are recognized and that he feels that the franchisor really cares about him, his problems and his success.

The managing or (in large systems) regional director of the franchisor should also take the trouble to visit franchisees regularly to cement the relationship and to ensure that the franchisee is really satisfied with the service he receives.

All field support visits by the franchisor to the franchisee's operational unit should be recorded on a form containing a checklist to verify compliance by the franchisee with operational standards and contractual obligations. The franchisor's representative must discuss the report with the franchisee to ensure that the franchisee knows and understands in what respect he is not regarded as performing correctly. He may have explanations which he must be given an opportunity to provide. Nothing could be worse than to have a franchisee think that unjustified secret reports are being made about him and his operations. Apart from monitoring compliance the franchisor should be using the information to help the franchisee to improve his standards and performance.

Written communications

It is likely that in many cases written communication from franchisors will be more frequent than personal contact. Because of the more impersonal nature of written communications it is more important to get the right message to the franchisee in an unambiguous way. In face-to-face contact misunderstandings can be discussed and resolved. A written communication which is capable of being misunderstood is like a festering sore which left unattended can become a major problem; what is worse is that the franchisor may not even realise the havoc its misunderstood communication has caused until the franchisee explodes into reaction. Even unintended carelessness can create the wrong impression, which underlines the need for extreme care in the preparation by a franchisor of written communications. The methods of written communication can vary from case to case but it is likely that there will be five basic categories of written communication:

- normal correspondence;
- newsletters;
- Internet communications;
- updates of manuals;
- field visit reports.

It is likely that the authors of these various communications will differ. There will probably be more than one author of letters, which could be written by any member of the franchisor's team; this will also probably be the case with updates of manuals, where the authorship will depend upon the segment of the manual which is being updated. The franchisor should have some system for checking that all authors of its written material appreciate the need for accurate, unambiguous communication and should introduce some internal method of checking material before it is despatched. Checking is more difficult with normal correspondence without impairing efficient operations but franchisors must take care because it is so easy to cause unnecessary offence with a thoughtless comment.

Franchisee meetings

Many franchisors take the trouble to organize meetings between themselves and groups of franchisees as well as meetings involving the whole network. Regional and national meetings can be a very effective means of keeping in touch with franchisees, their feelings, doubts, fears, ideas and complaints. These meetings also enable the franchisor to make presentations indicating how franchisees can improve performance, what new ideas are to be introduced, what is under research and development and what promotional and marketing activities are proposed. Franchisees rightly expect to be kept informed and if the right climate of cooperation can be created many ideas and suggestions from franchisees can be useful and make a positive contribution to the development of the network.

Franchisee associations

There are two types of franchisee association. There are those born out of the frustration and dissatisfaction by franchisees who adopt a hostile adversary position with the franchisor. This must be avoided at all costs. For an association to be set up by the franchisees in these circumstances must mean that the franchisor has failed in some of the following areas:

- adequately to communicate with its franchisees;
- to be receptive to its franchisees' ideas and concerns;
- to be supportive;
- to provide the right field support for its franchisees;
- in its marketing programmes;
- in its innovative functions – it has not kept the system and image up to date with market trends and competitive businesses;
- to organize advantageous purchasing arrangements;

- to develop and maintain the feeling in the network of mutual trust and interdependence between franchisor and franchisees which is so vital – the franchisor may have become overbearing or, by contrast, appear uninterested;
- in other material respects to discharge his obligations to its franchisees.
- to provide value for money – the franchisee should always feel that he is receiving services of a value greater than their cost to him in the payments he is making to the franchisor.

A franchisee association which develops in these circumstances is symptomatic of the problems; it will not solve them; it is an indictment of the franchisor. The franchise system will be attacked and the franchisor will find itself with either combined legal action or tremendous pressure, which could lead to the dismantling of its franchise system. Alternatively, the franchisees will try to lead the franchisor back along what they regard as the path of franchise righteousness. This could lead to franchisees seeking to impose their collective will and result in harm to the system and the weakening of the franchisor's ability to control the network.

In any event, all parties will have suffered traumatically in terms of personal relationship, confidence and undoubtedly financially. The amount of time and effort which franchisees and franchisor will have to spend on the areas of dispute will divert resources from their respective basic businesses, resulting in a downward spiral which will exacerbate the difficulties. This potential impact should not be lightly dismissed.

Concerted actions by franchisees on such a basis have a tendency to run into difficulties. Human nature being what it is there will inevitably be ringleaders (some of whom may be early unsatisfactory or dissatisfied franchisees) and those who will respond to peer pressure. Experience shows that when serious action is proposed many franchisees lose enthusiasm – those who responded to peer pressure step back and those who fear a loss of their business investment are not prepared to run the risk. Furthermore, since each franchisee's case and circumstances are different, a group of this nature can result in inter-franchisee disputes and differences which harm the whole network and can sour the atmosphere and the franchisees' relationship with each other as well as with the franchisor.

The franchisor will always, and quite rightly, take the view that it has a direct contractual relationship with each franchisee and that it will only deal with each franchisee on a one-to-one basis in resolving any problems or issues which the franchisee may wish to discuss. It is for the franchisor to evaluate what its franchisees provide as input, to balance the diverse issues which not surprisingly are likely to be based upon personal self-interest, and to produce solutions which are in the best interests of the entire network. Franchisees must accept that they are part of a team and as with all teams there is a leader – in this case the franchisor.

Getting the attention of the franchisor is all well and good up to a point, but franchisees who contemplate the route of establishing the 'trade union' type of association should give very considerable thought as to whether or not to adopt this approach rather than a more constructive and less confrontational route – the strategy is otherwise very high risk. There is a problem that in very large systems the pressure from franchisees may be sufficient to result in such an association being formed.

The other type of association is that which is formed either on the sole initiative of the franchisor or jointly by franchisor and franchisees as a means of improving communications and acting as a means of liaison when problems arise or to ensure that problems are avoided.[1] It is difficult to state when would be the right point in time in the development of any individual franchise to introduce such an association. Obviously in the early stages it will not be necessary or appropriate, but once the franchisor is established with some experienced franchisees in the field the advantages will become apparent. The association which is created in a spirit of goodwill with mutual advantage as its objective extends the climate of understanding which should exist into a practical reality, thus providing a strong weapon in cementing the franchisor and franchisees together in a powerful business alliance. It provides another method of bringing together the franchisor's and the franchisees' entrepreneurial talents for their mutual benefit.

There are those who do not believe that franchisee associations are necessarily the answer to the communications problem. There have been attempts by franchisors to establish associations which have failed owing to the apathy displayed by franchisees. One is inclined to wonder whether the reason for the lack of interest was that the franchisor's system for conducting relations with franchisees was so effective that an association was not felt necessary by franchisees. If a franchisor can devise a system which achieves that result an association may not be necessary. As with most techniques which are available there is no dogmatic rule that one should or should not have a franchise association. (Note: in countries which have franchise specific laws there may be a requirement to allow franchisees to form associations regardless of the franchisor's wishes.[2]) It may be a helpful business tool but it is only one of the options available to a franchisor and certainly does not, and cannot, replace direct personal face-to-face contact between franchisor and individual franchisees. If it is intended to result in, or does result in, a reduced level of such personal contact it is a misuse of the technique.

In considering the areas of activity for an association which follow it must be understood by franchisees that the franchisor owns the name under which the network trades and the system which it employs in doing so. The franchisor must inevitably take the final decision on all system and system management changes in the interests of all. The existence of an association is merely a method of informing and consulting with the network to ensure that the franchisor has available to him the maximum relevant information in his decision-taking process.

The areas of activity in which such a association can operate effectively are given below.

1. Communications. Practical difficulties and problems can be identified and discussed between the association and the franchisor. Style and content of communications can be discussed and improved. The franchisor can find out at first hand, and with constructive rather than destructive criticism, why his communications fail to achieve their objective. It may be that the association feels that the franchisor could introduce (if one is not already available) or improve a regular newsletter and make suggestions for topics to be included.

2. Franchisee experience in the field can be passed on to the franchisor and methods of coping with problems discussed. There is often a wealth of experience and ability among franchisees which the franchisor would be wise to tap. A limited size of group participation can make the discussion more fruitful than if all franchisees were present. One would hope that the franchisee representatives in the association will present a filtered distillation of their fellow franchisees' ideas and suggestions.

3. New ideas can be introduced by the franchisor for the association's considered views and reactions. The franchisor can either discuss the franchisees' views before market testing in company-owned stores or operations or report the experience in practice after pilot-testing has taken place. This could of course include innovations in products and services.

4. Suggestions can be made for the improvement of operational manuals if franchisees find that the explanations contained in them are not adequate or that there are areas which have been neglected. The manuals may also be expanded by the introduction of additional material to improve the range and scope of the available guidance.

5. Training or retraining procedures and facilities can be discussed by the franchisor with franchisees who are, of course, past 'pupils' of the franchisor's training facilities.

6. Discussion of detailed problems arising from the failure or inadequacy of field support staff procedures or the franchisor's other operational and support services.

7. Difficulties which may arise with regard to accounting and reporting procedures can be investigated and any remedial steps taken. Many franchisors are finding that the availability of computer systems which cope with the ever-increasing volume of accounting information with which they and their franchisees have to contend can be introduced to a network with cost-effective benefits to both franchisor and franchisees. In such cases, and often with little ongoing additional expense, a full accounting and information service can be produced and made available to franchisees. The introduction of such a service, its scope and capital cost as well as running costs, can be discussed with a franchisee advisory association and a scheme acceptable in its details can be agreed.

8. Proposals by the franchisor for the introduction of contractual changes. The reasons for such changes can be explained. The franchisor may wish to introduce new provisions to fill gaps revealed by experience or to adjust to changes in laws and the decisions of the courts, which must be reflected in the system and in the contractual documentation.

9. Most franchisees contribute in one way or another towards funding the cost of national advertising, local advertising, point-of-sale material, promotional activities and public relations. Invariably they are keenly interested to know how, where and when the funds will be spent and how much these activities will help each of them. Each year's proposed activities can be discussed with franchisees through the association. Frequently a franchisee will have a valid contribution to make because he will be looking at the proposals with his narrow self-interest in mind. This sort of grass-roots detail can escape the attention of the franchisor and its marketing, advertising and promotional advisers. Promotional activities, in the planning of which the franchisees have participated, will be greeted far more enthusiastically and with greater prospect of success than would be the case if they were forced upon the franchisees. It will also be possible to discuss such details as how long before the promotion starts the franchisee receives;

   (a) point-of-sale material;

   (b) any special range of stock, and so on, and on what basis.

10. There should always be continuing new product or services research and development which will necessitate market research and surveys. Franchisees through the association have a contribution to make in providing information for such research and surveys. Franchisees have in many cases introduced ideas for research and development of ideas. In the course of discussion about the introduction of the research and surveys franchisees could assist in the compilation of the terms of reference and the scope of the enquiries which may involve some of their members.

11. By liaison with a franchisee advisory association a franchisor can organize selective trials, by franchisees willing to participate, of new products or services to assist in their research and development.

12. Franchisees should also be given the opportunity to raise topics of concern or interest to them. Care should be taken to ensure that the association only deals with matters of concern affecting franchisees as a whole. It should not allow itself to be used as a vehicle for the promotion of any individual dissatisfied franchisee's complaints. It cannot act as advocate, judge and jury in what would inevitably be a two-sided story. The quality of the relationship between the committee and franchisor should not be placed in jeopardy for the sake of individual problems or disputes.

If the franchisee representatives in such an association try to become involved in such matters it will undoubtedly sour the atmosphere and be likely to lead to the dissolution of the association.

Concerning the organization of the association, it should be understood at the outset that while the association will be an association primarily comprising franchisees, the object will be to:

- improve communications between the franchisor and franchisee;
- provide a forum for the discussion of mutual problems;
- create a climate for improved liaison between the parties to the franchise relationship.

The franchisor must also be represented.

It is possible to establish a formally constituted association with a company limited by guarantee or an unincorporated association. Whichever is required, the franchisor should incur the expense and organize the franchisee advisory association. Most of the franchisee advisory associations which exist in the UK at this time, at the very least, have an informal constitution.

The document establishing the advisory committee should deal with the following matters.

The terms of reference

The terms of reference of the association can include all or some of the points already discussed above. Consideration should be given to whether one should establish more than one association or subcommittees in the association to deal with different aspects; for example, there could be an association or sub-committee which focuses on marketing and advertising and others which focus on operational issues and so on. The number of franchisees in the network will have some influence on the desirability of more than one association or the establishment of sub-committees. The terms of reference should exclude consideration of individual franchisees' disputes with the franchisor.

Membership

Membership should be open to all current franchisees.

How it should be managed

Normally one would expect to see some sort of representative committee which is kept to a manageable size. A large and unwieldy committee would be counter-productive. It is best to organize some form of regional representation so that each committee member can consult with the other franchisees within his region. Assuming that there is a nationwide network, one might contemplate the following regional representations:

- Scotland
- Wales
- Northern England
- East Midlands
- West Midlands
- South-east England
- South-west England
- Northern Ireland

There may be one representative from the smaller (in terms of numbers of franchisees) regions and two from the larger. When the differences in numbers are not as significant, one representative from each region would probably be enough. Each region should select its own representatives. A nominee (who should be another franchisee from within the same region) should attend if the selected representative is for some reason not able to attend any particular meeting.

Meetings

It should be sufficient to have two or three meetings each year with an agenda established by consultation with the franchisor. In that way all the subjects the franchisor and franchisees wish to deal with, or raise, can be discussed. One of the meetings could coincide with any national franchisee convention which the franchisor may organise. The franchisor should be represented at all meetings by senior staff relevant to the topics to be discussed.

Secretariat

The franchisor should provide and cover the expenses of the secretariat for the association. The individual franchisees' representatives will be responsible for keeping in touch with the franchisees in the region which he represents so that they are effectively informed of the association's discussions.

Finances

There should be little expense incurred in running the association. Mention has already been made of the franchisor funding the costs of establishing the association and of the secretariat. There will also be the cost to franchisee representatives of travelling to and attending meetings. This cost should be borne either by the representatives or collectively for each representative by the franchisees in his region. It is essential to bear in mind that the objectives of any franchisee association should be to work for the mutual benefit of all who participate in the franchise network by creating a harmonious atmosphere in which problems are dealt with quickly and new ideas are encouraged.

NOTES

1. Often called a franchise advisory council in the USA.
2. This is a common provision in the US franchise relationship laws.

10 Overview of contractual issues

The franchise contract is a very important document. Its signature is the moment of truth. The contract provides the franchisee with a document which enables him to see whether the franchisor's promises are being incorporated in the document which will regulate the dealings between franchisor and franchisee.

The contract is a legal commitment which is binding on both parties. The franchisee must therefore at this stage take competent legal advice as to the meaning and effect of the contract. In consultation with his solicitor he will check to see whether the contract confirms what he has been told. The franchisee should realize that the extent of the advice he is given is limited to the meaning and effect of the contract. It is the decision of the franchisee, and the franchisee alone, whether or not to proceed with any particular franchise opportunity. Decision-making is an essential part of his role as a businessman.

In this chapter account will be taken of the European Code of Ethics ('the Code') adopted by the British Franchise Association (BFA) in 1990. The Code is set out in full in Appendix B. The BFA has also published guidelines in a booklet entitled *The Ethics of Franchising* to what it considers to be compliance or non-compliance with the ethical principles of the Code. These guidelines are also taken into account in this chapter.

A franchise contract has to take into account a number of different issues which are now considered.

1. Although basically a contractual relationship between the franchisor and the franchisee, the operation of the franchise contract affects two other parties who are not joined as parties to the contract. The other parties are, first, all other franchisees within the network and, second, members of the public, the consumer, and it is to both of these parties that the franchisor and the franchisee owe responsibilities.

   It is simple to see how this arises. Each franchisee within the chain will be affected for good or bad by the actions of his fellow franchisees. If a franchisee runs his operation in a manner which is inconsistent with the standards associated with the franchisor's brand and image, it will damage the goodwill associated with them, thereby adversely affecting the business prospects of other franchisees. So each franchisee must accept a responsibility to the other franchisees who in turn will owe similar responsibilities to that franchisee. The restrictive provisions of the franchise agreement, which are concerned with the maintenance of the standards and the correct operation of the franchised business, are not merely tiresome chores, but the mechanism by which the franchisor can ensure that the reputation and integrity of the franchise chain is always maintained. What appears to be an onerous contract in some respects is therefore an essential feature which franchisees need the franchisor to have available to be in a position to ensure that the uniform system they are joining can be kept on course.

The consumer is not concerned with whether or not an outlet is franchised. A consumer is merely concerned with the brand and what it stands for in terms of the range and quality of service products and or services. A consumer will frequent a business which has given satisfaction in the past and will regard franchised businesses as being branches of a larger chain. If the franchisee fails to live up to the reputation of the brand the consumer will not accept as an explanation 'but this was operated under franchise and unfortunately we have problems with that franchisee'. All the consumer is concerned with is that when he deals with a business he receives the same standards of products and service which he has been led to believe he can expect from that particular 'branded' business. Consumers are becoming increasingly aware of franchising and its place in the business community because of the publicity which franchise systems are receiving. This, coupled with the increasing tendency for legal reasons to identify franchised outlets as being operated under franchise should result in the consumer knowing the identity of the trader with whom he is dealing. Franchisees therefore owe a great responsibility in the maintenance of these standards to ensure that the consumer is not misled and that, whichever outlet within the franchise chain the consumer patronizes, he is provided with the quality product and/ or services and the personal service he had reason to expect he would receive.

2. It has already been explained that the franchisor in a business format franchise will be contributing his 'blueprint', which embraces a package comprising trade secrets, methods of operation, use of trade marks, trade names and many of the other features to which reference has been made. The franchisor will be concerned in his agreement to ensure that provision is made for the franchisee (a) to use the 'blueprint', methods of operation, trademarks, trade names etc., and (b) to preserve the element of trade secrecy which is associated with the franchisor's particular methods and 'blueprint'. The agreement, in essence, is a licence permitting the franchisee to run the business only according to the blueprint. If the prospective franchisee wants the freedom to do only as he pleases then franchising is not for him.

3. It is inherent in discharging the four-way obligations outlined in item 1 above (i.e. the franchisor, franchisee, other franchisees and the consumer) that consideration is given to the establishment of standards, the manner in which those standards are instilled into the franchisee and what provision should be made to maintain and enforce them.

4. The term of the agreement has to be considered. As a basic principle one should expect the franchise relationship to be capable of subsisting in the long term as long as both parties observe their respective obligations. The BFA Code of Ethics provides that the 'duration of the agreement ... should be long enough to allow the individual franchisee to amortise his initial franchise investment'. This ethical principle, which is vague and anomalous in many respects, is thankfully expanded upon by the BFA in an 'Extension and Interpretation' attached to and incorporated in the Code, which states: 'It is recognized

   (a) that franchise contracts are ordinarily offered for a uniform term within a network;

   (b) that for a minority of the largest franchise opportunities amortising the initial investment may not be a primary objective for the franchisee. In such cases the objective should be to adopt a contract period which reasonably balances the interests of the parties to the contract;

   (c) that this section could be subject to national laws concerning the restraint of trade and may need to be met through renewal clauses.'

There may be legal reasons in some cases in the UK why the initial term should not exceed five years. In these cases the franchisee should ideally be given an option to renew the agreement. It is a requirement of the Code that the agreement should contain 'the basis for any renewal of the agreement'. Ideally, the relationship should continue as long as both parties observe their contractual obligations. Indeed, the BFA in its guidance in its publication *The Ethics of Franchising* expresses the following principle: 'franchisees, who are in compliance with the terms and conditions of their contracts, shall have the right to realise the value of their business on transfer'. The length of the time is also affected by the amount invested and the attitude of lending sources which will be concerned to ensure that the franchisee will have enough time to repay loans and still feel he has an asset worth all the effort.

Some franchisors do not like to grant too long a term in the belief that there may be developments in the law to which they would like to have the opportunity to respond sooner rather than later. In any event it is the invariable practice to grant franchisees an option to renew provided the franchisee has performed his obligations under the agreement, updates, refurbishes and re-equips the franchised unit, and enters into a new agreement in the form of the franchisor's then current agreement.

However, there are some franchisors who seek to use renewal time to impose wider conditions.

(a) A 'revamp' clause, which could involve the franchisee in going back to the shell of his shop and completely refitting it out to accommodate a new presentation with costs perhaps equal to or greater than those incurred when he originally set up; the franchisee can of course decide that he will not renew on those terms, perhaps because the franchisor cannot demonstrate that the required capital investment is cost-effective for the franchisee; the franchisee may not be able to raise the money from the banks, who are equally uncertain about financial viability; the franchisor, who will benefit from the possibly increased turnover in the form of product mark-up or franchise fees based upon gross sales regardless of the effect on the franchisee's net return, has a conflicting interest at this point in time. Such a revamp clause may be necessary in order for a franchisor to keep his business competitive and up to date.

The presence of such a clause in itself is not unfair but the way in which it is enforced can be. A franchisor who has such a provision should observe the following requirements. These requirements bear in mind the BFA membership criterion that pilot testing must be carried out. A revamp is analogous to opening a new operation in many significant respects.

(i) The 'revamp' should be previously tested by the franchisor in practice, who should be able to demonstrate the effect which it has on the financial performance of the units where it has been tested.

(ii) The testing should be in a sufficient number of representative operational units to ensure that there are sufficient comparables to enable an informed decision to be made by franchisees. The franchisor should make the decision as to the sufficiency of the number of units at which testing should take place.

(iii) The franchisor should be prepared to assist his franchisees in making arrangements with their banks for the financing or refinancing which they require for the purpose of revamping.

(iv) Revamps should not be required so often that a franchisee cannot reap the financial rewards for the expenditure he has made in terms of both recovery of investment but also increased profitability over a reasonable period.

(b) A 'relocation' clause, where the franchisor will make it a condition of renewal that a franchisee should close down at his present premises and move to fresh premises which the franchisor may decide offer a better trading opportunity or larger accommodation into which to fit the franchisor's new ideas. This is in essence requiring the franchisee to set up an entirely new business with all the inherent risks and considerable expenses plus the cost of the existing premises until they can be disposed of and the cost, which may be at a loss, of disposal.

This highlights a problem which can arise where a franchisor decides that a completely fresh approach is necessary. The franchisor may well be completely right and the changes essential but there are ways in which such issues can be handled properly. The following considerations should be applied in the circumstances.

(i) Is it really necessary for the franchisee to be required to move? Is it possible for the new concept to be installed in the existing location? A franchisee required to relocate may not be able to afford to do so and the franchisor does have a responsibility to him. The franchisee may well have a successful operation earning good profits for him and a good flow of franchise fees for the franchisor. A franchisor must in these circumstances exercise the utmost good faith consistent with his responsibilities, and should be prepared to demonstrate that the need exists in terms of future competitiveness and updating of the system. The introduction of a 'new' operation by the franchisor or another franchisee where it will adversely affect the 'old' operation because the 'old' franchisee cannot afford or does not wish to abandon the existing operation raises difficult issues for the franchisee, whose existing operation may be severely damaged. It may be possible for the existing operation to remain while the franchisee opens the new concept in a location where it will not cannibalize sales at the existing operation.

(ii) The franchisor must be able to demonstrate that the relocation is likely to be cost-effective for the franchisee from previous and adequate pilot testing by the franchisor.

(iii) The franchisor should be prepared to assist the franchisee in making his financing arrangements with his bankers.

(iv) In no circumstances should a franchisor use revamping or relocation as an excuse for unfairly ridding itself of any franchisee. The motive should be to enhance and promote the franchise system and its profitability equitably for both franchisor and franchisee.

5. Quite apart from the position on renewal of the agreement it will also be advisable that over the passage of years the freshness of the image appeal to the consumer and competitiveness in the market place are maintained. It will be necessary to ensure that provision is

made in the contract to require the franchisee to make provision, perhaps by setting amounts aside periodically, for investment in the modernization and the upgrading of the premises and equipment employed therein so that with the passage of time the appeal of the business and its attractiveness to the consumer do not fade.

6. In these days of rapid technological progress many franchisors have to consider the possibility that some new technology will have to be introduced in the future. The most common area in which this is likely to arise is where it is desired to introduce electronic point-of-sale systems which fulfil many functions, such as stock control and recording of gross income and categories of income. There is often a landline modem link with the head office computer, which can then provide franchisees with monthly profit and loss and stock order lists. These are undoubtedly the sort of services many franchisors wish to provide and they are welcomed by franchisees if part of the original package. However, if a franchisor wishes to have the right subsequently to introduce such a system it will also need to reserve the right to require the franchisee to spend whatever is necessary to install and run the system regardless of the benefits. This clearly is untenable since the franchisee would be exposed to an obligation, unilaterally imposed, to spend without limit. This means that the franchisor will have to be precise in his plan and proposals. One method of overcoming the problem is for the franchisor to delineate the scope of the planned requirements and to indicate limits of capital and running costs so that the franchisee can make an informed decision before undertaking a commitment.

7. The method by which the franchisor obtains his income and secures payment with the minimum opportunity for avoidance of the true extent of the franchisee's liability. Since the franchisor's gross revenue will largely, and in some cases wholly, be dependent upon the payment of franchise fees and/or management services fees by the franchisees, franchisors will be concerned to protect themselves against the franchisee not making full disclosure of all his income against which the management service fees are calculated. Obviously, there will always be those franchisees who see the payment of fees calculated by reference to gross income as a challenge but in franchising there is an overall structure which puts the cheat at a disadvantage.

The structure contains a number of features which will inevitably be reflected in the contract and the system which has been developed by the franchisor and is operated by the franchisees.

(a) The franchisor, in establishing the system by his experience in the market place, will have laid down the guidelines for financial achievement. He will be illustrating to franchisees, when training them and setting them up in business, what their gross and net margins should be at given levels of turnover and the percentage which each group of expense items should bear to turnover. Any concealment of gross income would inevitably distort those margins. The margins could, of course, also be distorted by incompetence or by leakage attributable to staff or customer theft or the franchise purchasing unapproved products without recording them through the system but, if any of these is the case, the franchisor should quickly be able to identify the cause and advise the franchisee so that appropriate remedial action may be taken.

(b) The franchisor will establish standard form accounting systems and reporting procedures so that it is informed about the performance of each franchisee's business and this will enable the franchisor to monitor the franchisee's performance and to detect warning signs if all is not well.

(c) The franchisor will require the right to do spot audits of the franchisee's financial records without prior warning being given.

(d) The franchisor's field support staff, who provide back-up to franchisees by regular visits, will have the opportunity of discussing performance with franchisees and making spot checks on stocks, books and other records to verify the accuracy of the information which the franchisee is reporting to the franchisor. These checks are part of the support which a franchisor provides, since inaccurate information, whether intentionally or unintentionally provided, hampers the franchisor's ability to provide assistance and guidance.

(e) The franchisor in collecting and collating the information from each franchisee is building up a record of each franchisee's performance and is able to establish an average for the whole network's results. Any franchisee whose achievements are markedly below average will be a candidate for special attention so that the cause may be identified and remedial action taken.

(f) The franchisee will be required to make a return of gross revenue to the Customs and Excise authorities for Value Added Tax purposes. Copies of these returns and any assessments to VAT made by Customs and Excise should be obtained by the franchisor and compared with the figures submitted to him.

(g) The franchisor will have access to the franchisee's supply sources. If it knows what the franchisee is buying it will have a very good idea of what his gross sales figures should be if the business is operated properly. The field support staff visits should reveal if the franchisee is purchasing products from non-approved sources which if not put through the system could provide the opportunity to falsify figures as well as distort the performance of the outlet.

(h) In some cases the franchisor may be able to obtain information from large customers of the network with whom arrangements have been made for the supply of goods and/or services by the network.

8. Consideration will have to be given to the question of the circumstances in which the franchise agreement can be terminated. In doing so, the position of the franchisee must be considered responsibly so that the franchise agreement cannot be terminated for anything other than good cause. The BFA Code of Ethics requires franchisors to give written notice to franchisees of breaches which can be remedied and to allow a reasonable time for the breach to be remedied. Consequences of termination also have to be clearly thought out in order that the franchisor's property rights are properly protected.

9. Of prime concern to franchisees will be the way in which the sale of the franchisee's business might be achieved. Obviously in a franchise system which requires the franchisee to be trained, as most do, or which may require a specialized area of knowledge or the application of particular processes, a franchisee can never be permitted freely to assign his franchise agreement when disposing of his business. Safeguards have to be built in to ensure that the new franchisee will accept the responsibilities, will undergo any necessary training and will provide the same standards of service and product as if, in fact, there had been no change of franchisee. Indeed, the new franchisee has to be as acceptable to the franchisor as if he had applied direct to the franchisor. The identification by a franchisee of a prospective purchaser of his business is the only occasion when a franchisee is recruited by someone other than the franchisor. There is no guarantee that the first prospective purchaser would be suitable franchisee material for a particular franchise. It is usual therefore to demand the same qualifications and standards for acceptance of a purchaser of the franchisee's business as are being applied to direct applicants to the franchisor for a franchise.

10. Thought has to be given as to what will happen if the franchisee, being an individual, or the principal shareholder and director of the franchisee if it is a limited company, dies. Most franchise agreements make provision to deal with these circumstances, although not all are satisfactory. There are some which make no provision at all. Clearly, it is an area of serious concern for both franchisor and franchisee that the right balance is struck so that the dependants of the franchisee are permitted (if they can satisfy the franchisor's criteria and pass any training course satisfactorily) to continue the business formerly carried on by the deceased or, alternatively, are able to turn the business to account by selling and receiving the capital value of the business. Key man insurance to provide a fund to act as a cushion and ensure the survival of the business may be worth considering.

11. The franchisee's expectations cannot be ignored. Quite apart from the consideration which is given to the franchisee's point of view on the aspects already dealt with, the franchisee must be satisfied that the contract offers him exactly what he has been led to believe he would receive. He should not leave anything to trust; he should ask the franchisor to write into the agreement, or perhaps as an amendment to the agreement, confirmation of all the obligations undertaken. Nothing should be left to implication. Most franchisors will not normally (and quite properly) accept amendments to their standard form so franchisees will only have their own lack of foresight to blame if they encounter difficulties where the promises are not reflected in their contract. Furthermore, although the tendency exists for a successful franchisee to forget what he owes to the franchisor for his success, the franchisor will invariably always know just that little bit more about the business than any one individual franchisee. In such a case the franchisor must be able to contain the franchisee within the scope of the franchise system by appropriate contractual provisions.

12. Some franchisors become involved in the property aspects of the transaction. This arises for a number of reasons.

    (a) The franchisor may already be a multiple outlet operator who is converting some of an existing chain to franchising. He is involved as a freeholder or lessee of the premises which are occupied for the purpose of his business. In granting the franchise he will grant a lease or sublease to the franchisee. He may, of course, decide to assign the lease to the franchisee.

    (b) The franchisor may decide, as a matter of policy, that in securing sites for outlets for the network he wishes to buy the freehold or become the leaseholder and grant a lease or sublease to the franchisee.

    (c) The franchisor may be more selective and only become involved in a property if it comes into the 'flagship' or 'irreplaceable' category. Into this heading would come scarce sites, such as existing light industrial uses close to residential areas, where, if the franchisee leaves the network, the franchisor may find it difficult (if not impossible) to obtain any suitable alternative from which to trade or in which to establish an attractive franchise.

    (d) The franchisor may decide that he will use the value of his covenant to obtain sites for the network which franchisees may not otherwise be able to secure at all.

    (e) The franchisor may find that he is forced into giving his covenant in order to secure a site since the landlord or his agent realizes that the franchisor's covenant may be worth having while that of the franchisee is not.

Each franchisor will formulate his own policy regarding involvement with property; but if he does get involved, the lease and franchise agreement will have to be linked with each other so that termination and/or renewal of one will result in the same treatment of the other. The rights given to tenants of business premises under the Landlord and Tenant Act 1954 (as subsequently amended) have to be considered in the formulation of a property policy. If the franchisor does become involved in property, the franchisee should be no worse off upon termination of the agreement than he would be if the franchisor were not his landlord except that it would not be able to use those premises which have been associated with the franchisor's brand and in which it may wish to install another franchisee.

13. On 30 November 1988 the European Commission adopted a block exemption regulation for categories of franchise agreements which, subject to compliance with its terms, exempted franchise agreements from the competition laws of the European Union, which are contained in Article 81 (then 85) of the EC Treaty. The UK has its own competition laws which apply to franchise agreements. The EC block exemption regulation referred to above expired on 31 December 1999 and the Commission has replaced it with another regulation. The new regulation applied from 1 June 2000 and the full text will be found in Appendix D.

The original regulation applied only to categories of franchise agreements. The new regulation applies to what are called 'vertical agreements', which are defined in the regulation in the following terms: 'agreements or concerted practices entered into between two or more undertakings each of which operates, for the purposes of the agreement, at a different level of the production or distribution chain, and relating to the conditions under which the parties may purchase, sell or resell certain goods or services'.

The exemption provided by the regulation from the prohibition in Article 81 only needs to be considered if the agreement contains restrictions of competition falling within the scope of Article 81. There are two expressions in the definition which need to be considered.

(a) 'Concerted practices' are agreements or understandings between enterprises that they will cooperate in an anti-competitive practice.

(b) 'Each of which operates, for the purposes of the agreement'. This is intended to allow franchise systems which operate 'company-owned outlets' that are at the same level in the 'chain' to benefit from the exemption provided by the regulation.

The scope of this regulation is wider than franchising and effectively is a 'one size fits all' regulation for all forms of distribution agreements. The reality, of course, is that one size does not fit all, since there are some fundamental differences between different distribution methods. This means that franchising is potentially affected by rules which may have no relevance to the way in which franchises are structured. The Commission in adopting this regulation made some changes to the law which applies to the procedures for obtaining individual exemptions and related matters. The most important of these changes was to enable the Commission to grant retrospective exemption to vertical agreements.

The Commission expects businesses to make an evaluation of whether or not they comply with the regulation and the Commission's approach as to whether or not their practices are within the policy which the Commission adopts when considering cases. To assist in this process the Commission has issued guidelines which explain the provisions of the regulation and how to assess whether or not one is infringing Article 81. The changes to the law now mean that there is no need to notify an agreement not covered by the regulation to seek clearance. An agreement may be notified at any time and the Commission can backdate the exemption (if it decides to grant it) to the date of the execution of the agreement. There is no need to explain why there has been no prior notification and each case will be considered on its merits. As the Commission points out in the Guidelines the amendment to the law 'should eliminate artificial litigation before national courts and this strengthens the civil enforceability of contracts'. Franchisees who assert as they have done in the past that the franchisor cannot enforce an agreement will have a heavy onus imposed on them to prove their case, while the franchisor can notify retrospectively if it considers it is at risk of non-compliance with the regulation.

The Commission also points out that 'no suspension is necessary in respect of injunction proceedings where neutral courts themselves are empowered to assess the likelihood of the application of Article 81 so far as concerns individual exemptions'.

The new regulation is much more complex in its application than the previous regulation and franchisors will need to be advised about how to benefit from the exemption which it provides.

The regulation exempts agreements where 'the market share held by the supplier does not exceed 30% of the relevant market on which it sells the contract goods or services'. There are definitions of relevant market and how to calculate the market share.

However, the exemption is not unconditional. There are two hurdles to overcome. The first is a set of prohibited restrictions whose inclusion in the agreement will prevent the franchisor's agreements from benefiting from the regulation. In many cases it will be possible to ensure that the agreement does benefit. The second is a set of obligations whose inclusion will only disqualify that individual obligation from benefiting from the regulation. So the difference simply is in the first case that the agreement will not benefit from the exemption and in the second case that only the obligation will not so benefit. As far as the obligations are concerned there may be difficulty in drafting post term restraints on competition but otherwise most franchisors should be able to achieve their objective.

One of the obligations concerns product ties. The regulation defines a 'non compete obligation' as 'any direct or indirect obligation causing a buyer not to manufacture, purchase sell or resell goods or services, or any direct or indirect obligation on the buyer to purchase from the supplier or from another undertaking designated by the supplier more than 80% of the buyer's total purchases of the contract goods or services and their substitutes on the relevant market, calculated on the basis of the value of its purchases in the preceding calendar year'.

The relevant obligation prohibits such a non-compete obligation which is of indefinite duration or which is for longer than five years. A tacitly renewable obligation beyond five years is regarded as indefinite. If the supplier is the buyers' landlord the obligation can continue for the five-year period or if longer the term of the lease.

The Guidelines do acknowledge that 'the transfer of substantial know-how usually justifies a non-compete obligation for the whole duration of the supply agreement as for example in the context of franchising.'

One must also not lose sight of the fact that in England and Wales the common law rules in relation to restraint of trade may affect the length of a product tie.

There is one case involving franchising which has been considered by the European Court of Justice but its judgment, which on the whole was sympathetic to franchising, is still valid and binding on the Commission.

There were two issues (among others) on which the European Court of Justice set out its judgment which are helpful in considering one's position in benefiting from the regulation. The first issue was its consideration of know-how.

'In a system of distribution franchises such as this, a firm which is established in a market as a distributor and which is thus able to develop a scheme of commercial methods, grants independent business men – for consideration – the opportunity to establish themselves in other markets using its sign and its business methods on which its success has been based. Rather than a system of distribution, it concerns a way of exploiting financially, without committing its own capital, a collection of skills. Moreover, this system makes available to business men, who do not have the necessary experience, access to methods which they would have acquired only after long efforts of trial and error and allows them to benefit from the reputation of the sign. Distribution franchise contracts are in this respect different from sales concession contracts or from those which link the appointed retailer in a system of selective distribution which includes neither the use of the same sign nor the application of uniform business methods nor the payment of royalties in respect of agreed advantages. Such a system, which allows the franchisor to share the success, does not in itself jeopardise competition. To enable it to function, a double condition has to be fulfilled'. (paragraph 15).

'In the first place, the franchisor has to be able to communicate to franchisees his know-how and to provide them with the necessary help in implementing his methods, without running the risk that this know-how and this help benefit, however indirectly, his competitors. Consequently the clauses which are indispensable to avoid this risk do not constitute restrictions on competition in the sense of Article 85(1). From this follows the prohibition on the franchisee on opening, during the period of the contract or during a reasonable period after its expiration, a shop having a similar or identical purpose, in a region in which it could compete with members of the network. Similarly, from this flows the obligation imposed on the franchisee not to transfer his shop without the prior agreement of the franchisor; this clause helps to avoid the benefit of the know-how provided and the help given passing indirectly to a competitor' (paragraph 16).

Paragraph 18 of the judgment is also relevant. 'Similar considerations apply to the obligation on the franchisee to apply the business methods developed by the franchisor and to make use of the know-how which has been provided.'

The other issue related to the brand and its protection. The Court stated 'in the second place the franchisor must be able to take appropriate measures to preserve the identity and reputation of the network symbolised by the sign. It follows from this that the clauses which institute controls indispensable for this purpose do not constitute restrictions of competition in the sense of Article 85(1) (now Article 81(1)).' Practices or provisions on franchise agreements which take advantage of the Court's judgment will not be infringing Article 81 and will therefore not need to be seeking an exemption from the regulation.

This regulation is important as far as UK competition law is concerned since any agreement which benefits from the exemption under the regulation will (at the time of writing, but this may change) be exempt from the UK competition law. One issue which arises in UK competition law is the grant of exclusive rights and this is the case under the Regulation. However there are commercial considerations which are by no means easy.

The commercial considerations revolve round the difficulties, particularly in the early stages of the development of a franchise business, of fairly defining a territory. The tendency is to allocate an area which is too large. Many franchisors who have tried to establish exclusive territories have created problems for themselves by having unexploited areas and an inability to force the franchisee to expand his business to fill the demand which has been created for the goods or services offered by the franchised network. The impact of such a situation affects franchisees as well as franchisors since there is an open invitation to others to provide the facilities which the network is not supplying. The obvious solution of establishing performance targets, allowing for the effect of inflation on true growth, is also not as easy to achieve. It is not a separate issue since the performance capability of any territory which is allocated must be related to the correct assessment of its potential, giving the franchisee the necessary scope for establishing and developing his business without inhibiting the growth of the franchised network. If the franchisor cannot fairly define the territory he is unlikely to be able to establish fair and realistic performance criteria to apply throughout the term of the contract. The ability to grant exclusive territorial rights without adverse competition law consequences will not affect the commercial considerations and while location clauses will continue to be used widely the grant of exclusive territorial rights will need careful consideration not only on legal but also on commercial grounds. The Guidelines also deal with the issues which arise from the Internet and the Commission's views of how they should be handled (see Chapter 12).

Structure of franchise agreements

It will be appreciated that not all the provisions referred to in this chapter will apply in every case, but some, indeed most, will feature in all franchise transactions.

The legal topics which have to be addressed in a franchise arrangement often involve a number of areas of law which are not usually dealt with by one practitioner. Indeed, some of the topics are quite specialized.[1] Although in business terms the contractual obligations can be split into two stages, which are dealt with below, in considering the approach to be made it is helpful to break the agreement into six separate phases:

1. The preparation of the franchise system for marketing. The development of the concept through the pilot operation during which are developed the industrial and intellectual property rights – the trade mark, the service mark, the trade name, goodwill and know-how. This is the stage at which advice about how properly to protect these rights must be taken. The development of the system, apart from solving business problems, must not create legal difficulties which may later cause the system to be changed. This is also the time to consider the structure of the transaction. Will one be involved in property? What will be the policy in relation to territories or catchment areas? What will be the range of services to be provided to the franchisee and so on?

2. The marketing of the scheme. This involves the promotion of the scheme: the preparation of the sales literature followed by the actual negotiations and discussions with prospective franchisees. When one considers the wide range of services to be provided by the franchisor, and the need to demonstrate to a franchisee the capacity of the business for success, the scope for the franchisor to make representations is very wide indeed. The larger the franchisor's organization, the more people there are involved in the selling effort, the greater the scope and the greater the risk of mistakes being made in such representations.

The above phases have been dealt with in detail in earlier chapters. The next four phases are:

3. The period from the recruitment of a franchisee to the opening of the franchisee's business.
4. The continuing relationship.
5. Termination.
6. Consequences of termination.

These are now dealt with in detail.

Phases (3) and (4) have to be dealt with within the contractual framework and can be accommodated within one agreement, although a few franchise companies have two contracts, one for each stage. In such cases the first-stage contract is frequently called a purchase agreement and the second-stage contract the franchise or licence agreement. Although the invariable practice is to use one contract it is convenient to consider each of the two stages separately, as they are dealing with different issues.

The first phase will deal with three aspects basic to taking the franchises from the period of signing the agreement to the opening launch of his business. It will deal with:

1. The franchise package.
2. The price.
3. The initial services to be provided.

Before examining each of these aspects it should be noted that it is not essential that the premises from which the franchisee is to trade should be finally agreed upon before the contracts are signed. As long as it is possible to pinpoint an area within which the premises are to be located, the agreements may be entered into conditionally upon a mutually acceptable site being found. This may appear at first sight to be potentially dangerous, but a successful franchise will usually attract more prospective franchisees than can be placed at any given time, as premises are not always readily available. A waiting list will develop. In such a case a prospective franchisee will wish to join the queue and reserve an area; indeed, it is possible in some cases to obtain an option from a franchisor for an area.

If a site is being sought the agreement will specify the area within which the premises are to be located and provide for the approval of the premises by the franchisor. If a decision has been made by the franchisor that it wishes to be involved in the ownership of the property the effect of that decision will need to be reflected in the contractual arrangements. The franchisor will usually provide assistance with the obtaining of any required planning permissions.

The franchise package

The extent, contents and subject matter of the franchise package which is being sold will be listed. The list is sometimes called an inventory or schedule of equipment or perhaps just an equipment list. It must contain all items which are included; all items which the franchisee has been told to expect. Some franchise companies regard this list as being confidential and stipulate in the contract that it must be so treated by the franchisee. In such a case there will also be a provision requiring the return of the list if the transaction does not proceed.

The franchise package may involve a number of options about how the premises will be dealt with or if there is a mobile franchise how the vehicle will be provided and equipped. The options in relation to the premises include the following.

1. The provision by the franchisor of standard plans and specifications for the franchised outlets which will be adapted by either the franchisor or the franchisee's own surveyor or architect and subject to approval by the franchisor. In many cases shopfitters are able to make adaptations.

2. The provision by the franchisor of a manual, with property specifications from which the franchisee's surveyor, architect or shopfitter will prepare detailed plans and specifications for the franchised outlet.

3. The complete service by the franchisor of the preparation of plans and specifications followed by the necessary works to convert the premises into the franchised outlet (a turnkey operation).

4. The hiring by the franchisee of a shopfitter, either from a list approved by the franchisor or freely chosen by the franchisee, who will be employed to convert the premises in accordance with the franchisor's plans and specifications.

In cases where the franchisor is not actually doing the work the quality and standards will be monitored by the franchisor for compliance with his standards while the franchisee will have the responsibility for ensuring the correct level and quality of day-to-day supervision.

Where there is a vehicle to be acquired as part of the package the manner of fitting out and equipping the vehicle will have to be detailed, with the franchisor either arranging for the works to be carried out or providing sufficiently detailed plans and specifications to enable the franchisee to organize it for himself. The specifications will include the colour scheme and a suitable livery for the vehicle.

The price

The price should be specified, as should the manner and timing of payment. This may be cash in full on signature, although this is rare. More often a deposit is required on signature with payment of the balance to follow on delivery of the equipment or at other identified stages, e.g. commencement of training or commencement of shopfitting.[2]

There may be allowance for the fact that finance has to be arranged. In this case the contract may be conditional upon satisfactory finance being obtained. What is to be regarded as 'satisfactory finance' should be defined carefully. If hire purchase finance is to be obtained for vehicles, fixtures, fittings etc., the contract must accommodate the necessary arrangements for the finance house to acquire title.

The price may not include delivery charges, installation charges, shopfitting works and VAT. If this is the case it should be made clear, particularly in respect of the shopfitting work, as the equipment list will often include equipment and fittings which will be incorporated in the shopfitting. The franchisee should be able to recover VAT upon the registration of his business.

If a deposit is paid at this stage, or indeed at any other, it should be made clear whether and in what circumstances it, or a part of it, is returnable to the franchisee. The franchisor will wish at this stage to retain the right to withdraw from the transaction. It may be that training will show the franchisee to be unsuitable for the particular type of franchise. In a case where the franchisor withdraws from the transaction the deposit should be returnable to the franchisee in full unless the reason is that the franchisee fails the training course, when the franchisor should be entitled to recover his costs to date.

However, a different situation obtains if the franchisee wishes to withdraw. The franchisor may be prepared to take a risk on his own withdrawal, but if the franchisee can withdraw without cost after having caused the franchisor a lot of trouble and expense, then the payment of the deposit will not amount to much evidence of good faith. Provision is therefore usually made for the franchisor to be able to retain the whole or part of the deposit to reimburse him for the expenses in which he has been involved. The BFA Code of Ethics permits this practice. The franchisee should insist, if a deposit is to be paid, that the circumstances in which he gets it back or in which the franchisor may keep some of it are very clearly and unambiguously set out in writing. Some franchisees have lost money by failing to read or understand what they were given or told. It is essential to take proper professional advice before parting with any money or signing any documents.

The initial services to be provided

The services which are to be provided to the franchisees are discussed in some detail in Chapter 4. The franchise agreement should reflect the obligation to provide these services and the franchisor should be prepared to undertake the commitment to provide what he has promised.

If there are two agreements the first agreement will contain the provisions relating to the initial training of the franchisee. This will mean that the franchisor will impose upon the franchisee a requirement to keep the franchisor's know-how, trade secrets and system private and confidential to ensure that if the transaction does not proceed the trained prospective franchisees cannot make use of, or disclose, the know-how acquired in training.

These are the main features to be expected in an agreement dealing with stage one of the transaction whether or not there is a separate contract.

The stage two provisions can conveniently be divided into nine sections.

Section 1. The rights granted to the franchisee.

Section 2. The length of the franchise agreement.

Section 3. The obligations undertaken by the franchisor.

Section 4. The obligations imposed upon the franchisee.

Section 5. The trading restrictions and requirements imposed upon the franchisee.

Section 6. Sale of business/death of franchisee.

Section 7. Dispute resolution.

Section 8. The termination provisions.

Section 9. The consequences of termination.

Section 1

The franchisee will be given a licence to exercise the following rights as far as may be relevant in the particular circumstances.

(a) To use the trademarks, service marks and trade names of the franchisor and to benefit from the goodwill associated with them.

(b) To use the brand image and the design and decor of the premises (including layouts, fixtures, fittings and equipment) developed by the franchisor in projecting that image.

(c) To use the franchisor's trade secrets, and confidential know-how, system and methods.

(d) To use the franchisor's copyright material.

(e) In appropriate cases to use the recipes, formulae, specifications, processes and methods of manufacture developed by the franchisor.

(f) The obligation to conduct the franchised business upon or from premises approved by the franchisor (usually premises are specified in the agreement) identified under the franchisor's name, branding etc. and in accordance with the franchisor's system and methods.[3]

Many franchise schemes carry with them the promise of exclusive rights (see the discussion of the commercial issues in relation to territorial rights in Chapter 10). These exclusive rights will vary according to whether the franchised business is physically immobile (e.g. a retail shop) or physically mobile (e.g. a ServiceMaster franchise). In the case of a retail shop the exclusivity would be based upon a radius within which the franchisor will not franchise another similar unit. In the case of a mobile franchise an area within which the franchisee may carry on his business may be exclusive or non-exclusive and the franchisee will be forbidden to solicit or tout for business outside that area. The grant of exclusive rights involves issues of competition law which are dealt with above. It is difficult to lay down any set radius, for what is reasonable will vary considerably from case to case. It is important to realize that the franchisor cannot hope for successful growth in his own business if his units are placed so close together that none can effectively operate on a profitable basis. Legal advice must be obtained if territorial allocations are made.

The nature and extent of the exclusivity granted needs careful consideration in the light of the different sales techniques which can be used and which do not necessarily require a fixed location. The Internet (see Chapter 12), which is now opening up sales opportunities from websites could enable a franchisor to by-pass the franchisee and defeat the protection which the franchisee believes he has. Mail order is another sales method which could have that effect. A franchisor who wishes to engage in sales methods other than those franchised should expressly reserve the rights to do so for two reasons: first, to disclose its intentions to the franchisee who can make a balanced evaluation of the effect on this proposed business venture under the franchise; second, to ensure that there is no confusion or dispute about what the exclusive grant amounts to.

    (g) The right (as well as the obligation) to obtain supplies of products from the franchisor and/or nominated suppliers at special prices. The franchisor can often obtain quite good reductions for franchisees using the weight of the bulk purchasing power of the whole of the franchised chain. The issue of product supply has been dealt with in detail above in the discussion on competition law.

Section 2

The length of the term of the agreement has been discussed in Chapter 10 when dealing with the provisions in the BFA Code of Ethics, including the BFA's ethical policy on renewals. In practice many franchisees are working for a business which will provide them with a good living and the possibility of making a profit on sale. On the whole this is achieved by many but it is not a guarantee. In a case in the High Court a judge has held that a franchisor cannot necessarily be expected always to be a franchisor so there can be a risk that the franchise system will not continue indefinitely. There have also been cases where the franchisor enters into a franchise agreement for a fixed term with no right of renewal. Again in such cases the franchisor may well offer a new franchise agreement when the fixed term expires. It is important for franchisees to appreciate that a franchise is a licence for a fixed term of years and in this respect analogous to a lease. The franchisor who wants to have a fixed term will probably limit his choice, as many prospective franchisees may well not wish to enter into a non-renewable agreement.

Section 3

The obligations of the franchisor in the continuing relationship which exists after the business has opened are dealt with in Chapter 4. As is the case with the initial obligations, the franchisor's ongoing commitments to the franchisee should be detailed in the agreement and the franchisor should be prepared to accept a legal obligation to provide them.

The Contracts (Rights of Third Parties) Act 1999 introduced a new concept to English and Welsh law by creating a right for a person who is not a party ('Third Party') to enforce in his own right a term of the contract if:

(a) the contract expressly provides that he may; or

(b) the contract purports to confer a benefit on him unless on a proper reading of the contract it appears that the parties to it did not intend the term to be enforceable by the Third Party.

In domestic franchising the parties are likely to exclude the operation of the Act but in international franchising the foreign franchisor, where there is a master franchisee in the UK, may wish to obtain the benefit of the Act in order to take action against under- or non-performing sub-franchisees.

Section 4

The franchisee is likely to have the following obligations or many of them imposed upon him:

(a) To carry on the business franchised and no other upon approved premises and strictly in accordance with the franchisor's methods and standards and in compliance with the operational manual. This provision may detail the range of products, their sources and/ or services which the franchises is permitted to sell or provide. In a fast food business a menu range is likely to be specified. The manual is likely to be changed over a period of time to reflect improvements in the system and responses to competitive market conduct.

(b) To observe certain minimum opening hours. These will usually be the hours which enable the business to be operated most profitably within the scope of the 'blueprint' and without incurring disproportionate overheads. For example, the franchisor may well through practical experience be able to demonstrate to the franchisee that the cost of staff and other overheads in remaining open for, say, a further two hours a day may not be covered by the additional trading which is likely to be done.

(c) To pay franchise fees. The various methods by which such fees are calculated and a franchisor receives payment of fees are dealt with in Chapter 7.

(d) To follow the accounting and reporting systems laid down by the franchisor. The purpose is twofold. First, the franchisor has a means of checking and calculating any fees to which he may be entitled. Second, these systems should be prepared in such a way that they will rapidly reveal vital management information and whether or not the projected gross and net profit margins are being achieved.

(e) Not to advertise without prior approval of the advertisements by the franchisor. As previously explained (Chapter 7), the franchisor will invariably handle all national advertising but this will not mean that there is no local or other advertising which cannot benefit the business. The franchisor will wish to have control of the contents of advertisements which make use of his trademark, service mark or trade name to ensure that the standards associated with them are maintained.

(f) To use and display such point-of-sale or advertising material as the franchisor stipulates. Also to use bags, boxes, wrappers and, in a food franchise, even such items as straws, cups and serviettes bearing the franchisor's name and trademark. Point-of-sale and advertising material may be supplied free of charge, within the framework of the advertising arrangements, but the other items would, of course, have to be paid for.

(g) To maintain the premises in a good, clean, sanitary condition and to redecorate when required to do so by the franchisor. This is a provision which often causes difficulty in practice. The franchisor will always be striving to ensure that the premises have the best possible appearance while the franchisee will be reluctant to spend his money.

(h) To maintain business insurance cover. The purpose of this provision is to protect the franchisee from the consequences of fire or public or employees' liability third party, product liability and other claims. It protects the franchisee's business and his livelihood. In some cases franchisors are able to arrange for insurance schemes to be established for the benefit of the network. Indeed, some insurance brokers have offered specialist services in this respect to franchisors.

(i) To permit the franchisor's staff to enter the premises to inspect and see whether the franchisor's standards are being maintained and whether the terms of the agreement are being observed.

(j) To purchase goods or products from the franchisor or his nominated suppliers (see competition law above).

(k) To train staff in the franchisor's methods and to ensure that they maintain the standards of service associated with the franchisor's branding and system.

(l) Not to assign the franchise contract without the franchisor's consent. All franchise contracts should be capable of assignment. If the contract is not assignable there is no incentive for the franchisee to invest and to build. The franchisor, however, will need to approve the purchaser. There is rarely difficulty in practice in arranging a transfer of the franchised business provided the purchaser of the franchisee's business matches the franchisor's selection standards and successfully passes through any necessary training. Many contracts provide for a fixed or percentage fee based upon the sale price to be paid to the franchisor to cover his costs of processing the transaction and of training and establishing the new franchises. Some franchisors are able to introduce purchasers from their waiting list of franchisees and make a charge for the introduction on a percentage fee basis, as would a business transfer agent. Some franchise agreements contain a grant of an option for the franchisor to purchase the franchisee's business when the franchises wishes to sell. Any such option should secure at least as good a deal for the franchisee as he would get if he were to do a bona fide arm's length sale in the open market. Any provision which requires the franchisee to sell to the franchisor at a value (e.g. net asset value) which is less than the real market value should be unacceptable.

(m) There will also be provisions calculated to make it plain that there is no partnership or agency created by the franchise agreement and that the franchisee has no power to act on behalf of the franchisor or to commit it in any way. The franchisee will also be required to make it clear to third parties with whom he does business that he operates the business under licence, and in accordance with the Business Names Act 1985 should display prominently a notice identifying the owner of the franchised business.

(n) It is not uncommon to find provisions requiring the franchisee to promote and improve the business. This may or may not be combined with minimum performance levels. The BFA Ethical Guide offers guidance on the ethical implications of performance clauses and indicates that a level set at 70% of the average performance of the particular system will not be regarded as unethical.

(o) There are also likely to be provisions in an appropriate system relating to customer lists and customer information subject to compliance with data protection legislation.

(p) Increasingly, there are controls or prohibitions relating to the registrations of domain names on the Internet and risks with material which may be published on the Internet (see Chapter 12)

Section 5

The restrictions imposed upon the franchisee are affected substantially by the European Commission's block exemption regulation and are detailed above.[4] The restrictions fall under four headings, the last of which is not dealt with in the Regulation.

1. Product sourcing, supply and control of range of products to be offered by the franchisee.
2. Restrictions on other competing activities both during the term of the agreement and after its termination.
3. Protection of the franchisor's know-how during the term of the agreement and after its termination.
4. A restriction on the franchisee to prevent him taking staff away from other franchisees.

The quality and range of the products to be sold by the franchisee are fundamental to the reputation of the brand and the franchise system. The Commission confirms the applicability of the judgment of the European Court of Justice in the Guidelines (see Chapter 10) in stating:

> a non-compete obligation [author's note: tied buying requirement] for the purpose on the goods or services purchased by the franchisee falls outside Article 81(1) [author's note: in other words it is not an anti-competitive provision] when the obligation is necessary to maintain the common identity and reputation of the franchised network. In such cases also the duration of the non-compete obligation is irrelevant under Article 81(1) as long as it does not exceed the duration of the franchise agreement itself.

The franchisor can require franchisees to devote the whole of their efforts to the franchised business and can prevent franchisees from soliciting or touting for business (active selling) outside their allocated territory. (See Chapter 10, where this issue is discussed.

Section 6

The question of assignability has been discussed in item 9 in Chapter 10 in the preliminary considerations.[5] The problem of what should be done in the event of the death of the franchisee, or the principal shareholder of the franchisee if it is a company, should be dealt with in the contract. The franchisee or principal shareholder should ensure that in the event of death:

(a) his personal representative(s) and/or dependant(s) will be able to keep the business going until one of them can qualify as a franchisee and take an assignment of the franchisee agreement or undertake the obligations formerly assumed by the principal shareholder; and/or

(b) that, if they cannot or do not wish to so qualify, arrangements can be made to keep the business going until a suitable assignee can be found at a proper price. In this respect the franchisor may agree to offer to provide management (for a fee) during the critical few weeks following the death. All reputable and ethical franchisors will be sympathetic and helpful whatever the contract provides, but it is best if the contract clearly specifies what will happen as is the invariable practice.

Section 7

Recent years have seen the introduction of formal ADR (alternative dispute resolution) mediation to add to the other methods of resolving disputes. Those other methods would include litigation, the decision of an expert and arbitration.

The vast majority of disputes which result in litigation are resolved by settlement which is a clear indication that disputes can be resolved ultimately by discussions between the parties; it is a question of timing and probably the growing expense of fighting a case which undoubtedly concentrates the parties' minds and makes them question the cost-effectiveness even of winning.

That is why ADR has become so popular. There is a difference between these various methods and some may be effective in certain instances but none is as all embracing as litigation in its remedies and each has its own drawbacks which may make it unsuitable for certain disputes.

So, what is arbitration and why should one consider it?

In basic down-to-earth terms arbitration is private litigation in which the parties appoint the judge and can lay down the procedure they wish to adopt. The Arbitration Act sets out a framework under which an arbitrator usually operates, as there are many cases decided by the courts which offer procedural guidance as well as establishing the rules under which arbitrators should operate. Does it overcome the disadvantages found in litigation? These disadvantages include:

- the time it takes, although the time scale has been streamlined with recent procedural changes;
- how much it costs;
- the judge may have no relevant expertise as it is likely that very few judges have heard any franchise cases; those who have, have sometimes shown their lack of experience in their decisions, while some have been 'spot on';
- litigation is public;
- litigation invariably spells the end of the relationship.

There are some pluses:

- the court can deal with parties who are not parties to the contract who can be joined in the litigation;

- the court can produce a decision whose effect can determine similar disputes in the future;
- the court can grant injunctions to enforce restrictive clauses in contracts and to restrain breaches of their terms;
- there is a mechanism for enforcing judgments of the courts in other countries through treaties and conventions.

Why use arbitration? There are a number of reasons why arbitration may appeal:

- arbitration is private;
- an arbitrator can be selected who has expertise in the subject matter of the dispute;
- procedures can be agreed which can reduce substantially the time and cost required to reach a decision;
- arbitration is binding on the parties and final, although there are limited rights of appeal to the court;
- the relationship stands a better chance of surviving the arbitration, although arbitration is as confrontational as litigation;
- arbitration awards are enforceable;
- there is a mechanism for enforcing arbitration awards in other countries through treaties and conventions.

There are some disadvantages:

- arbitrators on the whole have fewer powers than the courts;
- arbitrators cannot grant injunctions;
- unlike judges, who do not charge fees, arbitrators do;
- there is not likely to be any prospect of an appeal.

So litigation and arbitration are members of the same family – the parties still fight each other but the rules are different.

Alternative dispute resolution is altogether different in its approach. It seeks to assist the parties in the resolution of their dispute. The proceedings are entirely voluntary and informal. In essence the mediator is an independent third party whose function is to facilitate the negotiation of a settlement.

The discussions are without prejudice and the parties cannot be forced to reach agreement. The mediator does not give any decisions. If the mediation succeeds there will be an agreement recording the terms of the settlement. That agreement will be binding and can be sued upon to enforce its terms. Until the time that such agreement is signed either party can walk away and anything discussed or disclosed during the mediation cannot be used in the court proceedings unless by its nature it is something which would normally have to be disclosed in court proceedings.

ADR is usually a rapid procedure and far less expensive than litigation or arbitration. It is best to use it, if it is to be used, before court or arbitration proceedings are commenced, although it can be used at any stage.

Unlike in litigation and arbitration the parties stand a far better chance of continuing with their relationship after mediation if that is appropriate. Following the recent court procedural changes the courts are now actively promoting ADR and under the new civil procedure rules cases may be compulsorily stayed (legalese for put on hold) so that the parties can try to settle through ADR. Where the contract contains an ADR clause the courts are more likely to order a stay of proceedings and will oblige even an unwilling party to participate in ADR. The court can take into account any resistance and failure to try ADR when it considers who should bear the costs of litigation.

It should be appreciated that ADR does not produce any decision by the mediator, which means that none of the parties need fear that they will be subjected to a procedure which will result in an outcome which determines who is right and who is wrong. ADR will need to be taken seriously and will require the commitment of management time for the duration of the discussions. A day may be long enough to resolve many disputes but if it takes longer while progress is being made the time should be made available. According to the largest mediation organization in the UK, 82% of its cases were resolved in one day.

Litigation has been a part of the methods used to resolve disputes in franchising since franchising first emerged. Arbitration has been used sparingly.[6] The BFA has introduced an Arbitration Scheme as well as making ADR available.

What does one do if there is a dispute between franchisor and franchisee? First, it depends on which party feels the need to take action and what is the nature of the underlying problem.

Franchising done properly involves a dialogue between franchisor and franchisee. That dialogue should be effective in resolving differences between the parties. Disputes often revolve around the same issues:

1. Complaints by franchisees that:
   - the franchisor made pre-contractual representations which proved to be wrong particularly any profit projections;
   - the franchisor has not performed its contractual obligations either by not providing services at all or not providing them to a reasonable standard;
   - the franchisor has not innovated enough and the network is becoming outdated;
   - the franchisor has introduced changes which do not work;
   - advertising and promotion is ineffective and the franchisees are not enjoying any benefits from it.
2. Complaints by franchisors that the franchisee:
   - is not operating the system properly;
   - is not reporting as required by the contract or accurately;

- is late or not paying fees or advertising contributions;
- is not maintaining the quality standards;
- is not marketing the business properly;
- is not devoting enough time to the business;
- will not redecorate the premises;
- will not update equipment;
- has introduced an unapproved person to become involved in a joint proprietorial capacity;
- has set up a competing business to which he is diverting business.

It will be seen that there are some issues which could be the subject of discussion and debate with a view to settlement and there are some that could not be. Many of these which could not be are those involving franchisee practices.

The author remembers some years ago listening in the USA to a speaker with no experience of franchising extolling the virtues of ADR. He said that 'say, for example, if you have a Pizza Hut franchisee who introduces ingredients of his own to his pizza and Pizza Hut were unhappy about it that would be the sort of case where ADR would be appropriate'. In fact it is most unlikely that any franchisor would be prepared to tolerate such a breach of contract, let alone admit that it would be prepared to mediate. Apart from the flagrant breach of contract such a franchisee is disclosing a level of indiscipline which would worry many franchisors. Where would it stop?

So such matters as:

- failing to operate the system properly;
- not reporting;
- not paying;
- not maintaining quality standards;
- not devoting enough time to the business;
- not redecorating or updating equipment;
- involving others in the business without approval;
- directing business elsewhere

are not capable of resolution by mediation if not remedied within the time specified in a notice. All these issues go to the root of the relationship and are fundamental. Some are clear indications that the franchisee is unsuited to franchising: for example, false reporting, not following the system, setting up a competing business. Some of the issues affect the network's branding: for example, quality issues, not following the system, not redecorating or updating equipment.

A franchisor in such circumstances would probably wish to terminate the agreement and seek an injunction from the courts to enforce the post term restraints in the contract. Those are remedies which often require swift action. Arbitration and mediation would undoubtedly not be appropriate in such cases.

Many of the issues which franchisees raise may make them feel a loss of confidence and trust in their franchisor and that the relationship cannot continue. If such confidence and trust is lost the prospects of a continuing relationship are not good and the franchisee may not wish to mediate. However, some of the complaints which the franchisee has may form the basis of a claim for damages and that claim may well be capable of resolution by arbitration or mediation.

Franchisors and franchisees will undoubtedly be taking legal advice about the available options. Now the shopping list is longer:

- sue;
- arbitrate;
- mediate.

As lawyers often say, which to choose will depend on the circumstances and what might suit one person may not suit another. Given the court's new approach mediation may be forced upon the parties, but even so a judge would probably not be likely to tell a franchisor or a franchisee who has been cheated and has totally lost faith and trust that they should mediate to settle the differences.

Section 8

The agreement may be terminated in various ways. The agreement may be for a fixed term without any provision for renewal. If no offer of a new agreement is made the relationship is effectively terminated. There may be express provision for the termination following a breach of the agreement upon the service of a notice. Most agreements provide a machinery for the franchisee to be given an opportunity to remedy any defaults which can be remedied within a specific period before the franchisor can exercise the right of termination subject to safeguards to protect the franchisor against the habitual offender.[7] Indeed, as is mentioned above, the BFA Code of Ethics requires such a provision to be inserted in agreements.

Many franchisors treat breaches with varying degrees of seriousness, but many take a very strong view of breaches which raise questions of whether the franchisee can be trusted. Therefore, some regard false disclosure of gross income, and thus the amount of the fee to be paid, as fundamental and will wish to be able to terminate in such a case without giving the franchisee an opportunity to put matters right. Where the franchisee has provided misleading or false information in his franchise application a franchisor may wish to be able to terminate the agreement. A franchisor is also bound to take a very serious view of a franchisee who is found to be making confidential information available to competitors or potential competitors.

Even if a franchisee is in default under the terms of his agreement every effort should be made to investigate whether it is possible to find a solution which will not result in the termination of the contract. There are many steps which can and should be taken.

(a) Attempts should be made to persuade the franchisee to return to the performance of his obligations.

(b) Additional support should be offered to assist in a case where the franchisee is genuinely finding it difficult to cope. It may be necessary to provide the franchisee with additional training to try to improve his performance. If such a franchisee clearly has no long-term future it is best if both parties recognize the fact sooner rather than later so that a strategy can be developed to build up the business in order for it to be sold and the franchisee to receive the best possible recovery of his investment.

(c) If the franchisee is not responsive to the franchisor's attempts to help (and not all are) it may be worth suggesting that the franchisee sell his business.

(d) If all these approaches fail and the franchisee continues to be in default the franchisor should serve a default notice requiring the franchisee to remedy the breaches. A further attempt should be made to find a solution along one of the lines suggested above but if that fails the franchisor will be left with no alternative but to terminate the agreement.

Section 9

The termination of the agreement of a defaulting franchisee is always a sad time for the franchisor, but a bad franchisee will invariably cause disquiet among other franchisees, who could be adversely affected by his poor performance. Fairness and firmness should characterize the franchisor's dealing with all his franchisees but particularly with those with whom he experiences difficulties.

In whatever circumstances the franchise agreement is terminated the franchisee should be left with the assets of the business for which he has paid. He will be stripped of his right to carry on business under the trade name, and to use the franchisor's system and know-how, and he will lose all the other advantages made available to a franchisee. He may also have to move trading premises or substantially change his business in view of the post term restrictions on competition in the agreement.

In some cases the franchisor will own the freehold or lease of the premises and will grant a lease or an underlease to the franchisee. In such a case the franchisee may find that upon the termination of the franchise agreement he has lost his lease too. In such a case the franchisee should at the time of the signature of the contract consider whether or not there are safeguards for the cash investment he is making.

On termination in these circumstances the franchisee should be no worse off than he would be in the event of a termination where there is a third party landlord. It may be that he would be slightly better placed since if there is a third party landlord and the franchisee cannot trade from these premises he will have commitments under the lease until he can dispose of it. He would have no such post termination commitments if the franchisor is his landlord and retakes possession.

The franchisee must appreciate that the basic cause for him finding himself with problems on termination will invariably be his own default.

The objective in framing these provisions is to ensure that the franchisor recovers total control of his industrial and intellectual property rights, his system and his goodwill. This means that:

(a) the use of the brand name and goodwill associated with it must be discontinued;

(b) the use of the system and know-how must be discontinued;

(c) all outward signs, appearance of premises and vans must be changed to avoid confusion and to prevent the franchisee from cashing in on the franchisor's goodwill;

(d) customer contact must stop, as their custom is part of the franchisor's goodwill;

(e) the franchisee must be prevented from competing with the franchisor and the network from the premises on which he conducted the franchised business.

In view of the close working relationship that will exist between a franchisor and a franchisee all requirements must be clearly stated in the contract. This is a transaction in which no small print should exist.

Notes

1. The USA offering circular has an Item in chart form setting out the franchisee's obligations with a cross-reference to sections of the franchise agreement. Another item describes in great detail the franchisor's obligations with cross-references to sections of the franchise agreement.
2. The USA offering circular requires disclosure of all initial payments.
3. Many franchise agreements in the USA explicitly reserve all rights not granted to the franchisee in an effort to avoid an implication that, as a few court decisions have held, implied rights not specifically granted in the agreement may nevertheless arise.
4. In contrast, except for provisions which attempt to negate the statutory protections of franchise disclosure laws, neither US franchise registration/disclosure laws nor franchise relationship laws regulate the terms of the contractual relationship of the parties.
5. Some US state franchise relationship laws require the franchisor to permit transferability under certain circumstances. Further, the offering circular must disclose whether and how the agreement can be assigned or transferred.
6. In the USA, arbitration is a common dispute resolution system for franchise systems which want to keep their disputes private. ADR is becoming popular generally. Many

franchisors do not like arbitration because it is usually final and binding and not appealable. The offering circular must disclose whether disputes are to be resolved by arbitration or mediation, choice of forum and choice of law.

7. Many US state franchise relationship laws require notice to terminate, and some also require good cause to terminate and an opportunity to cure defaults. The offering circular must disclose how termination may be accomplished by both parties.

Information technology

Internet

The advances in information technology have not been ignored by the franchise community but they bring with them new challenges as well as new laws.

Franchisors now seek franchisees through their websites and through their links with the BFA website (if they are members). There are those who offer services through websites to franchisors to assist them in their search for franchisees but it does not stop there, as will be seen below.

The NatWest/BFA Survey provides us with an update on the use of information technology by franchisors and franchisees. In 2002, 91% of franchisors had a website and 41% an Internet site. Some 86% of franchisees use a PC, and 70% of franchisees need to use a PC every day they are trading. The most common uses include Internet access and sending e-mails (88%) and maintaining a customer database (78%). Franchisors and franchisees must take care to comply with Data Protection legislation.

Almost two-thirds of franchisors say their main reason for having a website is to provide general information to customers. Interestingly, only 9% of franchisors use their website for selling goods and services over the Internet.

The Internet has had to be taken seriously by franchisors since the European Commission (EC) considered the effect of the Internet on sales by franchises when it introduced the Block Exemption for vertical agreements (see also Chapter 10). In that regulation the EC provided that the exemption would not apply where the agreement has as its object:

> the restriction of the territory into which, or of the customers to whom, the buyer may sell the contract goods or services except ... the restriction of active sales into the exclusive territory or to an exclusive customer group reserved to the supplier or allocated by the supplier to another buyer where such a restriction does not limit sales by the customer of the buyer.

This protection of exclusively allocated territories or customer groups only applies to 'active' sales – 'passive' sales must be permitted.

In the Guidelines which the EC published in tandem with the

Regulation, the EC defines active and passive sales in the following terms:

'Active' sales means actively approaching individual customers inside another distributor's exclusive territory or exclusive customer group by for instance direct mail or visits; or actively approaching a specific customer group or customers in a specific territory allocated exclusively to another distributor through advertisement in media or other promotions specifically targeted at the customer group or targeted at customers in that territory; or establishing a warehouse or distribution outlet in other distributor's exclusive territory. 'Passive' sales means responding to unsolicited requests from individual customers including delivery of goods or services to such customers. General advertising or promotion in media or on the Internet that reaches customers in other distributors' exclusive territories or customer groups but which is a reasonable way to reach customers outside those territories or customer groups, for instance to reach customers in non-exclusive territories or in one's own territory, are passive sales.

The EC also provides guidance on Internet sales in the Guidelines:

(51) Every distributor must be free to use the Internet to advertise or to sell products. A restriction on the use of the Internet by distributors could only be compatible with the Block Exemption Regulation to the extent that promotion on the Internet or sales over the Internet would lead to active selling into other distributors' exclusive territories or customer groups. In general, the use of the Internet is not considered a form of active sales into such territories or customer groups, since it is a reasonable way to reach every customer. The fact that it may have effects outside one's own territory or customer group results from the technology, i.e. the easy access from everywhere. If a customer visits the web site of a distributor and contacts the distributor and if such contract leads to a sale, including delivery, then that is considered passive selling. The language used on the web site or in the communication plays normally no role in that respect. Insofar as a web site is not specifically targeted at customers primarily inside the territory or customer group exclusively allocated to another distributor, for instance with the use of banners or links in pages of provides specifically available to these exclusively allocated customers, the web site is not considered a form of active selling. However, unsolicited e-mails sent to individual customers or specific customer groups are considered active selling. The same considerations apply to selling by catalogue. Notwithstanding what has been said before, the supplier may require quality standards for the use of the Internet site to resell his goods, just as the supplier may require quality standards for a shop or for advertising and promotion in general. The latter may be relevant in particular for selective distribution. An outright ban on Internet or catalogue selling is only possible if there is an objective justification. In any case, the supplier cannot reserve to itself sales and/or advertising over the Internet.

So the position may be summarized as follows. Exclusive territories and customer groups can be protected from competition generated by active sales but not passive sales. Franchisees must be free to use the Internet to effect passive sales but there are controls which can be introduced by the franchisor.

If one refers to Chapter 10 one will be reminded of the European Court's judgment in which it decided that measures 'to preserve the identity and the reputation of the network symbolised by the sign ['brand']. It follows from this that clauses which institute controls which are indispensable for this purpose do not constitute restrictions of competition in the sense of Article 85(1) (now 81(1)).' This part of the decision should be borne in mind regarding what controls and safe-guards the franchisor can apply.

This approach by the EC can create problems for franchisors and their networks. Legal advice is essential to ensure that the law is complied with while franchisees, particularly those with exclusive territories, remain satisfied that their sales are not being cannibalized by fellow franchisees.

Not all systems will have a problem in any event because, on the whole, to take advantage of any opportunities which the Internet offers the business must be one which does not need attendance at the franchisee's business premises. For example, a ladies hairdressing salon would be such a business. The nature of the business and what it involves – the ambience created, which is essentially associated with the franchisor's brand and which cannot be provided or conveyed in the ether in which the Internet exists or through postal or courier services – may well take the issue outside Article 81.

The increasing use of the Internet presents other challenges. Trade marks are registered and granted nationally (although there is a European trade mark available) but the Internet is global. Trade marks are at risk of being 'stolen' and there have been cases in many jurisdictions which have not always produced the result which the trade mark owner would have wanted. Cybersquatting is where someone registers as a domain name the trade mark of others, particularly with the intention of trying to sell the name to the true trade mark owner. When registering a domain name the franchisor should consider extending its use to multiple addresses: .com, .co.uk and so on. Trade mark registration of trade marks owned and previously registered elsewhere by others has been a problem in some jurisdictions for many years, and the scope which the Internet provides can create (and probably has created) a greater problem for more brands than before.

The risks include metatags, which are pieces of HTML code invisible to a viewer but visible to a search engine that provides scope for diverting enquiries from their intended destination. Franchisors need periodically to check access to their websites to see if they are being hijacked, perhaps by one or more of their franchisees.

The Internet Corporation for Assigned Names and Numbers (ICANN) governs domain name registrations and has a Uniform Domain Name Resolution policy which is calculated to deal with the abusive use of names. There are also dispute resolution procedures in place through ICANN which have already been successfully used by many trade mark owners.

Consideration should also be given to the protection of one's copyright material, which is available to a far larger audience than it normally would be and thus likely to reach more of those who are happy to make infringing use of others' intellectual property rights.

Franchisors should remember that whatever is published on its website will lose confidentiality, so putting one's operational manual on the website would be a major error. This is not confined to operational manuals but applies to all matters which are secret and confidential to the network.

A franchisor needs to have a clear idea of how it wishes to use the website. Is it for any of the reasons set out above? Does the franchisor have other objectives?

Whatever the objectives, the franchisor must have a clear plan for its website and in preparing it should have the EC Block Exemption and guidelines in mind. Considerations include the following:

- What are the franchisor's objectives in establishing a website and how can it best achieve them?
- The website must be consistent with the reputation and identity of the franchisor's brand.
- Will those franchisees who wish to have a website be required to have a page on the franchisor's website, and how may that be achieved without infringing competition law?
- What quality standards will the franchisor impose on the franchisees' sites?
- Does the franchisor have objective justification for banning franchisees from selling on the Internet?
- The franchisor must comply with relevant e-commerce and distance selling laws and must ensure that its franchisees also do so, as otherwise the brand could be put in jeopardy.

Intranet

Franchisors may also wish to give consideration to the establishment of an intranet. According to the NatWest/BFA Survey, some 41% of franchisors have intranet sites which are used by franchisees and employees of the franchisor.

An intranet site is a private website. There are issues to consider, which include:

- The security of the site must be absolute. That means that access can only be available to those who are designated and authorized for the purpose.
- Access should only be given through a secure system with passwords. Preferably the passwords should be personal to each individual.
- All authorized users must at least be bound contractually to:

(a) maintain the secrecy and confidentiality of the information on the site;

(b) desist from disclosing to anyone else the means of access to the site and password.

- To what uses will the site be put?

(a) To provide regular communications between franchisor and franchisees and enhance the relationship.

(b) Would the franchisor want to put the operational manuals on to the intranet? There may be risks of it losing confidentiality if access to the site is improperly achieved and it is put into the public domain. There are advantages in having them on the site if safety can be guaranteed since updates can be put on the site, but will the franchisees read and digest them?

(c) Would franchisees be able to communicate with each other and exchange ideas?

(d) Newsletters can be placed on the site.

(e) Information can flow from franchisees to the franchisor, such as the regular reports etc. required to be sent by the franchise agreement.

(f) There can be direct downloading of software updates.

While the existence of an intranet can save time and money for the franchisor and perhaps for the franchisee, it should not and cannot replace personal and face-to-face contact between the franchisor and its franchisees.

E-commerce

At its simplest, e-commerce is the sale of goods and/or services through the Internet.

The EU competition issues referred to above are relevant, since e-commerce is the way the franchisor and/or franchisees sell using the internet. The franchisor must consider how it and the network can use the Internet in this way if appropriate.

Since the Internet is global no one selling through that medium knows in advance where in the world the customers will be.

Furthermore, the customer can be vulnerable to rip offs: place an order, give your credit card details and all you receive is a bill or faulty goods which come from a vendor in a jurisdiction where it may (probably will) be uneconomic to do anything about it. No franchisor would want any of its franchisees to engage in abusive conduct of this nature. This global element raises a number of legal issues and legal advice should be obtained to ensure that they are being handled properly:

- How is the contract formed? Under English law making contracts requires four elements – offer, acceptance, consideration and an intention to be legally bound. A shop in displaying goods is not making an offer; it is considered to be inviting prospective customers to offer to buy, which the shopkeeper accepts at the till. That method is not universal. When selling on the Internet it is essential to establish terms and conditions. These should specify in detail and unambiguously how a contract will be made. These terms and conditions should also be used by franchisees to avoid damage to the franchisor's brand. There have already been cases arising out of ambiguous wording on websites where it is not clear whether the vendor's acknowledgement of an order has the effect of being acceptance of the purchaser's order. This has been particularly relevant when the vendor has inadvertently put the wrong price on the product.

- Which law will govern the contractual relationship and which courts will have jurisdiction? When contracting with another business it is usual to specify which law will apply to the contract and which courts will have jurisdiction in the event of a dispute, but local laws may apply in any event, e.g. labelling requirements, competition law. The law is more protective in relation to consumers and also less clear cut. However, websites which have been tailored to attract consumers from a certain jurisdiction will almost certainly be subject to local law and jurisdiction regardless of any contrary choice of law and jurisdiction in the website terms and conditions.

- Are there any English law issues to consider? The data protection legislation will almost certainly apply to customer records at the very least. In addition there is now law in England and Wales relating to e-commerce, which is contained in the Electronic Commerce (EC Directive) Regulations 2002. This resulted from a Directive from the EU requiring all member states to introduce this law. It imposes obligations on service providers and lays down procedural steps. For example, orders have to be acknowledged without undue delay and by electronic means; and vendors must make available the opportunity for the customer to identify and correct input errors. Also resulting from an EU Directive are the Consumer Protection (Distance Selling) Regulations 2000, which apply to contracts for goods or services to be supplied to a consumer made exclusively by means of distance communication.

- Is there any EU law on the subject? See the regulations referred to above.

- Is there anything on the e-commerce website which might infringe intellectual property rights of third parties? This is almost stating the obvious but clearly while one may feel secure in one's domestic market, foreign systems may present problems.

- Are there any advertising issues in countries where the site can be accessed?

- Can any of these two latter problems be resolved by use of language or an indication that sales to certain countries are not available? One should address these issues by limiting one's offers to those countries about whose legal systems and relevant laws one can be certain in order to reduce one's exposure.

It is abundantly plain that internet, intranet and e-commerce have the potential to create problems for the unwary. Their use requires careful up-front consideration and legal advice.

13 Not for profit franchising

Over the past few years there has been significant growth in the establishment of not for profit franchises not only in the UK but elsewhere in the world. There is not much information available about this growing sector.

One feature which stands out is the way in which those involved seek to distance themselves from commercial franchises, while clearly recognizing and benefiting from the advantages and application of the principles established and practised by the commercial sector. This is an attitude shared by many universities which franchise courses.

There is some information in the form of research and academic studies available through the Internet with what seem to be various attempts, unsuccessful in the author's view, to demonstrate the differences between commercial franchises and the not for profit sector. Certainly in the author's experience on the whole universities in the UK have, in the past, and probably most even now, not appreciated that there are laws in some countries which impact franchising agreements, and these include not only universities operating commercial franchises but also the 'not for profit sector' franchise agreements. The Florence Melton Adult Mini-Schools (see Chapter 20) are franchised in the USA,[1] Canada and Australia, each of which has franchise laws, with no exemptions for 'not for profits' which, therefore, have to be complied with.

In the final analysis franchising is franchising – the fundamental differences between the two sectors are the financial arrangements and the nature of the franchisees' motivation. So, for the most part, it is a question of applying franchising principles and techniques to the specific issues involved.

In this context, it is worth recognizing that since commercial franchising first developed, the basic principles have not changed. Knowledge of how to apply them and the different techniques which have evolved have enabled franchising to cope with a vast range of business categories given the breadth and depth of experience and the many sources available in various publications to provide guidance.

The range of business categories to which commercial franchising has been applied is indicated in Chapter 2. These categories include teaching, medical and other professional services which have been the subject of some 'not for profit' franchises.

What franchising provides for any country is the introduction of valuable know-how, which can stimulate the development of indigenous businesses. Franchising involves training in how to run a specific business in all its aspects. In the developing world this enables a spread of the know-how to take place and filter through to the staff who will be employed in the franchised outlets.

This factor was well appreciated in the post-Soviet Central and Eastern European countries and led to the rapid arrival of foreign franchise systems spurring the development and growth of indigenous systems, resulting in what are now becoming fast maturing franchise communities. Many developing world countries do not have the financial and technical resources to enable them to provide services and products. The educational value of franchising is that it provides a method of making a significant contribution to helping those without knowledge to be better equipped to help themselves in the future. It will also enable the local population to find employment in franchised operations. This is where the franchising techniques enhance the capability to create and deliver the necessary services and/or products.

'Not for profit' franchises do not need to be confined to developing world countries. As our case study shows (see Chapter 20), they can succeed in the developed world.

Consideration will now be given to some of the issues to be addressed in 'not for profit franchising'.

'Not for profit' franchises have different objectives from the commercial sector. Certainly, they are looking to help others to benefit from the know-how and systems which they have developed so that their countries may have available services which they lack and in which the commercial sector may have limited interest.

A commercial franchise will identify a need or a demand for its products and for services, as will the 'not for profit' franchisor. In the former case, there is the profit motive. In the latter, the need and demand will be driven by social deprivation, gaps in the availability of services or products because there is poverty which needs alleviation and the availability to the financially less fortunate of essential services and/or products which would not otherwise be affordable or accessible at its true cost (see also below).

Franchising systems are usually developed to accommodate the circumstances of the business and how best to conduct it and to profit from it. Applying these techniques to the 'not for profit sector' enables it to maximize the value which it can introduce to the target area and to obtain the maximum benefit by the best use of what will invariably be scarce resources. This underlines the value which franchising brings with the licensing of developed techniques.

The next element is the franchisees. In the commercial franchise the franchisees will have different motivation from not for profit franchisees. The 2003 NatWest/BFA survey gives the following information about franchisees' likes and dislikes:

Satisfying aspects of being a franchisee

Being my own boss	37%
Franchisor support	28%
Decision-making freedom	8%
Making money	8%
Brand name of franchisor	6%

Franchisee dislikes

Long working hours	20%
Paying outgoing fees	15%
Having to adhere to the franchise system	13%
Lack of franchisor support	5%

The motivation and commitment of the not for profit franchisees may correspond with some of these likes and dislikes. For example, among the satisfying aspects one would not expect 'making money' to feature large and such a franchisee may not view the 'being my own boss' attitude with the same enthusiasm as his commercial franchising cousin. The franchisor may have the resources to establish its activity and to develop it to the point where it can franchise. It will need the resources to enable it to establish its franchise. If it is to seek funding from a third party it is likely to have to convince a funding source that it has something which is viable and can provide the voluntary sector with something which is needed. To do this it will be necessary to do what the commercial franchisors do and to operate a pilot first to make sure it has its system working effectively and to prepare financial projections to show the extent of the financial support needed.

The franchisor will need to decide what financial contributions (if any) it will require from the franchisees. In the commercial sector the franchisors' and the franchisees' businesses are reliant on the profitability of the franchisee's outlets.

The funds required by the franchisor may come from government or UK international funding agencies, and programmes, private donors, institutions, charitable trusts or foundations (if appropriate) and any resources it may have available. The franchisee may well be looking to similar sources for funding, probably in its country or region.

The degree to which a 'not for profit' franchisee will complain about long working hours is not likely to match to the commercial franchisees' attitude.

Paying fees, however low, will probably be disliked by many not for profit franchisees where they are charged, since that adds to their fund raising burden.

One would expect the 'not for profit' franchisee to be motivated by a desire to help others and to have a significant commitment to and belief in the cause which is the subject of the franchise. The franchisee may also be able to recruit volunteer workers who will be well motivated and committed and not require remuneration.

The International Director of FMAMS, Jonathan Mirvis, explains two approaches used by the not for profit sector in the following terms:

The funding of non-profit franchises may be similar to business franchises in that the franchisees cover their own expenses and pay a royalty to the franchisor, e.g. The Florence Melton Adult Mini-school, or a different system. One of the different models is used by 'Breaking the Cycle' in the UK. This model puts a heavier financial onus on the franchisor who not only covers their expenses but helps meet some of the deficit of the franchisee as well.

The onus of financial responsibility is not only a technical financial arrangement; it influences as well the dynamic between franchisor and franchisee. In the first model the franchisee is financially independent of the franchisor and thus in its relationship with the franchisor, similar to the business franchise, will aspire to as much independence as possible. Furthermore while the franchisee is dependent on the franchisor for the use of the system, the franchisor is dependent on the franchisee for its financial well being creating a necessity for a strong mutual partnership.

In the second model the franchisee is not only dependent on the franchisor for its use of the system but is dependent in its daily operation for meeting its financial commitments. This creates a dynamic of a high level of dependence of the franchisee on the franchisor tipping the relationship heavily in favour of the franchisor.

The first model strongly resembles the business franchise not only in the dynamic but in the relationship between franchisor and franchisee. The franchisor will always strive to maximise its income from the franchisee, try to assert a large degree of supervision to preserve the quality of the system and proliferate universally proven quality modes of operation. The franchisee on the other hand will try to minimise payments to the franchisor and practise maximum possible independence claiming its uniqueness and thus plead exemption from certain modes of operation.

The only major difference in this first model between the non-profit franchise and the business franchise will be in the area of semantics. Culturally non-profits do not favour the use of 'for profit' language and because of the strong 'for profit' connotations 'franchises' arouse, they will prefer not to call themselves 'franchises', opting instead for 'networks' or the like. Similarly even in those situations in which non-profits embrace the franchise openly they may opt to use 'non-franchise' terminology in operating the system. An example of this is Marie Stopes, the UK non-profit that franchises women's health clinics in developing countries. Instead of using the terminology 'franchisees', it calls the franchisees 'partners'.

The financial arrangements

In the commercial franchise the franchisee has to finance the acquisition and establishment of the franchised business and will be dependent upon the financial success of the business and whatever financial resources he has after making his investment.

In the 'not for profit' sector the contrast with the commercial sector is that the 'not for profit' franchisee will not be generating a profit. Indeed, it may be struggling to find adequate funding for its needs. The 'not for profit' sector on the whole requires its franchisees to obtain its funding from local or other sources which would probably not be otherwise available to the franchisor. So in a sense it mirrors the commercial approach where the franchisees provide the financial resources to open outlets. The local sources of funding from which the not for profit franchisee benefits enable it to establish its operations and units which deliver the services and/or products.

There can be tensions between the franchisor and franchisees where there are funding difficulties for one or the other but ultimately the way in which the funding structure works enables the franchisor to expand the availability of its service or products to those in need more rapidly, just as in the commercial sector.

While there are clear differences between the two sectors, they are both fundamentally operating within the same family of franchising. There is no shame in the not for profit sector being related to the commercial sector; quite the contrary, the use of what originally developed as a commercial technique for social, charitable and not for profit purposes is laudable.

Note

1. Not for profit franchises are not that common in the USA. The FTC has issued an advisory opinion holding that a not for profit organization was not covered by the FTC Franchise Rule because there was no 'continuing commercial relationship'.

14 The decision to franchise internationally

International franchising is not easy, but if done properly for the right reasons and with the availability of the right resources it can, in time, produce positive rewards.

However, many franchisors have made fatal mistakes in overseas operations and these mistakes have not been limited to small companies. Some well known and successful names in franchising have found to their cost just how difficult it can be to transplant and operate their formula in a new country. The larger of these companies have had the resources and time to enable them ultimately to sort out their problems. The smaller companies do not have the resources which would provide them with the luxury of time to remedy major errors. There are a number of business and practical issues which have to be considered in coming to the decision to begin franchising Internationally.

Fundamentally, there must be a sound business reason for overseas development. A mere ego trip in order to try to satisfy a craving to be in a position to boast that one is an international franchisor is simply not good enough. There have to be better reasons. For example, is the home market saturated or approaching saturation? Is the franchise so well established in its own country that the time is now propitious to broaden its horizons? Are there real market opportunities abroad which present themselves which are too good to miss? In the latter case one should not be deluded into an opportunistic deal unless all the other fundamentals are favourable.

In the same way that some domestic operations start up due to the pressure of interest from those who would like to take up a franchise, many successful franchisors find that they receive approaches from abroad from those who would like to introduce the franchise into their own countries. Such approaches are fine and very flattering, but whether or not one is in a position to accede to them will involve a proper and thorough evaluation of all the basic issues, including many of those referred to below. The fact that such an approach has been made does not mean either that the person making the approach is suitable or that the franchisor can by-pass taking the normal informed decisions or taking all the other safeguards to which reference is made in this work, which include ensuring it has the resources to cope. However, there have certainly been enough cases where deals have successfully been concluded to justify taking such approaches seriously.

There are, of course, franchises which particularly lend themselves to being operated on an international scale, such as product distribution franchises at retail or wholesale levels, and hotel and car rental firms and other businesses catering for international business travellers and tourists.

Is the reason or desire to become international in scope merely there in order to be able to claim one is ahead of competitors in the race for growth? Again, as with the ego trip, this can be a dangerous approach, particularly if the other relevant factors are ignored in a wave of blind optimism and an arrogant belief that it would be an easy task to achieve.

It is a principle that a company should not regard franchising as a panacea for the ills of an ailing business which will be solved by an immediate inflow of money. That does not work in the domestic market and as will become apparent it cannot work in the international market either. One cannot of course rule out the 'conman' prepared to sell a 'territory' for a large up front fee without the prospect of delivering what he has promised.

What can happen, of course, is that if the international expansion is not done at the right time or well enough, it can significantly drain the financial and manpower resources available to the domestic operation and hamper its development. The franchisor's reputation will be damaged by failure in one or more overseas countries and this may mean that those countries' business people will not be receptive to subsequent attempts to enter the market at least for a considerable time.

There are some prerequisites to franchising successfully overseas.

- The franchisor must have a sound and successful home base which is sufficiently profitable. The financial position of the franchisor must be secure and it must have resources which are surplus to, or which can exclusively be diverted from, its domestic requirements. The franchisor must appreciate that from the moment the decision is made to expand internationally there will be expenditure. Exploring which may be the best country and sending someone there to 'fact find' will cost money. No international deal worth doing can be signed so rapidly that the money is coming in from the time or even shortly after it starts to go out. In reality a realistic budget based upon an objectively prepared business plan has to be prepared to cover the probability that international expansion is long term, not short term, and that costs will be incurred for some realistic period of time before income may result.

- The franchisor must also have manpower resources available which can be devoted solely to the international operations, and, above all, it must be patient. Patience is a necessary attribute for franchisors operating in their own domestic markets. Entering into contracts with franchisees in haste often leads to repentance at leisure and at great cost. International operations are no different in terms of patience. In addition one would suggest that the franchisor must always feel secure enough to be able to say 'No' unless it is sure that the deal and the other party are absolutely right – the cost of making the wrong choice in the international transaction will be greater than is the case with a domestic operation. If things go really wrong the costs of extricating oneself can escalate rapidly particularly as one will be operating in a foreign country whose rules and business practices will inevitably be different from those with which the franchisor will be familiar.

- It is essential to find the right 'partner' in the target territory. This is not easy. It is difficult to make contact with those who may be most appropriate as franchisees, whichever structural approach is chosen (see Chapter 15).

On the whole, the development of international markets will always take longer and make greater demands on both the financial and manpower resources of the franchisor than is first anticipated. While it is difficult to generalize this is very much likely to be a case where it is 'take the figure one first thinks of and multiply by a factor of 3 and apply it to direct cost, manpower spent finding a local partner and the time one reckons it will take to be up and running in the first case.

It is quite likely that as one gains more experience it may be possible to speed up the process, but one must never do so at the expense of not taking all the same safeguards which should be taken at the outset in all subsequent cases. A belief in the maxim 'been there, done that, got the T shirt' can create a climate of comfort, confidence and indeed arrogance which can become very expensive. It is the author's experience that even the largest and most successful franchisors have 'war stories' which very much support a case-by-case approach applying the same basics each time. Never relax. Never become over-confident. Always be patient, and never get into the position where one cannot say 'No, this is not right' until one is absolutely and objectively certain that it is right.

The build-up of the international operation will take time because just as one is urged to operate pilot outlets in one's own domestic market, it is equally prudent to do so in the target country; who bears the expense of such pilot operations will be part of the negotiations between the parties (see Chapter 15). This concept of pilot operating is important in many cases not only to ascertain whether the business is viable in the new country, but also to fine-tune the operational side to conform to local customs, culture, habits, business practices and laws, and not least to cope with the problems which may arise through the need to use a different language, necessitating the translation and revision of operational manuals and other written material. There are other factors which can have an impact and to which consideration must be given.

- Is the target country one which has a history of political stability? The less stable the political climate, the more difficulties are likely to arise, particularly where there may be controls over the movement of funds, or over the involvement in the country of foreign companies. There can also be the risk of confiscation of a business in unstable countries. The instability in some countries which have been the subject of United Nations sanctions has caused many companies to withdraw, in some cases leaving trade marks and intellectual property rights unprotected.

- What degree of government control over, or interference with, the normal arm's length negotiating process between the parties can be expected? Will these requirements impose the reopening of negotiations and a dilution of the franchisor's bargaining power, with adverse financial consequences?

- Are there monetary exchange controls which might limit the amounts of franchise fees or prevent the repatriation of profits, or the remittance of funds? If so, can consents be obtained and will they be honoured over the long-term? How long will it take for funds to be remitted? Can one rely on a steady flow of cash or will it be intermittent? In some countries, funds can even be delayed when permission to remit does exist. These delays can sometimes be for long periods because the country's central bank does not have adequate foreign currency resources to enable the payments to be made. There are sophisticated methods of barter and counter-trade which have sometimes been used to overcome this problem, but there has to be a reasonable scale of business to justify these types of involved arrangements.

- Are communications and distribution systems good? As with domestic operations, the speed, effectiveness and efficiency of communications and distribution systems are an important factor. In the developing world problems are frequently found with such systems. Advances in technology and electronic communications have now overcome many of the communication problems.

- Many franchise operations rely on what is described as the discretionary spending power of their customers. The product or service supplied is not essential, and customers do not necessarily need to buy it. In such a case the question of how much money is available in consumers' pockets after they have met their essential living requirements can be an important issue.

The franchisor will also have to be able to provide the necessary training programmes. If it is geared up to provide a high level of training in its own domestic market place, it may find that it is well placed to extend the programme to cope with the overseas operations. Many consider it invaluable, certainly in the early days, to provide training at the domestic training facility so that an in-depth understanding of the operation can be achieved. It is essential, however, to be sensitive to the requirements and conditions in the target territory. The cost of sending personnel to the franchisor's territory may be inhibiting, particularly for sub-franchisees, and there may well be problems with language skills since one can scarcely impose on sub-franchisors the requirement that they can only recruit as sub-franchisees those who are sufficiently fluent in the franchisor's language to attend and understand the franchisor's training course. This would also mean that sub-franchisees would only be able to sell their businesses to those who are also similarly fluent. That would create a barrier to sales which would be untenable.

The last, and by no means the least, important factor is that the right person or company with whom it would be fitting to be associated has to be found for the target territory. After all, it is hardly surprising that it can be difficult to identify the right person in a foreign country, for as franchisors are well aware, it is often difficult even in one's own country to select the right franchisees. What is surprising is how many companies with significant experience in franchising have historically failed to recognize that this is a vital matter or to approach it with the serious attention to detail which it requires.

In the same way that many franchisors find it difficult to recruit the right people as franchisees and to display the patience which is necessary, so one finds that franchisors venturing overseas are confronted with a similar problem, but here it is compounded by the fact that they are operating in an unfamiliar environment and the difficulty which exists in making contacts. There have been many who have made bad choices which could have been avoided had they been patient and exercised the same degree of care in selection as they would have taken in choosing franchisees in their own country. A significant difference is that invariably in international development it will not be single unit franchisees who will be recruited but master franchisees or area developers with substantial financial resources and business ability.

If the prospect of expanding internationally continues to appeal after considering and evaluating the factors reviewed in this chapter, then one should move to a consideration of the business and legal issues with which one will be confronted.

Business and legal audits

Having taken the decision to go international, whatever the choice of country, the prospective international franchisor is well advised to learn something about each of its target countries if it wishes to be well equipped in its negotiations with prospective franchisees of whatever category with which it intends to do business.

There are two aspects – the business and the legal – but in considering them one must not lose sight of the other background factors which affect both of those aspects and which include government attitudes and policies which may affect both the business and the legal climate.

Some governments have an attitude towards franchising; some are intrusive; some are indifferent; many do not understand it. Apart from any particular attitude there may well be governmental initiatives from which incoming as well as indigenous businesses can benefit. These include special incentive schemes and grants which may be available for certain types of business or industry or in certain 'depressed' areas or regions. They may also be free trade zones which offer fiscal advantages.

We shall first consider the business aspects and what one would describe as the business audit. From the business point of view it should be appreciated that what the franchisor is doing, whatever structure it may choose, is establishing its business in a foreign country. The fact that it involves a franchisor franchising a franchisee in whatever capacity does not detract from that fundamental fact. As we shall see when we examine development agreements and master franchise agreements, there will be debate and agreement about who runs the risks inherent in establishing the system in the target country but the issue arising out of the establishment of a business in the target territory owes nothing to the fact that it is franchising which is involved.

A franchisor cannot, on the whole, expect that its franchisee 'partner' will readily materialize and accept everything at face value. The franchisor should not assume that anyone who expresses an interest in the franchise will be suitable. These statements may seem obvious but there are many franchisors (some significant and allegedly sophisticated in the ways of business) who have failed to give them the importance and credibility which they deserve. Since, depending on the route chosen, the franchisor may be dealing with any one of three types of franchisee it is difficult to generalize. If the franchisor decides directly to franchise to individual unit franchisees it will be looking more probably for people in the target country who are the counterparts of its franchisees in its domestic market. If its decision is to recruit area developers who will open a multiple number of franchised units it will be considering a different calibre of person or business entirely. If it decides to enter into a master franchise agreement with one person or company for each target country the calibre of person or business entity and resources available will be different again.[1] (These structures are discussed in Chapter 15.)

Finding and selecting the right local firm or business will be crucial to the franchisor's prospects of success. Unfortunately there is no easy way to match the franchisor seeking the local 'partners' and the local would-be 'partner'. In some cases this occurs because the would-be franchisee on his travels around the world sees a business concept which appeals to him and he makes a direct approach to the owner of the concept with a view to taking up a franchise in his country. Other methods of making contact include:

- Exhibiting at one of the increasing number of franchise expos which are held in various parts of the world. There have been significant increases in the number of would-be franchisees from around the world who attend the expos in the hope that they will be able to find suitable opportunities. Many expos now include international sections and there are increasing number of foreign visitors attending them.

- Advertising in the franchise media in the target county; in some countries the newspapers have 'business to business' and 'business opportunities' advertisements in which franchisors advertise their franchise. If the qualifications required by the franchisor require some form of previous experience or business exposure in the particular trade or industry with which the franchise is involved, advertising in the relevant trade journals may stand a better chance of success.

- Many countries have commercial officers attached to their embassies whose function is to help business people to become established in foreign countries. The use of such offices may enable appointments to be made with local business people if a visit to a targeted country is envisaged. The United States government is particularly good at supporting its franchisors in international development.

- Many professional providers of services, including, banks, lawyers and accountants, have contacts in other countries and may be able to help.

- Having editorial copy (not paid for advertorials) in the relevant media in the targeted countries may enable the franchisor to reach those who may be interested.

- Increasingly franchisors are finding that websites are producing enquiries. Some franchise associations' websites have significant success in providing leads for their members. There are also commercial sites offering a web service matching franchisors and franchisees.

Having the right person or business in place is extremely important and achieving this is fundamental to the achievement of the business audit.

There will be a number of factors to include, whatever the chosen method, and thus variable relevance and weight to be attached to them.

In all cases the franchisee will need to have the appropriate level of financial and manpower resources available to him. If it is a unit franchise the level of these resources will be less than will be the case where a development agreement is envisaged, and if there is to be a master franchise the level and nature of the resources will be greater.

The franchisor will also have to assess the ability of the prospective franchisee at whatever level is appropriate to cope with the needs of the business. A unit franchisee will not need the same skill levels or resources as a developer or a sub-franchisor. (See Chapter 15.)

The franchisor will need to familiarize itself with the business issues which are of importance to the acceptability and success of the system with the target country. In doing so it must recognize factors which could impact upon what it does in its own country and for which allowance must be made. This does not mean inevitably that such a factor will have an impact – merely that it should be taken seriously and given proper objective consideration. Hostility to what makes things tick in the target territory and an insistence that nothing can be changed will only make life more difficult for the franchisor.

We shall now consider some of these differences, some of which have been mentioned in the introduction.

- How does the market differ from the franchisor's home market or any other market in which it has experience? The franchisor may be forced by local laws to confront the issue of the differences in the target market. For example, in France (see below) in order to comply with the Loi Doubin the franchisor's disclosure document is required to make disclosure to the franchisee of the market in general, the regional market and the specific market. The expression 'the market' takes in a wide range of considerations.

- Those who sell the same or similar products or services, unless the franchisor is introducing products or a service which are new to the target territory. The former is much easier to assess, the latter much more difficult. The fact that there are those who sell the same or similar products does not mean that anyone can. For example, in Germany there exists a strong guild system, membership of which is essential in order to carry on certain types of business. The assessment of a market must be sufficiently wide to discover such arrangements where they exist and to assess whether they prevent or so restrict operations as to make franchising the particular business merely difficult but manageable, or impossible. The franchisor who takes the trouble to make its assessment thoroughly will be better placed in its negotiations with prospective franchisees.

- How the people live, what they like, what they dislike, what their culture is (which may extend to social structures and mores), how these might affect the franchise system, what their behaviour patterns are and how they might affect peak trading times, staffing requirements and thus costs.

What are the costs involved in running a business in the target territory? How will apparent cost differentials affect the outcome? For example, if the franchisor looks at approximately 10% of gross revenue for rental costs, should it be excited if rent costs appear low or depressed if they appear high? The answer will in all probability be reflected by lower gross revenue where rental levels are low and higher gross revenue where rental levels are high. Staffing costs may be affected by add-on social security costs, labour laws and trade union intervention, which in some countries can be considerably more important than in others, including the country of origin of the franchise (see legal issues below).

What are the relevant costs of construction? How practical and possible is it to reproduce the franchisor's designs and specifications in the target territory?

Are internal and external communication channels sufficiently good for the franchisor to communicate with its franchisees (whichever route is chosen) and, if there is a developer or sub-franchisor, for them to be able to communicate with franchised units? Internet and intranet communications now help to overcome many of the communication problems as well as the universal use of mobile (cell) phones.

Are there adequate reliable distribution systems in place to provide the supply channels which the franchisor or sub-franchisor will require?

Distributions systems may present difficulties in the most unlikely places but developing world countries have more than their fair share of problems related to the operation of such systems.

What level of 'street knowledge' does the franchisor need in order to operate in the target country? This can affect the choice of method of entry, as can the distance between the franchisor's home country and the target country.

Are there local suppliers of products and of services of the requisite quality available in the target territory?

Coping with language is a factor. No franchisor can expect to be able to recruit in its own operations those with a sufficient range of language skills that it does not need to recruit as franchisees those with whom it can communicate in its language or at least the main international business language, which is English.

Having considered the business issues the franchisor will need to consider legal issues, which include the following.

Contract laws

The basis upon which franchise arrangements are entered into is invariably contractual.

The law of contract will, of course, differ from country to country. The differences between the common law system and the civil law system are quite considerable. Under the former little is left to implication unless there is a law which specifically impacts part of the contract. Under the civil law system the civil codes imply terms in contracts depending on the nature of the transaction – some of these implied terms cannot be contracted out of.

One cannot assume that contracts can necessarily be entered into on the same basis from one country to another. Care must be taken before entering into any commitments to ensure that the correct form and procedures are followed. Indeed, one may find that it is possible to create a binding commitment where none was intended.

Legal status of the parties and the nature of legal relationships

Quite apart from an investigation and assessment of the capacity in which parties can contract, particularly if one of the parties is an overseas company, consideration must be given to whether or not there are local laws which might result in the franchisees being regarded as agents or employees of the franchisor. For example, in Dubai a franchise agreement is characterized as a commercial agency whatever the parties agreed and may have intended.

In most franchise arrangements, the parties go to great efforts to ensure the establishment of the franchisee as an independent contractor, to ensure that the franchisee has no power to bind the franchisor, and that the franchisee is not the agent or partner or employee of the franchisor. Laws such as those in Dubai can affect such efforts and also introduce the possibility that not only will it be difficult to terminate the arrangement but there may be compensation payable upon termination or otherwise at the end of the relationship.

There can be laws which are interpreted in such a way as to regard the franchisee as an employee of the franchisor and not as an independent undertaking, thus imposing upon the franchisor obligations, both to third parties and of a financial character in the form of social welfare contributions, which are not part of the normal calculations made, or considerations taken into account, when establishing a franchise scheme. Often such issues arise if the franchisee experiences business failure, leaving social security and tax liabilities outstanding. Sometimes claims can be made by employees of a franchisee under the same principle.

Government attitudes

It is important to ascertain whether the government has an attitude towards franchising and to the import of know-how and trade secrets (see also below).

One should investigate government attitudes and existing policies because it may be possible to take advantage of special incentive schemes and grants, which can be available for certain types of business or industry or in certain locations. This could make the franchise venture more certain of success and more profitable from the point of view of the franchisor and franchisee.

Competition laws (anti-trust)

The competition laws of the territory must always be considered. Many countries are now adopting competition laws, the stated objective of which is to make anti-competitive practices unlawful and thus stimulate competition. These laws are not directed at franchise transactions, but often affect franchising because of the generality of their application. In the European Union one should not be misled by the existence of anti-competition laws at the European level into believing that there are no such laws applicable in the member states. The European Union laws are concerned with the effect of such practices on trade between member states, while the laws applicable in the member states are focused on anti-competitive practices within the relevant state (see Chapter 10).

Apart from the statutory regulation of competitive practices, there are laws relating to contractual in term and post term restrictions on competition which should be found in every franchisor's checklist, and which have to be investigated. In some countries such post term restraints are not permitted.

Many of the practices inherent in a franchise transaction, such as exclusive rights, tied sales, price fixing and other controls, are capable of being affected by competition laws; their effect must, therefore, be very carefully considered.

Intellectual and industrial property laws

The expression 'intellectual and industrial property' includes patents, trade marks, the right to prevent unfair competition/passing off, copyright, design rights and know-how and confidential information. It is necessary to investigate the law in the target country to verify how correctly to deal with and protect those rights which are relevant for the franchisor.

Trade mark rights are territorial in nature and will generally only provide protection in the country under whose trade mark law they are registered. The exception is the European Community trade mark issued by the Community Trade Mark Office, which has pan-European effect. A trade mark may comprise a word, a logo or a combination of the two and in many jurisdictions may also include sounds, shapes and smells.

Copyright laws can offer some protection but only of the words used and not the ideas which they convey. The scope of the local laws should be investigated.

Most jurisdictions provide a trader with protection against a competitor who unjustly trades on the reputation and goodwill of another. In civil law jurisdictions, this is usually in the form of an unfair competition law, and in common law jurisdictions, a passing off action. Essentially, the law is seeking to prevent one trader from carrying on his business in such a way that the consumer believes it is the business of another trader.

The franchisor's know-how, trade secrets and confidential information are of course fundamental to it and the methods for ensuring their confidentiality both during and after the contractual term are not necessarily effective in every jurisdiction.

Taxation

The taxation effects on the franchise scheme have to be considered. There are two aspects. First there are taxes applicable to the operation of the franchise unit in the target territory. These may include:

- property-related taxes;
- sales taxes;
- taxes imposed upon business profits;
- whether payments of fees to the franchisor will be deductible from profits for tax purposes.

There may be variations in accounting and reporting systems and procedures which the business and tax requirements in the target territory require and which have to be considered.

Second, there are international tax considerations. Franchisors will wish to receive payments of franchise fees – that is initial fees as well as continuing fees (or royalties) – without deduction of any sum in respect of local taxes (withholding tax) or if that cannot be the case to receive credit for such taxes paid when calculating its tax liability in its own country. In many cases this will not be possible. However, one should investigate whether a double-taxation agreement exists between the franchisor's country and the target country to see what is its effect. If there are no direct double-taxation agreements, or if the terms are not thought sufficiently beneficial, then investigation should be made of the best route from target country to the franchisor's country for the income of the franchisor to enable the effects of multiple taxation to be eliminated or at least minimized.

Very often careful selection of the route through which the monies flow by taking advantage of double-taxation agreements can achieve a great deal in ensuring that the maximum amount of money reaches its ultimate intended destination. There are also cash-flow considerations, and if withholding taxes are imposed to any substantial extent it can have an adverse effect on the cash flow of the franchisor sufficient to affect its ability to finance its operations from the income generated in the initial stages. There can be unexpected traps even in double-taxation agreements where initial payments for the grant of rights may be regarded as advance royalty payments, or treated as if they were even if they are not, and thus subjected to withholding tax.

Corporate laws

In deciding whether to set up a branch or operational subsidiary, apart from the taxation implications of operating in this way, local corporate laws have to be considered to see what form of incorporation may be necessary, or desirable, or whether there are requirements for registration of foreign companies which establish a place of business in the target territory. Some countries have prohibitions against foreign nationals owning the majority of shares in companies which are incorporated in their jurisdiction.

Corporate laws also need to be studied to the extent that franchisees may choose to incorporate the business which is to be operated under franchise. The franchisor will have to ensure that those shareholders and directors cannot acquire the franchisor's know-how and trade secrets, and can be restrained from subsequently using them to compete with the franchisor.

There must be a clear understanding of the corporate laws, and the roles, duties and responsibilities of shareholders and directors. It is also wise to check whether a franchisor may be exposed to risk of claims if a franchisee fails.

Special franchise laws

The USA, with its federal and state system, abounds in a multiplicity of laws affecting franchising.[2] There are pre-contract disclosure requirements, registration requirements in some states (a minority) but not in others and in some states relationship laws affecting franchisors' rights to terminate or to refuse renewal of franchise agreements. As far as the

USA is concerned, one can almost be offending against some legal requirement even in discussing the grant of a franchise. Legal advice at the earliest point, even before discussions which may lead to negotiations, is essential. (See Chapter 16 for a full treatment of the US regulatory regime.)

There is a broad treatment of this subject below (see 'Franchise regulation around the world').

Special industry laws

The franchisor should investigate whether the target country has any laws which regulate the industry sector to which the franchised business belongs.[3]

For example, fast food or restaurant businesses will invariably be affected by legislation which regulates standards of hygiene and cleanliness in the interests of public health. These requirements must be carefully checked out by the franchisor to ascertain the differences between the requirements of the law in the target territory compared with the franchisor's home market. In the case of retail franchises there will frequently be labelling requirements which may necessitate their production in the language of the target countries, among other requirements.

Property laws

Laws affecting real estate and leasehold property vary from country to country and what may be permissible in one country may not be in another. In some countries, there may be protection for business tenants and in others there may not be; there are also some where 'key money' (a premium) is payable to secure a lease.

Careful evaluation has to be made of property laws to see whether the manner in which the franchisor's scheme is structured in its home country is capable of being repeated in the target country; for example, if the franchisor is involved in the property chain granting leases and sub-leases to franchisee. If it is not, adjustments may have to be made to take into account the differences and some fundamental rethinking may have to be engaged in. This is particularly the case where franchisors wish to retain the ownership or control of premises.

Exchange controls

Some countries have restrictions on the import and export of currency. It is necessary to ascertain whether such restrictions exist, and, if so, what they are and how the system works.

There may be a requirement that consent has to be obtained for inward investment, and that it may be given only on certain conditions. These conditions may affect the right of the investor to remit profits in whole or in part. Careful evaluation will have to be made to see how these laws affect the franchisor's investment and its ability to receive payments for goods and services (including franchise fees) in its home country.

There is little point in selling know-how and granting rights to others to exercise the opportunity to carry on business under a franchise arrangement if it is a profitless exercise for the franchisor, in the sense that it is unable to turn its entitlement to income into cash in its hand except in the target territory where it may have little use for it. There may be scope for barter arrangements but to be effective these sort of arrangements require a level of business to justify them.

Limitations on royalties

In some countries often as part of the exchange control regulations, there can be limitations imposed on the rate of royalties, and whether or not royalties can be paid at all.

Certain countries take the view that low grade know-how and trade secrets should not entitle the owner to any royalty income. Some take the view that the royalty income should be limited for a period of time, after which no further charge can be made.

One is not speaking of franchising in any denigratory sense when referring to it as 'low grade know-how', but compared with high technology manufacturing industries the know-how which a franchisor develops for the operation of a service business is usually regarded as much lower grade know-how by these authorities, which is their justification for their attitude.

Regardless of whether or not the franchisor is prepared to accept that its know-how is low grade, it is the attitude of the target country which is relevant. There are some which have very rough and ready guides which do not necessarily make sense when approached objectively. The possibility exists that the franchisor could well find that it is negotiating the fees with the government and not the franchisee, who may well encourage the government to bargain very hard.

Zoning/planning laws

It is necessary to investigate the extent to which there are any restrictions on the use to which premises can be put. Are there any building requirements or building regulations affecting the proposed fitting out of the premises for use for the purposes of conducting the franchised business? This difference between the franchisor's home and target countries can have a marked effect on the operation, the layout of facilities and the rate at which the franchise network can grow.

It often transpires that when the calculations (sometimes optimistic) of growth rate made by the franchisor take into account the differences, coupled with the difficulty in obtaining suitable sites for particular types of business and zoning problems, completely different financial and development schedule projections emerge from those which the franchisor originally anticipated.

Regulations in the target country in relation to building may require a higher standard of construction than is normally built into the franchisor's capital requirement projections. Unless a thorough investigation is made of these factors, the franchisor is not in a position to give the right guidance to franchisees or, indeed, to know the extent to which its operation is viable.

Employment laws

There are wide variations in employment or labour laws, as well as a wide range of add-on costs to the employer, depending upon the nature and degree of social security payments required in the particular country. There can also be legislation which inhibits the ability of the franchisor or the employer to dismiss staff without being liable for compensation payments.

Increasingly, one finds laws prohibiting discrimination against employees and prospective employees on the grounds of, for example, sexual orientation, race and disability. These laws must be assessed and realistic decisions made about how to cope with the differences which exist between countries.

Consideration may need to be given to whether there are immigration laws and/or work permit requirements which need to be complied with in order for the franchisor to make staff available in the target country.

Excise and duties

The cost of importing materials, equipment, plant and machinery must take into account (apart from shipping costs) any excise or other duties which may be levied on them in the target country.

This, coupled with the need to make technical changes in equipment, to which reference has already been made, may require the franchisor to use locally manufactured products, or products manufactured in the same trading area to which the excise taxes and duties may not apply or which may not bear such a high rate. If the franchisor is to provide the franchisee with products there may be import duties which are significantly high. If the franchisee is seeking to receive its income solely from mark-ups on products the franchisee may find it is paying duties on the mark-up which may make it more difficult to sell the products in the target country and make a sufficient profit. Such problems require imaginative solutions.

Import/export controls

Some territories have restrictions on what may or may not be imported or exported, and certain standards may be set which must be achieved before imports are allowed. There may also be quotas limiting how much can be imported from certain countries.

The franchisor must be sure that whatever it requires to import into a target territory, it must be possible to do so. Its product requirements must be capable of meeting the criteria established by the regulatory requirements in the target country in order to qualify for import, or alternative arrangements must be made.

Franchise regulation around the world

It could be said there are two types of regulation:

- regulation which is specifically focused on franchising because it is franchising;
- regulation which affects franchising because of its applicability to one or some of the elements of a franchise system.

There is not much regulation which is specifically focused on franchising. In fact, there are only somewhere between 15 and 20 jurisdictions in which such laws are to be found. It was not until 1970 when the state of California in the USA enacted its Franchise Investment Law that such focused laws existed. Since then in the USA some 14 other states and the Federal Trade Commission have added their contributions. For many years they were joined by only the province of Alberta in Canada. However, in recent years Albania, Australia, Brazil, China, France, Indonesia, Italy, Japan, Kazakhstan, Korea, Malaysia, Mexico, Ontario in Canada, Romania, Russia, Spain, Taiwan and Venezuela have joined this select club.

Before commencing any negotiation for a franchise in any of these countries one should take advice, even if the negotiations take place outside the country concerned, to ensure that the local law is not infringed and the franchisee is not unexpectedly able to exercise remedies for a failure to comply initially at requirements.

We shall briefly consider the position in a selection of these countries. The information provided is only a summary to give guidance of what is involved – proper advice should be obtained.

It is important to check the position as these laws can and do change. Indeed, China and Korea have introduced extensive changes since their original laws were introduced. Canada is considering a uniform franchise law for all its provinces.

Albania

Albania has adopted a Chapter in its Civil Code entitled 'Franchising'. The Chapter defines franchising in this way. 'The Franchising contract contains an account of continuous obligations by which independent enterprises are obliged to stimulate and develop together the commerce and competition of services in application of separate obligations.' One would imagine that something of the meaning is lost in this translation.

The Code has nine articles, of which the first is the definition. The others are:

- The obligations of the franchisor; which are to pass on knowledge and 'immaterial rights' (?) to protect the 'programme of obligations and support the franchisee'.
- There is a two-way fiduciary relationship in respect of the provision of pre-contractual information, with an indemnity for breach. The innocent party to the negotiations can claim expenses if the other intentionally does not allow a contract to be formed.
- The contract has to be in writing and contain all obligations and details of the programme.
- If the contract does not specify a term or if the term is for more than ten years either party can withdraw on one year's notice. The parties can agree to renewals to the contract.
- A franchisee can be restrained from competing for up to one year after termination but the franchisee may be entitled to compensation.
- The franchisor can be held liable if unable to deliver the rights and know-how on which the programme is based.
- The franchisor has a right to claim damages arising from the franchisee's breach of contract or failure to apply the franchise programme sufficiently.
- In the event of a breach (fundamental breach probably?) that puts the trade activity at risk the contracting party has the right of withdrawal regardless of the term.

This Code is, as will be seen, a superficial treatment of the subject matter and has the potential to create difficulties for franchise systems.

Alberta, Canada

The original law relating to franchising dates back to the early 1980s when a disclosure and registration regime was introduced. The regulatory body which administered the legislation was the Alberta Securities Commission Agency, to whom a form of disclosure document had to be submitted for approval. On approval being given and the franchise registered the franchisor could then offer its franchises for sale in Alberta.

This law was amended in 1995 when the pre-contractual disclosure requirement was continued but the requirement for registration and review by the Alberta Securities Agency Commission ceased.

The disclosure document must be received by the prospective franchisee at least 14 days before signing any agreement or paying any money. The document must:

- comply with the requirements of regulations which came into force on 1 November 1995 unless exempt;

- contain copies of all proposed franchise agreements;
- contain financial statements, reports and other documents in accordance with the regulations.

There are exemptions in both the statute and the regulations.
The law goes somewhat beyond disclosure and contains provisions

- imposing on both parties a duty of fair dealing in performance and enforcement;
- imposing a right for franchisees to associate with each other;
- imposing a right for the franchisee to claim damages for a misrepresentation in a disclosure document.

The law also permits the Lieutenant General in Council to appoint one or more bodies to govern franchising and to provide fair dealing, ensuring that franchisors and franchisee have the power to make regulations for their establishment.

Australia

Australia has been flirting with franchise regulation since 1985/6 when the federal government issued a Franchise Agreements Bill for comment. This step was taken in response to a decision by a judge that the sale of a franchise was the sale of a security and so subject to the Companies Codes. This resulted in the imposition of a disclosure requirement modelled on the rules applicable to companies. This was notwithstanding that another judge had disagreed with the first judge's opinion. The absence of an appeal to a higher court meant that the uncertainty continued. The Franchise Agreements Bill was widely criticized by franchisors and franchisees and replaced by a redrafted Bill which was published. This was equally criticized and abandoned. The government then passed a regulation exempting franchise agreements from the Companies Codes.

There followed more pressure for regulation which resulted in the establishment of a voluntary code administered by a company established for the purpose and supported by the government. This eventually collapsed, unlike the political pressure to do something. It had been clear that the Trade Practices Act which was robustly applied by the judges provided franchisees with adequate remedies. Indeed, many judgments were given about which many observers had doubts. However, this was not enough and the government introduced two changes to the Trade Practices Act. One of the changes was the introduction of a prohibition against unconscionable conduct by a franchisor. The other introduced a Code of Conduct which has the force of law.

In determining whether a company has engaged in unconscionable conduct the court may have regard to:

(a) the relative strengths of the bargaining positions of the supplier and the business consumer; and

(b) whether, as a result of conduct engaged in by the supplier, the business consumer was required to comply with conditions that were not reasonably necessary for the protection of the legitimate interests of the supplier; and

(c) whether the business consumer was able to understand any documents relating to the supply or possible supply of the goods or services; and

(d) whether any undue influence or pressure was exerted on, or any unfair tactics were used against, the business consumer or a person acting on behalf of the business consumer by the supplier or a person acting on behalf of the supplier in relation to the supply or possible supply of the goods or services; and

(e) the amount for which, and the circumstances under which, the business consumer could have acquired identical or equivalent goods or services from a person other than the supplier; and

(f) the extent to which the supplier's conduct towards the business consumer was consistent with the supplier's conduct in similar transactions between the supplier and other like business consumers; and

(g) the requirements of any applicable industry code; and

(h) the requirement of any other industry code, if the business consumer acted on the reasonable believe that the supplier would comply with that code; and

(i) the extent to which the supplier unreasonably failed to disclose to the business consumer:

  (i) any intended conduct of the supplier that might affect the interests of the business consumer; and

  (ii) any risk to the business consumer arising from the supplier's intended conduct (being risks that the supplier should have foreseen would not be apparent to the business consumer); and

(j) the extent to which the supplier was willing to negotiate the terms and conditions of any contract for supply of the goods or services with the business consumer; and

(k) the extent to which the supplier and the business consumer acted in good faith.

The court must not have regard to any circumstances that were not reasonably foreseeable at the time of the alleged contravention, although it may have regard to circumstances existing before the proposal becomes law but not to conduct engaged in before that date.

The Code contains four main parts and two annexures. The annexures contain the detailed guidance for the contents of the disclosure document which is required, not only on the original grant of the franchise but on the transfer of the franchise. The four main parts are:

Part 1: Preliminary

This sets out the name and purpose of the Code as well as a series of definitions. The definitions are wide in their scope of application. The Code applies to a franchise agreement entered into on or after 1 October 1998 and there were some transitional provisions for agreements entered into before that date.

Part 2

This lays the foundations for disclosure. It imposes the obligation to disclosure, requires disclosure to be in the form set out in the annexures, sets out the requirement to disclosure the former franchising agreement entered into and also requires a franchisee transferring a franchise business to provide the disclosure to a proposed transferee. The Code imposes the requirement that the franchisor must have received from the prospective franchisee signed statements that the franchisee has been given advice about the agreement or business by an independent legal adviser, an independent business adviser or an independent accountant. The franchisor must have received from the prospective franchisee a statement that he has been told what kind of advice should be sought but has decided not to seek it.

Part 3

This deals with what are described with the conditions of the franchise agreement. There is a cooling off period, there are requirements in respect of any lease between the parties, franchisee associations may not be prohibited, there is a prohibition on general releases from liability, there are requirements about marketing and other cooperative funds and there is a list of materially relevant facts which a franchisor must disclose to a franchisee or prospective franchisee within a reasonable time (but not more than 60 days) after the franchisor becomes aware of it. The list includes changes in majority ownership or control of the franchisor, proceedings by a public agency or a judgment in proceedings alleging certain conduct, civil proceedings against the franchisor by 10 per cent of the franchisees, judgments which are not satisfied within 28 days and so on.

A franchisee can request a copy of the current disclosure document at any time but not more than once a year. There are rules about affecting the transfer of the franchise and termination for breach and termination where there is no breach or where special circumstances exist. There is thus a very substantial level of intervention in the contractual relationship between the parties.

Part 4

This is concerned with the resolution of disputes. Mediation is officially sanctioned and a mediation advisor appointed by the minister. The franchise agreement must provide for a complaint handling procedure which complies with the Code and, although it is stated that these provisions do not affect the right of a party to take legal proceedings. One suspects that the courts may take a dim view of those who do not try the mediation process.

Franchisors who are domiciled or who are based outside Australia and who have only one master franchisee or one franchisee are exempt from the Code on the grant of the master franchise agreement or the franchise agreement. However, the way in which the Code is drafted imposes an obligation on the franchisor to make disclosure to sub-franchisees. This requirement is difficult to justify.

Brazil

The law introducing a pre-contract disclosure requirement was passed on 15 December 1994. The law does not regulate the relationship between franchisor and franchisee, which continues to be governed by Brazil's Civil and Commercial Codes.

The disclosure requirements are quite extensive and include:

- the business background and information about the franchise;
- financial information including balance sheets;
- what the franchisee will be expected to do;
- the status of the franchisor's trade marks;
- agreements with suppliers;
- list of franchisees;
- details of pending litigation;
- investment required.

The contract will also be attached to the disclosure document, which must be presented to the prospective franchisee at least ten days prior to the signing of the franchise contract or even a preliminary contract.

Failure by a franchisor to comply provides the franchisee with a right to rescind the contract, obtain a refund of fees and claim damages.

Brazil has amended its Civil Code which also has some effect on franchise transactions.

China

By a circular dated 14 November 1997 the Ministry of Domestic Trade promulgated 'Measures for Administration of Franchise Operations' (for trial implementation). These measures were introduced in accordance with instructions of the leaders of the State Council 'with a view to standardizing franchise operations and promoting the development of chain stores' and apply to franchise operations within the territory of the People's Republic of China.

Authorization of the use of the name to be given to the franchise enterprise and the amount of royalties to be paid for what is described as the use of the franchise right are to be governed by existing structures. The measures are also concerned with protecting the lawful rights and interests of both the franchisor and the franchisee. The measures seek to introduce a level of balance by dealing with not only the franchisor but also the franchisee.

The definition of franchising is somewhat basic but given its stage of development is probably adequate. The measure is stated to be for 'trial implementation' so one imagines that experience will bring improvements. There is a basic principal in that franchising issues are to be conducted in adherence to the principles of 'voluntariness, fairness, compensation, good faith and standardization'.

There are descriptions of:

- direct franchises;
- sub-franchises (regional franchises), which seem to include multiple franchising as well as master franchising.

The measures lay down requirements to be met by both franchisors and franchisees, as well as establishing their respective fundamental rights and duties.

The basic requirements for the contents of franchise agreements are listed, as well as the types of charges which a franchisor may make to the franchisees. These include:

- initial franchise fees;
- royalties;
- security deposits;
- other charges for services provided by the franchisor to the franchisee.

There is a requirement for a franchisor to make written disclosure to a prospective franchisee at least ten days prior to the signing of a contract. The minimum information to be provided includes:

- the name and basic facts of the franchisor's company, its business performance, the business consistency of its franchise;
- an investment budget for the franchise based on practice;
- methods of collection of royalties and various charges;
- terms and restrictions for supply of articles and goods.

Intellectual property rights are to be handled in accordance with other relevant provisions.

The measures also identify other bodies which are to be concerned in drafting policies, regulations and managing, guiding, planning and coordinating franchise operations, as well as codes of conduct.

The Chinese government has prepared a draft of proposed new law setting out 'Administrative Rules on Commercial Franchising'. This follows a different approach from the above legislation. The final version is not yet available and the comments which follow may not reflect the final outcome. The definitions recognize three types of franchise:

- direct franchise;
- regional franchise (development agreement);
- compound franchise (master franchise agreement).

This law will apply to 'franchise business activities involving retail, wholesale, restaurants, community services and industries that are non-administrative by nature performed within the territory of China'. It will establish principles of fairness and honestly.

The law establishes basic conditions, rights and obligations for both franchisors (e.g. the franchisor should have more than three pilot operations operating for one year within China) and franchisees which provide a checklist for provisions in the contract. There is also a list of the minimum contractual provisions. There is also a requirement to provide the franchisee with pre-contractual disclosure.

There is a section entitled 'Supervision and Administration of Franchising', which requires the registration of the contract with the 'trade and economy administration in its registered place'.

There will be penalties for breaches of certain requirements which may be levied on both franchisor and franchisee. These aspects are to be administered by the Administrative for Industry and Commerce.

France

The law focused on licencing of trade marks subject to the licensee accepting exclusivity or quasi-exclusivity, and thus affecting franchising, was adopted by the French parliament on 31 December 1989. The law is named Loi Doubin after the Member of Parliament who introduced it.

The basic law provides that prior to the execution of a contract there must be provided to the franchisee (licensee) 'a document giving honest information permitting the other party to make an informed decision'. The document, whose contents were to be specified in a regulation, must include:

- information on the franchisor's business, its experience and how long established;
- the market and its growth potential;
- the term and renewal;
- termination and conditions for the transfer of the business;
- scope of exclusivity granted.

The document has to be provided at least 20 days prior to the execution of the contract or the payment of any money.

The regulation followed (obviously urgency was not a consideration) on 6 April 1991 and provided that the document must contain the following information about the franchisor and its business:

- The registered office, its legal form, the nature of its activities the identity of its management and its share capital.
- Its registration number on the Commercial Companies' Register or its registered number on the Register of Independent Entrepreneurs.
- The record of any trade mark registration or licences relating to their use by the licensor at the Trade Mark Registry.
- The address of the bank branches which it uses (limited to five bank branches).
- The date of the establishment of the business, its history, the history of its network and all information necessary to assess its business and its management's experience. This may be limited to the preceding five years.
- A description of the market in general and the local market and the prospects for its development.
- the following details of the network:
  (a) a list of franchisees;
  (b) their addresses;
  (c) the dates of signature and renewal of agreements.
  This may be limited to the 50 franchisees closest to the location proposed for the prospective franchisee.
- If applicable, the catchment area or territory of the proposed franchisee and other franchised (licensed) establishments which are in the same area.
- A description of the term of the contract and conditions for renewal, termination, assignment and exclusivity.
- A description of the nature and amount of expenses and capital investment.

Non-compliance is a criminal offence. The franchisee also has a range of remedies under the Civil Code.

Indonesia

The Indonesian government issued a regulation on franchising on 18 June 1997. The basic law provides a framework for pre-contract disclosure and for registration of new agreements as well as existing agreements; the former within 30 days from the date of the agreement and in the latter case within six months from the date of the regulation. Failure to register results in the revocation of the franchisee's business licence.

The implementing regulation provides more detail of the required pre-contract disclosure, which must be truthful and in writing and provide information about:

- the franchisor and its business activities;
- the IP rights;

- the franchisee's obligations;
- the franchisor's support;
- the respective rights and obligations of the parties;
- termination, cancellation and renewal of the contract.

There are other non pre-disclosure requirements:

- priority has to be given to local sourcing of products and services;
- the franchisor has an obligation to nurture, guide and train the franchisee;
- a sub-franchisor is required to operate at least one unit.

There is a peculiar provision which, while permitting pan-Indonesian development, restricts implementation to stages, with account to be taken of social and economic development in the framework of the development of small and medium-sized business. The Minister of Industry and Trade will stipulate implementation provisions after consultation with the minister and heads of relevant government agencies.

Italy

On 21 April 2004 the Italian Parliament passed a franchise specific law. The law will come into force on the day after its publication in the Italian Official Bulletin.

Existing agreements will have to be amended to comply with the new law within one year from the date upon which the new law comes into force.

The definitions borrow from those which the European Commission has used in its competition law approach to franchising. The law also expressly applies to master franchise agreements. Curiously, it also applies to what are described as 'corner franchising' which is defined as an arrangement 'whereby the franchisee sets up a space exclusively dedicated to the commercial activity mentioned in Article 1, paragraph 1 (that contains the definition of a franchise agreement) in an area at his disposal'. This description sounds more like a concession where a large store enters into agreements under which space in the store is licensed to an operator. What is not clear is whether this applies to a franchisee or whether the person taking the concession becomes a franchisee in doing so.

The third article of the law deals with the form and content of the agreement:

- the agreement must be in writing;
- the franchisor must have pilot tested the concept;
- the minimum term of the agreement must be three years or, if longer, a term related to the period of amortization of the franchisee's investments. This latter provision follows the EFF Code of Ethics.

The agreement *must* contain the following:

- sets up costs;
- fee calculations and payment and, if applicable, minimum performance targets;
- rights to territorial exclusivity (if any) granted to other franchisees and a franchisor's outlet;
- details of know-how provided. It is not clear whether this means the manual must be in the contract or in a separate document which can be varied as is the invariable practice;
- criteria (if any) for acknowledging the franchisee's contribution to the know-how;
- details of technical and commercial assistance provided by the franchisor;
- terms for renewal, termination or assignment of the agreement.

The fourth article contains a range of disclosure requirements. The Ministry for Production Activities is to issue a decree within 90 days from the date the law comes into force with more disclosure requirements.

The fifth article details obligations of the franchisee:

- not to change its registered office in the agreement without the prior consent of the franchisor;
- to maintain the confidentiality of the franchisee and to procure that employees and collaborators do so even after termination.

The sixth article deals with pre-contractual behaviour obligations imposing on both franchisor and franchisee the requirement to exercise goodwill, fairness and good faith. Each is also required to provide the other with information which is necessary or appropriate for the purposes of the franchise agreement.

The seventh article requires the parties to attempt conciliation before commencing arbitration or court proceedings.

The eighth article provides the remedy of annulment of the agreement and damages if one party supplies false information to the other.

Korea

On 7 April 1997 the Fair Trade Commission issued a notice setting out the criteria for establishing what constitute unfair trade acts in franchising under the Korean Monopoly Regulation and Fair Trade Act.

In 2002 Korea enacted an 'Act of Fairness in Franchise Transactions' and an 'Enforcement Decree of the Act on Fairness in Franchise Transactions'.

The rationale for the Act is expressed in the following terms: 'This Act has been enacted to establish fairness in franchise transactions and promote balanced and mutually complementary development on even terms between a franchisor and a franchisee for purposes of advancement of consumer welfare and a sound natural economy'. When one starts with such a muddled and grandiose ground rule, which demonstrates a level of confusion about what is the nature of a franchise, its effect and the franchisor/franchisee relationship, the rest can only be an uphill struggle.

The Act covers a wide range of topics:

- Definitions.
- Basic principles of franchise transactions which include:
  (a) principle of good faith;
  (b) franchisor's duties;
  (c) franchisee's duties.
- Fairness in franchise transactions.
- Dispute conciliation.
- Disposition of cases under the Fair Trade Commission.
- Penal provisions.

To come within the definition of a 'prospective franchisee' a person has to make a written application to receive information regarding a franchisee's obligations etc. A disclosure document is 'a document in book form'.

Among the duties of a franchisor we find 'install shop facilities ... at reasonable prices and costs'. Does that mean the franchisor has to carry out shopfitting works for the franchisee? Curiously, the franchisee has to 'consult with the franchisor prior to altering the business activity of the products and services'. Did the draughtsman of the Act not understand franchising?

> The Fair Trade Commission, in order to establish a sound and orderly franchise transaction system and prevent the circulation of franchise agreements containing unfair terms and conditions, may encourage the drafting and use of a franchise agreement that is to be used as a standard in specified franchise transactions.

This sounds a little too intrusive and could well be a disincentive. How well qualified and relevantly experienced would the Fair Trade Commission be to intervene in a constructive manner?

The position of franchise consultants is also dealt with: 'a person who possesses the necessary qualification related to the consultation in the area of the franchise transaction as specified by a Presidential Decree may become a franchise transaction consultant'. The inclusion in the list of matters on which 'The consultant shall provide consultation' of 'matters related to the preparation and revision of a franchise agreement', rather than leaving it to the legal profession where it properly belongs, is puzzling.

The enforcement decree contains more definitions and deals with other issues specifically stated in the Act as to be determined by Presidential Decree. It largely provides a greater level of detail than the Act.

This legislation in its totality is very lengthy and complex, with perhaps too much left to official bodies, which are not likely to have the experience necessary to intervene effectively and in the best interests of the sound development of franchising.

Malaysia

An Act regulating franchising has been enacted in Malaysia and came into force in 1999. It covers:

- a registration requirement and the establishment of a registrar;
- franchise agreement provisions;
- conduct of the parties and termination of franchise agreements;
- the establishment of a Franchise Advisory Board;
- offences and penalties;
- enforcement.

The Act applies to the sale of any franchise in or to be operated in Malaysia, wherever the transaction is concluded.

There will be a minister who will be responsible for matters relating to franchises. He will presumably have other responsibilities. The minister will appoint a registrar of franchises and such numbers of deputy registrars and assistant registrars as may be necessary. It is clearly envisaged that the registrar's office will be of a significant size.

A franchisor will be required to register its franchise with the registrar before it can make an offer to sell the franchise. A failure to do so will be an offence. The information which will be required to be submitted to the registrar is:

- an application in the prescribed form;
- completed disclosure documents;
- a sample of the franchise agreement;
- operations and training manuals;
- a copy of the latest audited accounts and financial statements;
- such other information as the registrar may require.

Failure to submit within the time requested will result in the deemed withdrawal of the application, necessitating a fresh application. The submission of false or misleading information will constitute an offence.

The registrar may approve with such conditions as he imposes or refuse (with reasons) an application and may require the payment of the prescribed fees. Registration is by no means automatic as even reputable and successful foreign franchisors have surprisingly discovered.

Registration will normally be effective on the date specified by the registrar. The registrar will have the power to suspend, terminate, prohibit or deny the sale or registration of a franchisor but before doing so must give notice of his intention to do so with details, and provide the franchisor with an opportunity to make written representations. The franchisor is required to notify the registrar of material changes to the disclosure documents. Franchise brokers (i.e. those who sell franchises for franchisors) are required to register.

A franchisor is required to submit to a prospective franchisee a copy of the franchise agreement and disclosure document at least ten days before the franchisee signs the agreement. Failure to do so will constitute an offence.

Each year the franchisor is required to submit a report to the registrar in a prescribed form, including an updated disclosure document. The registrar may require the inclusion of additional information or a deletion from the disclosure document, or issue an order suspending, terminating, prohibiting or denying the sale or registration of the franchise until any deficiencies specified have been corrected.

There is a right to appeal to the minister in respect of any decision of the registrar.

A franchise agreement must be in writing and contain at least the following information or provisions:

- the name and description of the product and business to be franchised;
- the territorial rights granted to the franchisee;
- the franchise fee, promotion fee, royalty or any related type of payment which may be imposed on the franchisee;
- the obligations of the franchisor;
- the obligations of the franchisee;
- the franchisee's rights to use the mark or other intellectual property;
- the conditions under which the franchisee can assign his rights;
- a cooling off period of not less than seven days when the franchisor may retain, out of any initial sum paid, the reasonable expenses incurred by the franchisor;
- a description of the mark and other intellectual property to be franchised;
- if there is a master franchise agreement details of the franchisor and the rights of the master franchisee;
- the type and particulars of assistance provided by the franchisor;
- the duration of the franchise (which must be not less than five years) and the terms of renewal;
- the effective termination or expiration of the franchise agreements.

The agreement may also contain provisions to protect confidential information and to restrain competitive activities. There is a prohibition against a franchisor unreasonably and materially discriminating between franchisees in charges offered or made for the franchise fees, royalties, goods, services, equipment, rentals or advertising services if such discrimination causes competitive harm to a franchisee who competes with a franchisee who benefits from such discrimination. There are some exceptions, such as 'discrimination' arising from and related to franchises granted at different times.

Where a franchisee is required to make a payment for promotion the franchisor will have to establish a promotion fund into which such payments are made. The fund will have to be audited and the accounts filed with the registrar. Failure to comply is an offence.

There is a section of the Act devoted to the 'conduct of [the] parties and termination of franchise agreement' which has a number of interesting approaches, not all of which would be universally acceptable:

- The franchisor and franchisee have to act in an honest and lawful manner and pursue 'the best franchise business practice of the time and place'. The latter phrase is somewhat lacking in precision and will be open to varying interpretation.
- In their dealings with each other the parties have to avoid:
  (a) substantial and unreasonable over-valuation of fees and prices;
  (b) conduct which is unnecessary and unreasonable in relation to the risks to be incurred by one party;
  (c) conduct that is not reasonably necessary for the protection of the legitimate business interests of the franchisor, franchisee or franchise system.

One can imagine the problems which these provisions will raise in terms of the day-to-day conduct of the franchisee's business and the contention which they will introduce into the relationship.

The franchisor has to give the franchisee an opportunity to cure breaches of the agreement, which shall not be terminable except for good cause which is defined.

A franchisor will commit an offence if he refuses to renew a franchise agreement or to extend the term without compensating a franchisee by repurchase (or by other means) at a price to be agreed after considering the diminution in value of the franchised business caused by expiration where:

- the franchisor refuses to waive any post term non-competition provisions or
- the franchisee has not been given at least six months' written notice that the franchisor does not intend to renew the agreement.

On the other hand, the franchisee does not have to give any notice at all that he does not intend to renew the agreement.

One could, of course, argue that there is no diminution in the value of the business caused by expiration since if the agreement is for a fixed term it should be amortized to nil value over the length of that term. There is an inherent unfairness in asking a franchisor to buy a business or surrender the protection of a non-compete clause. The franchisee may have acquired the business by purchase from an existing franchisee, where the expression 'repurchase' is scarcely appropriate. There is no mechanism to deal with a failure to agree a price, which must make a franchisor extremely vulnerable to prosecution. A franchisee's leverage on these circumstances is disproportionate to the perceived problem, especially when extension of a term will be a statutory right and the terms of the extended agreement must not be less favourable than the existing agreement.

A franchisor is required to provide assistance to a franchisee to operate his business, such as the provision of a supply of materials and services, training, marketing and business or technical assistance. The fear may be that the expression 'provide assistance to a franchisee to operate his business' could be interpreted to mean that the franchisor has to be providing a more 'hands on' service than franchisors normally provide or factor into their system.

There is also a provision which requires a franchisor and franchisee to protect the consumer's interests at all times, which seems to be a curious imposition of consumer protection law on to franchise law.

There is to be a Franchise Advisory Board comprising up to 15 members who have wide knowledge and experience in franchising. The Board will advise the minister and registrar, who will not be bound to act on that advice.

There is a wide range of penalties, from 2000 rinngit to five years' imprisonment. The court may also order that the franchisor refunds any form of payment which he has obtained from any franchisee. This is the case despite the fact that the franchisee may have had full value for and profit from the payment and that the contract must continue for at least five years and be automatically renewed. A payment to a franchisee of seven or eight years' standing could well have a significant adverse effect on a franchisor and the system.

It will not be possible to contract out of the law.

This proposed approach is fraught with difficulties. It upsets the balance between the parties and could well create far more problems than it will solve.

Mexico

Franchise disclosure was introduced in June 1991 and implemented by a regulation coming into effect on 8 December 1994. The law also requires registration at the Mexican Institute of Industrial Property, apparently for trade mark purposes

There are ten headings under which information has to be given:

1. The franchisor's name, domicile and nationality.
2. A description of the franchise.
3. How long the franchisor has run the business.
4. Details of any relevant copyright.
5. The nature and amount of payments to be made by the franchisee.

6. The nature and extent of services and technical support to be provided by the franchisor.
7. A description of the franchisee's territory.
8. Whether or not the franchisee has the right to sub-franchise and if so on what basis.
9. The franchisee's obligations to maintain confidentiality.
10. A general statement of the franchisee's rights and obligations.

Ontario, Canada

After many years of considering the regulation of franchising the legislature of the Province of Ontario passed a pre-contractual disclosure law which came into effect on 1 July 2001.

Apart from the disclosure obligations in the Act the opportunity was taken to introduce a duty of fair dealing on the parties to the franchise agreement. Fair dealing means for the purpose of the legislation a duty to act in good faith and in accordance with reasonable commercial standards. This formula obviously provides much scope for judges. Franchisees are also given the right to form a franchisee association.

The disclosure requirement follows a familiar pattern:[4]

- the document must contain all material facts, financial statements and copies of the franchise agreement and ancillary documents;
- the document must be provided to a prospective franchisee not less than 14 days before any money is paid by the prospective franchisee to the franchisor or the signing of the contract;
- the consequences of failure to provide the disclosure document or of misrepresentation include recission and damages;
- damages can be claimed if there is a failure to observe its fair dealing duty or franchisees are prevented from associating with each other;
- the Act applies if the business is to be operated entirely or partly in Ontario.

As one might expect, the Act contains definitions of 'franchise' which are wide enough to include businesses which may not normally be considered business format franchises.[5]

There are some exemptions from the Act (e.g. employment relationships, partnerships) and from this requirement to make disclosure (e.g. the grant of a franchise to an existing franchisee, a renewal of a franchise agreement) and in both cases where there has not been any material change since the current franchise agreement was entered into.

The Act is a very detailed treatment of the subject matter.

Romania

Romania has passed an 'Ordinance regarding the legal status of franchising'.

As has so often proved to be the case with countries with little franchising experience (and others who should know better), the law clearly suffers from an imperfect understanding of the subject matter and an unfortunate level of inflexibility. The legislators appeared to have borrowed provisions from the EC block exemption regulations, which were, of course, framed with competition and not relationship issues in mind.

A franchisor is defined as a trader who:

- owns a registered trade mark which will be valid throughout the term of the franchise agreement;
- grants the right to operate or develop a business or product or technology;
- trains the franchisee for the operation of the registered mark;
- promotes the mark and through research and innovation ensures the development and validity of the product.

This muddled thinking sets the tone for what follows.

'A franchise' is a marketing system based on continuous cooperation between financially independent persons whereby the franchisor grants the franchisee the right to develop a business, product, technology or service. 'A franchisee' is a person selected by the franchisor who adheres to the principle of uniformity of a franchise network as defined by the franchisor. 'Know-how', which does not appear as a term in the other definitions, is the entirety of elements serving the manufacture and sale of a product. 'Franchise network' means an assembly of contractual relationships between a franchisor and several franchisees to promote a technology, product or service and for the development of the production and distribution of a product or service.

There is no registration requirement. The law is concerned with pre-contractual, contractual and post-contractual relations.

The pre-contractual stage is concerned with the provision of information. A franchisor has to provide the franchisee with information relating to:

- its transmittable experience;
- the financial terms, not only initial fees, ongoing fees and advertising fees, but how the purchase price of services and products will be determined;
- the elements which enable the franchisee to make projections and a financial plan;
- the area of exclusivity;
- the duration of the agreement and the provisions relating to renewal, termination and assignment.

A franchise agreement must reflect the interests of the members of the franchise network and protect the franchisor's industrial or intellectual property rights by maintaining the common identity and reputation of the network. The agreement must state, without ambiguity, the parties' obligations and liabilities. There are obligations imposed on both franchisor and franchisee. The franchisor must:

- effectively run a pilot operation;
- own intellectual and/or industrial property rights;
- train the franchisee and provide commercial and technical assistance for the duration of the agreement.

The franchisee must:

- develop the network and maintain its common identity and reputation;
- provide the franchisor with information to enable it to analyse performance and financial statistics;
- not disclose the franchisor's know-how to third parties during and after the franchise agreement.

The franchise agreement must include clauses detailing:

- its object;
- the parties' rights and obligations;
- financial requirements;
- its duration;
- conditions governing amendment, extension and termination.

A franchise agreement has to observe a set of principles:

- its term must be long enough for the franchisee to 'recover the investments specific for any franchise';
- the franchisor must notify the franchisee long enough in advance (without saying what it has to be enough for!) if it intends not to renew;
- conditions for termination which must be precisely defined;
- conditions for the transfer of rights arising from the agreement must be clearly defined;
- a pre-emption right must be provided if the interests of marketing and expanding the network require;
- there must be a non-competition clause to protect the know-how;
- the franchisee's financial obligations must be clearly defined.

The agreement enables the franchisor to control its trade marks. The franchisee has to publicize that he is financially independent from the franchisor. A franchisee has to be given reasonable time to remedy any breach of the agreements.

Post-contractual relations have to be based on rules of fair competition. The franchisor may impose strict obligations to protect the confidential nature of the business and the non-use of the know-how by a competing network.

There are some provisions dealing with exclusivity which seem to assume that there will be an exclusivity fee and that it will be pro rata to the admission fee and in addition to it (one might be excused for having difficulty in understanding this provision). An exclusivity agreement must contain a termination clause accepted by both parties, which will deal with reimbursement of the exclusivity fee.

There is a curious provision borrowed partially from Article 85(3) of the EC Treaty, which states that 'By its organization and development a franchise network must contribute to the improvement of products and/or distribution of products and/or services.'

The law also deals with advertising for franchisees, which must be free of ambiguities and inaccurate information. Any advertising documents prescribing financial projections of a franchisee must be objective and accessible. Presumably, this is intended to refer to profit projections.

The franchisor must ensure that the franchise network maintains its identity and reputation.

Russia

Russia does not have a disclosure law – it does have a registration requirement but its law does not explain how one should register the agreement or what is the purpose of registration.

The fact that Russia has a law relating to franchising is an oddity since when it was introduced there was not a lot of franchising in Russia. This is a case where the law has come before the commercial practice and it contains provisions which many franchisors will regard as discouraging. The law was adopted as Chapter 54 of the Russian Civil Code on 22 December 1995 by the State Duma and approved by the Federation Council on 25 January 1996. Although the law is clearly aimed at franchising, it describes its subject matter as 'commercial concessions'.

In discussions in Russia with those involved in drafting the legislation various explanations were given:

- there is a practice in Russia to use the law as a textbook providing guidance and education;
- the law indicates that such a transaction is permitted;
- it may assist in dealings with the tax authorities.

The code does not educate – it directs and is prepared from a knowledge base which is so limited that it contains many provisions which are inhibiting rather than encouraging growth.

The definition of a contract of a commercial concession is confusing and does not really come to terms with franchising techniques.

The contract has to be registered with two separate organizations and a failure to do so renders it void or unenforceable, which seems a rather drastic outcome for a failure to follow a course which appears to have no object but to feed beaurocracy.

The franchisor, described curiously as the 'rightholder', is obliged to:

- ensure registration;
- provide continuous technical and consulting assistance to the franchisee (user), including training and advanced training of employees;
- supervise the quality of goods (work and services) manufactured (performed, rendered) by the user in compliance with the contract.

This is a very onerous list. The list of user's obligations is more extensive but scarcely addresses the real issues in franchising.

The concept of exclusivity is enshrined in the provisions.

A rightholder (franchisor) is vicariously liable for claims against the user (franchisee) for failure to maintain quality standards.

There is an automatic right to renewal of the contract on the same terms although the rightholder can refuse such renewal and if it does it cannot operate a franchise in the relevant territory within three years from the expiry of the contract unless it compensates the outgoing user. The automatic right to renewal 'on the same terms' has the effect of perpetuating the position which obtained on the date the first contract was signed, thus preventing the rightholder from updating the contract to take into account business issues as well as changes in the law. If the rightholder dies his contractual rights and obligations are transferred to his heir provided the heir is registered or becomes registered as an entrepreneur within six months. What a great qualification as a franchisor!

These are but a few examples of an ill conceived legislative exercise. One wonders when it may be reconsidered.

Spain

The basic law was enacted on 5 January 1996 and was implemented by a regulation adopted on 17 November 1998 which came into force on 27 November 1998.

The basic law requires that 20 days before a contract is signed or money paid by the franchisee to the franchisor the latter must provide the franchisee in writing with all information regarding the franchise network, with the object of enabling the franchisee to be in a position to decide freely and knowingly whether or not to enter into the contract. The basic law lists the following information required:

- essential identification regarding the franchise;
- a description of the market;
- the exploitation structure and extension of the networks;
- the essential provisions in the franchise agreement.

As one might expect, the regulation provides the essential level of detail. The regulation provides for both pre-contract disclosure and registration. The registration requirement seems to be concerned with providing the central and regional governments with details of all franchisors operating within their territories. This should provide some statistical evidence of the extent of franchising and its growth in Spain as it is expressed to be for the sole purpose of information and publicity. The regulation defines what it means by 'trading under the franchise regime' and achieves it by borrowing heavily but not entirely from the EC Block Exemption regulation, whose provisions it appears to be adopting as a benchmark. The regulation also defines a master franchise agreement, which it describes as a 'principal franchise agreement'. One is inclined to wonder whether the effect of adopting the definition in this form will lead to franchisers drafting agreements which do not meet the requirements of the definition to ensure that the regulation does not apply to them.

Disclosure, which must be accurate and not deceptive, must be made at least 20 days prior to signature of the franchise agreement or a provisional agreement (e.g. deposit agreement) or the payment of any money (this is similar to the French requirement). The information to be disclosed includes the following.

Details of the franchisor

- Corporate name.
- Registered address.
- Details of inclusion in the register of franchisors (see below).
- Paid up share capital.
- If a foreign franchisor, details of inclusion in the register of franchisers in which they are obliged to register under the laws of their country (or state) of origin.
- In the case of a principal franchisee (sub-franchisor), details of the above in relation to the principal franchisor (franchisor).

Trade marks

Evidence of ownership or rights to use (and for what period) and any possible legal proceedings.

Franchise activity

A general description of the sector of activity and its most noteworthy features.

Experience

Details of the franchisor's experience, including:

- date of incorporation;

- the main stages and history of the development of the franchise network.

Content and characteristics of the franchise and its exploitation.

These include:

- a general explanation of the system of business;
- the characteristics of know-how and permanent commercial or technical assistance to be provided to franchisees;
- an estimate of setting-up costs;
- if profit and sales projections are given (this is not obligatory) they must be based on experience or studies and be sufficiently justified.

Structure and system of the network in Spain:

- The form of organization of the network.
- The number of outlets in Spain:
  (a) company owned;
  (b) franchised.
- The location of outlets.
- The number of franchisees who have withdrawn in the preceding two years, stating why.

The franchise contract

The essential elements include:

- the rights and obligations of the parties;
- its duration;
- conditions for termination;
- renewal provisions (if any);
- economic considerations;
- exclusivity agreements;
- restrictions on the sale of the franchise by the franchisee.

Confidentiality

The franchisor shall be entitled to require a franchisee to enter into an undertaking to keep pre-contractual information confidential.

The following provisions relate to the register.

Its creation

- The register is created for the sole purposes of information and publicity and has a public and administrative nature and character.

- The register will be administered by the Directorate General for Domestic Trade of the Ministry of Economy and Finance.
- Registration must be made of the persons who intend to perform the franchise in Spain prior to the sale of the franchise when the franchise to be operated is in more than one autonomous region.

Franchisors

- The inclusion of franchisors on the proposal of the automonous governments in the region where they have their registered office. An identity code will be allocated by the state registrars.
- Regular updating of the list of franchisees and the preparation of statistics.
- Cancellation of franchise if required by the automonous government.
- The issue of certificates of registration.
- Provision of access to the register for automonous governments.
- The provision of information about franchisors of a public nature to interested parties.
- The inclusion of franchisors who have no registered office in Spain.

Documentation to be filed

Application for inclusion in the register shall be filed with the competent authority in the autonomous government where the franchisor has its headquarters. At least the following details have to be provided.

- Particulars of the franchisor:
  - (a) name/status;
  - (b) registered office;
  - (c) details of inclusion in the mercantile register;
  - (d) taxpayer's number or business identification number.
- Details (including ownership or entitlement to use) of industrial or intellectual property rights to which the agreement refers, their duration and any legal disputes.
- A description of the franchised business and its activity:
  - (a) number of franchisees and their outlets;
  - (b) number of company owned outlets;
  - (c) including where the outlets are located;
  - (d) how many franchisees left the network in the previous two years.

- Where there is a sub-franchisor it must provide particulars of its franchisor, comprising name, corporate status, registered address, legal status and the duration of its agreement with its franchisor.

Obligations

Where there is a change in the information provided relating to the particulars of the franchisor, the industrial or intellectual property or the franchised business and its activity, it must be notified within three months. If the franchisor ceases franchise activity this must be notified forthwith. In any event the information must be updated in January of each year.

The register may be computerized and the registers operated whether centrally or by regional governments have to be coordinated.

Transitional provisions

Franchisors whether based in Spain or not who sell franchises in Spain have one year to register (i.e. before 27 November 1999).

The USA

The United States has both federal and state laws which directly affect franchising. What follows is a brief introduction to what a is complex web of legal requirements. There is a much more detailed treatment of this subject in Chapter 16.

At the federal level there is a pre-contract disclosure requirement created under statutory authority by the Federal Trade Commission ('FTC Franchise Rule').[6] The rule applies throughout the states except where state laws are more restrictive. Fourteen US states require registration or filing and disclosure. The North American Securities Administrators Association ('NASAA') has devised a Uniform Franchise Offering Circular (UFOC) to enable a standard format to be used which complies with both federal and state disclosure laws. The FTC allows use of the UFOC format to comply with the requirements, of the FTC Franchise Rule. There are a variety of state legal requirements the most stringent of which are those which require registration of the franchise offering as well as the delivery of a pre-contract disclosure document. One other state requires disclosure but not registration; the other 35 states have neither regulation nor disclosure laws. There are also 21 states and two territories with franchise relationship laws and 25 states with business opportunities laws.

The following is a brief list of the information which has to be included in the UFOC:

- the identity of the franchisor, its trade name and trade marks;
- the business experience of the franchisors, directors and officers;
- the franchisor's business experience;

- the franchisor's litigation history (to include that of its directors and executives), with litigation covering criminal, civil and administrative procedures;
- the bankruptcy history of directors and executors;
- a description of the franchise;
- initial funds required to be paid by a franchisee;
- details of persons affiliated with the franchisor with whom the franchisee is required or recommended to do business;
- obligations to purchase;
- revenues received by the franchisor in consideration of purchases by a franchisee;
- financing arrangements;
- restrictions imposed on the franchisee in regard to sales;
- personal participation required by the franchisee in the operations of the franchise;
- termination, cancellation and renewal of the franchise;
- statistical information concerning the number of franchisees and company-owned outlets;
- site selection;
- training programme;
- public figure involvement in the franchise;
- financial information concerning the franchisor.

There are no private rights to enforce compliance with the FTC rule. The FTC is the enforcement agency and can apply for (among other things) injunctions to prevent continued non-compliance.

The state laws provide franchisees with remedies, which include the right to rescind and claim damages

Discussion

The worrying trend which is emerging is that legislation, particularly in Indonesia, Korea, Romania, and Russia, shows significant signs that those introducing the legislation either do not have a sufficient understanding of the subject or have an agenda for which franchise legislation is used as an excuse. There are criteria to consider before legislating: see the 'health warning' below.

It is almost beyond belief that a country with a significant successful franchise community like Belgium has legislators who can produce such appalling Bills. UNIDROIT (International Institute for the Unification of Private Law) has produced two publications which need to be considered.

The first is a *Guide to International Master Franchise Agreements*. This was published in 1998 and was the product of hours of discussion between some of the world's most experienced franchise practitioners. The end product is a comprehensive review of all aspects of master franchising. The guide is exactly that; it does not seek to take a position on the issues its sets out. With that knowledge the parties can reach the deal which suits them.

The second is *A Model Franchise Disclosure Law with Explanatory Note*. One of the dangers of such a publication is that it will be used because it is there. The explanatory note comes with a 'health warning' in the following terms:

'The International Institute for the Unification of Private Law (Unidroit) recognising that franchising is playing an ever greater role in a wide range of national economies, being mindful of the fact that in the legislative process, state legislators may wish to consider a number of different elements including:

- whether it is clear that there is a problem, what its nature is, and what action, if any, is necessary;

- whether prospective investors are more likely to protect themselves against fraud if they have access to truthful, important information in advance of their assent to any franchise agreement [this assumes that a would be fraudster would be likely to provide truthful information even if he produced a disclosure document];

- whether the nation's economic and social interests are best served by legally requiring a balance of information between the parties to a franchise agreement;

- whether there is a pattern of abusive conduct, or whether this conduct is isolated or limited to particular industries;

- the nature of the evidence of abuse;

- whether existing laws address the concerns and whether they are adequately applied;

- whether an effective system of self regulation exists;

- the financial burden the new legislation will place upon franchisors and investors as compared to the benefits of legally required disclosure;

- whether the proposed legislation inhibits or facilitates entry to franchisors, and its effect on job-creation and investments; and

- the views of interested organizations including national franchise associations.

The preamble also states 'that the model law is an example that is not compulsory for state legislators and as an instrument intended to be a recommendation for states that have decided to adopt franchise specific legislation' (emphasis added).

We now turn to the second category of regulations which impacts on franchising in some way or other without being specifically focused on franchising. Some examples have been referred to in Chapter 00 such as the Commercial Agents Law in many of the Middle East Gulf states, which is interpreted so widely that it applies to non-agency transactions regardless of whether the parties are intended to be principal and agent.[7] As explained above, the French Loi Doubin applies not only to franchising but to all licences of trade marks with exclusivity or quasi-exclusivity. Another law in some countries which often affects franchise systems is aimed at trading schemes which have more than one tier, e.g. franchisor, sub-franchisor, sub-franchisee. This law is aimed at pyramid selling, multilevel marketing and network marketing, some of which systems are fundamentally founded on fraud. The way these laws are structured often catches franchise systems. In the UK the original legislation of this nature was contained in the Fair Trading Act 1973 but that Act was recently amended by the Trading Schemes Act 1996, which had a change of emphasis. Under this Act virtually all trading relationships, i.e. distribution systems, agency franchising and the 'pyramid etc. schemes' have to comply with regulations unless they come within one of the two exemptions. These exemptions are:

- single tier systems;
- non-single tier systems provided all participants are at all times registered for VAT.

The legislation is unhappily wide and the regulations are clearly only drafted with pyramid type schemes in mind, which means that many businesses affected cannot make sense out of complying with the regulations. Certainly franchise systems could not do so.

There are also dangers lurking for franchisors who impose controls in their agreements which are inconsistent with the franchisee's status as an independent contractor. There are jurisdictions in which the courts have held that what was intended as a franchise agreement was in reality a contract of employment.

There are also potential problems in some countries where the courts have applied consumer protection laws to business transactions, and therefore also franchise agreements, e.g. the German standard terms in consumer contracts law.

The legal audit (see above) must be taken seriously – there are many hidden pitfalls in many connections, and investigations must be wide. Fortunately the would-be cross-border franchisor is better placed than his predecessors since there is now more published information as well as those with the experience to provide guidance.

Notes

1. In the USA the term 'master franchise' historically had a different meaning, often applying to franchisees who service other franchisees in exchange for remuneration from the franchisor but see Chapter 16.
2. Some US lawyers that may not directly affect franchising may nevertheless have to be dealt with, such as the federal and state business opportunity laws.
3. The USA, for example, has industry-specific laws in a variety of areas, such as for gasoline dealers/service stations, farm and industrial equipment dealers, automobile dealerships etc.
4. Ontario modelled its definition and many of its disclosure obligations on the US FTC Franchise Rule.
5. Among other things, Ontario borrowed the US FTC Franchise Rule's definition of business opportunity.
6. The FTC Franchise Rule covers both the typical written franchise arrangement and certain types of business opportunities.
7. In the USA, 35 states have sales representative laws that cover similar commercial agency relationships. They would not apply to the typical franchise relationship.

15 International franchising: structuring the arrangements

Having taken the decision to operate in a foreign market, the franchisor then has to consider the method by which such an operation will be established. It should be appreciated that what in effect is happening is that the franchisor is taking a business into another country. Its intention is to use franchising as its method of expansion. There are a number of different approaches which are commonly in use. These include:

- a company-owned only operation;
- direct franchising;
- a master franchise arrangement;
- a joint venture.

The mechanism by which the chosen method is implemented may involve the franchisor in establishing:

- a branch operation;
- a subsidiary company.

Either of these may be involved in running a store or stores and/or operating a regional office in due course.

Company-owned operations

In this case, the franchisor establishes its own operation directly owned and run. In order to do this, the company would need to have the manpower and financial resources to establish and sustain such an operation, which many franchise companies do not possess or to which they do not wish to put their resources.

It is, however, a convincing way of entering a country since a successful company-owned network would in the future provide the basis for the introduction of franchising should the franchisor wish to do so. Indeed, the franchisor that establishes its own operation keeps all its options open. It can expand the company-owned chain; it can use its experience and results to enable it to recruit prospective direct franchisees or master franchisees. Quite apart from the need to have the resources to establish a business in a target territory a franchisor may decide that to attempt to develop internationally in this way would be too slow since the number of countries which could be entered would be quite low. One must also consider the point already made that establishing an international programme will require both financial and manpower resources – using them to open company-owned operations in one country may prevent the franchisor from achieving the rate of growth which would otherwise be available to it. Expanding by opening its own operations in all targeted territories may face the franchisor with a number of business problems. These will include particularly:

- recruiting and training local staff;
- adapting to the business methods, the culture and the language, and acquiring 'street knowledge' of doing business in the target territory, the franchisor will inevitably need local people to provide the right direction in these respects (it cannot be done by remote control);
- acquisition, conversion and/or construction expenses;
- the problems of day-to-day supervision and control of operations from a distance.

Direct franchising

This will involve the franchisor entering into a franchise agreement with each individual franchisee in the target country, and providing the basic back-up and continuing support directly. As a technique it is normally limited in scope because the further away the franchisor is from the target territory, the more difficult it becomes to service franchisees. The use of the direct franchising route also makes the franchisor vulnerable to the possibility that it will fail to recognize the differences which exist between its home country in which the business originated and the target country. Pilot operations are advisable in order to achieve the transition.

For those intending to do business with or within the European Union it is relevant to appreciate that although much progress has been made in eliminating fully internal barriers which formerly existed – that is, those which are physical (e.g. the movement of people and goods), technical (e.g. product specifications, professional qualifications) and fiscal (e.g. harmonization of tax rates) – there will remain some vital differences throughout the EU. These include:

- language barriers;
- local laws which could impact upon franchising, franchise operations and agreements (see below), although special industry laws should be increasingly standardized;
- cultural and lifestyle differences;

- the tastes and habits of the inhabitants of the individual member states will continue to be different;
- national characteristics will not change at all;
- the need to adapt the franchise system to local conditions.

However much the politicians strive to regard the EU as one market the reality is that when one considers entry into one member state it will not follow that entry into another member state will be the same; it will either be free from the same restrictions or have a set of its own hurdles to be overcome.

Area development agreements

The territorial scale of the EU may make it more feasible for franchisors to consider the use of area development agreements. The use of area development agreements, under which the franchisor enters into an agreement with a developer who will open an agreed number of franchised units within an agreed time frame within a defined area, is another form of direct franchising. There are some franchisors for whom this is the preferred route: some will have one developer per country; others will have a number of developers within a country. As a method of covering a country using direct franchising it can have some advantages, in that there will be far fewer franchisees for the franchisor to deal with. On the other hand, if things go wrong the problems can be spectacular and involve a large number of franchised outlets in the country or indeed in some cases all the outlets owned by one developer.

An example of the scope which the use of this technique presents is as follows. Take country x where it is reckoned that the market would sustain 100 franchised units. The franchisor wishes to use direct franchising because it provides it with more control over operations and advertising than the other methods available. However, it finds the prospect of dealing with 100 individual franchises somewhat daunting. It also believes that it would take a long time to reach critical mass and achieve the level of market penetration which it would like. It therefore decides to seek ten area developers, each of whom would be required to develop ten franchised outlets. The franchisor believes that by only having ten franchisees it will be able to use its resources better in assisting them to become established; it will obtain franchisees of a higher calibre who will be able to introduce substantial resources and obtain prime locations without the difficulties often encountered by individual franchisees; and it will be able to train each franchisee's core team to train their managers and staff. In terms of control and the expenditure and generation of advertising it will be better placed only having ten franchisees which whom to deal. It accepts the risk that one mistake can have a disproportionate adverse impact and that it may be difficult to cope with the problem of dealing with ten failed units if one of the developers for whatever reason fails to succeed.

There are other dangers, since it is easier for a smaller group to pool resources and 'take on' the franchisor, particularly if they are discontented with the franchisor's performance and are contemplating breaking away from the franchisor's network. As the franchisee will be of a different calibre from the individual franchisee it will tend to be more confident of its own knowledge and ability, which may present the franchisor with different forms of control, management and people handling problems from those with which it is more familiar.

Master franchise arrangement

Under this arrangement the sub-franchisor will have the right either to open its own outlets or to sub-franchise, but it will probably be required to concentrate on sub-franchising. The sub-franchisor will be expected to establish its own outlet or outlets to pilot-test so that it can demonstrate the success of operations in the territory to the prospective sub-franchisees. The sub-franchisor, in essence, stands in the shoes of the franchisor in the territory and is to all intents and purposes the franchisor of the system in the territory.

As is always the case, there are advantages and pitfalls. The franchisor has to consider the following.

- it is difficult to identify and select the right person or company as sub-franchisor;
- the need to have a strong profitable home base to sustain the demands which will be made upon the franchisor;
- the effect which the necessary diversion of manpower and financial resources from domestic operations will have on the franchisor's business;
- it must again be emphasized that it will always take more people and cost more money than one would anticipate;
- the time factor: it will also always take much longer than one anticipates it might.

The franchisor has only one entity with which to deal in the target country. All its dealings will be with the sub-franchisor and it will not be concerned in the day-to-day direct dealings with the sub-franchisees who operate the outlets. The similarity with domestic operations where the franchisor is not concerned with the day-to-day problems of the franchisee's operations is not coincidental. However, the franchisor must not ignore the sub-franchisees – they are the lifeblood of the network and the quality of their operations will either bring credit to the franchisor's name and system or harm its reputation.

The quality of the sub-franchisor's services in the selection and training of sub-franchisees, site selection and all the other services it provides to its sub-franchisees is vital. The franchisor needs to be satisfied that the sub-franchisor will ensure that these services are provided to the requisite standard. It must also have an interest in the ongoing controls and the supervision of standards which the sub-franchisor will provide. Any neglect of these areas will mean that the franchisor will find itself with a sub-franchisor who is not properly performing its obligations. This will require action to be taken and could ultimately lead to a termination of the master franchise agreement. The franchisor will then be left with a troublesome sub-standard sub-franchisee network to be coped with. Experience demonstrates that it is a time consuming and expensive exercise to deal with all the issues which arise. There is a likelihood that there will be a significant loss of sub-franchisees who are disaffected and who may break away and try to compete. In an extreme case the franchisor may find it cheaper, although difficult to accept, to abandon operations in the territory. The maintenance of standards and the control of the quality of the network's operations is crucial and difficult to maintain and its achievement is regarded by many as one of the fundamental problems with master franchise arrangements. It is therefore important to recognize that this is an issue both to be confronted and to be dealt with in the contractual arrangements and in the way the franchisor manages the relationship.

The franchisor should make some effort to attend sub-franchisee meetings organized by the sub-franchisor and encourage foreign sub-franchisees to attend the franchisor's franchisee meetings in its domestic market at least on a annual basis. This form of contact, together with the normal regular support and 'quality control' visits, will demonstrate to the sub-franchisees that the franchisor is indeed interested in them and that they are part of its global network and family of franchisees. The franchisor, however, should never put itself in the position where it risks being regarded as usurping the functions of the sub-franchisor as long as the sub-franchisor is running the operation correctly. There is a balance which has to be maintained which will not lead to sub-franchisees playing off the sub-franchisor against the franchisor.

In the same way as the franchisor operating in the domestic market expands his network using the resources of its franchisees, so does the franchisor under the master franchise agreement. Indeed, he does it at two levels instead of one. At the one level, the sub-franchisor will be required to provide the financial resources to establish and exploit the system in the target country. Whatever financial resources are needed to establish the system and operate it in that country, they will have to be found by the sub-franchisor. Part of the franchisor's selection process will involve an assessment of the sub-franchisor's financial resources. Additionally there will, of course, be the other level – the operation of the outlets for which the financial resources will be provided by the sub-franchisees who are operating these outlets.

The sub-franchisor should, of course, be making his own financial calculations to see whether he considers the proposition to be financially worthwhile. There will be some discussion in a later chapter on the piloting of operations which is necessary, but decisions will have to be taken during the course of the negotiations as to the nature and extent of pilot operations, as well as what contribution will be made to their establishment by each of the parties. The sub-franchisor will be responsible for the recruitment of staff for the pilot operations, as well as for the establishment of the infrastructure of the sub-franchisor's own business organization.

The arrangement encourages the blending of the franchisor's developed system with all the relevant factors to which reference has already been made, which are to be found in the target country by the application of the sub-franchisor's local knowledge. This sort of knowledge cannot be acquired sufficiently quickly by a 'visitor' to the target country. The local businessman will have the basic knowledge and experience of local business practices, the law affecting business, banking and financial sources, and may be able to help the franchisor to identify potential suppliers of products or services who may be suitable for approval as suppliers to the local network.

A franchisor in a domestic operation will earn less in cash terms from a franchised outlet than it would from its own operational outlet. This is also the case with master franchising when the fee income generated by sub-franchisees is divided between franchisor and sub-franchisor. The sub-franchisor will be charging franchise fees to its sub-franchisees and from these fees it will have not only to finance its own operations, but also to make a payment to the franchisor. What that fee will be, and how it is calculated, will be a matter for negotiation. It is unlikely that the fee charged to sub-franchisees in the target territory will differ much from that charged to franchisees in the franchisor's domestic territory, so the amount available to be shared will be limited.

Mention has already been made of the vulnerability of the franchisor to any fall in standards of the network run by the sub-franchisor. The franchisor must, therefore, develop a strategy for the establishment and maintenance of the quality standards which it has established and which are associated with its brand and system. This may be achieved by a combination of the continuation of training through imposing requirements in the contract, inspection visits and general alertness by paying attention to the market place. There will be a need to have sanctions which can be enforced if standards lapse, probably by feedback from disgruntled sub-franchisees, but while this cannot be ignored the franchisor cannot risk its relationship with the sub-franchisor without involving it in investigating whether the feedback is an accurate reflection of a real problem or issue or a sub-franchisee trying to create problems for the franchisor – that would not be unheard of.

The problems which arise when the franchisor feels that it has no alternative but to terminate the sub-franchisor are many and varied. It is likely in such circumstances that the franchisor will inherit problems because termination will result from the sub-franchisor having done his job badly or because he is not doing very well financially and in both cases he will have neglected or otherwise failed the network. Franchisees always find a change of ownership in their franchisor to be unsettling, but often in a master franchise arrangement there are mixed feelings. On the one hand, the sub-franchisees may be pleased that the franchisor (the creator of the system and responsible for its health) has taken over the reins, but, on the other hand, there inevitably will be a feeling that perhaps it should have done so sooner. Undoubtedly, whether or not it is justified the sub-franchisees will feel that they have in some way been let down and will blame the franchisor even though it will equally be a victim of the sub-franchisor's failure. There will invariably be a level of hostility and resentment from some sub-franchisees, who may well be supported by many fellow sub-franchisees. There is likely to be a 'can of worms' uncovered by the franchisor and the issues may well include mishandling by the sub-franchisor of advertising contributions made by sub-franchisees.

Whatever the problems are, the network will have to be carefully listened to and handled. Sympathetic treatment of their complaints must be seen to be available – although the franchisor may also be a victim of the sub-franchisor's failures, it is unlikely to find any sympathy from the sub-franchisees. Most franchisors can expect an attrition rate whatever steps they may take, as well as the expense of preventing future infringement by breakaway sub-franchisees of its intellectual property.

Joint venture

It is not the purpose of this chapter to consider the advantages and disadvantages of joint venture arrangements, only the issues which are particularly relevant to franchising. The franchisor which enters into a joint venture at whatever level – master franchise with the sub-franchisor or with a developer – will still find that many of the problems we have discussed will exist. The need to identify and do a deal with the right person is just as much of a problem. But there is more to it than that. The franchisor will have to negotiate what share it wishes to take up and decide how it will finance its contribution.

The joint venture company will become either an area developer or a sub-franchisor of the franchisor's system and will have to enter into the appropriate development or master franchise agreement with the franchisor. There may be particular reasons to consider a joint venture as many companies do when contemplating dealing in developing world countries. Some countries provide tax incentives and liquid capital may not readily be available to even established businesses, at interest rates which are affordable.

In some instances, the franchisor's contribution to the share of the joint venture has taken the place of the front-end fee normally payable, and on occasions the front-end fee is paid, but returned by the franchisor to the joint venture as its contribution. Sometimes a value prepared by a professional valuer is placed on the services provided by the franchisor and this value is taken as the measure of the franchisor's contribution to the capital of the joint venture.

The joint venture company will establish the system in the target territory as a franchisee or sub-franchisor. It will be as involved in all the issues as if it were not part owned by the franchisor. The franchisor will, however, find that it has become involved in the risk of operational losses which it would otherwise have avoided and perhaps the need to find or assist in finding additional capital. It may also discover that there is much scope for disagreement on operational matters with joint venture partners who will resent the fact that the development or master franchise agreement will give the franchisor (who is also its joint venture partner) the last word on many such issues. This highlights the two roles which the franchisor has in this type of arrangement and which creates scope for friction in the relationship.

Finally, the franchisor which is confronted with a buy-out situation, or the need to terminate the joint venture, the development agreement or the master franchise agreement, will find itself in a potentially difficult position. The joint venture partner will be established in the territory in operational control, and locally in command of the situation. The franchisor needs to have already established a presence in the territory, or the ability rapidly to put the right person or team in position (which will be rare), or it will be at a considerable disadvantage in trying to take over the operation or assert control. Indeed, if a franchisor is contemplating becoming involved in a joint venture, it would be wise to have its own staff working in the joint venture company in roles which ensure that they are able to run the joint venture company if on termination they wish to take over third parties' share of the ventures.

It is infinitely more difficult to divest oneself of an unsatisfactory joint venture partner than it is to terminate a developer or a sub-franchisor (not that the latter is an easy option). To have to face the prospect of coping with both at one and the same time is something to contemplate long and hard.

Many refer to branch operations and subsidiaries as if they were methods of franchising internationally. Of course they are not – they are ways in which a franchisor may choose to formalize a presence in a country or region.

Branch operation

The establishment of a branch operation can arise in two sets of circumstances where the franchisor:

- franchises direct into the target territory and has established a branch operation to service franchisees; or
- has established the branch as a regional base to provide services to franchisees within the region.

Whether or not a branch is established may well be affected by fiscal or legal considerations, rather than those of the business. These considerations may lead the franchisor to follow the next course available to him, the establishment of a subsidiary.

Subsidiary company

The involvement of a subsidiary company may fulfil any of the following four functions.

- the franchisor could be franchising directly from its territory into the target territory and use the subsidiary to service franchisees;
- the franchisor may grant master franchise rights to the subsidiary (see below), and the subsidiary will be either opening its own operations or sub-franchising, or both;
- the subsidiary may be involved with a joint venture partner;
- the subsidiary may be used as a regional base, to provide services either to sub-franchisees, or to sub-franchisors in the region, or to both.

The service which the branch or subsidiary would provide would be similar in nature to those provided by the franchisor and would cover the whole range of franchisor services, including, as the network develops, a training facility.

The correct choice of partner and type of arrangement, as well as properly structured and drafted legal documentation are absolutely essential in international operations.

Direct franchising and development agreements

Despite the difficulties which direct franchising presents in terms of local knowledge and language some franchisors use this technique. There are a number of businesses which use the franchise marketing method, ranging from those whose businesses thrive by a massive presence to those whose businesses are aimed at the luxury brand segment of the market place. In the former case the level of resources available may make direct franchising, often using a subsidiary, a very viable proposition. In the latter case the franchisor's strategy may only involve opening 'flagship' outlets in selected markets – in some smaller countries perhaps only one. Between these two extremes there are many businesses which cannot afford to franchise direct or to be so selective as far as opening outlets is concerned. They will probably need to achieve certain volumes of sales in the foreign operation to make it worthwhile. There are also businesses based on specialist skills which require an innovative approach which may blend many of the available techniques without fully adopting any of the recognized categories. Some have an approach which is tailored more to the particular market and use one technique in one country and another in a different market. One must always retain the option of flexibility.

The technique of the development arrangement has as its intention the more rapid growth of the network; it is widely used in the US market and increasingly in international transactions. There are many similarities between this technique and that of international master franchise agreements. The basic approach creates an arrangement in which the developer is given the right to open a multiple number of outlets in accordance with a predetermined schedule and within a given area. In some arrangements, which are called development agreements, there may be a right to sub-franchise to some franchisees. This is of course much closer to a master franchise agreement – there are regional master franchise agreements which provide both options.

In the USA there is a concept of a development agent, which basically provides someone with an area of operations for the purpose of recruiting franchisees for the franchisor and then providing them with the rest of the franchisor services instead of or on behalf of the franchisor.[1]

The area development arrangement in domestic markets is usually only employed in large countries; it is effective in countries which cover a large area but with few significant concentrations of population. Development arrangements are not commonly found in the UK, although some do exist.

There are issues for a franchisor to consider in expanding through area development agreements which are equally applicable in domestic and foreign markets.

- As with the franchising of individual units, the franchisor will be making use of the financial and manpower resources of the franchisees. However, an area developer needs more resources because it will be opening a number of franchise units. If the cost of opening an individual unit is, say, £100,000 and the developer has undertaken to open 25 outlets it will need to find at least £2.5 million to meet its obligations within a given period of time.

- The £2.5 million is not the whole story of course. The developer will need to develop a business infrastructure because it will need a 'head office' organization and its staff will have to be recruited and found. Premises will have to be found, professionals retained and fees paid. It will take time for the business to build up and reach break-even. There may quite easily be another £0.5 to £0.75 million at least required in terms of financial resources. One may be able to plan for the possibility that once profitability is achieved the profits may be ploughed back (cashflow permitting) so that the total capital requirement is reduced.

- The financial resources of the area developer will therefore have to be geared up to permit the rapid growth of the required number of outlets so as to obtain the maximum benefit from the rapid saturation of its marketing area and the utilization of the organizational infrastructure which it will be creating, as well as to ensure compliance with the development schedule.

- Given the nature and extent of resources which will be required and the commitment which will have to be undertaken, the area developer will have to be far more experienced in business than an individual unit operator.[2] The selection process and the selection requirements in the case of an area developer will be very different from those which apply to the selection of unit operators. They will also be difficult from those which apply to the selection of a sub-franchisor.

- The fee arrangement in respect of the grant and exploitation of development rights would invariably fall into one or more of the following four categories.

  (a) A lump sum payment to secure the development right to open an agreed number of outlets. This payment, in some cases, may be treated as a payment on account of the initial franchise fees to be paid in respect of each outlet, or it may be a payment totally unrelated to initial franchise fees. (The receipt of such a front-end payment can provide a franchisor with a welcome cash injection but that should never be the main reason for entering into such an agreement.) A franchisor in structuring the fees should bear in mind that the larger the initial fee to be paid the greater the cost to the franchisee in terms of interest and the longer it will take it to reach break-even. The discussion of fees in Chapter 7 has some relevance and should be reviewed.

  (b) An initial franchise fee to be paid on the opening of each outlet at the same rate as applies to individual outlet operations. These may be discounted by an agreed amount to reflect the fact that a lump sum payment has been made for the development rights which are to be exercised over a period.

  (c) Continuing franchise fees.

  (d) Advertising contributions.

  In the case of both of the latter fees the franchisor will normally expect to receive the same as it receives from individual unit operators.

One can expect the developer to claim that the fees should be lower since there will be so many outlets in operation and that since the area developer will have its own management structure, the franchisor will have less to do in return for the fees. Superficially this is an attractive argument and indeed there may be some saving in this respect, but it will more often than not be less of a saving than might be suggested, so the argument is not as one-sided as may be claimed.

A franchisor should on the other hand not expect that it will be able to provide less in the way of services to an area developer than to an individual outlet operator. All the normal range of services will have to be provided, as will periodic visits from field support staff to ensure the maintenance of standards and quality of operation, as well as providing assistance with problems, either on site or at the area developer's central office.

Furthermore, if an area developer encounters problems they will have a greater impact than will be the case with an individual unit operator. The franchisor will find disproportionately heavy demands upon its resources which it may find difficult to cope with economically. A franchisor who has accepted lower fees from a developer and scaled down its support capabilities will be caught out when there are problems. Resources taken on to service the other franchisees paying full fees will have to be diverted to the developer with problems. This leads to a situation in which the other franchisees are in effect subsidizing the area developer. In the case of advertising contributions, an area developer may argue that as in aggregate its contribution is disproportionately high it should have some concession. Of course, compared with any other franchise on a store by store basis the disproportionate claim fails. Any such concession would inevitably mean that those who did not benefit from the concession would be making a proportionately higher contribution to the aggregate spend, which they would resent. Further, it is sometimes argued that part (if not the whole) of the area developer's contributions should be concentrated in its marketing area. This, of course, is what every franchisee would like and, if followed, would result in a loss or watering down of the benefits of co-operative network advertising and promotion.

The fundamental principle that franchisees should be dealt with on an equal and consistent basis must be observed even where there are area developers involved in the network. Special cases make for discontent and resentment and lead to broader problems and conflicts.

While, in theory, it should be easier for the franchisor to control the network operated by an area developer, the reality may well be different. Of course, the area developer will have its own management infrastructure and should want to ensure that all outlets operate the system properly and that full advantage is taken of the opportunities to develop the business. But while the area developer and some of its senior staff may well be extremely well motivated through capital investment and share option schemes, each outlet will be, in fact, under management, and that management has to be provided with the right degree of motivation and subjected to a proper level of supervision.

The franchisor still has a responsibility to ensure that everything which should be done is functioning properly in the developer's head office as well as in the operating units. Care must be taken to ensure that the franchisor is not caught between an area developer's head office, who refers it to a unit which is in need of assistance, and the manager of the outlet, who blames his head office for all the problems at his unit. Unit managers will often resist directions from the franchisor unless his head office agrees and so directs him. This is an issue to be addressed in the area development agreement.

The area developer should have, or will acquire, a broader based local knowledge, extending throughout the whole of his marketing area, which should enable him better to capitalize upon the opportunities. There will be greater scope than exists for individual outlet operations, given the larger area, for a comprehensive saturation of the market place and the benefits from the greater concentration of exposure which will be obtained in the area developer's market area.

The area developer's own business organization should provide substantial back-up to the franchisor's efforts. Since the area developer's presence at each outlet will be staff and not an owner, the need for supervision will be greater and so will the need for constant training and retraining, as well as the recruitment of personnel. The area developer will have to provide these facilities in some respects in addition to the services provided by the franchisor. The area developer will not be replacing the franchisor in the areas of training and supervision, but will be able to provide these services more economically, given his scale of operation, than can each individual outlet operator. The area developer will have to bear in mind that it will need to have these resources available or it may not be able to ensure that it can perform its contractual obligations to the franchisor.

Contractual documents

The franchisor who seeks to benefit from the advantages of offering area development agreements will have to face the burden of complex contractual and structural arrangements. There will invariably be two, and possibly three, contractual documents.

1. **Development agreement**. This will have two distinct aspects. First, it will contain detailed provisions in relation to the development programme and the procedure for selecting, approving and fitting out locations. Second is the detailed infrastructure to be established by the area developer; the area developer will have to undertake certain central obligations in terms of business organization and functions. Its senior staff will have to undergo specific training, and it is likely that the franchisor would require that the person who is appointed managing director (general manager) will have to be approved by the franchisor and to have passed the franchisor's training course. In addition it is not uncommon to find a requirement that the managing director (general manager) should have a minimum equity stake in the business.

2. **Operational unit agreement**. This will usually be on the same basis as that used for individual unit operators, adjusted to avoid unnecessary overlap with the development agreement. The operational unit agreement will be signed when each location is approved, at which time any initial fee applicable to that unit will also be payable.

3. **Funding agreement**. Unless the area developer has considerable resources it is possible that, in addition to the above agreements, there will also be a funding arrangement. Funding may be provided by anyone, ranging from one investor through a syndicate of

investors to a venture capital fund. Apart from the conflict which is at the centre of every franchise arrangement, the involvement of any third party investors creates more scope for conflict and tension. Franchisor and franchisee see a common purpose in their relationship, while a third party funding source will not be viewing the arrangement in the same way as a franchisee. The investor will be looking for a return in terms of income and a capital gain with a secure exit route. It will not necessarily be that interested in the principles of franchising and may expect the franchisor to submit to its demands, which of course the franchisor cannot do. This approach is not uncommon but the investor has to appreciate that the investment is being made in a franchised operation and that such operations are not tailor made to investors' requirements, which could be destructive of the fundamentals of franchising. There is another factor, which is that the franchisor is not in a relationship with the investor at that stage. Indeed, even if the investor proceeds the relationship is likely to be indirect through the investor's shareholding in the franchise. There are two relationships: one between franchisor and franchisee and the other between the franchisee and its investors. The investors have to accept, if they want to invest, that the franchisee is operating as part of a franchise system with which it will have to conform. Depending on the size of the investment it may be necessary to factor in the possibility of the franchisee's shares being listed on a stock exchange to provide the investors or venture fund with an exit route, while not compromising the franchisor's need to protect its interests by having control move to a competitor or its intellectual property (including its confidential information and trade secrets) put at risk. Sometimes the investment is in the area developer's entity itself and sometimes in individual franchised units.

The investors will otherwise have to accept that if dissatisfied with the working partner they may have to convince the franchisor of their case, since the franchisor may consider the partner is doing well. They will also have to accept that any sale of the franchised business (other than a market listing but see above) will require the franchisor's approval.

Structuring the area development agreement

There are a number of issues to be considered.

- What are to be the number and density of the outlets?
- Are exclusive or non-exclusive rights to be granted?
- Will the area developer be limited to opening the number of outlets agreed upon in the contract, or will it be permitted to open more? If so, on what basis?
- What degree of transferability will there be? Will the area developer

be permitted to dispose of his right to develop the area? That would be unusual, as most franchisors would expect an area developer to complete the development schedule before seeking to sell the business. The franchisor is unlikely to want to enter into a development agreement merely to create an asset for the developer to profit commercially from by selling it. The franchisor is essentially seeking a relationship with those who will develop the area and who will have been selected for that purpose. The franchisor would not expect the area developer not to be involved in the crucial development stages of the system, for which purpose he was expressly recruited. Such a course of action would be fraught with problems which may extend beyond the relationship between the franchisor and its developer; they will undoubtedly also involve its investors and venture fund which have put up the funds for the area developer's business. One cannot of course rule out the possibility that pressure for a sale may come from the investors or venture fund who believe they can find a quick profitable exit route or because they are dissatisfied with the returns being achieved.

Would the franchisor really want to permit a change, before the network is fully in position, in the person who has negotiated the development schedule and who is, in reality, the person to whom the franchisor is looking for performance? The break in continuity may prove a stumbling block and the individual may be difficult to replace. A change may also result in difficulty being experienced in meeting the development schedule. The area developer's team of senior executives may well lose interest if the person who recruited and motivated them is to depart before the development phase is complete. On the other hand, those who have provided the financial back-up will not want to be prevented from changing that person if they have lost confidence in his ability to take the business forward effectively (the possibility of the conflict arising between franchisor and investor in this scenario has already been mentioned). These are all difficult matters which will have to be considered and for which common ground will have to be found in the course of negotiations.

Again, it is necessary to emphasize that in structuring these arrangements, the fundamental features and requirements of a franchise transaction must be maintained no matter what pressure the area developer and its funding sources try to impose. Once the integrity of the franchise concept and system is undermined, the future development of the franchise is put at risk. As is the case with individual outlet operations where uniformity of treatment is essential, so it is with area developers – once the format for dealing with area developers is established it should remain the same for them all.

To what extent will the area developer be permitted to dispose of individual units without affecting the development obligations and on what conditions? Bear in mind that each unit operated by the area developer should be on the same contractual basis as those operated by individual franchisees. The issue is not whether the area developer can sell individual units, but whether it can do so before it has fully developed the schedule (as required by the contract), or if it does so thereafter, must it replace the outlet sold with another? If so, on what terms? It should be borne in mind that if a developer can develop and then sell units without restraint the franchisor will end up with large numbers of single unit franchisees rather than few, developing each with many units. The franchisor must be able to remain in control of what category of franchisees and structure it wants.

The issue of the possible advisable closure of a non-performing unit will also need to be considered. There may be many reasons for non-performance, which include a site selection error of judgement, redevelopment in the area, parking restrictions or reorganization of traffic flows.

When one considers the problem of termination of these arrangements, the position becomes even more difficult. There are three possible arrangements to terminate: (a) the development right, (b) the whole agreement, and (c) individual outlet agreements. Let us consider each in turn.

The development right. One would normally expect this right to be capable of termination in the event of a failure to perform the development schedule. But there may be a range of options to consider. If the area developer has exclusive rights should it merely lose its exclusivity? Whether or not it has exclusive rights, should it lose the right to continue to exploit the development schedule in the future? If so, are there ways in which it might be able to protect itself against a slower rate of progress than the parties had planned and the developer had committed to? These are issues which must be considered.

One should remember that the franchisor will attach great importance to the maintenance of the development schedule and may feel that the failure to do so would operate too much to the detriment of the development of the network in the target territory. Whichever way the franchisor decides to approach the problem there is no clear answer. At worst the franchisor would have parallel systems being operated by the original area developer and one subsequently appointed. The practical problems which can arise in such circumstances where there are in essence two developers, within a given territory, may lead some franchisors to require that the defaulting developer should be capable of being terminated for a failure to sustain the development schedule. (There is discussion of this issue in relation to master franchise agreements later in this chapter).

The whole agreement. This would apply where there is failure by the developer to observe and perform the 'non-development right' provisions in the development agreement, i.e. the detailed infrastructure referred to earlier (see above under the development agreement). One would normally expect that such failure would not lead to termination unless the developer had been given an opportunity to put matters right. However, given that despite warnings and in the face of a failure to remedy the default, the franchisor terminates the agreement, one would expect such termination to bring the development agreement to an end, including the development right. This would have to be the case, since if the general provisions relating to the area developer's business structure are ignored it would be futile to permit it to continue to develop by opening further outlets. Similarly, such a breach would also be expected to lead to a position where the individual outlet agreements would also be capable of being terminated, since the business structure, designed to provide the basis for the supervision and control of those outlets, would not be in existence. The franchisor would also find that it had a direct contractual relationship with the individual units, but the unit agreements will have been prepared on the basis that the development agreement was to be in existence. The unit agreements in these circumstances may well not be sufficiently complete, which requires a renegotiation and a reappraisal by the franchisor of its strategies for those units.

Individual unit agreements. One might expect that there could be problems with the operation of individual units, which could lead to termination of the agreement relating to such a unit. Whether or not that termination should affect the main agreement must depend upon:

- why the agreement is terminated;
- how many of such agreements are terminated within any given period of time;
- whether or not the breach of the individual unit agreement involved a sufficiently serious breach of the main agreement.

Consequences of termination. One then has to consider what should be the consequences of termination of each of these three agreements.

- Would the loss of the development right affect the continued operation of the individual outlets then in operation, and if not can the developer still apply to open new outlets, but independently of the development arrangement? What would be the consequences if it did?
- If the whole of the development agreement is terminated, should the individual unit agreements also be in jeopardy (see above)?
- One would also expect that all the normal consequences of termination of a franchise agreement would be equally applicable. In cases where the franchisor has an option to purchase on termination, the scale of the business to be purchased could cause problems for it because the amount of the money involved could be considerable, particularly if there is a premium value in the real estate occupied by the developer for the purposes of the business.

A franchisor would need to develop a strategy for coping with such an issue before finalizing the documentation so that it has the necessary contractual options in place.

Further considerations

So much for the complexity of the contractual and structural arrangements, but there are other important issues for the franchisor to consider when entering into area development agreements. Some have been raised already but they are important enough to warrant inclusion in a summary of this nature.

- Entry into development agreements has to be handled with great care so that a proper balance of power is maintained between the franchisor and his franchisees. A franchisor with, say, four area developers covering the whole of the UK and with no other franchisees is clearly vulnerable to challenge. Each of the area developers will represent a substantial part of the franchise, and if two or more 'gang up' on the franchisor it could be in great difficulties unless it has considerable resources. A franchisor should, therefore, never structure its arrangements so that it is creating a franchisee network where the franchisees or a small group of franchisees could have such power that it is at a serious disadvantage. A balance must be maintained between single unit operators (or company-owned units) and area developers so that the franchisor has a powerful business base from which it can operate without a threat with which it cannot cope through lack of resources and the ability to manoeuvre.

- Having chosen to select area development as an expansion method, a franchisor is committing itself to that one franchisee to exploit an area and open a number of outlets, consistent with the size of the area. If the area developer does not proceed at the agreed rate of openings, then the growth of the franchisor's network will be inhibited. It may be difficult later on to regain the impetus and put the network back on course.

- If an area developer proves unable to cope, the problems for the franchisor will be that much greater, depending upon the size of the area developer's operation at the time when the problems arise. Dealing with individual unit operations which experience difficulties will always be part of life for the franchisor, but normally those operators will only represent a small percentage of his network. Dealing with the area developer whose operation has gone sour will probably involve all the area developer's outlets, which in aggregate will be a larger percentage of the whole network, and these problems will have to be coped with in addition to the normal volume of problem cases from individual unit operators.

- These factors emphasize the need to ensure that the developer's management team is of the right quality (see also below).

- The existence of a large organization as a franchisee, with the likely transient nature of its employees, makes it more difficult for the franchisor to protect the spread of its know-how and confidential information. Care will have to be taken by the franchisor to ensure that the correct steps are introduced to protect its know-how and confidential information from unauthorized exploitation by competitors.

- The elements of motivation and incentive at operational unit level, which are important fundamental features of franchising, are considerably diminished because the outlets are operated not by franchisees but by managers. The supervisory ability of the area developer's management team and the existence of incentive schemes are, of course, valuable aids to the solution of this problem. It is, therefore, vital that a way is found to provide incentives and motivation at outlet level, as well as training and operational supervision, and to encourage the stability and long-term loyalty of the management staff. This is an issue particularly where increasingly one finds franchisees with multiple operating units – some even large enough to obtain stock exchange listings. This is found most frequently in the USA. These franchisees with stock exchange listings have additional pressures which can feed back to and put pressure on the franchisor arising from investors' expectations of capital and income. The franchisee is still restricted, even though listed, to operating its business as laid down by the franchisor. These pressures can put the relationship between franchisor and franchisee under great stress

- The introduction by the development agreement system of a layer of management between the franchisor and the operational unit staff can create difficulties. The franchisor must be in the position of being allowed to intervene at the operational unit level if standards are not maintained.

Area development arrangements present challenges as well as benefits. However, the issues which they raise also have relevance in other 'multiple franchisee' arrangements, such as situations in which a franchisee through his ambition and ability becomes the owner and operator of a significant number of operational outlets. Where a franchisee is permitted to develop his business in this way, the franchisor should consider whether an umbrella agreement is necessary once the number of outlets reaches a certain size.

Master franchise agreements

Before considering the provisions which one can expect to find in an international master franchise agreement, it is advisable to delineate the functions and purposes of the arrangement as well as the consequential requirements.

The master franchise agreement will reflect the commercial bargain which has been struck by the franchisor with the sub-franchisor to:

- introduce the franchisor's system to the target territory;
- evaluate the viability of the franchisor's system in the target territory;
- equip the sub-franchisor to become the 'franchisor' in the target territory;
- develop the growth of the franchisor's system in the target territory;
- result in the sub-franchisor providing the full range of the franchisor's ongoing services to sub-franchisees in the target territory.

It should be understood that in these transactions the aspirations of the parties and balance of negotiating power will vary from case to case, as will the skills, financial resources, knowledge and experience of the prospective sub-franchisor.

Negotiations for these agreements are prone to failure for the following reasons.

- The franchisor's initial fee requirements require the payment of a sum which bears no resemblance to the reality of the prospects for the business in the territory or the value of the services and know-how which are being provided.
- The franchisor requires payment of too high a proportion of the unit operations and continuing franchise fees which sub-franchisees will be paying to the sub-franchisor.
- The prospective sub-franchisor (and this is particularly the case where it is a large company) cannot come to terms with the conceptual issues involved in franchising on this basis and the controls to which it will inevitably be subjected. Whatever the nature of the agreement, the fundamentals of franchising do not change and cannot be compromised, however much of a culture shock they may be for the prospective sub-franchisor.
- The prospective sub-franchisor has underestimated the capital requirement and the time frame involved before the operation will generate profits.
- The franchisor will not accept the need to consider if, how and to what extent the system and manuals require adjustment to the business, legal and other relevant factors (including the market realities) which are to be found in the target territory.

Structure of the master franchise agreement

The master franchise agreement will have to accommodate the issues which the commercial discussions will have confronted. In many of these issues, there is no such thing as the right answer, since these agreements, unlike unit agreements, are all negotiated.[3]

However, the fundamental principles must remain, as is the case throughout all franchise transactions. It is necessary to emphasize, yet again, that in structuring these arrangements the fundamental features, characteristics and requirements of a franchise transaction must be maintained. Once the integrity of the franchised concept and the system is undermined the future development of the franchise is put at risk.

The main issues to be dealt with in negotiating and preparing master franchise agreements are as follows:

1. The rights to be granted and the term.
2. Territory.
3. Exclusivity.
4. Performance schedule, piloting, adapting the system.
5. Franchise fees.
6. Withholding tax and gross-up provisions.
7. Training.
8. Advertising.
9. Trade marks and other industrial and intellectual property.
10. Sale of the sub-franchisor's business.
11. Protection against misuse of know-how and unfair competition.
12. Default issues.
13. Post-termination consequences and requirements.
14. Choice of law and forum.
15. The nature of the sub-franchise agreement the sub-franchisor will have.

We shall now look at each of these subjects in turn.

1 The rights to be granted and the term

These will always include the use of the franchisor's trade marks, service marks, trade names, know-how, confidential information, copyright material and all the usual elements which one finds in franchise transactions. The nature and extent of the rights, and the obligations attached to them, are dealt with separately later in this chapter. The length of the term for which the rights are granted must also be specified.

The agreement of the length of the term does not usually present too many problems in negotiation. However, the author has seen drafts with what is clearly an unrealistic five-year term proposed. Since the nature of the transaction involves establishing the sub-franchisor as the franchisor in the target territory with a corresponding investment, the longer the term, the greater the opportunity to develop the territory properly. With a five-year term, in many cases a sub-franchisor would have a shorter term available to him than the sub-franchisees would expect. That is clearly unworkable when one considers how long it can take to:

- train the sub-franchisor;
- find the first location or open the first outlet;
- pilot-test the first outlet (pilot-testing may involve more than one outlet);
- reproduce with agreed amendments local operational manuals with any necessary translations;
- recruit and establish the first franchisees.

There will not be much of a five-year term remaining after all that is achieved.

The clauses in the contract which will deal with these issues will have to recognize and cope with the problems involved in the grant by the sub-franchisor of a longer term to sub-franchisees than the sub-franchisor has left under its agreement. This can happen sooner rather than later if the sub-franchise agreements are for a ten-year term since any sub-franchise agreement granted after 15 years where the master franchise agreement is for 25 years will create a problem unless the issue is dealt with properly in the master franchise agreement. The more realistic terms are from 25 to 50 years with rights of renewal. The safeguards for the franchisor will be in the performance criteria which are laid down for the development of the network and the control mechanisms and their enforcement should it become necessary. The length of the agreement takes not only the above issues into account, but also the need to provide the sub-franchisor with the opportunity to get a return on his investment which makes it worthwhile, as well as the opportunity, having built a business successfully, to sell it and obtain the benefits of the value of the end product.

Assuming that it is agreed that the sub-franchisor should have a right of renewal, there will be the normal issues to consider. In what circumstances should the right of renewal be denied? On what terms should it be granted? Will there be scope for the franchisor to introduce changes to the contractual terms? It is common in unit franchises to provide that on renewal the franchisee and the franchisor will enter into the form of franchise agreement being offered by the franchisor at the time of renewal. Since master franchise agreements are individually negotiated, a more flexible approach needs to be found in such cases. One must bear in mind the likely time scale, since the original master franchise agreement was entered into. Indeed, over the lengthy period for which a master franchise agreement exists there will probably be changes in the applicable laws to which the parties may be obliged to respond and reflect in amendments to their agreement.

Will any charge be made for the extended rights which are to be granted, and if so how will the charge be calculated? Leaving it to be negotiated at the time the right is exercised could effectively leave the sub-franchisor with no rights at all, since if the charge cannot be agreed there could be no contract. What will be provided for as the ongoing development schedule? How will one cope with changes over the years in the method of exploitation of the franchised business, e.g. one could find larger regional franchise units with satellite operations instead of smaller stand-alone units. As many development schedules are created with 'today's' system in mind, such changes can make a nonsense of the development schedule. The number of outlets which are required by the schedule to be opened and kept in operation become obsolete and there could be a breach of the contract, though turnover may be enhanced using the new formula. An issue of this nature emphasizes the need for the parties with a long-term agreement to recognize how important it is to be flexible.

2 Territory

As is the case with operators of individual units who seek the comfort of territorial rights, most sub-franchisors also seek the widest possible territorial rights. In agreeing the extent of the territory to be exploited by the sub-franchisor, regard clearly has to be paid to the franchisor's overall international marketing strategy and how each of the individual sub-franchisors will fit into the pattern of that strategy.

Ideally, the territory should be one in which the sub-franchisor has the knowledge, experience and capacity to cope. One of the reasons already stated for master franchise agreements is to have the sub-franchisor stand in the shoes of the franchisor in relation to the market place. It somewhat defeats the objective of the exercise if territories are granted of such a nature and/or extent that the sub-franchisor is not capable of achieving proper exploitation. The question of exploitation and the degree of exploitation will be dealt with later, under the heading of performance schedules.

Care should be taken not to add on a nearby territory merely because the sub-franchisor wants it or because it is geographically close. This can have the effect of sterilizing an area. In the past, this has sometimes been the case in Australasia, where Australian sub-franchisors commonly asked for the rights to New Zealand to be included and often succeeded in obtaining them. However, New Zealand is a long way from Australia. It is a different market and it was neglected. There are other areas where a similar approach is adopted by some would be sub-franchisors, of which a classic example is the whole of the Middle East.

3 Exclusivity

Most sub-franchisors expect to have exclusive rights to the agreed territory. This enables them to invest with the comfort of knowing that they are investing in a market in which they will be the sole exploiters of the opportunity. Exclusivity is normally tied to performance criteria and can be lost if these criteria are not met. This can lead to practical problems if one has a network which is being developed by a sub-franchisor who fails after a period of time to meet the performance schedules.

The consequences of such failure need to be carefully thought through since they will have a critical effect on the future of the network in that territory. Many sub-franchisors would consider the franchisor to be behaving extremely unfairly if the whole contract were to be terminated. Many might say that loss of exclusive rights merely because there is perhaps a temporary hiccup, which can be attributed to economic circumstances, resulting in a shortage of prospective franchisees or unavailability of suitable premises, is a harsh and unjust outcome for a sub-franchisor which is otherwise performing its obligations.

Terms can sometimes be negotiated to provide for a sub-franchisor, who expresses these concerns, to make payments to the franchisor to compensate it for the loss of revenue by the non-achievement of the performance schedule in cases where the sub-franchisor wishes to preserve his position. This method is only a temporary expedient and does not necessarily compensate the franchisor for the fact that there has been a loss of impetus, unless, of course, it can be recovered later.

In practical terms, the mere loss of exclusivity without the loss of the continuing right to grant further sub-franchises could result in parallel networks being operated – one by the sub-franchisor, and the other by the franchisor or by another sub-franchisor (recruited by the franchisor to replace the one in default). This is also the practical effect which occurs when the sub-franchisor loses not only exclusivity but also the continuing right to grant sub-franchises. The presence of two sub-franchisors in a market will also create other difficulties:

- The two networks may result in two different sets of standards. Indeed, the first sub-franchisor whose development rights have been restricted may not be as sensitive to the need to keep standards high.
- If a sub-franchisee of the first sub-franchisor is to move premises for reasons beyond its control it may need to encroach on the catchment area or territory of a sub-franchisee of the new sub-franchisor.
- It may be difficult to achieve cooperation between the two sub-franchisors in advertising and marketing activities.
- The prospective sub-franchisees of the new sub-franchisor may be more difficult to recruit, since they will know that the first sub-franchisor's rights were terminated and its sub-franchisees may well deter such prospective sub-franchisees.

The likelihood of one or all of these problems arising means that careful consideration has to be given to the issues. In many cases franchisors favour the clean break and so invariably would the new sub-franchisor. Indeed, the continual presence of the first sub-franchisor could well inhibit interest from other prospective sub-franchisors.

4 Performance schedule

The agreement of a performance schedule which sets out the projected annual and cumulative rates of growth of the network in the targeted territory is a common feature of these agreements. Indeed, without it, the franchisor would not have the confidence that a commitment exists which can result in the proper exploitation of the territory. Unless a sub-franchisor is prepared to accept a realistic performance schedule for the establishment of operational units, the master franchise route can lose some of its attractions. Where exclusive rights are granted the performance schedule is obviously of great importance because this is the franchisor's insurance policy against under-exploitation.

There are practical difficulties in establishing performance schedules. It may not be possible at the time the contract is being negotiated to have an accurate idea, or sufficiently accurate knowledge, to enable the parties to judge what would be a realistic achievable rate of expansion. One thing that is certain is that the franchisor's requirements are likely to be very bullish, while the sub-franchisor's expectations will tend to be more modest. However, most sub-franchisors will prepare business plans in the process of deciding whether or not to take the opportunity on board and these must include some assessment of the growth rate which the business is capable of achieving. Without this, the sub-franchisor would not be able to make a balanced business judgement about whether or not to go into the proposition, and the level of resources which would need to be committed to it. Regular updating of such business plans can help the parties better to judge performance and to take into account market trends and economic dips and surges which could affect the realistic rate of growth which the sub-franchisor should be able to achieve.

Furthermore, one has to consider the transition from the way in which the business is conducted in its country of origin to what is required in the target territory. A number of differences may have to be recognized, considered and resolved before one can be certain that the concept actually works and has been 'fine-tuned' so that it meets the requirements of the market place in the target territory. The variations required may be slight, they may be subtle, they may be fundamental, but whatever the category they can have a sufficiently significant effect on operations to make the difference between success and failure.

To identify what is required usually requires the establishment of one or more operations (pilot operations) to achieve the necessary degree of knowledge and to demonstrate to would-be sub-franchisees in the target county that there indeed is a business which has been proved successful in the new market place. The experience so obtained of the market place can determine whether the development schedule which has been agreed will be effective, or whether it is in need of change by mutual agreement to reflect the reality which has become apparent. Indeed, the sub-franchisor may conclude that it does not wish to continue in the light of the results obtained in the market place from the operation of the pilot units. The master franchise agreement has to be sufficiently flexible to accommodate the practical realization of the parties' expectations. There will also be the issues of who will bear the cost and run the risk of establishing and running the pilot operations.

As far as the piloting is concerned, the franchisor must be sufficiently receptive to suggestions and face up to the need to recognize that there are differences. They are likely to be people related; attitudes will be different; social and cultural attitudes may have an effect. The ultimate outcome may not result in the franchisor compromising the way in which the basic business is operated. The changes may have to be made in marketing methods, staff recruitment, training, management, accounting and procedural methods.

There may be different business flows during the course of the opening hours. This could result in the outlet being busy in the target territory at different times of day from those which are most popular in the original territory. This can affect staff numbers and schedules. This may mean that not enough business is generated overall to make the business in the current form a viable proposition. This will require experimentation in order to resolve the problems and gear up the business to be successful in the target territory. It may also require changes in product mix, introducing local products which are consistent with the system's overall offering.

All franchisors will use the existing operating manual as their starting point. How much change will be necessary will depend upon the nature, range and scope of the manual's coverage. If, for example, it deals in detail with the hiring and firing of staff, with an explanation of the legal issues and procedures, this will need to be changed for use in the target territory.

After the initial shock to the franchisor and its system has been overcome, it will be necessary for both franchisor and sub-franchisor to liaise with regard to the future development of the system in the target country. The franchisor's development of its system in the country will have to be shared with the sub-franchisor; the sub-franchisor's response and input must be considered and appropriate changes introduced.

The franchisor will always wish to retain control over whatever changes are made to the manuals and system in the target territory. The franchisor will also require that the copyright and ownership of the manuals (including translations) and the system are retained by it.

The provisions in the contract have to be drafted to allow sufficient flexibility to:

- leave the franchisor with control, but
- provide for the cooperation which will be necessitated by the requirement to allow the business to develop as the years pass.

Part of this aspect of the matter will include developing the operational franchise agreement into which the sub-franchisor will enter with sub-franchisees.

Normally, the franchisor will start with the form it uses in its domestic operations and try to keep to it as far as possible. This is often not possible since legal systems differ (common law versus civil law), as does the terminology and the approach adopted to certain issues, e.g. corporate law, real estate law and competition (anti-trust) law.

The important issue for many franchisors is to ensure that contractual requirements can, in substance, be enforced in the target territory. The franchisor will always want to have the ultimate control over the form and text of the operational agreements which are so crucial in protecting its name, reputation, trade marks, service marks, know-how and systems. The franchisor will also wish to have confidence in the operational agreements it may inherit on termination.

Agreement will have to be reached about how much continuing support will be provided by the franchisor to the sub-franchisor and whether this is included in the fees payable or will have to be paid for separately.

How the parties initially come into contact with each other will also have a bearing on the negotiations, as there are many instances in which the prospective sub-franchisor, having seen a business in another country, makes a judgement that the concept will undoubtedly succeed in his own country and subsequently approaches the franchisor for the master franchise rights. Many large and well known multinational franchisors find that they have many would be sub-franchisors and franchisees approach them. Lesser franchise systems have to work to obtain leads. The enthusiasm by a prospective sub-franchisor or franchisee who approaches a franchisor should not result in the franchisor accepting him without question. Great care has to be taken in selecting sub-franchisors. It must be understood that they are expected not to open only one operational unit but fully to develop the market and to adopt the role of franchisor in the target country. For a franchisor venturing abroad for the first time this means that it is looking for a different calibre of franchisee from those with whom it has so far dealt. For those who do not franchise in their own country and for whom the selection of a franchisee is a novel experience there may in reality be no difference since neither type of franchisor will have had relevant experience. The greatest caution must be exercised, since the cost of making a mistake could be extremely significant. The decision must not be rushed and, however impatient the franchisor may be to get on with it, it must always, right up to the point of agreeing everything, be capable of withdrawing unless it is absolutely certain that the sub-franchisor has the necessary qualities and resources.

5 Franchise fees

See 'International financial considerations' below.

6 Withholding tax and grossing-up provision

See 'International financial considerations' below.

7 Training

Training of a sub-franchisor should go beyond training in the running of an operational unit. The sub-franchisor needs training and assistance in how to be a franchisor. To do this one needs to examine the range of services which the sub-franchisor needs to provide and to educate the sub-franchisor in those areas. This is important to the arrangement, for without them the sub-franchisor would not be able to maximize the benefits to be obtained from the franchisor's experience. While sub-franchisors are trained in how to run an operational unit, it is rare to find a franchisor which provides training in how to be a franchisor. It is also rare to find a manual which is provided to a sub-franchisor focused on how to be a franchisor. The areas in which the sub-franchisor will need assistance will include:

- Site assessment, evaluation and choice. The franchisor will not have the detailed knowledge in the target territory of premises and the market, which is possessed by the sub-franchisor, but it will know the type and size of premises required for the concept's equipment and furnishings. There may also be some common criteria for the evaluation of sites which may emerge. Some franchisors reserve to themselves the right to approve premises but this is often impracticable and the franchisor will rarely have the know-how to be able to make the decision at long distance. Where the demand for premises is high, the franchisor may not be able to respond quickly enough to enable the sub-franchisor to secure the premises.

- Use of plans and specifications and the way in which they have to be adapted for use in the territory so as to ensure that they comply with local construction laws and building codes and accommodate the franchised business.

- Providing the sub-franchisor with operational assistance:

  (a) in developing the pilot operation on the commencement of the business, and

  (b) on an ongoing basis to help to monitor performance and offer advice.

- The preparation of criteria for the selection of sub-franchisees. The franchisor cannot expect to be involved in the recruitment and selection of sub-franchisees, but it may have some valuable guidance to offer to the sub-franchisor on selection methods. It may assist in the selection of some of the early recruits to the network. As is the case with premises, some franchisors seem to reserve to themselves the right to approve prospective sub-franchisees. This is equally impracticable. It should be noted that a franchisor who does have these rights can, by refusing approval of premises and/or franchises, prevent the sub-franchisor from achieving the development schedule.

- The selection and approval of suppliers may be an important feature of the franchise. The franchisor will need to help the sub-franchisor to identify suppliers and the criteria to be applied in their selection. If the franchisor has products which are to be sold by sub-franchisees and which are fundamental or products for which a proprietary specification exists or there are secret formulae (e.g. recipes in fast food), the franchisor may, if it cannot supply at reasonable prices from its country, have to grant rights to manufacturers to produce the products to the franchisor's specifications in the target country to enable the franchisor's trade mark to be affixed. Indeed, many franchisors seek to achieve local suppliers of products.

- The provision of marketing, promotional and advertising materials used in the territory of origin, which may be useful in the target territory. Language and regulatory requirements can restrict the usefulness of such materials.
- Access to the ongoing research and development which the franchisor may be conducting. Local market research and testing may be necessary.
- The ability to participate in franchisee seminars and franchisee get-togethers organized by the franchisor.

The degree of formal training support will, of course, vary from case to case. However, many franchisors find it sensible, particularly in the early stages, to ensure that both the sub-franchisor's staff and the sub-franchisees and their staff are trained at the franchisor's domestic training facility. There are many who find that the quality of training at the domestic base just cannot be reproduced and, even though there have to be changes to accommodate local requirements, this degree of training is essential:

- it provides an in-depth orientation coupled with visits to operating units which cannot be provided elsewhere;
- one would expect that the contract would contain the details of how, and how many of, the sub-franchisor's team will be trained.

In appropriate cases, the franchisor may provide an opening crew for the first few units which are established in the target territory. This crew will provide on-site training for the sub-franchisor's staff. Normally, the cost of training is included in the front end fee but there are also those who charge separately for such training. The sub-franchisor and its sub-franchisees would in any event be expected to pay all their expenses relating to getting to and from the training location, their subsistence and other expenses which may be incurred during the provision of the training.

The intensity of training and support which is given during the piloting stage in the target country can be quite high, depending on how complex and extensive are the operational requirements. The agreement may provide for the sub-franchisor to establish its own training facilities in the course of time, and for the franchisor to provide the necessary back-up and training aids to enable this to be done.

8 Advertising

See 'International financial considerations' below.

9 Trade marks and other intellectual property rights

The trade marks, service marks, trade name, goodwill, copyright, know-how, confidential information and other industrial and intellectual property rights should always belong to the franchisor.

The sub-franchisor may have to prepare translations of the operational manuals and other written material, when care should be taken by the franchisor to ensure that the copyright in such translations will belong to him.

The contractual provisions will have to deal with the licensing of these property rights in accordance with the legal requirements of the target country. The sub-franchisor would be expected to control and police the use of these rights by sub-franchisees and to report to the franchisor any infringements which may take place of which it becomes aware. The franchisor would naturally accept responsibility for taking such relevant legal action at its own expense as may be necessary to protect and preserve its intellectual property.

10 Sale of the sub-franchisor's business

The master franchise agreement will contain provisions dealing with the basis upon which the agreement may be assigned and the sub-franchisor's business sold.

The basic principles are the same as those which apply to the sale of a franchised business by a franchisee or a sub-franchisee. No franchisor would want to admit to its network a franchisee who did not meet its selection criteria. The same principle applies in the case of a sub-franchisor However, there are differences to be taken into account without compromising standards because the level of investment will inevitably be much greater, and the skills which the purchaser will require will not be the same as those which are required for the operation of a franchised unit.

A purchaser of a sub-franchisor's business will have to demonstrate not only his financial capacity, but also his ability to understand the franchise system and to manage the business of a sub-franchisor. The basic requirements which will be applied should be specified where possible, as should any conditions which are considered appropriate. The prospective sub-franchisor to be accepted should at the least match up to the franchisor's selection requirements for sub-franchisors.

One should bear in mind the possibility that an interested purchaser could be a competitor with which the franchisor would not wish to deal. The purchaser might also be a large company, which is wishing to expand and diversify its business. In these circumstances, special considerations may have to be given as to how the franchisor's know-how and confidential information can be confined to the franchised business, and not made available elsewhere within the purchaser's organization, or group of companies. Another factor which may need to be considered is that the sub-franchisor's business could become significantly large and it may wish to have the ability to have its shares dealt in a recognized stock exchange. If the sub-franchisor's financing is provided by venture funds or other financial institutions they may require this option as an 'exit route' for their investments. This will raise control of ownership issues which must be dealt with in the master franchise agreement (see more on this above).

It is often provided in master franchise agreements that the sub-franchisor must appoint a managing director, chief executive officer or general manager of its business whom the franchisor must approve and train. It is also sometimes provided that this person should have a minimum equity stake in the business. If business changes hands this requirement will understandably continue and provision should be made in the agreement that the appointment, subject to approval and training, will be made by the purchaser of the sub-franchisor's business.

11 Protection against misuse of know-how and unfair competition

Most countries permit in term prohibitions against competition and post term prohibitions, provided, in the latter case, that the length of time and the area of operation of the restraint are reasonable. Clearly, an investigation has to be made in each territory to ascertain what are the rules, and in this respect, one also has to have regard to competition laws (anti-trust), which increasingly affect these covenants. There are some countries which either do not permit such restraints or which apply narrower principles to their application than is commonly found elsewhere.

It is also relevant to consider the know-how relating to the systems, methods etc. which the franchisor is also entitled to protect. Normally, one could expect a greater degree of protection to be available at law in respect of know-how than would be permitted where non-competition provisions are concerned.

Effective control on the use of know-how can complement a franchisor's protection against unfair advantage being taken by franchisees of what they have learned from a franchisor. One must, however, always be aware of the difficulties in enforcing clauses aimed at protecting know-how. It is often difficult to establish that the know-how is sufficiently secret and confidential to be capable of protection. Copyright as a method of such protection is not entirely satisfactory because it does not protect the substance of the information or the ideas the words convey, only the way in which it is expressed.

In the EU, the competition (anti-trust) laws have been held by the European Court of Justice to apply to franchising. Exemption is, however, available for franchise agreements, provided that they comply with the terms of a regulation which (among other things) establishes the basis and parameters for the protection of know-how, and in term and post term restrictions on competition. This regulation has to be taken into account within EU member states. There are also anti-trust laws in the member states of the EU which have national rather than pan-European effect. These can also affect the scope and extent of the protection available (these issues are discussed in Chapter 10).

12 Default issues

One of the difficulties for a franchisor in master franchise arrangements is that it is no longer in a position to exercise day-to-day control of the operations of the franchised units. It is therefore crucial to the franchisor that the sub-franchisor monitors and controls the quality and standards which are achieved by its sub-franchisees. It is appreciated that the sub-franchisees are trading, using the franchisor's know-how and systems, and are benefiting from the goodwill associated with the name.

The franchisor runs the risk of events occurring which are adverse to its interests and it may not learn that there is a problem until it has become a big problem. The sub-franchisor as the custodian of those interests in his territory has to recognize its responsibility. Provision should be made in the agreement for the policing of those standards by the sub-franchisor, but if it fails to do so, the franchisor has to have remedies. These would obviously be built into the default provisions in the contract.

One often finds attempts are made to introduce into contracts wording formulae, using expressions such as 'material or substantial defaults', but these are often difficult to interpret. In the absence of any proper explanation of what the expression means, what a franchisor regards as 'material or substantial' a sub-franchisor may not regard as being so 'material or substantial', and how a court would determine the dispute could be open to question. What is certain is that a franchisor who believes that the correct standards are not being observed needs to have access to rapid remedies and not to be locked into a lengthy lawsuit while a judge decides whether he thinks the default is sufficiently serious.

It is advisable if one is minded to use an expression, such as 'material default', to have a precise definition, which may, for example, describe it as 'any default under the agreement of which the franchisor has given notice to the sub-franchisor to cure and which remains uncured after a fixed period of time', which depending on its nature may be as much as 30 or 60 days or in a food operation much less where health hygiene and safety issues are concerned.

Money defaults will usually be treated more seriously by franchisors with a shorter period of notice. Quality control defaults may need a longer period in order for the default to be put right, because it may involve the sub-franchisor taking action and enforcing rights against sub-franchisees.

The failure by the sub-franchisor to ensure that its sub-franchisees comply with the terms of their contracts is a serious issue, but one which may require reasonable time to cure. The problems may also not always best be solved by requiring the sub-franchisor to undertake legal proceedings. The solution of operational problems leading to a lowering of standards can often be dealt with by direct discussion and persuasion, rather than by resorting to law. The parties must acknowledge that there are a wide range of methods available to cope with these problems. Ultimately, of course, the franchisor must be able to bring matters to a head to protect its interests. The franchisor may well be influenced in what course of action it wishes to adopt by what the sub-franchisor did or failed to do which caused or allowed the breach complained of to occur.

There will, as in most commercial agreements, be provision for termination in the event of insolvency, bankruptcy or liquidation of the sub-franchisor.

Consideration must be given to whether the sub-franchisor is to have the right to terminate the agreement, and in what circumstances. In some cases, the sub-franchisor is given the right to terminate in the event of the insolvency, bankruptcy or liquidation of the franchisor. It is comparatively rare to find that the sub-franchisor has a contractual right to terminate.

13 Post-termination consequences

The consequences of termination are usually drastic. In brief terms, one would expect that the sub-franchisor will lose the right to continue to offer or operate the franchise, will have to de-identify his business and will be bound by effective post-term restraints on competition and the use of the franchisor's know-how.

There are other considerations and one of the most important is, of course, what is to happen to the network of sub-franchisees.

- Will the sub-franchise agreements survive the termination of the master franchise agreement?
- Will the franchisor be entitled to take them over?
- Will the franchisor be obliged to take them over?
- Will the sub-franchisor be able to make a virtue out of termination and claim payment of a sum of money by way of 'compensation' for 'the take-over of its business'?
- Will the franchisor, now that it has terminated the sub-franchisor for good cause, want to take over what could be a badly run network of disgruntled sub-franchisees, who are intent on making difficulties, and be faced with considerable expense to put the business right? Rather than the sub-franchisor expecting to be paid something (as mentioned above) should it, on the contrary, be liable to pay the franchisor for the costs the latter will have to face in coping with the problems which it will inherit?
- What is to happen to any real estate (including freeholds and/or leases) which the sub-franchisor has acquired for leasing or subleasing to the sub-franchisees, and which may have a capital value which the franchisor cannot afford to pay? The thought that a bitter terminated sub-franchisor could be the landlord of the sub-franchisees does not bear thinking about. The franchisor should take steps in structuring the contract to avoid this.

The issue of whether the master franchise agreement should terminate as a whole if the development schedule is not maintained has been touched upon earlier.

What should be the consequences for the sub-franchisor and its network if it has a contractual right to terminate which it exercises? Should the sub-franchisor be entitled to continue as before, using to the full the franchisor's intellectual property rights, including the name and know-how, and, if so, on what basis? Is it right that the sub-franchisor may have to run the risk of losing its business when the franchisor is at fault, whether the fault arises voluntarily or involuntarily? Given the obligations of the franchisor in the particular agreement should the failure by the franchisor to perform any or all of them be fatal to the agreement, given the continuing ability of the sub-franchisor to use the intellectual property and other rights?

The issues are many and varied, and the list provided is far from complete, but it will serve to indicate the complexity of this particular subject and the substantive issues with which the parties are confronted when negotiating. The ultimate problem is that no one can say that any particular outcome is the right solution. The right solution in any negotiation is what the parties agree to after their negotiations, having fully considered the potential impact of what they have agreed. If they get it wrong they may come to regret their decisions – so they must be ultra cautious.

14 Choice of law and forum

All contracts really should specify the law to be applied to the contract, and the venue for the resolution of disputes. Consideration should also be given to whether the parties wish to have disputes referred, or capable of being referred, to arbitration. The recent development of alternative dispute resolution, which is a form of mediation, may also be considered.

The choice of law is a difficult decision and affected by many considerations. There is a spectrum ranging from countries which respect the contracting parties' choice of law to those which will not enforce a foreign law contract against their own nationals. Franchising arrangements involve some legal requirements which cannot be contracted out of.

- In most countries the courts will not enforce 'public policy issues' provisions in contracts in accordance with foreign laws. Restrictive covenants, competition law and exchange controls are the type of provisions which fall into this category.
- The treatment of intellectual property rights, which the sub-franchisee is licensed to use, will fail to be dealt with under the law of the country in which the business operates. The laws of State A where the franchisor is based relating to trade marks would not affect the treatment of trade marks in State B where the sub-franchisee is carrying on business. There are also other laws

created by statute in the country in which the business is conducted which cannot be avoided and which can impact the rights of the parties.

- Another factor to be borne in mind is that the sub-franchise agreements would undoubtedly be subject to the law of the country in which the sub-franchisee is operating. There may well be legal difficulties in having the master franchise agreement (out of which all sub-franchise rights are granted) governed by a different legal system from that which governs the contracts for the operational units.

- The choice of forum will depend on a number of considerations, not the least of which is whether the courts in the country of choice of law dispense justice fairly. There are countries in which judges are bribed and there are some in which foreign franchisors may find it difficult to win against local nationals. The choice of law does not commit the parties to use the courts of that country. The issue is whether the judgment, obtained in whichever country provides the forum, can be enforced effectively against the other party in the country in which it carries on business or has assets sufficient to discharge its liability.

- The subject is too wide and too legally complex to be given fuller treatment in a work of this nature. It is necessary to obtain legal advice which will take into account the issues raised and the existence of treaties for the enforcement of arbitration awards and court judgements.

15 The nature of the sub-franchise agreement the sub-franchisor will have

Most franchisors would expect the sub-franchise agreement to follow the same pattern and contents as the agreement which it uses in its country of origin as far as the local laws do not impact its enforcement.

Co-branding

Another technique which is being increasingly used in the USA and spreading elsewhere is that described as co-branding. This has potential in domestic as well as international franchising.

This is where the same franchisee operates a number of complementary franchises from the same premises. An example which illustrates the technique would be a franchisee with, say, three different fast food franchises each with a service counter and a common area for sitting and eating, similar to a mini food hall in a shopping mall. With increasing cost and scarcity of accommodation in city areas the technique may have some appeal. This technique is not limited to franchising. Owners of different trading brands may find that it will bring benefits to their businesses.

There are a number of variations which are capable of being considered.

1. Two franchisors from Country A go together to Country B to franchise to:
   (a) one franchisee who will operate both franchise systems in one facility; or
   (b) two individual franchisees in one facility each operating one of the franchise systems.
2. One franchisor from Country A enters the market in Country B where it will franchise to the franchisees of an existing Country B franchisor.
3. One franchisor from Country A enters the market in Country B where it will franchise to a company to operate its system through the company-owned network (this could equally apply where the company based in Country B has a global company-owned network).
4. Two franchisors from Country A and Country B go to Country C where they and a Country C franchisor franchise to:
   (a) one franchisee who will operate all their franchising systems in one facility; or
   (b) three franchisees in one facility one for each franchise system.

   (This scenario could equally apply where one franchisee with three brands enters country C from country A.)
5. A franchisor in Country A does a deal with a franchisor either in Country A or elsewhere which has a system with franchisees across the world for those franchisees to operate the other franchisor's system in their outlets.
6. Two franchisors in the same country do a deal to co-brand their systems wherever in the world they chose to operate.

All these arrangements envisage that, whatever combination of franchise systems and franchisees, they will result in two or more branded businesses being operated from the same premises by one or more franchisees.

However, there are pitfalls in such an arrangement which all franchisors and franchisees must consider. There are two ways in which the arrangement can be structured. In the first the physical facility would be occupied by different franchisees who would each occupy part of the premises under franchise from different franchisors. This type of arrangement presents the least of the difficulties as long as each franchisor ensures:

- that each franchisee operates the franchise properly from his portion of the premises;
- that the areas used in common are compatible with the franchisor's branding and image;

- that there are adequate contractual obligations to ensure that this common area is properly maintained;
- that the facilities available are consistent with the franchisor's requirements; and
- that the franchisor is able to enforce his standards.

There is clearly room for conflict between the franchisors or the franchisees over the way in which the common areas are fitted out and maintained. There is also the problem of who will be the tenant of the total facility as well as of the common area.

1. Will one franchisor or franchisee lease the area and sublet to the others or license them to use it?
2. Will the other franchisors and/or franchisees be able to exercise the level of control which they require over the common area?
3. Will the other franchisees operate to a standard which will not detract from the standard imposed by one of the other franchisors?
4. Will the association with the franchise operation in one section of the property harm the others?
5. What should happen if one of the franchisee's operations fails?
6. With whom would it be replaced and who would have the responsibility for ensuring this?
7. What would be the position if one of the franchisors or its franchisee decides that the location is wrong for them or that they are not doing as well as they should?
8. Should they be able to 'opt out'? If so, on what basis?
9. By whom should they be replaced, on what terms, and whose responsibility should it be to deal with the problem?
10. If the franchisor and franchisee whose operation is not doing well decide that the location and/or conceptual approach is wrong, who will find the replacement and should the other franchisors and/or franchisees have any say in who replaces them and what their operation should be?
11. If one of the franchisees runs his operation within the facility on a substandard basis so that the other franchisees suffer, what redress should there be and who will enforce it?
12. Similarly, if one franchisee does not meet his obligations for the maintenance of the common area, who will enforce these obligations against him and secure his compliance?

Should there be an overall agreement between all the franchisors to regulate the operations? If there is such an agreement should the franchisees also be a party to it so that they can enforce its provisions?[4]

The second arrangement is where there is one franchisee for all the operations to be conducted from the common facility. In this case there are further difficulties to consider. The most striking disadvantage appears to be a risk of the loss of control with a consequent lowering of standards. It is not difficult to see how this happens since the arrangement has built into it some fundamentals which are likely to give rise to these difficulties unless they are resolved.

1. The franchisee is not under the control of any one franchisor.
2. The franchisee is entering into the arrangement to maximize the utilization of space and staff and minimize expense.
3. The common area is not strictly under the control of any of the franchisors to the point where one of them can impose standards of uniformity, supervision and cleanliness which match those found in a unit wholly dedicated to that particular franchise.
4. The franchisee is in a position to play one franchisor off against another and to display a degree of independence to each (because he has other franchisees in the same location) which undermines control and standards.
5. The franchisee has no incentive to promote all operations if he can achieve the financial result he seeks by concentrating his efforts on the one which he considers will produce the best results for him.
6. Each franchisor's position in relation to the franchisee is weaker, since the existence of the others may be a viable fall-back situation for the franchisee.
7. The franchisors are placed in a situation in which conflicts of interest can develop between them; even businesses which appear to be complementary can be competing and can have overlapping product, service or menu items.
8. Where such overlapping exists, the temptation for the franchisee to standardize the product, service or menu item – despite the normal differences imposed by the franchisors by buying the cheapest products which meet the requirements of one franchisor regardless of the requirements of the others in terms of quality of product supply and methods of preparation – is considerable and difficult for each franchisor effectively to monitor on a regular ongoing basis.
9. It is difficult, if not impossible, to contemplate the sale by the franchisee of each franchise individually. The criteria for franchisee selection by each franchisor may differ and a prospective purchaser from the franchisee may not satisfy the approval requirements of all the franchisors involved.
10. Each franchisor and its franchisees run the risk of being associated with another franchisor whose business may:
    - fail;
    - suffer a loss of credibility;
    - fall into disrepute; or
    - become heavily involved in litigation with franchisees.

It is likely that the impact of any of these events could adversely affect the innocent franchisors not only in terms of the consumer's association with them but also because they may become involved in any litigation arising from these factors, particularly where bankruptcy or liquidation may be involved.

11. The participation by the franchisee in any of the franchised network's, marketing, promotional and advertising campaigns, particularly those involving point-of-sale material, may be in question since the others may resent the promotion of one franchise without the other. Liaison between all within the framework of their own marketing, promotional and advertising strategy may well be impossible bearing in mind the size and spread of their own networks. To try to establish contractual commitments in this area would not make sense or be practicable.

12. The franchisors will probably have put themselves under the pressure of seeking to use this technique as a method of achieving quicker growth than would otherwise be available to them, thus putting themselves under what might be the wrong pressures. In addition it would probably be difficult for them to resist further growth by this method by their common franchises within the area of this operation or the surrounding area.

Experience tends to show that there are many who do not devote the time and thought which is necessary to consider and resolve these issues. This can only lay the foundation for problems. Any franchisor with an established network who is considering such an arrangement must give particular thought to how he can safeguard that network if the arrangement fails.

Anyone considering this particular method of growth must take considerable care in structuring the arrangements and should seriously question whether the likely benefits in terms of any 'improvement' over their normal method of expansion as well as the benefits likely to be available to franchisees are worth the undoubted risks. This approach has the potential to be very high risk.

International financial considerations

The starting points for the consideration of the financial aspects of the master franchise agreement are:

- What level of business and profitability will the franchised operational units be able to generate? In reality it is only out of the business which can be created at that level that all the parties involved can benefit, which should ensure a sober approach by both parties.
- What is the value of the franchisor's trade mark and/or trade name

and what value does it add at the operational level as well as in assisting the sub-franchisor to sell sub-franchises?

- What is the value of the franchisor's system embracing its secret and confidential know-how and information?
- What will it cost to:
  - (a) establish the franchisor's name in the target country so that it is as valuable there as it is in its domestic market?
  - (b) develop the franchisor's system so that it is fully effective and operative in the target country?

The sources of income to which a franchisor can look in the operation of a domestic network usually include one or more of the following:

- an initial fee;
- a mark-up on product sales;
- a continuing franchise fee (also rightly or wrongly sometimes called a royalty).

There may be other opportunities for a franchisor to secure an income flow

- by becoming involved in the real estate chain and deriving a 'profit' rent, i.e. it receives more than it pays out;
- by receiving payments of commissions or overriders, including retrospective rebates from suppliers to the franchise network;
- by leasing equipment to franchisees.

Whatever sources of income or combinations are the chosen method they will provide the financial pool, which will have to be enough to make the transaction worthwhile for franchisor and sub-franchisor under the master franchise agreement.

Let us examine what the franchisor is likely to expect out of the agreement. The most obvious is that it wants a sufficiently attractive result to make it worthwhile to do the deal. However, the income flow from the operating units will not increase just because there is a master franchise agreement. The franchisor cannot expect the sub-franchisor to be able to pay over so much that it is not in a position to run its own business profitably. The franchisor will invariably expect to be paid:

- an initial fee; and
- continuing fees or royalties (which include possibly some of the other types of payment referred to above).

There is no answer to the question of what these fees should be. Very often one suspects that there is little science applied to these calculations and that they result from 'horse trading'.[5] The problem is that if the fees are set at the wrong level this is likely adversely to affect the growth and development of the sub-franchisor's network. Every pound the sub-franchisor pays in an initial fee is a pound less for network development. Every pound paid in continuing fees or royalties is a pound less for network services and profitability. It is important that the right balance is struck and that both parties recognize that they should be looking for a steady medium- to long-term growth rather than a short-term 'killing'.

There are, one would suggest, some general principles which need to be considered when seeking to establish what the fees should be. The best way to approach the establishment of the fair level of fees is for the franchisor to acquire a significant level of understanding of the target market and costings to enable it to prepare projections, ideally covering at least a five-year period, to demonstrate what the sub-franchisor may realistically expect to achieve and to prepare from that a similar plan to demonstrate to the franchisor that it will be worth his while financially to enter that market. If the franchisor can prepare a ten-year plan it will be providing a more realistic view since many of the costs and expenses incurred in the first two to three years will have been absorbed and amortized. It is not suggested that the franchisor should present these projections to the prospective franchisee who should be encouraged to prepare his own projections. The franchisor will, however, be better equipped to deal with the issues arising from the sub-franchisor's projections and, very importantly, to set its financial requirements at levels which its own projections justify. This should enable the parties' discussions to avoid many of the contentious discussions which can otherwise arise where, as is often the case, the franchisor has plucked figures out of thin air which may bear no resemblance to what might be achievable. Many franchisors have lost good prospects and in some cases years of development in a good territory because their demands could not be justified and they had no figures of their own realistically prepared to counteract the prospective sub-franchisor's doubts. This approach will assist in the next fee issue, which deals with initial fees.

Initial fees

As will be appreciated, it is not easy to agree what the franchisor should receive for:

- the grant of the rights;
- the transfer of know-how; and
- assisting in setting up the sub-franchisor in the target country.

If this was easy it would not cause the problems with which one is so often confronted. Indeed, there are many franchisors whose expectations are such that any would-be sub-franchisors are frightened off. The author is aware of a significant number of such cases. There are also instances in which unrealistic figures have been agreed only to be resented by the sub-franchisor when it realizes that it cannot make money at all, or, at least, sufficiently quickly to justify the high level of the initial cost.

It seems that there are a number of factors which should be taken into account when trying to calculate what would be a proper level of initial fee to be paid to a franchisor. The degree of importance to be attached to each will differ from country to country, depending upon the practices to be found in each and their relative impact on the parties in their discussions. The factors are:

- The actual cost to the franchisor of dealing with the sub-franchisor, having assisted it in setting up its business and helping to prove that the concept works within the target country.

- How much it would cost and how long it would take the sub-franchisor to acquire the requisite know-how and skills to operate a similar business in its country assuming it set it up by itself. If this can be done as quickly and for less or at not much more cost, the prospective sub-franchisor may question whether it needs the franchisor.

- The value of the territory as estimated by the franchisor. Many franchisors tend to have their ideas about what the territory is worth coloured by their experience in their own country. In their country their name is known, their system is well established (if it is not they should not be venturing abroad) and franchisees will merely accept the value and cost of entry but may also be prepared to pay a premium for entry. When moving to another country the franchisor is often offended to be told 'We have never heard of your brand.'

- How do you know that your system and networks will work here? From perhaps being tracked down by eager franchisees in their domestic sellers' market they find that they are in a buyers' market and are faced with unfamiliar attitudes. There are a significant number of franchisors who attempt international development when their domestic operation is not sufficiently matured and does not have the resources to justify trying to enter the international market.[6] The franchisor has to accept that under a master franchise agreement it will be for someone else to have an act of faith and to establish the franchisor's name, reputation and system in its country. That act of faith can best be found where the franchisor is a significant success and can demonstrate its confidence. A patronizing 'we are the greatest – we don't understand your reservations' has no place in such a scenario. The franchisor has to be mindful of the problem and sensitive to the views and reservations of those with whom it will be negotiating.

- The estimated aggregate amount of the initial franchise fees which could be charged by the sub-franchisor to its sub-franchisees in the development of the network in its country. To explain this, let us assume a country where there is a potential to charge by way of initial fees (excluding goods or services which may be provided initially) of £5000. The country has the potential to accommodate 100 outlets of the franchised business. This provides an aggregate potential initial fee income of £500,000 ignoring the fact that the franchisor may be able to increase the fee gradually as the network grows and membership of it is more highly sought after. One has to take into account the fact that to earn these initial fees the franchisor will be incurring expenses. One cannot assume that the country rights are worth £500,000. A lump sum payment would in any event have to be discounted to take into account the cost of earning it as well as the time it will take for the market to be fully exploited.

- The value which accrues from the franchisor having developed and run its system in its own and perhaps other countries with success. Experience of opening in other countries should provide a franchisor with the realism which flows from experience. Whatever lessons may be learned from establishing the pilot operation in the target country will be based on what has already been learned and may reflect lessons already learned in the course of the franchisor's previous experience of international development. This enables the parties to have a starting point which may or may not require adjustment – it may then only be a question of degree rather than a fundamental issue.

Franchisors who are based in those countries where high initial fees are charged to franchisees tend to have much higher expectations and, therefore, tend to demand far more than may be considered realistic in the target country. As the medium- to long-term interests of the franchisor probably are best served by having a well motivated and successful sub-franchisor, a franchisor with this attitude will need to recognize that its attitude is counter-productive and has to be reconsidered.

Whatever considerations (including horse trading) are used to finalize the negotiations and reach agreement on the amount there are methods of structuring payments which may spread payments over a period of time or be related to the opening of operating units.

The way in which whatever is agreed as being an initial fee is structured will be affected by other considerations, including taxation and exchange or other financial controls which apply in the target country. For example, the tax treatment of initial fees in some countries (even where a double taxation treaty exists if there is an applicable treaty) may result in them being regarded as advance royalty payments and subject to withholding tax. Exchange and other financial controls in the target country may require registration with and approval by a finance ministry or other governmental body. This may result in a challenge to the level of the initial as well as continuing fees. Despite the fact that the initial fee may be related to the provision of initial services in the form of training or support services the authorities may still treat the payment as a royalty.

Continuing fees

Continuing fees or royalties are normally calculated as a percentage of the aggregate amount of the gross network sales to the ultimate consumers in the target country. The level at which they are fixed obviously has to provide the franchisor with a good economic reason to be involved, but it must be appreciated that in a master franchise agreement these payments represent a straight deduction from the gross income of the sub-franchisor, and that if they are too high, the sub-franchisor will not be able to run its business profitably. In such circumstances, the network of sub-franchisees will not be given the proper support and cannot succeed.

In the case of direct franchising, either on a unit-by-unit basis or under the framework of a development agreement, the franchisor will no doubt expect to be paid the same continuing fees as it charges in its domestic market; the issue may be whether it will be providing the same range of support and other services to the foreign franchisee as it provides to its franchisees in its domestic market. The issue may go even deeper into whether the franchisor has the resources to provide the same range of support and other services in the target country.

One often sees an initial presentation to prospective sub-franchisors by franchisors (who operate their domestic operation on, say, 5 or 6% of gross sales paid by fee their unit operators) in which they ask for a fee equal to 3 or 4% of gross network sales from the sub-franchisor. That sub-franchisor in market terms may not be able to charge more than 5 or 6% to its sub-franchisees. Indeed, if it were to be receiving an income based on that sort of percentage, and there was no involvement by the franchisor, it would be able to run a very viable and profitable business. However it is doomed to failure if it loses what would be 60 to 80% of its gross income to the franchisor, which is what the effect would be of the franchisor's demands. In many cases it is difficult to succeed as a sub-franchisor if the franchisor's continuing fee represents more than 10 to 20% of the income the sub-franchisor generates from its sub-franchisees. It should be borne in mind that whatever is paid to the franchisor is a first call on the sub-franchisor's income. How many businesses can operate sufficiently profitably to make the business proposition worthwhile when they lose more than 20% of their gross revenue unless they are receiving for that sum a significant range of cost saving services?

The financial effect on the sub-franchisor's business of establishing the level of continuing fees has to be thought through very carefully. Proper financial projections and a business plan must be prepared to demonstrate the effect which the level of fees payable by the sub-franchisor will have on the viability of its business. There are sometimes different approaches to fees; for example, variable levels according to turnover, fixed fees, minimum fees. These are very much an exception.

There are those franchise systems in which the franchisor is the manufacturer of products or a supplier of products made to its specification by licensed manufacturers. There are some cases where the sub-franchisor is licensed to manufacture the franchisor's products and to supply its network of sub-franchisees. Some franchisors enter into licensing agreements with local manufacturers in the target country for the supply of products to the sub-franchisor and the sub-franchisees within the network. In each of these cases the franchisor and sub-franchisor would participate in the mark-up on the products. This may be the sole income of each of them (although this is more rare) or it may be part of their income together with one of the other methods of charging continuing fees or royalties.

The method of making payments also has to be carefully related to the way in which the sub-franchisor will be dealing with sub-franchisees. For example, if sub-franchisees pay their fees monthly by the tenth day of the month, an obligation on the sub-franchisor to make payments to the franchisor monthly on the tenth day of the month would not be capable of being performed. Yet one sees provisions of that nature. The payment periods and accounting periods at both levels have to tie in with each other so that the sub-franchisor has the opportunity to collect fees from sub-franchisees, check them against reported revenues and prepare and submit reports and payments to the franchisor. Where product supply is a feature the terms and conditions of supply and payment will have to be dealt with separately in the agreement.

Another question to be considered is whether the sub-franchisor is to be responsible for paying franchise fees to the franchisor whether or not the sub-franchisor has been paid by its sub-franchisees. This will be a subject for negotiation. It is unlikely that the franchisor will wish to act as banker to the sub-franchisor and accept its credit risk. As far as products are concerned the sub-franchisor will have to be prepared to fund purchases from the franchisor or other supplier and ensure that sub-franchisees pay promptly so that sub-franchisors' exposure to risk is kept as low as possible.

There should always be a provision in the master franchise agreement requiring the sub-franchisor to ensure that sub-franchisees observe and perform the terms of the sub-franchise agreements. This would inevitably mean that a failure by the sub-franchisor to collect fees and financial reports would be a breach of contract. In practical terms, a defaulting and non-paying sub-franchisee will not only not be paying fees, but will also probably not be submitting returns of gross sales, which, of course, will mean that no one will know what should be remitted. There are techniques for coping with this sort of problem.

The franchisor will invariably stipulate the currency in which it wishes payment to be made. In most cases, the franchisor would like payment to be in its own currency. This requires the establishment in the agreement of a conversion date. It is also sensible to identify which bank's quoted rate will be used on that conversion date, so that there is an accurate method for the parties to ensure that the right amount of currency has been remitted. Provision will usually be made for the cost of remittance and conversion to be borne by the sub-franchisor.

There may be exchange control requirements to be complied with in some countries. The mere fact that exchange control permission has been obtained does not necessarily mean that payments will be made with any degree of regularity because payments can be delayed administratively by the country's central bank when it assesses the anticipated total outflow of funds from the country during any particular month compared with the available resources. Furthermore, the banking system combined with the local bureaucracy may well cause further delays in payment. These possibilities need to be considered where appropriate and dealt with in the agreement.

A franchisor might consider the establishment of a bank account in the target country to ensure the quick flow and availability of funds as the bankers do not always move funds as rapidly as the needs of the parties require. Very specific provisions have to be written into the agreement to avoid any payment problems which can be anticipated.

If, by reason of exchange controls, currency conversion cannot take place, provision should be made in the agreement to establish what will be the alternative.

Bearing in mind the long-term nature of these contracts, often one has to insert provisions to allow for the possible introduction of exchange controls, as the mere fact that a country has no controls at the time the contract is negotiated does not mean that at some time during the life of the contract such controls will not be introduced, albeit temporarily.

Withholding of taxes, and gross-up provisions

In dealing with the payment provisions in the contract, the way in which payments will be treated and characterized for the purposes in both the franchisor's country and the target country should be considered.

Any double taxation agreement which exists should also be examined to ensure that if the franchisor wishes to receive payments which are free of withholding tax, this can be done as far as possible. Provision should be made in the contract to enable the franchisor to obtain the benefit in its own country of any double taxation agreement by the provision of evidence of payment in the target country in such form as may be necessary to enable the relief to be claimed. This avoids paying tax twice on the same amount.

Some franchisors insert what are called gross-up provisions in their contracts, which provide that if tax is deductible, effectively it has to be borne by the sub-franchisor increasing its payment to the franchisor so that the franchisor receives the same amount net as he would have received had there been no deduction. The effect of such a provision is to increase the level of fees payable by the sub-franchisor, as it is effectively paying the franchisor's tax liability on the payments which are remitted to it. This would be a cost which would not be recoverable from the franchise network, and if a sub-franchisor is forced into accepting such a provision, then the sub-franchisor should check its projections and cash-flow forecasts to ensure that this additional burden does not make the proposition unacceptable.

Advertising

Most franchise systems provide for advertising to be organized by its franchisor, financed by contributions made by franchisees of the operational units. There are three basic alternative arrangements which are found in domestic arrangements.

1. The franchisor charges the franchisee a sum calculated as a percentage of the franchisee's gross income rather in the same way as the continuing franchise fee (management services fee) is calculated. The sums received by the franchisor from the franchisees are spent by the franchisor on advertising and promotion. Most franchisors will want to have complete control over the nature and extent of the advertising and promotional activities upon which the sums recovered are spent.

2. The franchisor includes the advertising expense within the continuing franchise fee and undertakes to spend not less than a minimum percentage of such fee on advertising and promotion. Again, most franchisors will wish to have the same degree of control over advertising and promotional activities.

3. The franchisor undertakes to do advertising and promotion to the extent he thinks fit without collecting a contribution or allocating a fixed sum for the purpose. This approach is often adopted where the franchisor is a manufacturer which is already a substantial advertiser on its own account and the franchisee will inevitably benefit.

There are some cases where advertising concentrated more in the area in which the franchisee is operating is more appropriate and effective than national advertising. This often results in authorized local advertising, with the franchisee obliged to spend a fixed percentage of its gross revenues on such advertising activities. The franchisee may also be required to make some small contribution to a limited amount of national advertising.

In some countries, notably the USA, regional advertising with franchisee participation in regional advertising committees is to be found.

Many franchisors expect their sub-franchisors to follow the same advertising procedure in the target country as operates in their own country.

There are some systems where international advertising may be particularly appropriate. This approach, for example, is essential if there is a system which is transnational, such as car rentals and hotels, where an international directory is a common feature of the international marketing of the system.

The advertising arrangements need to recognize the market place and the best ways in which to exploit it. While use may be made of materials prepared in the franchisor's domestic market, the sub-franchisor may take care to ensure that the franchisor is not spending advertising contributions from the target country's resources without producing material which is usable, which saves at least as much as it costs and which does not need a significant amount of money spent on it to prepare it for the local market.

The franchisor and sub-franchisor should ideally be able to work closely with each other in relation to advertising in the target country. After all, the local knowledge of the sub-franchisor is an important element in the relationship – the franchisor cannot expect to know more about the sub-franchisor's market than its sub-franchisor.

Notes

1. Historically, this type of arrangement was called 'master franchising' in the USA.
2. Some area development arrangements in the USA allow the area developer to raise capital for expansion by taking in minority investors on a unit-by-unit basis.
3. Sub-franchise arrangements exist but are not that common in the domestic USA market.
4. In the USA, the franchisee is likely to receive two offering circulars, one from each franchisor. However, sometimes one franchisor offers multiple brands to its franchisees.
5. Some US franchisors going into a foreign market admit that they simply charge for the initial fee as much as they can get from the local franchisee.
6. Many foreign master franchisees are quite sophisticated with substantial resources. It is not uncommon to see a foreign master franchisee acting for a number of franchised concepts in its territory.

16 The British Franchise Association

The British Franchise Association Ltd (BFA), a company limited by guarantee, was incorporated in 1977. There were eight founder members.

1. Budget Rent-a-Car (UK) Ltd.
2. Dyno-Rod plc.
3. Holiday Inns (UK) Inc.
4. Kentucky Fried Chicken (GB) Ltd.
5. Prontaprint Ltd.
6. Service Master Ltd.
7. Wimpy International Ltd.
8. Ziebart Mobile Transport Services Ltd.

Five of these companies, Budget Rent-a-Car, Holiday Inns, Kentucky Fried Chicken, Service Master and Ziebart, had clear origins in the USA. Wimpy originated in the USA, although the franchise development was devised and executed in the UK. Dyno-Rod, the idea of an American, was also developed in the UK, while Prontaprint was the only one devised and developed in the UK, by an Englishman.

The BFA has clearly defined membership criteria, and in joining all members, whether full or associate, commit themselves to comply with the terms of the following policies and procedures published by the BFA:

- the Code of Ethical Conduct;
- the disciplinary procedure;
- the complaints procedure;
- the appeals procedure;
- the terms of triennial reaccreditation.

(The current terms of these policies, procedures and the Code of Ethical Conduct are contained in Appendix B). Members also agree to comply with the Code of Advertising Practice as published by the Advertising Standards Authority.

In addition, members agree to provide to the BFA any non-confidential information relating to their franchise business, or relating to the standing and qualification of their directors, as may be requested by an authorized official of the Association. Members also agree to grant a full-time official of the BFA authorized access (at reasonable times and on reasonable notice) to confidential information relating to the franchise and its standing (on the understanding that such information remains confidential to the authorized official).

The BFA offers a mediation service, and an arbitration scheme specifically designed for franchisors and franchisees who jointly agree to use the service. The BFA also has rules under which a member may be required to go to arbitration under the Association's scheme as a condition of continued membership. The safeguards against the abuse of these provisions are substantial.

In the author's view the BFA is likely to create problems with this approach. Arbitration is not necessarily the correct form for the resolution of all disputes. A franchisor may well receive legal advice that proceedings through the courts are more appropriate than arbitration in the circumstances. The BFA will have to be careful about the way in which it approaches mandatory arbitration on pain of expulsion. There may also be potential liability issues for the BFA in going down this route.

Members of the BFA also comply with the spirit and intent of the Guidelines to Best Practice as published by the Association from time to time. While the BFA will use its best endeavours to establish the eligibility of an applicant, the onus for demonstrating that its criteria have been met on initial accreditation or reaccreditation lies finally with the applicant or member.

The BFA has three categories of franchisor subscriber: full members, associate members and provisionally listed companies. Full members are fully established franchisors with a substantial and successful track record. Associate members are on the whole more recent entrants to franchising, with successful franchisees but who have yet to establish a proven trading and franchising record. Provisionally listed companies are those at the point where the business has been well prepared for its entry into franchising but which are only just at the point of establishing their first fully fledged franchise operation. The following four specific terms of membership apply to both associate and full members. Provisionally listed companies may not be able fully to demonstrate their compliance with the 'replication' requirement (term 2). Each term sets out a general condition which the applicant must fulfil. Each general condition is followed by examples of how applicants will ordinarily be expected to demonstrate that the condition has been met.

1. **Demonstrate that the business itself is viable.** The production of the most recent 24 months' audited accounts, including trading accounts, which show that the business is capable of being run at a profit which will support a franchised network.
2. **Demonstrate that the operating units in the business can be successfully replicated.** The production of the most recent 12 months' audited accounts for a managed arm's length pilot

operation, or a fully fledged pilot or franchise operation, which show a trading performance at least in line with the business plan set for it and which is supported by a developed operating system.

3. **Demonstrate that the contractual terms to be offered to prospective franchisees comply with the BFA's Code of Ethical Conduct and such other terms as it may publish from time to time.** Lodge with the BFA for its accreditation, and make available for inspection by appointed franchisees, a copy of the then current agreement and any changes thereto.

4. **Demonstrate that the offer documents to be used with prospective franchisees present a full and realistic picture of the franchise proposition.** Lodge with the BFA for its accreditation, and make available for inspection by appointed franchisees, a copy of the then current offer documents and any changes thereto.

Applicants who comply with the general conditions of membership and the specific terms 1 to 4 set out above will be eligible for admission as associate members. Applicants who comply with the following additional specific conditions will be eligible for admission as full members.

5. **Demonstrate that the franchise network has developed over time with a proven trading and franchising record.** Provide a record of franchise openings, withdrawals and disputes (which required external intervention to resolve) together with evidence of the profitability of individual units and of the network as a whole sustained over a period of 24 months.

Associate and full members and provisionally listed companies may refer to themselves as such in their offer documents, advertising and other published material. Each category has a specific logo attached to it.

Franchise operations which form part of a larger group or company will be required to submit evidence concerning the franchised network, on a confidential basis if necessary, which is confirmed by a director of the company as representing a true and fair picture of the franchised network. Additionally, such franchised operations will be required to provide a statement from the holding company or group confirming its intention to maintain the franchised operation for at least the forthcoming year. Overseas franchisors franchising directly into the UK, and the master licensees of overseas franchisors, are eligible to apply for associate or full membership in respect of their UK operation.

The BFA now has full members, associate members and provisionally listed companies whose business classifications are set out in Chapter 2. The BFA also has an affiliate listing membership which permits those who provide professional services to franchisors to associate themselves with the BFA. The affiliates include solicitors, accountants, exhibition agencies, media and communications, surveyors, bankers, patent and trademark agents, insurance brokers, development agency and franchise consultants.

The Association is as concerned with the standards of professional advice available to franchisors and franchisees as it is with the standards of good practice adopted by franchisors, since, in many cases, the later follows from the former. In consequence, the Association's affiliated professional advisers are also required to meet entry criteria, primarily based on professional references but also with entry routes through interview and confidential review of work done.

The BFA was originally promoted to achieve three objectives: to provide recognition for franchisors who met industry standard of good practice; to provide franchising with a collective voice and to perform the normal functions of a trade association; and to counteract the adverse publicity which business opportunities wrongly calling themselves 'franchises' had attracted. The ways in which the founder members sought to achieve these objectives are reflected in the BFA's main objectives, which are contained in the Association's Memorandum of Association. It will be noted that these objectives incorporate the definition of franchising commented on in Chapter 1. The objectives for which the Association is established are the following.

1. To promote, protect and further the interests of franchisors, i.e. those who in the course of their business grant a contractual licence (a franchise) to another party (the franchises) which:

   (a) permits or requires the franchisee to carry on during the period of the franchise a particular business under or using a specific name belonging to or associated with the franchisor; and

   (b) entitles the franchisor to exercise continuing control during the period of the franchise over the manner in which the franchisee carries on the business which is the subject of the franchise; and

   (c) obliges the franchisor to provide the franchisee with assistance in carrying on the business which is the subject of the franchise (in relation to the organization of the franchisee's business, the training of staff, merchandising, management or otherwise); and

   (d) requires the franchisee periodically during the period of the franchise to pay to the franchisor sums of money in consideration for the franchise or for goods or services provided by the franchisor to the franchisee; and

   (e) is not a transaction between a holding company and its subsidiary (as defined in section 154 of the Companies Act 1948) or between subsidiaries of the same holding company or between an individual and a company controlled by him.

2. Without prejudice to the generality of subclause (1):

   (a) the recognition of the BFA in the UK and internationally as the single authoritative, self-regulating and representative body for UK franchising;

   (b) the development and recognition of franchising within the European Union in partnership with European National Franchise Associations.

The BFA has now, some 27 years since its birth, grown into a significant and respected organization in franchising; respected by practitioners (franchisors and franchisees), by professional advisors, by the major banks, by government both in the UK and in Europe, by those few business schools which have so far taken a real interest in franchising, by the media, but perhaps most importantly by the general public as potential investors in the business of franchising.

The Association works across a broad front of activity, but all its activity comes down in the end to the Association's foundation in standards. Standards on their own are no use, of course, unless the people who need to benefit from them know about them. So the promotion of the good franchising practice the Association represents is the other side of its work. The BFA sets out its activity in seven functional areas.

Accreditation. The BFA accredits its members on entry and reaccredits them on a triennial basis. It also vets entrants to the major BFA sponsored franchise exhibitions held around the UK. The due diligence work the staff of the Association carry out is overseen by its Accreditation Committee, which also oversees the operation of the BFA's mediation and arbitration schemes. Those schemes are also supported by the BFA's Legal Committee, whose particular concern is to ensure that the Association's ethical standards for franchise agreements, and the increasingly numerous and increasingly complex clauses they contain, are kept at the forefront of developments in this field. The Association's dispute resolution practice begins with a complaints procedure under which attempts are made to bring a member franchisor and a complaining franchisee back into direct and constructive communication. These interventions by the Association are often successful and the remaining number of disputes that require more substantial negotiation are fortunately few.

Legislation. The low incidence of substantive disputes between franchisors and franchisees is one of the underlying strengths in the Association's relationships with government and legislators. Where there is so little evidence of abuse, there is no need for heavy handed intervention through formal regulation. Franchising must of course, like all business, meet the requirements of general, competition, trading and contract laws and the BFA works with government and its officials to ensure that developments in the general legislative environment do not unnecessarily restrict the continued growth of franchising. It is equally important that legislative initiatives intended to restrict the damage which can be done by abusive arm's length schemes – like pyramid selling – do not accidentally restrict legitimate franchising. One such Private Member's Bill before the UK Parliament would have done just that without the guidance given by the BFA and its advisers to government officers in framing what eventually became the Trading Schemes Act.

International. These days, the more robust regulatory threats are likely to originate in the European Commission, not least in the shape of the regulations – the Block Exemption Regulations – which exempt trading agreements which would otherwise have to be regarded as anti-competitive under the terms of the Treaty of Rome. The Association and its advisers have been very active, directly with the European Commission and through the UK government, in influencing the shape of European regulation. Perhaps most importantly the BFA has taken a leading role in the work and governance of the European Franchise Federation (EFF), which has now grown to represent the 17 leading franchise nations within the European Union and its applicant countries. In the renegotiation of what was the Block Exemption Regulation for Franchising to its successor, the Block Exemption Regulation for Vertical Agreements, the EFF won for itself a special place at the negotiating table with Commission officials. The BFA was a member of the EFF's four man negotiating team and played a central part in securing a beneficial outcome. The BFA also played a central role with the French in the EFF's and the American Association's (the International Franchise Association, IFA) work with UNIDROIT, an organization whose purpose is the unification of commercial law internationally. UNIDROIT produced a draft model law for franchising which, in its early draft, would have been disastrous wherever it was adopted.

Training. The BFA has always played a very active role in putting on seminars for prospective franchisees and training workshops for existing franchisors. Now, with a development investment from the Business Link organization in Hertfordshire, the BFA runs monthly training days for both prospective franchisees and franchisors. Further programmes are in development and the BFA has also become a leading partner in a European Social Fund supported project to increase access for disadvantaged groups to enterprise through franchising. The BFA has also tried, with others in the sector, to take the lead in developing formal qualification routes and career paths within the increasingly professional field of franchise management. The results so far are patchy and the Association recognizes that much work remains to be done in this area.

Promotion. Recognition for franchisors and their networks of their professionalism and achievements does not just happen by itself. Fortunately the industry provides a host of remarkable individual success stories that, if the media can be introduced to them, would command the attention of national, local and trade newspapers and magazines. At this individual story level the Association's annual awards schemes for franchisors and franchisees, sponsored and organized by HSBC and the *Daily Express*, play a very important role. The basic statistical facts, the extraordinarily good success rates of franchising, also play an essential role in commanding the attention of the press, government and business. The BFA is a partner in this area with NatWest, which sponsors and organizes an annual survey of franchising which is now in its second decade of production. No other country in the world can boast of such a continuing research project on the contribution its franchising sector makes to the economy. The awards scheme and the research results both take their place in the annual National Franchise Week which the BFA first organized in the millennium year and which is now a permanent feature of the Association's promotional calendar.

Exhibitions and the world wide web. Franchise promotion is not just about spreading good franchising practice, it is also about recruiting individual franchisees to the right franchised businesses for them. That takes the BFA's educational initiatives on the one hand – to make sure that prospective franchisees are well informed – and efficient marketing vehicles for individual franchisors on the other hand. The franchising trade press has a great role in informing prospective franchisees and marketing franchisors and the BFA works closely with the trade magazines. Its relationships with the major exhibitions are even closer. The BFA's job in this area is a difficult one: to win the right with the organizers, in the name of the long-term benefits of quality, to turn away companies who wish to pay to exhibit because they do not meet industry standards. The BFA has been able to secure such a veto under contracts with successive organizers for the past twenty years. The results are evident in the quality of franchising shows in the UK. A new marketing opportunity for the franchise sector has been opened up through the world wide web. For the first time the BFA was able to approach a marketing media without the realities of its costs forcing the need to take advertising from businesses outside the BFA. The BFA's franchise website, which is limited to BFA approved organizations, is cooperatively sponsored by the UK's major clearing banks, and is one of the most successful franchise sites in the world. Many BFA member franchisors now recruit a substantial number of franchisees through the BFA website, some the majority of the number they recruit each year.

National Franchisee Forum. There have been many attempts around the world to bring franchisees more centrally into the work of national franchise associations. The Americans, with their many big business multiple franchisees, have gone as far as to make them equal voting members of the IFA. The real problem is not what standing franchisees will have in associations, it is how to get the ordinary franchisee, busily going about the everyday requirements of their particular business, to give any attention at all to the issue of 'franchising' as the means through which they own their business. The BFA made a first stab at the end of the 1990s with an all inclusive consultative body approach. Every franchisee of a BFA member could join – more than 15,000 were thus eligible. With a big marketing spend membership got up to 316, without it numbers dropped to 81. In 2002 the BFA thought again and devised a new Franchisee Forum which drew something from the French model of a consultative committee but with the added dimension of a little democracy. Now, when BFA member franchise companies vote each year for their representatives on the governing body, they also thereby vote for those companies to put a franchisee on the independently chaired National Franchisee Forum. The Forum has proposed modifications to the complaints procedure and improvements in the Association's guidance on minimum performance clauses in franchise agreements, which have been adopted. The Forum's independent Chairman is the Association's Honorary President, Sir Bernard Ingham. His contribution to the development of the BFA over the past decade should not be under-estimated.

One should not assume that the BFA's progress has all been achieved without difficulties. Some member companies have had their problems and withdrawn. Some disputes between franchisor members and individual franchisees have emerged and the BFA has assisted in the resolution of these disputes without the need for costly and lengthy litigation. It would be impossible to achieve the Utopian state in which all problems and difficulties would cease to exist. There will be BFA members who fail and there will be franchisees of BFA members who are disgruntled and dissatisfied. The strength of the BFA will be dependent upon:

- its skill in investigating applications for membership and in conducting its re-accreditization process so as to ensure that no questionable franchisors are admitted or continue in membership;
- the observance by its members of the Code of Ethics, not merely in principle, but also in spirit;
- rigorous attention to warning signs about members which emerge from complaints and criticism;
- its ability to persuade members to change undesirable practices;
- the maintenance of its reputation so that membership is an achievement which enhances the status of the member.

In its 27 years of existence the BFA has made significant progress first under the full-time directorship of Tony Jacobsen, ably assisted by his wife, Dr Christine Jacobsen. Their dedication to the BFA was a significant factor in its establishment and early growth. On 1 January 1984 Tony Dutfield, who was Chairman of the BFA in 1983 in his capacity as representative of Wimpy International Ltd, succeeded Tony Jacobsen as Director of the BFA. Tony Dutfield retired in 1989 and was succeeded by Brian Smart as Director, who remains in that role. Under his direction the BFA has undergone many improvements and greatly improved its professionalism. One expects that with its sound foundations it will continue to fulfil its objectives, particularly in the light of the changes which have been made to strengthen its evaluation and reaccreditation procedure. The BFA has also played a considerable role in the activities of the European Franchise Federation and the World Franchise Council. The BFA has grown considerably in stature and influence in the past 27 years, not only in the UK and Europe but also in the worldwide family of franchising.

17 Franchising in the USA[1]

Most people acknowledge that the United States is the 'birthplace' of franchising as the world knows it today. As you read this chapter, keep in mind that the USA has a federal system. That means that in addition to any federal laws that might apply on a nationwide basis, a person doing business in the USA might also have to deal with the laws of 50 states, the District of Columbia and each territory or possession. This overlap has created a crazy quilt work of franchising regulation in the USA.

The US franchise disclosure and registration regulatory environment

Franchise experts often argue about when franchising first got started, but from a business perspective it became prevalent in the United States in the 1950s and 1960s. From a legal perspective, franchising in the United States as we understand it today started with the enactment of the first franchise disclosure and registration law in 1970.

When were they adopted?

The first franchise law in the United States was the California Franchise Investment Law which was adopted in 1970 and became effective 1 January 1971. In response to what it perceived as widespread abuses relating to the sale of franchises, the California legislature decided that persons investing in franchised businesses needed protection because 'California franchisees have suffered substantial losses where the franchisor or his representative has not provided full and complete information regarding the franchisor-franchisee relationship, the details of the contract between franchisor and franchisee, and the prior business experience of the franchisor.'

The California Legislature then said:

It is the intent of this law to provide each prospective franchisee with the information necessary to make an intelligent decision regarding franchises being offered. Further, it is the intent of this law to prohibit the sale of franchises where such sale would lead to fraud or a likelihood that the franchisor's promises would not be fulfilled, and to protect the franchisor by providing a better understanding of the relationship between the franchisor and franchisee with regard to this business relationship.

Following the lead of the already existing so-called 'blue sky' securities laws referred to in the above recital, California decided that disclosure of certain relevant information was necessary in order to allow an investor to make an informed decision when buying a franchise.

But California did not stop at disclosure. The state also decided that it would be unlawful for any person to offer or sell any franchise in the state unless the offer of the franchise has been registered or exempted. The application for registration had to be accompanied by a proposed 'offering prospectus' which was to contain certain material information in over 20 categories. We will review below how the California Franchise Investment Law defined 'franchise' and what its disclosure and registration obligations are.

Within the next ten years, 14 other states adopted their own franchise disclosure and registration laws, in the following order (by approximate effective date): Washington (1 May 1972), Virginia (1 July 1972), Wisconsin (1 July 1972), Rhode Island (11 May 1973), Minnesota (23 May 1973), Oregon (21 July 1973), Illinois (1 January 1974), South Dakota (25 February 1974), Michigan (15 October 1974), Hawaii (1 January 1975), Indiana (1 July 1975), North Dakota (1 July 1975), Maryland (1 January 1978) and New York (1 January 1980).

What is interesting about these 15 state disclosure and registration laws is that they were all adopted within a relatively short period of time (from 1971 to 1980, most from 1971 to 1975) and they all provided that a disclosure document (or offering prospectus) had to be provided to a prospective franchisee prior to sale. And, except for Oregon, all these laws provided for some type of registration or filing with the state authorities. Most of the laws were to be administered by the state's corporate or securities authority, but in several states the attorney general's office received that assignment.

What is also interesting and significant is that no new state franchise disclosure and registration laws have been adopted in the USA since 1980, although most of the existing laws have been amended or revised since then, several significantly.

At the same time that the states were adopting laws, the USA Federal Trade Commission (FTC) was methodically promulgating its own rule on franchising under Section5 of the Federal Trade Commission Act (FTC Act), which prohibits unfair and deceptive acts and practices. Starting with a notice of proposed rule-making issued in 1971, it took the FTC seven years to promulgate its own rule entitled 'Disclosure Requirements and Prohibitions Concerning Franchising and Business Opportunity Ventures' (FTC Franchise Rule). The FTC Franchise Rule finally became effective on 21 July 1979.

In its 132-page Statement of Basis and Purpose explaining the rationale for the FTC Franchise Rule (small print in three columns per page), the FTC explained that there were a multitude of complaints regarding the conduct of franchisors within the franchise relationship, that those complaints frequently involved both material misrepresentations and non-disclosure of material facts on the part of franchisors, that a large number of complaints involved fraudulent conduct and that a 'serious informational imbalance exists between prospective franchisees and their franchisors'. The FTC said the informational imbalance was particularly acute in franchising, where many prospective franchisees possess a low level of business sophistication, and concluded that a lot of these activities constituted unfair and deceptive acts or practices under Section 5 of the FTC Act.

But, unlike most of the states, the FTC opted to require disclosure only and not registration. The FTC Franchise Rule requires disclosure of material facts and does not regulate the substantive terms of the franchise relationship, although it does contain a number of prohibitions which forbid franchisors from using certain deceptive acts or practices, such as failing to refund fees or deposits in accordance with contractual obligations, making earnings claims unless they meet certain criteria set forth in the FTC Franchise Rule, or providing information which is contradictory to the information set forth in the disclosure document.

What is interesting about the FTC Franchise Rule is that the FTC did not adopt one of the definitions of 'franchise' used at the state level, and, as will be discussed below, did not pre-empt the state laws in most respects. The use of a different 'franchise' definition and the lack of federal pre-emption has led to some confusion over the years on the franchisor's disclosure obligations.

How do these US laws define 'franchise'?

The definition of 'franchise' in the USA is similar to that described in Chapter1, although no jurisdiction in the USA uses the term 'know-how' in its definition, and there are essentially six different definitions of 'franchise' used in the USA.

Let's start with the first US law. The California Franchise Investment Law defines 'franchise' as having three elements:

> 'Franchise' means a contract or agreement, either expressed or implied, whether oral or written, between two or more persons by which:
> (1) A franchise is granted the right to engage in the business of offering, selling or distributing goods or services under a marketing plan or system prescribed in substantial part by a franchisor; and
> (2) The operation of the franchisee's business pursuant to such plan or system is substantially associated with the franchisor's trademark, service mark, trade name, logotype, advertising or other commercial symbol designating the franchisor or its affiliate; and
> (3) The franchisee is required to pay, directly or indirectly a franchise fee.

The California definition has become the commonly accepted United States definition of 'franchise'. It requires that all three elements be present in order to have a franchise.

Essentially the same definition of 'franchise' was adopted by the other 14 states adopting franchise disclosure and registration laws, with the following modifications:

- Illinois, Rhode Island and Washington provide that the marketing plan can be 'prescribed or suggested.'
- Hawaii, Minnesota and South Dakota substitute the concept of a 'community of interest' in the business of offering, selling, marketing or distributing goods or services for the 'marketing plan or system' element.
- New York has only two elements: either a prescribed marketing plan and franchise fee, or trade mark association and franchise fee.
- Oregon substitutes 'valuable consideration' for the franchise fee requirement.

All these state laws or their implementing regulations have a dollar threshold for the franchise fee requirement, and typically exclude coverage of franchises where there are payments of less than $500 (or some lesser amount, the lowest being $100). The dollar exclusion was included in these laws after extensive lobbying primarily to exclude direct sellers (like Amway and Avon) from coverage under the laws. But do not be deceived by these dollar thresholds. As was pointed out in a famous case construing the Illinois law, in some states that minimum dollar threshold can be reached by cumulative required payments made over a number of years.

All the state franchise laws have provisions excluding from the 'franchise fee' definition the purchase of goods at a bona fide wholesale price. The purpose of this exclusion was to make sure that the typical selective distribution system or authorized dealer programme would not be ensnared in the coverage of these laws. The states recognized that there is no need to regulate relationships where there is no other payment to the supplier for the right to represent the supplier in distributing its goods or services.

Most of the states have a variety of other exemptions that are too detailed to describe here. Suffice it to say that many large sophisticated franchisors can avoid many of the hassles and burdens associated with the registration (but not the disclosure) obligations of these laws by claiming a 'large franchisor' exemption which is available in most of the states. Most of the states also have a 'fractional franchise' exemption which allows avoidance of both the disclosure and registration requirements by franchisors of programmes where the franchisee has been in the type of business before and the parties anticipated at the time the agreement was reached that the sales from that relationship would not represent more than 20% of the franchisee's sales in dollar volume for at least one year.

The FTC, which was watching the state developments with interest, ignored what the states did with respect to the definition of 'franchise' and decided to develop its own definition. The FTC Franchise Rule defines 'franchise' as follows:

(a) The term franchise means any continuing commercial relationship created by any arrangement or arrangements whereby:

(1)(i)(A) a person (hereinafter 'franchisee') offers, sells, or distributes to any person other than a 'franchisor' (as hereinafter defined), goods, commodities, or services which are:

    (1) Identified by a trademark, service mark, trade name, advertising or other commercial symbol designating another person (hereinafter 'franchisor'); or

    (2) Indirectly or directly required or advised to meet the quality standards prescribed by another person (hereinafter 'franchisor') where the franchisee operates under a name using the trademark, service mark, trade name, advertising or other commercial symbol designating the franchisor; and

(B) (1) The franchisor exerts or has authority to exert a significant degree of control over the franchisee's method of operation, including but not limited to, the franchisee's business organization, promotional activities, management, marketing plan or business affairs; or

    (2) The franchisor gives significant assistance to the franchisee in the latter's method of operation, including, but not limited to, the franchisee's business organization, management, marketing plan, promotional activities, or business affairs; Provided, however, that assistance in the franchisee's promotional activities shall not, in the absence of assistance in other areas of the franchisee's method of operation, constitute significant assistance; or

(ii)(A) A person (hereinafter 'franchisee') offers, sells, or distributes to any person other than a 'franchisor' (as hereinafter defined), goods, commodities, or services which are:

    (1) Supplied by another person (hereinafter 'franchisor'); or

    (2) Supplied by a third person (e.g. a supplier) with whom the franchisee is directly or indirectly required to do business by another person (hereinafter 'franchisor'); or

    (3) Supplied by a third person (e.g. a supplier) with whom the franchisee is directly or indirectly advised to do business by another person (hereinafter 'franchisor') where such third person is affiliated with the franchisor; and

(B) The franchisor:

    (1) Secures for the franchisee retail outlets or accounts for said goods, commodities, or services; or

    (2) Secures for the franchisee locations or sites for vending machines, rack displays, or any other product sales display used by the franchisee in the offering, sale, or distribution of said goods, commodities, or services; or

    (3) Provides to the franchisee the services of a person able to secure the retail outlets, accounts, sites or locations referred to in paragraph (a)(1)(ii)(B)(1) and (2) above; and

(2) The franchisee is required as a condition of obtaining or commencing the

franchise operation to make a payment or a commitment to pay to the franchisor, or to a person affiliated with the franchisor.

What exactly did the FTC definitions do? The first part of the FTC's definition (starting with (i)(A) above) has three elements that are similar to, but are expressed differently from, the definitional elements used by the 15 disclosure and registration states. Arguably, the FTC definition provides for broader coverage. The FTC explains that under its definition there are two types of franchise arrangements: package franchises and product franchises. Package franchises are those most familiar to the public and involve situations where a franchisee is licensed to do business under a prepackaged business format established by the franchisor and identified by its trademark, and there is some payment to the franchisor. In the product franchise relationship, the franchisee merely provides an outlet for products produced by the franchisor. Automobile and gasoline dealerships were given as the most common examples. The franchisee invests capital in the form of a franchise fee or other initial or recurring payment.

In addition, however, the second part of the FTC definition (starting with (ii)(A) above) provides that the FTC Franchise Rule also applies to a limited class of business opportunity programs which the FTC viewed as a 'major variant' of franchising. (We discuss business opportunities in more detail below.) This is undoubtedly the result of the fact that the majority of the complaints in the FTC files at the time the FTC Franchise Rule was adopted involved business opportunity scams rather than franchise complaints.

The FTC Franchise Rule definition of 'franchise' is unique and has not been adopted by any of the state disclosure and registration laws or by any other state for any purpose. As a matter of fact, only the Arthur Wishart Act (Franchise Disclosure) in Ontario essentially copied the FTC definition of 'franchise', including its business opportunity provision, and Malaysia seems to have borrowed part of it.

Like the states, the FTC Franchise Rule also provided for a variety of exemptions and exclusions. Under three of the exemptions, the FTC Franchise Rule does not apply: (a)to a fractional franchise, (b)if total payments are less than $500 within six months after commencing operation of the franchise business, or (c)if there is no writing.

For no discernable reason, the FTC Franchise Rule as originally adopted was not only different in many respects from the state laws which preceded it, but created a lot of ambiguities in coverage. For example, as originally promulgated, it did not exclude from the consideration element the purchase of goods at a bona fide wholesale price, even though the FTC acknowledged that 'product franchising involves more … than a selective method of branded product distribution'. That omission caused 15 selective distribution companies (including auto manufacturing, gasoline companies and three other entities) to sue the FTC when the proposed Rule was adopted. As a compromise to settle the suits, the FTC provided in its Interpretive Guides which were issued to clarify the Rule that 'required payments' do not include payments made at a bona fide wholesale price for reasonable amounts of merchandise to be used for resale. Thus, the typical selective distribution system or authorized dealer program was excluded from coverage.

The FTC's failure to follow the state lead in defining what is a 'franchise' has led to confusion over the years, which even today is still not yet resolved. But the FTC's failure to follow the state lead in other respects has caused even more confusion.

What are the disclosure and registration obligations?

All the state registration and disclosure franchise laws or their implementing regulations require that an offering circular be provided to the prospective franchisee prior to sale. In addition, while Oregon simply requires that the franchisor provide a disclosure document that complies with one of two formats,[2] all the other states require some type of registration or filing.

For many years, all of the states have followed a prescribed disclosure format known as the Uniform Franchise Offering Circular ('UFOC Guidelines'). The UFOC Guidelines were developed by the North American Securities Administration Association ('NASAA') and its predecessor, the Midwest Securities Commissioners Association ('MSCA'), as a method of creating uniformity for disclosure by franchisors. The original UFOC Guidelines were adopted by MSCA in 1974. The UFOC Guidelines have been amended many times since, most recently by NASAA in 1993.

The 1993 UFOC Guidelines provide for disclosure of information in 23 categories. The categories (by item number of the offering circular) and a brief summary of the disclosure requirements are as follows:

Item   *Description*
1.   **The franchisor, its predecessors and affiliates**
Disclose prescribed information about the franchisor and its predecessors and affiliates (as those terms are defined), including the franchisor's business and the franchises to be offered, all of their prior business experience, the general market for the product or service to be offered by the franchisee, any specific industry regulations and the competition.
2.   **Business experience**
Disclose a five-year work history for all directors, trustees and/or general partners, principal officers and other executives or subfranchisors who will have management responsibility relating to the franchises. All independent franchise brokers have to be listed.
3.   **Litigation**
With respect to the franchisor, its predecessor, a person identified in item 2 or an affiliate (as defined in this Item), disclose all pending litigation alleging a violation of franchise, anti-trust or securities law, fraud, unfair or deceptive practices or comparable allegations and any other material litigation. There must also be

disclosure of any felony convictions, final judgments in cases involving the foregoing types of cases and settlements of an action if the franchisor paid material consideration, for the past ten years. There must also be disclosure of any currently effective order or decree relating to the franchise or under a US or Canadian franchise, securities, anti-trust, trade regulation or trade practice law.

4.   **Bankruptcy**

With respect to the franchisor, its affiliate, its predecessor, officers or general partner, disclose any bankruptcy by the franchisor, its ffiliates, predecessors, officers or general partners during the past ten years.

5.   **Initial franchise fee**

Disclose the initial fee and any other required payments to the franchisor or its affiliates before the franchised business opens. If the fee is not uniform, the formula or range of initial fees paid in the last fiscal year have to be disclosed, as well as any installment payment terms.

6.   **Other fees**

Disclose all other recurring or related fees or payments that the franchisee must pay to the franchisor or its affiliates, as well as any payments the franchisor or its affiliates impose or collect on behalf of a third party.

7.   **Initial investment**

Disclose the initial investment the franchisee has to make to begin operation of the business and operate the franchise business during the initial phase (at least three months), using a high–low range.

8.   **Restrictions on sources of products and services**

Disclose all obligations the franchisee has to purchase or lease from the franchisor or its designated suppliers, how specifications are issued and the precise basis by which the franchisor or its affiliates will derive revenue from approved suppliers.

9.   **Franchisee's obligations**

In chart form in 25 prescribed categories, list the principal obligations of the franchisee under the franchise and other agreements.

10.   **Financing**

Disclose the terms and conditions of any financing arrangement that the franchisor, its agents or affiliates offer to franchisees.

11.   **Franchisor's obligations**

Disclose the franchisor's obligations before the business opens, and after the business opens; how the location of the business is determined; time from signing the agreement to opening; the training programme; the franchisor's advertising programme and use of funds in a marketing fund; cash register and computer requirements; and the table of contents of the operations manual.

12.   **Territory**

Describe any exclusive territory, the conditions for keeping it and the franchisor's right to compete.

13. **Trade marks**
Disclose the principal trade marks to be licensed and their registration information and any limitations on the right to use the marks.

14. **Patents, copyrights and proprietary information**
Describe any patents or copyrights that are material to the franchise.

15. **Obligation to participate in the actual operation of the franchise business**
Describe whether the franchisee has to participate personally in the business.

16. **Restrictions on what the franchisee may sell**
Disclose restrictions on what the franchisee can sell.

17. **Renewal, termination, transfer and dispute resolution**
Disclose in chart form, with a summary of each provision, information in 24 prescribed categories relating to renewal, termination, transfer and dispute resolution.

18. **Public figures**
Disclose if any public figures are being compensated to use their name and whether they are involved in the management of the business.

19. **Earnings claims**
As an option, the franchisor can make an earnings claim about actual or potential sales, costs, income or profit from franchised or non-franchised units, if these claims can be substantiated.

20. **List of outlets**
Disclose in three separate charts the franchised units that are operating or have been sold or transferred over the past three years, the status of company-owned stores for the past three years and projected openings for the next fiscal year. The franchisor must also list the name and address of the 100 franchisees closest to the state, and all franchisees who have left the system in the past fiscal year. The franchisor also has to report whether there are any franchisees it has not communicated with within ten weeks of the application date.

21. **Financial statements**
Attach audited financial statements in US GAAP form, including balance sheets for the past two fiscal years, and statements of operations, stockholders' equity and cash flow for the past three fiscal years.

22. **Contracts**
Attach copies of all agreements the franchisee is likely to sign.

23. **Receipts**
The last two pages of the offering circular and two receipt pages to be signed by the franchisee, one of which is to be returned to the franchisor.

The UFOC Guidelines also require that there be a cover page that lists the franchisor's name and address, has a sample of the primary mark to be used, describes the franchised business, gives the total amounts from items5 and 7 of the offering circular (initial fees and initial investment), has certain statements and risk factors and states an effective date. There must also be a table of contents.

The UFOC Guidelines also contain registration application forms that are used to file registration applications with most of the 14 states. However, each state has its own registration filing requirements and procedure, which may vary slightly. While initially all of the 14 states required filing of registration applications together with the prospective offering circular, the registration requirement has evolved over the years. Michigan since 1984 only requires the filing of a simple notice of sale. The other 13 states still require the filing of both the offering circular and registration materials. We will discuss below in the 'burden' section how the other 13 states deal with the review of these documents.

Although the states have essentially adopted a uniform format to follow for disclosure, when the FTC adopted the FTC Franchise Rule, it again decided to formulate its own disclosure format of 20 categories. Those categories were similar to the UFOC Guidelines, but different again. The FTC also provided that earnings claims would have to be disclosed in a separate document. We are not reprinting its table of contents for reasons which will be discussed below. Contrary to popular belief, the FTC did *not* adopt a registration or filing procedure and does not review the disclosure document.

As a result of the FTC action, franchisors in the USA have been faced with a decision as to whether to use the FTC disclosure format or the UFOC Guidelines format. The dilemma for franchisors selling on a nationwide basis in the USA was that some of the disclosure and registration states would not accept the FTC disclosure document for filing. As a result, the FTC had to provide in its Interpretive Guides that franchisors could use the UFOC Guidelines format to comply with the FTC Franchise Rule. As a matter of fact, the FTC provided that the UFOC Guidelines format could be used in lieu of the FTC Franchise Rule disclosure document in any state, 'notwithstanding the presence or absence of a state franchise law'. The manner in which it can be used, however, depends on whether there is a currently effective state registration.

In setting up its elaborate guidelines on how the UFOC could be used in lieu of the FTC disclosure format, the FTC proclaimed some limited pre-emption of the state laws. In its Interpretive Guides, the FTC said it would not pre-empt the state laws, except that in six areas the FTC Franchise Rule would still apply:

- **Scope of the rule**: disclosure is needed for all transactions covered by the FTC Franchise Rule.
- **Persons covered by the rule**: franchisors obligated under the FTC Franchise Rule have to comply even if not covered by state law.
- **Timing of disclosures**: the FTC timing requirements apply, unless a state law requires earlier disclosure.

- **Contracts to be executed**: prospective franchisees must be given copies of completed contracts proposed to be executed at least five business days before signing.
- **Certain prohibitions**: franchisors and franchise brokers cannot make representations contradicting what is in the disclosure document.
- **Refunds**: it is a violation not to refund fees as provided in the contract.

Once the FTC conceded that franchisors could use the UFOC Guidelines format everywhere, hardly any franchisor who franchises on a national scale in the USA uses the FTC disclosure document format. For that reason, we have not provided you with the table of contents of the FTC Franchise Rule disclosure requirements.

The FTC Franchise Rule also imposed two 'cooling off' periods. First, the disclosure document must be given to a prospective franchisee at the earlier of the 'first personal meeting' or ten business days before signing any agreements or paying any money. The 'first personal meeting' is a face-to-face meeting between the prospective franchisee and a franchisor or its franchise broker to discuss the sale of a franchise. It does not include telephone or mail contacts. In addition, execution copies of all documents to be signed by the franchisee must be provided to the franchisee with all the blanks filled in at least five business days before the documents are signed. These two periods can run simultaneously (but as a practical matter seldom do).

In 1999, the FTC finally decided that it should amend the FTC Franchise Rule to adopt essentially the UFOC Guidelines. More on that below.

Why are these laws so burdensome?

If most franchisors in the USA are using the UFOC Guidelines to prepare their offering circulars, why are these laws so burdensome? Doesn't this provide the desired uniformity? There are a variety of reasons why these laws are so burdensome, most of which are related to the detailed disclosure obligations, the prerogatives of the state examiners reviewing those documents and the lack of actual uniformity.

Despite the detailed disclosure obligations contained in the UFOC Guidelines and its instructions, drafting an offering circular is not a precise endeavour. It takes a considerable amount of business judgement to determine what has to be disclosed and how to disclose that information. And, when the franchisor has completed its offering circular and files its document with the states, many of the state franchise regulators may not agree with the manner in which certain information is disclosed and will require revisions before the registration is approved.

While at one time all the registration states reviewed offering circulars filed with them, over time five of the 14 states requiring registration or a filing have essentially opted out of the review process:

- Michigan since 1984 only requires the filing of a simple notice of sale.
- Wisconsin and Indiana require the offering circular to be filed, but do not review it, and it becomes effective on filing.
- South Dakota and Hawaii require an offering circular to be filed, but no longer review it. In South Dakota, the registration becomes effective ten days after filing and in Hawaii seven days after filing.

The remaining nine states (California, Illinois, Maryland, Minnesota, New York, North Dakota, Rhode Island, Virginia and Washington) review the offering circular in various degrees and provide comments of one sort or another. Typically the franchisor filing an initial registration with all these states can expect a large number of disparate comments, sometimes showing no consistency of review among the nine states. Although the states are mandated by statute to reply to an application within set time limits (e.g. 30 days), it can take 60 to 120 days or longer after filing to receive all the state approvals. To try to achieve some uniformity in the comments provided so that the franchisor can develop a uniform document to use in all states, eight of the states now participate in an optional coordinated review process where one state collects all the comments and deals with the franchisor to finalize the offering circular. The ninth state, California, does not participate in the coordinated review process.

Almost every franchisor in the USA desires to use one offering circular in every jurisdiction, but that seldom is possible for a start-up franchisor. Yet many franchisors will not participate in the coordinated review process because it takes longer and the statutory timelines for reply by the states are extended and/or waived. Thus, it is not uncommon for a start-up franchisor who avoids the coordinated review process to have different offering circulars for different jurisdictions.

The state review process is often the most burdensome part of the disclosure and registration process and it has to be repeated every year. Most states have the franchise registrations expire a set time after the franchisor's fiscal year end (typically 110 to 120 days), but some have the registrations expire one year after approval. The coordinated review process is not used for annual renewals or material change amendment filings. The FTC Franchise Rule, on the other hand, requires updating 90 days after the close of business franchisor's fiscal year end.

Because of the disparity in the timing of renewal applications, many franchisors try to get their renewals on a cycle that coincides with their fiscal year end. This can usually be done by requesting the states that have a renewal date that does not coincide with the franchisee's fiscal year end to adjust their expiration dates consistent with the other states that have renewal filings based on the franchisor's fiscal year end. Most franchisors have a 31 December fiscal year end, so most franchisors have to revise their offering circulars in March for filing in late March or early April. The date when the renewal document has to be filed varies from 30 days prior to the expiration date (in Indiana) to one day before expiration.

For outside counsel who represent a number of clients, this 'March madness' is a real burden, but it is even worse for the state franchise examiners who are literally inundated with hundreds of filings at the same time. Eight of the 14 states review the annual renewal filings in the same manner as new filings. Illinois law says the renewal is effective on filing, but the state has been reviewing filings anyway several weeks or several months after the filing under its administrative authority. Annual renewals are effective upon filing in Indiana, South Dakota and Wisconsin, and seven days after filing in Hawaii. In Michigan, another simple notice of sale has to be filed. But in the other eight states, the renewal process can take up to a month or two to complete.

In addition, if there is a material change in any of the information contained in the offering circular during the course of the year, a material change amendment has to be filed with most of the states, but not with Michigan or Indiana. The states and the FTC have different definitions of what is a material change (some have none) and different time periods for when a material change amendment has to be filed, but the filing must be made promptly. The longest time periods are the FTC's timetable, which says the disclosure document has to be updated on at least a quarterly basis, and Illinois, which says the material change amendment has to be filed within 90 days after the occurrence of the material change. Most of the states review material change amendments, perhaps with less vigour, but they are effective upon filing in Illinois, South Dakota and Wisconsin, and seven days after filing in Hawaii.

Clearly, however, the UFOC Guidelines require more disclosure than any other jurisdiction in the world.

Lack of pre-emption

As described above, the US federal system has created a crazy quilt of compliance with the franchise disclosure and registration laws. Uniformity is difficult to achieve and the process of preparing the offering circular, making material change amendments and annual renewal fillings, and dealing with the state examiners who will review and comment on the documents, is a time consuming, expensive and oftentimes frustrating process.

A large part of the burden could be cured if the FTC asserted federal pre-emption over the disclosure and registration process. In its proposed revisions to the FTC Franchise Rule, however, the FTC has again indicated that it has no intention of asserting pre-emption when it modifies the FTC Franchise Rule, so the burden on franchisors will not be likely to be lessened.

But an interesting development is happening quietly. Several of the disclosure and registrations states have essentially dropped out of the review process in recent years, and it is possible that others may follow suit. But that leaves the nine states that review offering circulars in the enviable (or undesirable, depending on your views) position of dictating what the contents of an offering circular should be for essentially the entire country. Why should these nine states be appointed the public guardians of franchise disclosure for the whole country?

What are the penalties for failing to comply with these laws?

Failure to comply with the FTC Franchise Rule is a violation of Section 5 of the FTC Act, subjecting violators to civil penalties of up to $10,000 per violation. However, the FTC Franchise Rule does not provide a private right of action to a franchisee. However, in several states, franchisees have successfully sued franchisors for rescission or damages under the state's 'Little FTC Act' for violation of the FTC Rule.

At the state level, it is typically unlawful to make untrue statements or false representations in the disclosure documents. The state statutes usually give the franchisee the right to sue for damages and/or rescission if the law is violated. The franchisee can seek damages or injunctive relief and usually can recover his or her attorneys' fees. In some states, a wilful violation of the law can also subject the franchisor to criminal penalties.

It is critical to understand that at both the federal and state levels, the penalties can apply not only to the franchisor, but also to its officers, directors and persons actively involved in the sales process

How have franchisors and franchisees benefited?

Presale disclosure

In the early days of franchising, there was considerable resistance by many franchisors to the disclosure process. Many thought legislation was not necessary to address franchisee concerns. However, it was difficult to ignore the fact that there were a number of fraudulent scam artists engaged in selling franchises to unsuspecting and unsophisticated franchisors prior to enactment of the first franchise disclosure and registration laws.

After living with the disclosure and registration process over the years, and due in large part to the International Franchise Association's commitment to disclosure, the legitimate franchise community in the United States has come to accept, and indeed rely on, the pre-sales disclosure process. The IFA Code of Ethics requires its members to obey the laws and provides:

> IFA's members believe that the information provided during the presale disclosure process is the cornerstone of a positive business climate for franchising, and is the basis for successful and mutually beneficial relationships.

From the franchisor's perspective, the disclosure process provides material information to a franchisee prior to sale and makes it difficult for a franchisee to argue later that it did not know what it was getting into. From the franchisee's perspective, it gives him or her access to a wealth of information on the franchisor and its programme to allow the franchisee to make an intelligent choice of whether to proceed with the purchase of the franchise.

The registration process

It is more difficult to see how the franchise community has benefited from the registration process. At one time, the registration process may have been a necessary adjunct to the disclosure process. But all that registration does is to provide a central filing system for franchisors selling in a state (which could be achieved by a simple notice filing as in Michigan) and to get state examiner comments on whether they believe the franchisor has properly disclosed in accordance with the UFOC Guidelines. The state examiner comments are seldom consistent and often are trivial.

In this author's opinion, the states can prevent fraud or other improper acts without having to use the registration process to achieve that result. However, the current Deputy Securities Commissioner for Maryland, who is the Chair of the Franchise and Business Opportunities Project Group of NASAA, argues that the intended beneficiaries of the state franchise laws are franchisees and that the relevant assessment should be the costs of review in relation to the benefits afforded franchisees. He points out that states routinely receive registration applications from unsophisticated start-up franchisors, often without the benefit of legal counsel, and do not begin to approach substantial compliance with the UFOC Guidelines. For these franchisors and their prospective franchisees, the review function conveys a critical benefit.

According to various studies, there are approximately 2500 to 3000 franchisors in the United States, but only 1100 to 1200 typically are registered in the disclosure and registration states. In a study conducted for the IFA by FRANDATA, the study found that in 1996 there were 1156 registered franchising companies in 12 states studied and 1178 registered franchising companies in those states in 1997. The study also found that 321 franchise systems registered in 1996 were 'missing' in 1997 and had been replaced by 339 'new ones'. In an attempt to explain the 'missing' companies, the author said there may have three reasons why a company was missing: (a) some may have stopped offering franchises in a registration state; (b) the registration may have been filed in 1996 and been valid for part of 1997, but not renewed; or (c) the authors may not have been able to obtain the company's UFOC's in time for the study.[3]

There are different ways to interpret these data, but one way is to conclude that 1700 (more likely 2000) of the franchisors in those years escaped any review by a state examiner because they did not register to sell in one of the registration and disclosure states, and, in those states, there was a swing of 600 franchisors. Yet the number of franchisee complaints received by the FTC is decreasing.

Extraterritorial effect of the US laws

The existing FTC Franchise Rule is not clear as to whether it applies to the sale of a franchise by a United States franchisor to a franchisee located in another country that operates a franchised business in the other country. Arguably, the FTC Franchise Rule was not intended to apply to such transactions. However, a sale to a United States citizen or resident to operate a franchise in a foreign country is likely to be covered by the FTC Franchise Rule. Some confusion on the situation was created when a Florida federal district court (trial court) upheld a claim under the Florida Deceptive Trade Practices Act that the failure of a US franchisor to give a South American prospect an offering circular violated the FTC Franchise Rule, but that case was subsequently reversed on appeal.

In its notice of proposed rule-making to revise the FTC Franchise Rule, the FTC makes clear that the revised Rule will apply only to the sale of franchisees to be operated in the United States, its territories and possessions. A proposed new provision would limit the scope of the revised FTC Franchise Rule to the sale of franchises in the United States, its possessions or territories. The FTC says the record supports its finding that mandated pre-sale disclosure in international franchise sales 'is unnecessary, may be misleading and may impede competition'. In addition, the FTC believes that franchises are sold internationally 'to sophisticated investors who are generally represented by counsel or who can otherwise protect their own interests'.

At the state level, the US franchisor needs to review each applicable law. In Illinois, for example, the sale by an Illinois based franchisor to a foreign franchisee to operate a franchised business in a foreign country would not be subject to the law's registration and disclosure requirements, but will still be subject to the law's antifraud provisions. In New York, however, a New York based franchisor would have to provide a New York registered offering circular.

Foreign franchisors selling into the USA

A foreign franchisor selling to a US citizen or resident to operate a franchised business in the USA would have to comply with the FTC Franchise Rule and any applicable state disclosure and registration requirements. The FTC recently complicated the life of foreign franchisors by saying that the financials attached to the offering circular must meet United States GAAP requirements. That might force foreign franchisors to set up a US subsidiary to engage in US franchise sales so that subsidiary can provide the necessary financials in accordance with US GAAP. There may be other good reasons for a foreign franchisor to use a United States subsidiary rather than sell directly into the United States from a foreign country, but that is beyond the scope of this book.

A sale by a foreign franchisor to a foreign franchisee to operate a franchised business in the USA, however, may not be covered by the FTC Franchise Rule but it might be covered by some of the state franchise disclosure and registration laws.

Foreign franchisors attending trade shows in the USA

Many trade show promoters will not allow a domestic franchisor to participate in its trade show without having an effective offering circular. The same would be true for a foreign franchisor seeking to sell its franchises to a US citizen to operate a franchise in the USA. If the foreign franchisor were only going to sell franchises to be operated outside the USA, however, compliance with the US franchise disclosure and registration laws probably is not necessary and this requirement is not likely to be imposed by the trade show host. The foreign franchisor, however, would be well advised to consult with franchise counsel to determine whether the law of the state where the show is being held might cover its appearance at the trade show.

IFA advises that its policy regarding the International Franchise Expo (IFE), which is currently licensed to Mart Franchise Ventures, is that foreign franchise systems may exhibit at the IFE, but must prominently display a statement that indicates that their interest is in attracting investors for operation of units outside the USA only, and disclaim any interest in attracting investors to operate similar businesses in the US. IFA believes that many of these exhibitors are not necessarily interested in USA investors anyway, and may be attending the IFE because of the large number of international visitors and delegations that participate in the show.

What does the future hold for disclosure and registration in the USA?

Will the proposed revisions to the FTC Franchise Rule be less burdensome?

The proposed revisions to the FTC Franchise Rule are designed to replace the FTC's originally promulgated disclosure requirements with modified versions of the UFOC Guidelines. It is good that the FTC disclosure requirements will finally mirror the disclosure requirements in the UFOC Guidelines that franchisors have been following for years anyway. It really did not make sense for the FTC to keep a disclosure regime in place that hardly anyone is following.

But as usual the FTC did not simply accept the current UFOC Guidelines. It decided to tinker with them and to revise them in numerous respects. Many of the FTC's proposed revisions will modernize the UFOC Guidelines provisions, but many are controversial and precipitated 40 detailed written comments in late 1999 and early 2000. As of the date of this book, the franchise community has been waiting for almost three years for the FTC to announce what the final revisions will look like. There is little likelihood that we will see their revisions until 2004 at the earliest. And then, when they are announced, there will be another short comment period and yet another interval before they can be promulgated and made effective. It is impossible to guess a timeline.

We do not have space to digest all of the FTC's proposed revisions, but some of the positive things they may do are the following:

- Business opportunities will be broken out into a separate rule of their own.
- The FTC Franchise Rule will be limited to the offer or sale of a franchise to be located in the USA, its territories or possessions.
- The FTC would enable franchisors to comply with the revised Rule by using electronic media to furnish their disclosure documents.
- A sophisticated investor exemption would apply to large investments (US$1.5 million) and large corporate franchisees (in business for five years with a net worth of US$5 million).
- The first personal meeting disclosure requirement would be dropped in favour of giving a disclosure document 14 days before signing an agreement or paying any consideration.
- Execution copies of documents would have to be given five days before signing.
- Earnings claims can be made in the text of the offering circular.
- Numerous other modifications of the offering circular disclosure requirements.

Besides recognizing the reality that the UFOC Guidelines are the preferred disclosure vehicle, perhaps the most beneficial revision proposed by the FTC will be to allow electronic disclosure of offering circulars (the USA can now catch up with its friends in Australia). Perhaps the most disappointing thing is the failure to provide for effective pre-emption. The states will be left free to impose additional require-ments that allegedly provide equal or greater protection for franchisees, but in reality simply clutter up the disclosure process.

Are the states going to help the franchise community achieve uniformity?

As noted above, there have been no new state disclosure and registration laws since 1980. State efforts in the 1980s to achieve uniformity among themselves went nowhere.

But the trend in recent years indicates that many of the states that have been involved in the registration process no longer feel the need to devote their resources to reviewing disclosure documents. While they still happily accept registration applications and a large filing fee, five states have essentially opted out of the review process (Michigan, Wisconsin, Indiana, South Dakota and Hawaii) and a sixth is supposed to have been statutorily opted out of the review process for renewals and material change amendments (Illinois, although the state is using its adminis-trative powers to review after the fact). A seventh (California) is going to move to a risk-based review process.

Does this trend mean that the remaining states are going to roll over and play dead too? It is not likely, but it will be interesting to see how the franchise disclosure and registration states respond (either directly or through NASAA) when the final revised FTC Franchise Rule is finally promulgated (if ever). In order to make their laws consistent with the revised FTC Franchise Rule, the 14 states that have disclosure and registration requirements will have to revise their laws and/or implementing regulations to conform to the FTC's revisions. This will give the states a mechanism and opportunity to help the franchise community to achieve more uniformity, but this is unlikely to happen.

If the states are going to remain involved in the disclosure and registration process after the FTC Franchise Rule is finally revised, expansion of the NASAA coordinated review programme to include all states still providing reviews would be a useful step in helping start-up franchisors to achieve uniformity, and extension of the process to material changes amendment and annual renewal filings would be helpful.

Business opportunity laws

Twenty-five states and the FTC have adopted so-called business opportunity laws or seller-assisted marketing plan laws. Three other jurisdictions cover these types of arrangements in their consumer protection laws. They are often misdescribed as 'distributorship' laws. These laws are designed to protect innocent investors from being lured on the basis of false or misstated information into buying a business to sell goods or services at retail using racks or vending machines at locations procured by the seller, such as greeting card displays, candy machines and the like, or entering into questionable business ventures, such as worm or mink farming. However, if a seller offers a marketing plan to start a business, or makes certain enumerated representations in connection with the sale of the business opportunity, these laws are likely to apply to the relationship. Trademark association is not required.

The state business opportunity laws

The following 25 states have business opportunity laws: Alaska, California, Connecticut, Florida, Georgia, Illinois, Indiana, Iowa, Kentucky, Louisiana, Maine, Maryland, Michigan, Minnesota, Nebraska, New Hampshire, North Carolina, Ohio, Oklahoma, South Carolina, South Dakota, Texas, Utah, Virginia and Washington. The following three jurisdictions have consumer protection laws that cover business opportunities: Alabama, District of Columbia and Tennessee.

The definitions used in the state business opportunity laws vary considerably. The Illinois Business Opportunities Sales Law of 1995, for example, defines a 'business opportunity' as a written or oral contract or agreement whereby the seller provides products, equipment, supplies or services to enable the purchaser to start a business where the purchaser is required to pay more than $500 and in which the seller represents that he or she will:

1. provide locations or assist the purchaser in finding locations to install vending machines, racks, display cases or similar devices on another person's property; or
2. provide or assist the purchaser in finding outlets or accounts for the purchaser's products or services; or
3. buy all the products made, produced, fabricated, grown, bred or modified by the purchaser using the supplies or services sold to the purchaser; or
4. guarantee that the purchaser will derive income which exceeds the price paid; or
5. refund all or part of the purchase price or repurchase the goods sold if the purchaser is dissatisfied with the business; or
6. provide a marketing plan, provided that the law does not apply to sale of a marketing plan made in conjunction with a federally registered trademark.

The 25 state business opportunities laws generally require the seller to file or register with the state and to disclose certain specified information to the purchaser prior to the time the purchaser pays any money. The seller usually must be able to substantiate by documentation any earnings claimed. Some states require the seller to post a bond or register with state authorities. If the seller violates these laws, the purchaser can void the contract and obtain a refund of the purchase price paid. In most states, the injured purchaser can also sue for injunctive relief and/or damages and usually can recover attorney's fees.

Most state business opportunity laws can apply to certain types of franchise programmes. Generally, however, franchisors with federally registered trade marks or service marks or those that comply with the FTC Rule or local franchise disclosure laws are exempt from the state business opportunities laws. However, the exemption may not apply if the franchisor makes earnings claims in connection with its offering or offers to refund the buyer's money if the buyer is dissatisfied with the business opportunity. In several states – Florida, Kentucky, Nebraska, Texas and Utah – it is necessary for a franchisor to file a notice of exemption to avoid application of the business opportunities laws. In Connecticut, if the seller's trade mark or service mark was registered after 1 October 1996, a copy of the trade mark must be filed with the state to claim the exemption.

The FTC business opportunity regulation

The FTC Rule also regulates such operations (and calls them 'franchises') and does not pre-empt the state laws except to the extent that the disclosures required to be made may be inconsistent. Unlike its franchise definition, which is broader than the state definitions, the FTC Rule business opportunity definition is more limited than the state definitions. The FTC Rule applies when there is a continuing commercial relationship whereby: (a) a seller, defined as a 'franchisor', sells goods, commodities or services which are supplied either by the franchisor or by another person with whom the franchisee is required or advised to do business; (b) secures for the franchisee retail outlets or accounts for the goods, or locations or sites for vending machines, rack displays or other product sales displays, and provides the services of a person to secure those outlets or sites; and (c) requires the payment of $500 or more within six months after the business is commenced as a condition of obtaining or commencing the operation. Again, all three elements must be present.

The FTC Rule, which applies in all states and US territories and possessions, requires the seller to provide a disclosure document to the purchaser prior to the time the sale is consummated. It is an unfair or deceptive act or practice under Section 5 of the FTC Act to fail to furnish the information.

In its rule-making proceeding to revise the FTC Rule, the FTC announced that it plans to promulgate a separate business opportunity trade regulation rule. No time table has been set, but the FTC advises that it will not start work on a new business opportunity rule until it revises the franchise portion of the FTC Rule.

Termination/non-renewal or relationship laws

There are 23 states, plus two US territories, that have passed laws which in one way or another regulate some aspect of the relationship between franchisors and their franchisees, particularly with respect to the termination or non-renewal of the relationship. The jurisdictions with relationship laws include: Alaska, Arkansas, California, Connecticut, Delaware, Hawaii, Idaho, Illinois, Indiana, Iowa, Louisiana, Maryland, Michigan, Minnesota, Mississippi, Missouri, Nebraska, New Jersey, North Dakota, South Dakota, Virginia, Washington, Wisconsin, Puerto Rico and the Virgin Islands. The Alaska law was adopted in 2002 and the Idaho and Louisiana laws in 2003.

The scope of coverage of these laws varies considerably. Some of the earliest state laws passed, and the laws of Puerto Rico and the Virgin Islands, apply generally to just about every selective distribution relationship, including franchises. However, many of the more recently adopted laws often use a definition of 'franchise' similar to that used in the franchise disclosure laws and thus would not apply to the typical distribution arrangement. Each state's definition must be examined to determine its scope of coverage.

For example, the California Franchise Relations Act uses the same definition of 'franchise' used in its disclosure law. In Illinois, the relationship law is physically incorporated into the Illinois Franchise Disclosure Act of 1987, so the same definition applies. As a result, these laws would apply to the typical uniform business format or package franchise, but would not apply to the typical distribution agreement if the seller does not require a fee to be paid by the distributor. The Arkansas

Franchise Practices Act requires the agreement to have an 'exclusive territory' in order for there to be coverage.

On the other hand, Connecticut, New Jersey, Wisconsin, Missouri and Mississippi have laws of broad applicability, as do Puerto Rico and the Virgin Islands. For example, the Connecticut franchises law covers 'franchises', which are defined as a franchisee being granted the right to offer, sell or distribute goods or services under a marketing plan or system prescribed in substantial part by a franchisor, and the operation of the business pursuant to the plan is substantially associated with the franchisor's mark or trade name. No fee is required.

The New Jersey Franchise Practices Act covers 'franchises,' which are defined as written arrangements in which one person grants to another person a licence to use a trade name, trade mark etc., and in which there is a community of interest in the marketing of goods or services at wholesale, retail, by lease agreement or otherwise. However, the Act applies only to a franchise which contemplates or requires a place of business in New Jersey, where gross sales of the products or services covered by the franchise exceed $35,000 for the prior 12 months, and where more than 20% of the franchisee's gross sales are derived from the franchise.

The Wisconsin Fair Dealership Law applies to 'dealerships', which are defined as expressed or implied agreements, oral or written, by which a person is granted the right to sell or distribute goods or services, or use a trade name, trade mark etc., in which there is a community of interest in the business of selling or distributing goods or services at wholesale, retail, by lease, agreement or otherwise. The Alaska law applies to distributors who provide merchandise or services to a dealer.

The termination/non-renewal and relationship laws vary considerably in the subject areas regulated. Many of the laws deal with the relationship between the franchisor and franchisee during the term of the agreement, and cover matters such as the right of the franchisee to associate with other franchisees of the franchisor, competition by the franchisor and a ban on discriminatory treatment.

Some of the laws, such as the Missouri and Mississippi statutes, which have very inclusive definitions of what constitutes a 'franchise', only require 90 days notice to cancel, terminate or fail to renew a franchise. Most of these laws, however, including those in Connecticut, New Jersey and Wisconsin, deal with the ability of the seller, manufacturer or franchisor to end the relationship with the distributor, dealer or franchisee. Typically, the agreement can only be terminated or not renewed for 'good cause', as that term is defined in the statute. There usually must be notice given within a specified time before the termination, cancellation or non-renewal takes place; for example, 90 days in Wisconsin, 60 days in Connecticut and New Jersey and 180 days in California. Often, the distributor, dealer or franchisee must be given the right to cure the alleged deficiency. In Wisconsin, the notice requirements also apply to a substantial change in the competitive circumstances of the agreement.

There is also often a provision requiring the franchisor to repurchase the franchisee's inventory, if the termination actually takes place, at a price specified in the statute, such as 'fair wholesale market value'. Some laws also permit the heirs of the franchisee to inherit the agreement and continue the relationship indefinitely. Under the California law, a franchisee who has received a notice of non-renewal has the right to sell his business to a person meeting the franchisor's current requirements. The most comprehensive law is in Iowa, which covers most of the subjects discussed above plus transfers of franchises, encroachments, terminations, non-renewal and other matters.

If the agreement is terminated by the franchisor without complying with these laws, the franchisee is usually given the right to sue for damages and/or injunctive relief and generally can recover his or her attorneys' fees in addition. The net effect of some of these laws often means that the relationship will exist for as long as the franchisee (and his or her heirs) may want, as long as they continue to comply with the terms of the franchise or distribution agreement until the agreement expires of its own force without renewal rights.

The two laws adopted in 2003 have quite narrow focuses. The Idaho law simply provides that any condition, stipulation or provision in a franchise agreement that purports to waive venue or jurisdiction in that state's court system is void, but the law allows the franchise agreement to make a choice of law. The Louisiana law just prohibits as a deceptive or unfair trade practice any business franchise agreement, including any written modifications, amendments or addendum, from requiring franchises located within ten miles of each other to honour or accept reciprocal agreements.

Efforts have been made several times over the years to adopt a federal relationship law. In fact, Bills have been introduced and hearings held in Congress frequently. The definition used in most of those proposed federal Bills has been broad enough to regulate most franchising and many selective distribution arrangements. No Bill has passed Congress so far because of substantial opposition from the industry and many franchisees.

Special industry laws

There are also laws that relate to specific industries, such as wholesalers or dealers selling motor vehicles, petroleum products, farm and industrial equipment lawn and garden equipment, outdoor power equipment, hotels, campgrounds or liquor, wine or beer.

A number of states have adopted disclosure laws or regulations regulating only certain specified industries. Some of those industries and the number of states with such laws are as follows: gasoline station operations (ten), automobile dealerships (two), hardware distributors (one) and real estate (one). There are also four states which do not have franchise disclosure laws, but have general statutes prohibiting misrepresentations when selling a franchise.

There are also a number of specific termination/non-renewal or relationship laws relating to particular industries. For example, Missouri has a law relating only to campground franchises. Automobile dealership relationships are regulated by the Federal Automobile Dealer Franchise Act (often called the 'automobile dealer day-in-court' law) and 50 separate state laws. Gasoline station operations are covered by the Federal Petroleum Marketing Practices Act and 42 separate state laws.

Farm machinery dealerships are covered by 45 state laws; recreational vehicle dealerships are subject to five state laws; and liquor, beer and/or wine distributorship are regulated by 45 state laws.

What can be franchised?

What can be franchised in the USA is essentially similar to the types of businesses described in Chapter 2. Franchising is a method of distributing products and/or services, and the IFA says on its website that 'more than 75 industries operate within the franchising format.'

In response to the question 'How widespread is franchising?', IFA's website[4] says:

The answer may surprise you. In 2000, most analysts estimated that franchising companies and their franchisees accounted for $1 trillion in annual US retail sales from 320,000 franchised small businesses in 75 industries. Moreover, franchising is said to account for more than 40 percent of all US retail sales. Industry analysts estimate that franchising employs more than 8 million people, a new franchise outlet opens somewhere in the US every 8 minutes, and approximately one out of every 12 retail business establishments is a franchised business.

How to go about being a franchisor or franchisee

The descriptions of why to franchise your business (Chapter 3), why to take up a franchise (Chapter 4), how to become a franchisor (Chapter 5) and how to become a franchisee (Chapter 6), apply equally well to a US franchise situation. The one difference, of course, is that the franchisor selling franchises to a US citizen to be operated in the USA will have to comply with the federal and state franchise laws described in this chapter.

Chapter 7 dealing with the financial aspects of franchising is generally applicable to the USA to the extent it discusses how fees are calculated, but the role of the banks in the USA is much different from that in the UK. US banks are not as eager to participate in the franchise lending business.

Chapter 8 dealing with franchisor–franchisee relations and Chapter 9 dealing with channels of communication and franchisee advisory associations are generally applicable to franchises in the USA. However, because of the existence of the US franchise relationship laws described in this chapter, there may be a more adversarial relationship between franchisors and their franchisees than exists in some other countries. It is always the goal of a successful franchise system in the USA to have satisfactory relationships with its franchisees, but that usually requires hard work on both sides to achieve the desired balance in the relationship.

The chapters on overview of contractual issues (Chapter10) and the structure of franchise agreements (Chapter 11) also reflect to a large degree similar considerations in the US franchise system.

The chapter on information technology (Chapter 12) does not fully address the ongoing battle in the USA over the use of the Internet by both franchisors and franchisees to sell products and/or services, and whether the franchisor has adequately reserved the right to compete with its franchisees through Internet sales, or whether the franchisee's franchise agreement allows the franchisee to make Internet sales either within or outside its territory.

Not for profit franchising (Chapter 13) applies only to the UK. Not for profit franchises are not that common in the USA, and the FTC has issued an advisory opinion holding that not for profit organizations are not intended to be covered by the FTC Franchise Rule.

The chapters dealing with international franchising (chapters 14 and 15) are equally apropos to US franchisors seeking to expand internationally. The only question the US franchisor faces in going international that is different is whether the FTC Franchise Rule or one of the state franchise laws might apply to that transaction.

Litigation in the USA[5]

Some foreign franchisors may be reluctant to do business in the USA because they fear becoming embroiled in litigation in the US courts. There is no denying that the USA's system of using juries for all types of civil actions, allowing class action lawsuits and permitting plaintiff's lawyers to take cases on a contingency fee basis has resulted in more litigation with larger damage awards than anywhere else in the world.

Unfortunately, it is also true that there is a considerable amount of litigation in the USA in the franchise area, although perhaps the consequences for franchisors are not as dire as the large number of lawsuits may suggest.

Litigation involving franchising seems to have followed trends or patterns over the years. In the early years, there were many claims relating to outright fraud in the sale of franchises, particularly unregistered franchises. Most state franchise laws give the franchisee a private cause of action for violation of the state's registration and disclosure laws. In later years, there have been numerous actions alleging anti-trust violations, breach of the duty of good faith and fair dealing or breach of fiduciary duties, and class action suits by franchisee associations on behalf of their members.

Despite a lot of franchise litigation, franchisors are likely to be found liable to franchisees only for fraud or significance breaches relating to the franchisor's contract obligations. Franchisees generally have not been successful in proving anti-trust violations, breaches of the duty of good faith and fair dealing (it is not a breach of the duty of good faith for a franchisor to do what the contract says it can do) or breaches of fiduciary duties (fiduciary duties normally do not arise in the franchise relationship), or in filing class actions by an association of franchisees on behalf of its members (a franchisee association may not have standing to request the individual claims of its members). Obviously, there are exceptions to this general statement.

The fact of the matter is that franchisor-franchisee relationships in the USA have improved over the years. To avoid the litigation quagmire, many franchisors have used alternative dispute resolution (ADR) procedures. ADR can consist of mediation, an internal claims resolution procedure and/or arbitration. The idea is to provide a mechanism for an early resolution of disputes at a minimum of cost.

Many franchisors use arbitration for all dispute resolution with their franchisees, partially because the procedure is supposed to be confidential. That is misleading, however, because an adverse arbitration award or settlement may have to be disclosed in item 3 of the franchisor's offering circular. Moreover, arbitration in the USA may or may not be faster and/or cheaper than litigation, and it has the disadvantage generally of being final and binding with no right of appeal (except for procedural errors).

The so-called litigation explosion in the USA should not deter a foreign franchisor from franchising in the USA. As relations between franchisors and franchisees continue to improve in the USA and as ADR becomes more popular to resolve disputes, a franchisor who follows sound business practices is not likely to be exposed to burdensome litigation.

Notes

1. This chapter is based on a paper given at the Annual Conference of the International Bar Association in San Francisco, September 2003.
2. The Oregon law essentially prohibits fraudulent misrepresentation in connection with the offer or sale of franchises, but the implementing regulations require a disclosure document to be given to prospective franchisees.
3. Kathryn Morgan, The 'Missing Companies Study', Appendix B to FRANDATA and IFA Educational Foundation, Inc., *The Profile of Franchising, Vol. III: A Statistical Abstract of 1998 UFOC Data*. The study can be found at IFA website (http://www.franchise.org). Go to 'Sitemap', then to 'Education Foundation', then to 'Research', then to 'The Profile of Franchising Volumes I-III', then to 'Appendix B: Missing Companies Study' (visited August 4, 2003).
4. http://www.franchise.org/resourcetr/faq/q4.asp, 'ABCs of Franchising,' 'Answers to the 21 Most Commonly Asked Questions About Franchising' (visited 25 November, 2003).
5. This subsection on litigation in the USA was based in part on a paper given by Charles G. Miller, Bartko, Zankel, Tarrant & Miller, San Francisco, at the Annual Conference of the International Bar Association in San Francisco, September 2003.

Case studies: UK franchises

In this chapter we examine three franchise operations, one of which was featured in the sixth edition of this work, one of which was featured in the first edition and the other of which is new.

1. Countrywide Gardens.
2. Recognition Express.
3. Wimpy.

None of the companies is based in London. Wimpy is in the Home Counties, Recognition Express is based in the Midlands and Countrywide Gardens is based in the North of England. All these companies are well established and are active members of the British Franchise Association (BFA). Wimpy and Recognition Express have provided Council members of the BFA and Wimpy has had three Chairmen of the BFA, while Recognition Express has provided a Vice-Chairman of the BFA who also represented the BFA on the European Franchise Federation and represented that federation on the World Franchise Federation.

Two of the companies, Wimpy and Recognition Express, have been voted 'Franchisor of the Year'. All the companies came from a small beginning and none of them is what one might describe as big business, although Wimpy started as a member of a large group and was subsequently owned by two other large groups before a management buy-out. The company had in the meantime bought the rights to Europe from the US franchisor. Recognition Express started in the UK under a master franchise agreement from a US company called 'Badgeman', was owned by a large company and was subject to a management buy-out. Countrywide Gardens is a family business which was commenced in 1980 and in 1984, when a decision was made to expand nationally, franchising was the chosen route.

Despite their moderate size, by 'big' business standards, they have all made a significant contribution to small business activity and employment.

All these franchise systems are organized along traditional business format principles. They represent the hard core of franchising activity and have experienced growing pains along their path, as do all businesses. Not all dealings with franchisees go smoothly, as will be apparent from reading about their experiences, but what also emerges is that good communications and a concerned approach with franchisees do pay dividends. Despite the inevitable problems at various times all have managed to develop and grow with basically sound and successful formats. They would all agree from their experiences with many, if not all, of the principles set out in this book but they have undoubtedly each found their way to the achievement of their objectives by different routes within the established framework of franchising's basic principles.

There are three factors which call for some comment. First, all three of these franchise companies point to franchise exhibitions as a source of new franchisees. In the sixth edition of this work, which featured six UK franchisors, only one found exhibitions an effective recruitment method. Clearly exhibitions are becoming more effective than they were. Second, considering the size of operations all three franchisors manage to sustain operations with relatively low 'head office' staffing levels. All of them involve a lot of their 'head office staff' resources in contact with and support of franchisees, which helps the 'belonging to a family' feeling which exists in many franchise networks. Third, all three have concluded that considerable effort has to be put into franchisor–franchisee relations. This is a lesson which must be taken seriously (see Chapters 10 and 11). There is a similarity in approach to handling such relations, with a heavy emphasis on communications and regular meetings. The case in practice for and against franchise associations appears to be supportive of the views expressed in Chapter 11 of this book.

Case study 1

NAME OF COMPANY	YEAR ESTABLISHED BUSINESS
Countrywide Garden Maintenance Limited	1980

YEAR COMMENCED FRANCHISING	TYPE OF BUSINESS
1984	Garden and grounds maintenance to nationwide organizations, businesses and the domestic market places.

NUMBER OF OUTLETS OPEN BEFORE FRANCHISING	UK COMPANY-OWNED OUTLETS	UK FRANCHISED OUTLETS
1	1	41

Employees

IN FRANCHISING ACTIVITIES	IN COMPANY-OWNED OUTLET	IN FRANCHISED OUTLETS
15	12	450

Countrywide commenced business in 1980 and evolved from a Manchester business which offered grounds maintenance to both commercial and domestic customers. In 1984 a decision was made to expand the business on a national basis.

Having made the decision to expand, Countrywide considered the various options ▶

and decided to conduct an in-depth investigation to consider and decide whether the business could meet the basic requirements of a franchise system. Among these requirements they selected the following:

1. A long-term demand for their services.
2. A broad customer base.
3. An easy to learn system.
4. Good sustainable profits.

The Countrywide franchise package costs £29,950 plus VAT and includes the following items:

Computer
Software (*Windows*, *Word*, *Excel*, *Sage Accounting*)
Printer/fax
Stationery pack (business cards, letterheads etc.)
Sales literature
Vehicle deposit (Ford Transit)
Vehicle sign writing
Marketing launch
Training
Franchise manuals (on loan)
42 inch rotary cut ride-on lawn tractor
22 inch rotary cut lawnmower
19 inch rotary cut lawnmower
Hover mower
Strimmer
Hedge cutter
8 by 5 foot trailer
Sprayer
Hand tools
Uniforms
Protective equipment

The ongoing management services fees are 8% plus 2% for marketing and support. In addition to the 2% for marketing franchisees pay for Yellow Pages and Yell.com advertising.

Contact is made with prospective franchisees mainly through:

- franchise exhibitions;
- franchise press;
- BFA website;
- whichfranchise.com;
- the Countrywide website.

Supplemented occasionally through locally based recruitment campaigns.

Franchisee qualities

When Countrywide recruits franchisees it is crucial to both parties that the personal chemistry is right. For both to be successful it is imperative that the franchisee has a will to succeed, is conscientious, can deal with the general public, has a strong sense of customer care, has some management experience and realizes that hours of work will vary and that he will need to have the backing of his family.

Training

Countrywide's training programme for new franchisees comprises three to four days at head office to become familiar with the manuals. There are three manuals:

1. Franchise Business Manual. This covers:
   - accounts;
   - business planning;
   - writing a business plan;
   - employing staff;
   - sales and marketing.
2. ISO 9002 Manual. This covers:
   - the ISO system;
   - how the work is done;
   - all paperwork to control the business.
3. Health and Safety Manual. This covers:
   - the health and safety policy;
   - all aspects of health and safety;
   - risk assessment;

- accident procedures;
- reporting.

Approximately eight to ten days are spent working with at least two existing franchisees to see how the business operates in practice. Franchisees also learn to price work and undertake *Sage Accounts* training. Three days are spent in a horticultural college to acquire a chemical operator's license (PA1 and PA6a).

Countrywide provides a range of ongoing support services to its franchisees.

Head office support

Franchisees are backed by our experienced and professional head office staff who are all directly involved in supporting the franchise network.

Business planning

Continuous business and financial planning support ensures that franchisees always remain in control of their business as it grows and increases in success.

Marketing support

Franchisees benefit from the comprehensive range of sales and marketing support which the head office staff provide, including a fully computerized telesales team, tender sourcing, client presentations, contract negotiating and after sales support.

Accounts support

Invoicing, debt collection and credit control are often the most difficult and time consuming aspects of running of any new business. Countrywide head office staff handle all these tasks.

Telephone answering

Countrywide maintains a 'golden' free phone number (0800 234567) which appears in all Countrywide promotional material. All calls are directed to head office, from where each enquiry is immediately forwarded to the appropriate franchisee.

In the field

Experienced guidance is always available from field support staff whom the franchisee can call upon to provide help and assistance as required.

As is so often the case Countrywide had initial problems in recruiting franchisees into its new system when it first marketed its franchising. After the first two or three franchisees had become established recruitment became easier. Again, once the network became established Countrywide found that it had made some selection errors, resulting in poor quality franchisees who were restricting the overall growth of the business. This is not uncommon in many systems and new franchisors take time to gain the experience necessary to choose the best franchisees. Countrywide acknowledges that it should have helped these franchisees by helping them to sell their areas but eventually did so, replacing them with a new breed of franchisee. This was so successful that new franchisees were able to improve turnover by as much as twelve times in only a three-year period.

Countrywide has a franchisee association which has a chairman and regional representatives who meet with Countrywide and provide feedback from regional franchise meetings.

The association was established by Countrywide, as it believed it would be of great benefit to the franchisees and the franchisor. The association's role apart from enhancing franchisor–franchisee relations covers many aspects, including reviewing new contracts and dispute resolutions and some franchisee work groups, who examine specific issues and new projects.

The Countrywide story reveals that its experience mirrors what others have found when selecting the early franchisees in a network. Fortunately they recognized their

▶

problems in time to make the necessary changes, which have made such a significant different to the business. This underlines how important it is to take great care in the early choice of franchisees. The emphasis on support and the fostering of good relations with franchisees though a franchisee association is a plus considering how vital the franchisor–franchisee relationship is to a healthy franchise system.

In 2001 Countrywide added a new service branded 'Countrywide Lawn Doctor', which as its name implies is lawn treatment which includes a year round regular fertilization and weed service plus moss treatment, scarifying and aeration during the winter. Franchising commenced in 2002 and there are now 16 franchisees.

The initial package which Countrywide provides includes everything needed by the franchisee to start in business:

Computer
Software (*Windows*, *Word*, *Excel*, *Sage*)
Printer/fax
Mobile phone
Stationery pack (business cards, letterheads etc.)
Sales literature
Vehicle deposit (Renault Kangoo or similar)
Vehicle sign writing
Marketing launch
Training
Franchise manuals
Scarifier
Spiker
Fertilizer spreader
Walkover sprayer
Sweeper
Hand tools
Measuring wheel
Supply of fertilizers and chemicals
Uniforms
Personal protective equipment

Countrywide provides comprehensive head office support to its franchisees.

Business planning

Continuous business and financial planning support.

Marketing support

A sales and marketing team. Franchisees benefit from the comprehensive range of sales and marketing support which the head office staff provide and which includes a fully computerized telesales team.

Telephone answering

The company maintains a golden freephone telephone number (0800 234567) which appears in all Countrywide promotional material. All calls are directed to head office, from where each enquiry is immediately forwarded on to the appropriate franchisee.

In the field

Experienced guidance is always available from field support staff who will call on franchisees to provide help and assistance as required.

Franchisee qualities and training

See above on page 344.

Case Study 2

NAME OF COMPANY	YEAR ESTABLISHED BUSINESS
Recognition Express Limited	1979

YEAR COMMENCED FRANCHISING	TYPE OF BUSINESS
1980	The manufacture and sale of personalized name badges, small signs and other corporate recognition products.

COUNTRIES IN WHICH COMPANY OPERATES	OUTLETS OUTSIDE UK
6	5

NUMBER OF OUTLETS OPEN BEFORE FRANCHISING	UK COMPANY-OWNED OUTLETS	UK FRANCHISED OUTLETS
1	1	30 franchise territories

Employees

IN FRANCHISING ACTIVITIES	IN COMPANY-OWNED OUTLET	IN FRANCHISED OUTLETS
12	7	120 +

The business concept was started in the USA in 1972 by Dick Ferguson when Recognition Express, then called Badgeman, was the first company to promote the concept of wearing of personalized name badges. The business grew quickly and by the late 1970s many retailers were requiring their staff to wear a name badge to promote a professional and friendly image to their customers. Several of these retailers were also franchised businesses and many were taking their concept overseas. Kentucky Fried Chicken (KFC) was one of the largest customers of Recognition Express and the KFC business in the UK was purchasing name badges from Recognition Express in America. KFC suggested to Dick Ferguson that he should seek a master franchise holder to cover the UK to make it easier for KFC to buy badges in the UK. While Dick Ferguson had, by now, developed a good knowledge of franchising in America he had no knowledge or experience of franchising internationally. KFC offered their experience and helped to find the first master franchisee for Recognition Express in the UK. Recognition Express Limited opened the first company-owned outlet in Chiswick in 1979 and, following the proven format of the Americans, appointed its first three franchisees in 1980.

Recognition Express supplies to its franchisees all the production equipment they require to produce a range of personalized name badges, signs and promotional products. The equipment costs approximately £10,000. There are additional packages of equipment if they wish to expand their manufacturing potential. In addition Recognition Express has sourced a large number of preferred trade only suppliers and negotiated the best possible terms. They can provide additional promotional products which are outside of each franchisee's manufacturing capability. Recognition Express also supplies an initial stock of consumables, samples, sales and marketing material, stationery and business software.

The franchisee is provided with an induction training programme over a 12 working day period which covers product knowledge, graphic design, business administration, sales and marketing and methods of production.

In the UK Recognition Express enters into direct franchise agreements with each franchisee. In European countries the company enters into master franchise agreements.

Field support is standard and franchisees receive regular visits from the marketing, technical and financial support staff of Recog-

▶

nition Express. Weekly e-mail newsletters are sent to franchisees. Regional meetings are held every three or four months. Every two years a conference is held for all master franchise holders and franchisees to attend. These are subsidized by Recognition Express. Recognition Express supplements the above contacts with franchisees by regular mail, memos and telephone contact to ensure regular communication.

Franchise exhibitions, presentations and websites are the company's most successful means of recruiting new franchisees. Other methods used with less success include advertising in newspapers and in franchise magazines such as *Business Franchise Magazine*.

Regardless of the source of the enquiry, the procedure for recruiting franchisees then follows the same process. Initially, the company sends a franchise information pack and invites the prospective franchisee to submit a preliminary two-page application form. If a prospective franchisee at this stage or at any later stage decides that Recognition Express is not the business for him, he is encouraged to self-select himself out of the recruitment process. If the prospective franchisee returns an application form it is reviewed to ensure two key issues: first, that the prospective franchisee has the financial resources to acquire the franchise; second, that he has suitable work experience gained in a business to business environment, which Recognition Express knows from experience is necessary for him to become a franchisee. Provided he meets these criteria he is invited to attend a seminar at the company's offices in Hinckley.

This seminar may be attended by a group of prospective franchisees or may be a seminar arranged for just one person. The seminars take the following format:

- Prospective franchisees are required to sign a confidentiality undertaking.
- A board director (usually the managing director or marketing director) gives a

presentation explaining the product range, the market for the products and the way the franchise system operates. If an individual prospective franchisee is clearly well informed from reading the information pack then this stage can be dropped.

- Structured questions are asked of the prospective franchisees to help to determine whether they meet the minimum criteria required by the company.
- The production manager conducts a tour of the production facilities, distribution warehouse and offices.
- At the end of the day the seminar is reconvened to answer any questions and the prospective franchisees are handed a sheet which states 'Prospective Franchise Owners Next Stages' and which summarizes the requirements the company has for prospective franchisees and the information and assistance which will be given to them prior to joining the franchise.
- If the prospective franchisee meets the company's criteria and wishes to proceed to conducting further investigations themselves, then they must provide a more detailed financial statement of their personal finances.
- The company requires prospective franchisees to visit and talk to existing franchisees, as well as seeking advice from banks and solicitors who are experienced in franchising. This is usually only from affiliates of the British Franchise Association.

Recognition Express provides a range of ongoing support services.

New equipment is reviewed and evaluated as it comes on the market and any recommendation made to franchise owners will have been as a result of careful appraisal of its performance and cost measured against sales potential and profitability.

The company has an ongoing programme of new product development to maintain its position as market leader and to provide new opportunities for its franchise owners to grow their business.

Wherever possible Recognition Express looks to negotiate special bulk purchase rates for raw materials and any price savings are passed on to the franchise owners.

Recognition Express implements a continuous marketing support programme designed to provide sales aids and high quality sales brochures and to maintain a high profile in the trade media serving the prime target markets of its customer base. The company has a centralized direct marketing programme which ensures that every month, each franchisee that takes part has marketing material sent to a mixture of existing customers, lapsed customers and prospects. Each franchisee provides the database, and the company organizes the design, printing and posting of the material. This material includes postcards, a quarterly newsletter and direct mailers which are followed up by a telemarketing company.

The company has a very successful website, and each franchisee has his own website. These produce sales enquiries which are e-mailed direct to each franchisee.

Sales leads resulting from media activity and exhibitions are collated and passed to the relevant territory.

Recognition Express retains the services of advertising and design agencies, PR agencies and telemarketing companies who offer their services to both the company and the individual franchisees. The company also designs a lot of its own marketing material to submit to franchisees, especially when presenting new product or new market segment opportunities.

Commercial mailing lists of potential new customers by market sector and territory are purchased as necessary. Using the latest contact management software individual franchise owners can operate their own mailing lists, combined with a selection of standard sales letters written and adapted through the central marketing department. Low cost sales literature is produced centrally to keep direct marketing overheads to a minimum.

Recognition Express exhibits at trade shows attended by potential customers in its core markets. The exhibition display modules used at these national trade exhibitions are available for franchise owners participating at regional events, enabling them to buy into exhibitions on a space-only basis. The modules are pre-displayed and easy to erect so setting up time is minimal.

Advertising, PR, websites, design work and other marketing services are financed through the marketing fund. This fund is contributed by the franchisor, with the balance spread across the network on a pro-rata to turnover basis.

The company has a franchise advisory council. The purpose of the council, which meets at least three times a year, is to provide a forum for communication between the Franchisor and Franchise Owners, enabling a free exchange of views on matters relating to the Recognition Express business, and in particular:

- to provide a vehicle for franchise owners to offer their views, opinion and advice to the franchisor on maximizing business performance and profit potential, market opportunities, competitive threats, network development, sales and marketing activities.

- To enable the franchisor to raise matters which it considers relevant to franchise owners and on which their opinion is sought; to present proposals for new strategies, procedures or system developments which require support from the franchise owners to be successfully implemented.

The council comprises four representatives from the UK franchise owners who are elected by the franchise owners, two representatives of the franchisor and one invited representative from the international franchise owners.

The cost (in 2003) of establishing a Recognition Express franchise is £30,000 (plus working capital), which includes £10,000 for production equipment. The initial franchise fee is £10,000 (included in the set-up cost of £30,000). The continuing franchise fee is 10% of gross sales from which the franchisor makes a marketing contribution of a sum equal to 1% of gross sales. The marketing contributions by franchisees vary between 0.5% and 3% of gross sales.

The product range that Recognition Express provides to its customers has continually expanded throughout its trading history in the UK. From the introduction of name badges to a then non-existent market in 1979, the potential market size for its current product range in the UK has expanded to an estimated £1.2 billion.

The aim of any new franchise is to offer nationwide coverage as soon as possible. That,

combined with the original size of the market, contributed to Recognition Express allocating only 28 territories in 1979. In recent years it has become obvious that the original territories are far too big to ensure successful market penetration at the required levels. The current market size is capable of supporting a much larger network of franchisees. It is far too easy for competitors to gain market share if there is not an adequate number of franchisees proactively selling.

Recognition Express has now commenced the process of negotiating with existing franchisees who own original size territories with a view to buying back areas that they are not exploiting fully. These will then be resold to new franchisees. As a result, Recognition Express is targeting a minimum of 75 territories and a maximum of 100.

Case Study 3

NAME OF COMPANY	YEAR ESTABLISHED BUSINESS
Wimpy International Limited	This company established its business in July 2002 when there was a management buy-out but the original business of which this is a successor commenced in 1985.

YEAR COMMENCED FRANCHISING	TYPE OF BUSINESS
1954	Table service restaurants, express units and kiosks featuring the Wimpy hamburger.

COUNTRIES IN WHICH COMPANY OPERATES	OUTLETS OUTSIDE UK
2	11

NUMBER OF OUTLETS OPEN BEFORE FRANCHISING	UK COMPANY-OWNED OUTLETS	UK FRANCHISED OUTLETS
n.a.	5	295

Employees		
IN FRANCHISING ACTIVITIES	IN COMPANY-OWNED OUTLET	IN FRANCHISED OUTLETS
Not provided	60	4000

Wimpy International Limited (then owned by Pleasure Foods Limited) was the subject of a case study in the first edition of this work, which was published in 1970. Wimpy started

life back in the mid 1950s in the ownership of Joe Lyons and was bought by United Biscuits in the mid 1970s. Up to this point Wimpy had been purely table service restaurants and under the ownership of United Biscuits a new wing was added in the form of counter service. In late 1989 United Biscuits sold off all its restaurant interests including the largest operation, namely Wimpy, to what was then Grand Metropolitan. The large counter service units were absorbed into a rival brand then owned by Grand Metropolitan and the table service and brand in total was bought by three of the ex-Wimpy Board this management buy-out (MBO) being funded by venture capital investors, the lead investor being 3i. The MBO proved very successful and expanded the business quite dramatically and in July 2002 a secondary MBO led by John Davison, the managing director, was undertaken with the funding provided by the Bank of Scotland Integrated Finance.

The Wimpy business is probably the most mature franchise system in the UK, having been established 50 years ago, so the issues which arose in its early years are not relevant to what it now is. Even the 1970 study was prepared 15 years after the company commenced business, when it already had a substantial network with highly successful franchisees, many of whom owned a multiple number of outlets. The original concept, which was 'table service', is now one of three propositions which Wimpy offers in the market place at the present time.

The three offerings are:

1. **Table service restaurant**

   This typically will be found in the high street or in shopping precincts. It has been updated and includes several new items which include:

   - free-standing tables and chairs;
   - wood effect flooring;
   - overhead menu boxes for the takeaway menu;
   - new coffee machine and a speciality tea and coffee menu.

   Customers continue to be served by a waiter/waitress at the table with crockery and cutlery, not polystyrene and plastic. There is a wide ranging menu including the Wimpy beef hamburger. Although this is described as a table service restaurant it also offers a take-away service. Occupying 1500–2000 square feet, the table service restaurant requires an investment starting from £140,000, which includes a franchisee fee of £7500.

2. **Express units**

   These offer customers a rapid service from a limited take-away menu while offering an extensive selection of meal 'deals'. Express units are typically found in leisure venues such as bowling centres, leisure complexes, motorway service areas and food courts. This concept has been a major growth area for Wimpy in recent years. These units require from 500 square feet of retail space and require an investment from £90,000, including a franchise fee of £5000.

3. **Kiosks**

   This is a new concept using a minimum of space and a limited take-away menu to provide freshly cooked food to order. This fits in well where there is a high volume of foot traffic and not much space in such locations as convenience stores, forecourts, leisure complexes, sports arenas and cinemas. The kiosks require a total area of 260 square feet and an investment from £45,000, including a franchise fee of £5000.

Wimpy recruits franchisees in a number of ways:

- it exhibits at the franchise exhibitions in the UK which are supported by the BFA, of which the largest is at the NEC in Birmingham in September/October in each year;
- adverts in national newspapers and franchise magazines monthly;
- the Wimpy website, which is linked to the BFA website from which it obtains leads;
- word of mouth from existing franchisees.

▶

The selection process evaluates the applicant's attitude, management ability, financial standing and a desire to work hard to please customers. For those who have no previous catering experience some work in a Wimpy operation usually helps to determine suitability.

The initial services to the franchisee include:

- assistance with site selection, negotiation and rent levels;
- training for the franchisee and management;
- design;
- equipment specification;
- an illustrative financial proposition for a financial plan for the bank;
- assistance with initial recruitment and training of staff;
- operational manual which covers areas of health and safety, personnel, administration and all other operational procedures;
- opening assistance and marketing support until the franchisee is 'free-standing'.

In terms of ongoing support the Wimpy system is designed to be simple to operate. The franchisee need only make two phone calls to order, one for frozen and dry goods and the other for beverages. Local purchase of a few salad items is left to the franchisee. Wimpy provides:

- marketing support, which is a combination of national promotions with media and local promotions agreed with the field team to suit individual sites;
- operational support, which includes regular restaurant audits, food quality and safety checks, training videos on site and training;
- human resource information;
- updates on health and safety issues;
- assistance with any problems which may arise with the local environmental health office.

With all these support services the franchisee is aware that 'head office' is only a phone call away.

Wimpy is not without issues which arise from time to time with franchisees but it finds that they tend to be related mainly to product delivery problems, which are usually dealt with swiftly. The main reason for this is that there is an emphasis on communication which is regarded as the key to ensuring that the parties pull together. Wimpy organizes franchisee conferences.

Each district manager is responsible for approximately 30–40 units in a territory, and is the direct link with franchisees, who also have direct dial phone numbers at Wimpy headquarters. There are regular mail-outs to franchisees, including the in-house magazine the *Wimpy Times*.

Wimpy does not have a franchisee association. There is an informal system of restaurants around the country that among other matters test new products or systems as well as those tried out in company owned restaurants. Feedback is obtained from these franchisees in relation to operational procedures, recipe mix and other matters.

It is interesting to note how much emphasis this mature franchise system places upon communications, the way in which franchisees are encouraged to interact and the two-way nature of communications and how well it is working for it.

Wimpy has been operating as a franchise for some 50 years yet it still retains its enthusiasm and is not frightened to extend its scope by introducing new concepts and exploiting new market opportunities.

It is no coincidence that the range of services provided to franchisees and the manner of their delivery epitomizes what many advocate should be done but do not achieve. Wimpy's comparative longevity and current freshness of approach shows it can be done.

As a matter of interest the text of the original study, in the first edition (1970) of this work, is set out below.

Pleasure Foods Limited

Wimpy Proposition

1. A Wimpy is a high class snack bar selling a pure beef hamburger (a Wimpy) as its main item and generally conforming to a selective menu.

2. Our Franchise Negotiators will advise on suitable locations. We provide free, on loan, the equipment for cooking the Wimpys, together with certain items of advertising.

3. Our Technical Department produces plans for the conversion of approved premises and will furnish technical advice.

4. Complete 'know-how' on the administration, general running and equipping of the bar is given by our Catering Advisors who also attend at the opening of Wimpy Bars to supervise generally and train staff for 2/3 days until things are running smoothly.

5. There is no charge for the services of the Technical and Operational Departments.

6. The costs of shopfitting, equipping and conversion are borne by the licensee and he is responsible for staffing and administration.

7. Wimpy Bars must conform to an agreed specification providing a general high standard of appearance which, of course, accentuates the national appeal.

8. The gross profit in Wimpy Bars averages 60–62% of the turnover. The approximate percentage of overheads against turnover are as follows:

Rent and rates	10%
Wages (including NHI, Graduated Pensions and SET)	23–27%
Other items (electricity, telephone, Insurance, etc)	7½%
Food costs	<u>38–40%</u>
	<u>78½–84½%</u>
Net profit (before tax, depreciation)	15½–21½%

On this basis a net profit of £62–86 can be achieved with a turnover of £400 per week.

In cases where the anticipated turnover is in excess of £500 per week, it is permissible to consider a slightly higher figure than 10% for rent and rates and this fact will be taken into consideration when a specific site is discussed with our Franchise Negotiators.

9. Pleasure Foods Limited reserve the right to accept or reject a site after a careful assessment of its trading potential together with the overheads involved.

10. The size of a Wimpy Bar, including service area and wash-up, may be as little as 600 sq. ft, but average size is 1000 sq. ft and the costs of converting and equipping the premises is between £6500 and £10,000.

11. The name 'Wimpy' is the property of Pleasure Foods Limited and a licence fee of £300 is payable to this Company for its use at any one site.

12. The licensing of a Wimpy Bar is covered by an agreement between Pleasure Foods Limited and the Licensee. This agreement is for an initial period of 5 years and is signed as soon as negotiations for the site are completed. The licensing fee is payable on signature of the agreement.

13. It is not practicable to list all salient points of the agreement but this should be a matter for discussion between the Franchise Negotiators and the potential customers when all details can be fully covered.

14. At no time do we reserve areas for prospective licensees unless they have a specific approved site. We are, however, prepared to reserve a site for a reasonable time while negotiations are taking place in order to allow time for manoeuvre in negotiations.

15. It is not our policy to license new Wimpy Bars close enough to affect business of any existing bar.

▶

16. If you cannot secure a specific site because the lessors require a multiple covenant, Pleasure Foods would, in certain instances, consider taking the head lease and sub-letting to you. The Estate Department is also prepared to discuss the purchase of freeholds of existing leases where premiums are being asked.

The Wimpy franchise is, of course, the largest franchise in this country. It has been operating for a number of years and has had a most spectacular success. This is a franchise which involves the franchisee in the payment of an initial licence fee of £300. The company does lend to the franchisee a number of items of equipment which exceed in value the £300 and for which no charge is made to the franchisee.

The income for Pleasure Foods Limited from the franchise is obtained through the sale of product to the franchisee. The franchisee is obliged by his contract to purchase all his requirements from Wimpy Hamburgers and certain other items from the franchisor and the price at which they are sold includes a mark-up to cover the franchise fee.

The Wimpy franchise is a model of simplicity. Taking full advantage of a number of years of practical experience the company has developed its scheme to an extremely advanced stage. For example, virtually everything sold by the franchisee is obtained by him in packs which contain the correct portions. The amount of portion control which the franchisee has to exercise to maintain his profit levels is therefore negligible.

Indeed, Pleasure Foods go so far as to telephone through to franchisees before making deliveries to ask what the franchisee requires.

The investment in a Wimpy is fairly considerable as franchise propositions in the UK go, but, nevertheless, the company has been able to sustain a very rapid growth rate and achieved a great number of startling successes. There are quite a number of chains of franchises owned and operated by individuals or companies. Indeed, some franchisees own more than fifteen.

One should perhaps state the obvious in pointing out that the value of the pound has changed somewhat since 1970.

19 Case studies: international franchises

Case Study 1

NAME OF COMPANY
Mothercare UK Limited
(trading as Mothercare)

YEAR ESTABLISHED BUSINESS
In UK 1961
Internationally 1968

YEAR COMMENCED FRANCHISING
1984

TYPE OF BUSINESS
The company is a specialist retailer of clothing and equipment for the expectant and new mother through the first weeks and years of life of the child up to pre-school age at about five or six years of age. The company strives to be the natural first choice in meeting all the needs of the new mother and her children for childrenswear and equipment: in other words, 'Everything for the mother to be, her baby and young family'.

OUTLETS WORLDWIDE WHICH COMPANY OPERATES	OUTLETS IN UK IN WHICH COMPANY OPERATES	NUMBER OF COUNTRIES
421	247	36

(The company operates an international mail order system with ordering facilities via a catalogue and on-line through the Internet, which serves customers in over 130 countries.)

INTERNATIONAL OUTLETS	INTERNATIONAL OUTLETS COMPANY-OWNED	INTERNATIONAL OUTLETS FRANCHISED
174	0	174

Employees

IN COMPANY-OWNED OUTLETS	SUPPORTING INTERNATIONAL OUTLETS
3075	30

The international franchising activities of Mothercare are organized within an International Division of its parent company, Mothercare plc.

The Mothercare business was originally founded by Selim Zilkha in 1961 when he perceived there to be an opportunity in the market for selling everything required by the mother to be and her baby under one roof. The concept was essentially simple. By focusing on convenience, choice and value for money he presented the mother with one shop to visit and a uniform format. Zilkha had realized that the way in which maternity clothing was then sold in predominantly women's fashion outlets, while cots, push-chairs, prams and the multitude of other items required were sold in many different stores, was neither convenient nor cost effective to the consumer.

Zilkha purchased a business (W & J Harris), a small chain of stores in and around London which sold nursery hardware, such as prams and pushchairs. He sold half the stores and converted the others into Mothercare stores. In 1962–3 he published the first Mothercare catalogue with a circulation of 51,400 copies. The prime purpose of providing the catalogue was to enable the mother to plan her purchases as well as to provide her with advice and support during the time of her pregnancy and through birth and the early years of her child's life. The catalogue was, as we shall see below, an important factor in the growth of the business.

Growth of Mothercare was rapid. It only took eight years to open the first 100 stores, by which time the age range had extended to include children under five years old. Over the intervening years, the age range was extended to eight years old in 1990 and later to ten years old but is now focused on the core of mother and baby and children up to pre-school age.

The first foreign store was opened in 1968 in St Gallen, Switzerland. That store was not franchised; the first franchised store opened in 1984 in Kuwait, by which time the company had obtained more international exposure, as it had by then opened stores in Austria and Belgium and acquired a chain of stores in the USA, where it opened the first Mothercare store in 1977 in Langhorne, Pennsylvania.

On the domestic UK front, the company became public in 1972 and merged with Terence Conran's Habitat chain. These two companies were joined by British Homes Stores (now Bhs) in 1986 when the holding company was formed. Bhs was subsequently sold in 2000, since when Mothercare has been, once again, a standalone business.

From the opening of the first franchised store in 1984, the following six years to 1990 was a period of intensive development of the franchise system. During that period, Mother-care established franchises in 15 countries. The catalogue played a significant role in the rapid growth in both the domestic UK market and foreign market. Its wide circulation both in the UK and abroad increased awareness of the brand and its concept, creating a demand for stores.

The Habitat business was sold in 1992. Mothercare sold its US operations in 1991 and although they continued for a while under a franchise type of operation that relationship ended in 1996.

The company has won a number of awards over the years. In 1977 it received the Royal Society of Arts Presidential Award for Design Management and the 1977 Marketing Award. In 1979, it received the Queen's Award for Export Achievement. In 1996 it again received the Queen's Award for Export Achievement in recognition of the rapidly growing interna-tional operations which had also developed its system in foreign markets using the franchise method of marketing. In 1998 the company was the *Retail Week UK International Retailer of the Year*.

Mothercare has been consistently recog-nized over the years for its key role in parenting in the UK by being awarded such accolades as Tommy's Campaign Parent Friendly awards for the Best Children's Clothes Shop and the Best Organization for Dads.

In 1996, 57 Children's World stores were purchased and converted into Mothercare stores. These stores are larger than traditional Mothercare stores.

Mothercare decided to franchise in interna-tional markets after careful consideration of the options available to it. It realized that franchising would enable it to grow rapidly in overseas markets. Local franchisees provide the capital to establish the stores, and the synergy between their local knowledge and experience and the Mothercare product range, systems and methods were expected to produce results. Indeed, they have done and fully justify Mothercare's decision. Mothercare has also found that the authorities in the countries in which their franchisees operate regard their businesses as domestic and not foreign owned.

The international development of the business has been focused in three regions in the world: Europe, the Middle East and the Far East. The growth to 174 stores in 36 countries, given the size of a Mothercare store, which is invariably not less than 150 to 200 square metres, and the range of inventory, is significant.

The company does not currently use master franchising arrangements; it prefers direct franchising using area development agreements under which it grants exclusive rights to a local business to develop the Mothercare business in a country. It does not rule out the possibility that something short of a whole country may be appropriate in some cases. There is an agreed development schedule for the exploitation of the territory. Mothercare favours the direct relationship which provides them with more control and a closer working relationship with their franchisees.

Mothercare is a supplier of products to its franchisees and, given the nature and range of products which mother and baby are likely to need, issues of local regulatory approvals arise. Some countries have a considerable bureaucracy to overcome and policies differ on what are health products and how they can satisfy local requirements. Obviously, these approvals can take time.

Mothercare in common with many other franchisors is seeking quality franchisees and in view of its chosen route of development arrangements these franchisees need to be well resourced financially. The company receives many unsolicited approaches from around the world but many are from individuals who wish to open one store and do not realize what Mothercare's requirements involve. The company finds that a combination of its reputation and the maintenance of contact with trade organizations overseas, the Department of Trade and Industry, banks and networks of contacts through its lawyers, accountants and individuals often assists in making contact with franchise prospects.

Not unnaturally, the company regards training as a key element. It requires at least the manager of the first store and other key players in the franchisee's business to be trained in the UK. The training is in-depth and for long enough to ensure that the franchisees fully absorb the Mothercare ethos. They are made to feel that they are part of the Mothercare family wherever they may be operating, and the training is calculated to help them to achieve the ability to 'think' Mothercare throughout their business operations. They are encouraged to ignore the distance between their operations and the UK and deal with their support team by maintaining close contact. Each franchised territory is supported by a franchise development manager based in the UK. Regular visits are made to each territory throughout the relationship. As will be appreciated, the opening of new stores is a period of intensive support when a start-up opening crew is provided. Support is also provided with overall store design and layouts as well as ordering and the opening inventory. Mothercare has a sophisticated Internet-based ordering system.

Mothercare also conducts a series of product selection meetings in the UK giving franchisees the opportunity to exchange views and promote best practice.

Mothercare's franchise fee structure is simple. It does not normally charge initial fees. Its approach is to rely on a mix of product mark-up and royalty on gross sales for its income stream.

Recent developments

Mothercare is now a relatively mature franchisor, the first franchisee having been appointed in 1983. After a period of territorial expansion, the period since 2000 has been characterized by a focus on the consolidation and upgrading of the businesses within the franchise territories, rather than seeking new markets. The process of improving operating methods and disciplines has been successful in developing the return from many of the existing markets, but inevitably there have been cases where franchises have closed, often in marginal markets where the expected economic conditions did not materialize and/or or the returns have been elusive.

In addition a small number of franchises have changed ownership. Handled sensitively and ensuring that the new owner meets the required criteria as a franchisee has often provided the catalyst for renewed operational vigour and investment.

Case Study 2

NAME OF COMPANY	YEAR ESTABLISHED BUSINESS
Pirtek	1980

OUTLETS WORLDWIDE WHICH COMPANY OPERATES	OUTLETS IN AUSTRALIA IN WHICH COMPANY OPERATES	NUMBER OF COUNTRIES
258	67	10

INTERNATIONAL OUTLETS	INTERNATIONAL OUTLETS COMPANY-OWNED	INTERNATIONAL OUTLETS FRANCHISED
191	0	191

Employees

IN COMPANY-OWNED OUTLETS	SUPPORTING INTERNATIONAL OUTLETS
0	Not available

Pirtek provides on-site replacement of hydraulic hoses. These hoses are usually the most vulnerable part of any machine, as the hoses are made of rubber and can easily perish or become damaged. In normal operation, when an expensive and often critical piece of machinery has been put out of action, what is also often critical is the amount of time it takes to get the machinery back into action, as its inaction may have a costly knock-on effect on the whole project in which it is employed.

Pirtek's service is defined by operating 'mobile service vehicles' which can be called out to visit a work site, factory or plant to repair or maintain the hydraulic equipment. Over 50 per cent of all turnover is accounted for by providing this urgent service and 17 per cent by 'on site' convenience mobile vehicles. The balance is accounted for by trade sales and product sales by the network or centres.

Pirtek, which is well known in the UK, has twice won the British Franchisor of the Year Award, in 1998 and 2000–1, and the International Franchisor of the Year Award in 2000–1. The UK franchise community may well consider that Pirtek started in the UK, but it did not.

Pirtek was launched in Australia in 1980 by Peter Duncan and Wally Davey, who had previously been involved in a business which had a mobile distribution and service system in hydraulic hoses. The name Pirtek came from Pir in Pirelli (a hose supplier) and Tek, representing technology. Peter and Wally commenced their business in Sydney and began franchising in 1981/2. By 1987 they had approximately 20 franchisees.

At around that time Peter Brennan, who had just left Prontaprint in the UK, was acting as a consultant. A fellow consultant in Australia invited him to Australia to help him with a print franchise. Just after Peter arrived the company went into liquidation and the consultant introduced him to Pirtek. Peter spotted a good opportunity and introduced Forbes Petrie (also a former Prontaprint man) to the opportunity.

They liked the business and wanted to take it to the UK. Peter Duncan did not want to grant master franchise rights, he wanted to have a joint company with the Australian shareholders holding 50% and Peter and Forbes owning 50%.

Pirtek UK opened a pilot centre in Park Royal in London in late 1988/early 1989 and within nine months it had two franchisees. Park Royal was franchised in 1990/1 and a head office was established in Acton, West London. By 1997 the Pirtek UK network had grown to 50 franchisees. It was in this year that Pirtek UK took the decision to enter the European market. At that time additional funding was raised, some of which was invested in the business and the rest released to the shareholders for some of their shares.

By then the Australian network had grown to a maturity of 67 franchisees. Pirtek Australia had also developed a network in New Zealand by direct franchise from Australia, which has grown to 12 franchisees. In 1999 Peter Duncan entered into a joint venture with an expatriate South African living in Australia to open up in South Africa, where they now have 11 franchisees. Following the same pattern of co-ownership in 2000/1 a joint venture with local interests led to the establishment of a Pirtek operation in Singapore.

In 1997, following an introduction from Forbes Petrie, a master licence was entered into by Pirtek Australia with a newly formed US company, in which Peter Duncan became a minority shareholder. Following a successful pilot in Minneapolis the company began franchising and in the USA there are now 23 franchisees with ten in the pipeline.

Pirtek UK embarked on its European expansion plans by opening three company-owned operations at around the same time in

France (Ile de France Paris), Germany (Cologne) and the Netherlands (Rotterdam). These markets now have the following numbers of franchisees:

France   21
Germany   21
Benelux   16 (of which 12 are in the
            Netherlands and four in
            Belgium)

The European expansion led to a corporate structure, with Pirtek Europe Ltd as a holding company with four subsidiaries:

Pirtek UK Ltd (England)
Pirtek Deutschland GmbH (Germany)
Pirtek BV (Netherlands)
SARL Pirtek (France)

Pirtek has shown steady growth supported by the commitment of one of its founders to supporting its international development by taking a significant shareholding interest. Australia is also concentrating on New Zealand, South Africa and Singapore and is clearly well placed to spread through the Pacific Rim. Pirtek UK is the hub for European growth and the USA, having been initiated from the UK, is a large enough market to stand alone.

The equity participation as the major shareholder in the franchise is an unusual feature in international expansion of franchise systems. Unusual or not it seems to be working well. The system has been well refined and the quality of the hose fittings and couplings and of franchisees in having the competence to ensure the safety of the work they do is crucial to Pirtek's success.

Pirtek provides its franchisees with the usual complete range of initial and continuing services in each of the countries in which it operates:

● **Sales and marketing**. Negotiations with national trading accounts, innovative marketing programmes including advertising, sales promotion, corporate image, PR and trade exhibition activities.

- **Operational**. Acquisition of vehicles and equipment, centre site selection, development and fitting out of a franchise centre.

- **Training**. Ongoing product and sales training courses for both the licensee and his staff. Product and system training at both the main centre and throughout the country. Pirtek employs a number of field trainers who support staff directly in the field.

- **Technical and product support**. Customer advice and problem-solving arrangements from Pirtek's international and national supplier group. Technological advancements and new product ranges. Technical advice and support.

- **Administration/management**. Operational manuals, insurance packages, administration packages (e.g. staff terms and conditions, confidentiality undertakings), policy and procedure maintenance.

- **Financial**. Analysis of trading patterns and trends. Supporting data for leasing or finance applications. Assistance with both initial and ongoing business planning, advice on continuing financial ratios of the business and assistance in monthly management accounts preparation. Introduction to banks, leasing companies and providers of financial facilities.

- **Legal**. There is a legal hotline for problems which crop up to ensure each franchisee is protected in the field.

20 Not for profit case study

NAME OF ORGANIZATION
The Florence Melton Adult
Mini-School (FMAMS)

YEAR COMMENCED ACTIVITIES
1980

YEAR COMMENCED FRANCHISING
1987

NUMBER OF INTERNATIONAL OUTLETS
63

NUMBER OF COUNTRIES IN WHICH ORGANIZATION OPERATES
4

All outlets are franchised. FMAMS does not operate any outlets and there are at present no outlets in Israel, although it is due to commence activities there in 2005.

FMAMS is a non profit making organization which provides adult Jewish education courses. It considers that a unique aspect of a non profit franchise is the need to subsidize the operation at the level of franchisor and/or franchisee. FMAMS explains that while in the commercial franchise sector areas of conflict can arise over the division of profits, in the non profit franchise conflicts may arise over the discussion of the responsibility for the deficits.

FMAMS was founded on the initiative of Florence Melton, an inventor and philanthropist from Columbus, Ohio, USA. In 1980 she submitted a proposal to the Melton Centre for Jewish Education at the Hebrew University of Jerusalem to create a two-year sequential programme of study for adults in the area of Jewish studies. Florence Melton felt strongly that while children's education was a high priority in the Jewish community, adult education was neglected.

Based on the assumption that the vast majority of adult Jews in North America had not received any Jewish education beyond primary school, she called for the creation of a two-year programme that would enable adults to study the fundamentals of Judaism in an intellectual environment. Florence Melton was also troubled by the growing polarization among the different Jewish religious strands and therefore stipulated that this programme should be community based and inclusive of all strands. Florence's choice of the Hebrew University came in the wake of her being rejected by leading academic institutions in North America who felt that this programme would not have a market. Despite the university's geographical and cultural distance from the field, Florence was convinced of the university's ability to initiate this project based on its impressive track record in the field of Jewish education research and development. Apparently even at Hebrew University's Melton Centre there was a level of scepticism regarding the marketability of this project.

Florence chose the name 'mini-school' for the following reasons. She liked the 'school' concept as opposed to a programme concept, since this reflected permanence, stability, professionalism and impact. However, since only an evening a week commitment was required she chose the term 'mini-school'.

From 1980 to 1985 the courses were developed and tested in the field in three pilot sites in the United States in 1985. In 1987 the school was launched nationally. In 1992 the school spread to Canada, opening in Montreal. In 1993 the school opened in Sydney and then opened in London in 1998. Negotiations are under way to open in Cape Town and the school is due to open in Israel in 2005.

There are currently 50 franchisees in the United States, three in Canada, two in the United Kingdom and two in Australia. Some of these operate more than one school. Three are satellite schools and three are second schools of existing school franchisees. Over 20,000 students have thus far graduated from the programme and there are currently over 5000 students enrolled and attending on a weekly basis.

The decision to franchise was taken primarily for economic reasons. The size of the initial grant which was made available forced the university to seek partners in North America to run the programme. Thereafter other advantages of the franchise method to the franchisor emerged. The local organizations were already entrenched in their community and therefore access to staff and students was far easier than it would have been if the Hebrew University had built a chain organization from scratch. Furthermore, since this was a non profit project which required funding on both the international and local levels, local partners with established ties with local donors and foundations proved to be highly effective fund raisers for their local schools.

The original assumptions regarding the market for these courses in the United States were true for other English speaking countries with large Jewish populations. While the level of Jewish literacy may be proportionately higher in Canada, the UK and Australia compared with parts of the USA, a similar level of ignorance and intellectual curiosity exists among many Jewish adults in these countries.

Most of the 63 franchisees house the mini-school within existing institutions (multifractional), while a small number are single unit. The choice to opt for multifractional franchisees is due to their proven ability financially to support the franchise at the local level. This allows the franchisor to focus efforts on support for the system without having to expend major resources in seeking funding for the local franchisees. This format, however, has two major drawbacks as far as FMAMS is concerned. The first is the organizational stability of the franchisees, their changing leadership and set of priorities. When a franchisee's organizational director leaves the position, there is no guarantee that his or her successor will have the same level of affinity and commitment to the franchise as the predecessor. A second disadvantage is that the franchise has a unique culture which must blend in with the local organizational culture. When there is no blend this can lead to a number of tensions. This problem proved to be potentially acute when the franchisee was a provider of other adult education courses. In two situations the mini-school was perceived to be a counter culture within the organizations, resulting in the ending of the franchise relationship with both organizations.

There are currently two single unit format mini-schools. In these mini-schools FMAMS has found that both of these drawbacks do not exist at all. However, both single unit franchisees face tremendous economic pressures threatening their existence due to their inability to raise funds.

There has been international cooperation between directors of the different schools resulting from them meeting at the annual conferences. The degree of staff cooperation is far smaller. While there is a staff list service the level of interchange is highly limited.

FMAMS has so far experienced two areas of tension:

1. The first was in the area of cultural adaptation. Australia and the UK raised serious doubts regarding suitability of a curriculum written for North America. Once the courses were implemented, the level of suspicion dissipated.

2. The second area was regarding the payment of franchise fees. Canada and Australia requested that the franchise fees be quoted in local currency as opposed to the policy of the franchisor to quote US dollars. This issue has continued to be an area of contention, with the FMAMS not willing to compromise.

The recruitment of franchisees has to be geared to the size or structure of the Jewish community in each country.

In North America, FMAMS appears at conferences and attends workshops where prospective local franchisee professional or lay leaders are present. In addition potential franchisees apply to FMAMS based on word of mouth. In the UK and Australia, the market is far more limited and there franchisees are targeted and asked to submit applications.

FMAMS provides an orientation seminar for new directors on an annual basis. Thereafter, the director is given a system manual. In addition, there is an initial site visit to the local school where an orientation is given to the lay board and prospective faculty.

FMAMS also provides ongoing support:

- a member of the international staff pays an annual site visit;
- there is an annual directors' conference;
- there is annual in-service training of staff;
- directors and staff have a toll free number to a national office in the USA and the international office in Israel;
- an interactive closed website with support for directors and staff;
- a weekly list serve update for directors and staff.

Newly recruited franchisees pay an initial $1000 signing on fee. Thereafter each year an annual fee of $8950 is paid before the beginning of each academic year.

The Natwest–BFA Annual Survey

In each year since 1984 a survey of franchising in the UK has been commissioned by the British Franchise Association and sponsored by NatWest UK. The survey is now conducted by Business Development Research Consultants who took over in 1992. The latest information provided was published in February 2003 and covers the calendar year 2002.

Number of systems

Franchising is continuing to expand. In 1987 there were 252 franchise systems; in 1990 the number had risen to 379 in 1997 there were 568 systems; and in 2002 there were 677 systems identified. In the period from 1997 to 2002 this represents a 19% increase.

Number of franchisees

The number of franchised units has also grown to 30,800. The comparative figure for 1997 was 24,000, showing an increase of around 28%. The increase in the number of systems should result in increasing franchised units over a period of time, as has been the case in the past.

Volume of sales

Sales in 2002 reached £9.5 billion, compared with £7.0 billion in 1997, which represents an increase of around 39%.

Number of employees

The number of people employed in franchised units rose in 2002 to 326,000, which compares with 273,800 in 1997, an increase of almost 20%. If franchising continues to grow as it has done, we can expect significant increases in job creation. One statistic which is not available is the number of people who work in businesses which supply goods and services to franchised businesses. The total job creation by franchising also includes those who work for franchisor organizations. When all are added together it may not be a surprise to find that franchising's contribution to jobs in the UK is probably not less than 425,000.

Franchisee profitability

In 2002, 91% of franchisees claimed to be profitable. Some 79% of franchisors and 62% of franchisees expect business to improve in 2003.

Failure rates

The number of unit failures as a percentage of all units operating in 2002 was 2.2%.

Turnover levels

The mean average turnover of franchisees has risen to £299,000 per annum, even with just over a quarter of franchisees reporting turnover of up to £50,000. This no doubt reflects the significant number of small franchise operators. On the other hand, just under a quarter claim their turnover to be £500,000 or more. When one considers different categories the following average turnover figures emerge:

Store retailing	£541,000
Hotel and catering	£534,000
Transport and vehicle services	£384,000
Personal services	£211,000
Business and communication services	£146,000
Property services	£1,230,000

Barriers to growth

The two most significant barriers to growth are reputed by franchisors to be lack of suitable franchisees (40%) and lack of suitable sites for franchised businesses (11%).

In 1997 franchisors believed that by the year 2002 they would be operating more than double the number of units that currently operated. This has proved to be an ambitious target. No doubt in reaching the conclusion they failed to take into account the many factors which affect forecasts and which are outside the control of franchisors.

Franchisors abroad

Some 27% of franchisors claim to have operations in overseas markets. However, 18% plan to be operating abroad. Given the fact that one of the principal barriers to expansion outside the UK is identified by 19% as being 'legislation in some countries', there is clearly some education needed. This reason becomes more puzzling when 15% definitely expect to be franchising in France, 15% in Germany, 17% in Spain and 12% in the USA. As will be seen elsewhere in this work, most other countries do not have franchise-specific laws, while France, Spain and the USA have pre-contract disclosure laws and the USA other laws which directly impact on franchising. Germany has a difficult legal regime for those who are accustomed to a common law jurisdiction like that in the UK.

These figures for growth expectations have reduced significantly over the past five years. It is also significant that the claimed numbers for European markets have reduced over the years, as have expectations. There are 8% of operations in Spain, 7% in France, 7% in Italy and 5% in Germany. Those operating in Italy will now know that there is a franchise law (see Chapter 14).

Broader aspects of franchising

The fact remains that if one compares the numerous franchise systems in the USA with the number in the UK *pro rata* to the population numbers, the potential for growth in franchisor numbers and prescribed outlets is considerable. The potential in franchisor numbers is more than double the current number and in franchise units something in excess of 80,000. One may doubt the capacity of the UK market to achieve that. However, if one carries on with the same exercise in relation to the European Union (shortly to be enlarged), the scope for growth throughout that area is considerable and that of course is a prime market place for UK franchisors.

Financial aspects

The overall average initial outlay of franchisees is £59,200. This includes:

- initial franchise fee in 96% of the cases;
- equipment in 56%;
- stock in 44%;
- working capital in 68%.

Ongoing fees payable by franchisors to franchisees include:

- management services fees in 70% of cases, averaging 8.1% of sales;
- advertising contribution in just under a half of cases, averaging 1.6% of sales, which seems very low;
- IT support fee in 13% of cases, averaging 2% of sales;
- other charges in 13% of cases, averaging 4.1% of sales.

Borrowings by franchisees

2% of franchisors provide finance to their franchisees, while just under 58% help arrange the monies needed to start up. Just over half of franchisees needed to borrow monies. The average amount involved was £38,100.

The percentage of the market share of bankers to franchisees is split up as follows:

NatWest	30%
Barclays	17%
Lloyds/TSB	14%
Royal Bank of Scotland	12%
HSBC	13%
Bank of Scotland	2%

Of other sources, relatives at 9% is the highest. The amounts of the loans split as follows:

- up to £10,000 in 24% of all cases;
- £10,001 to £50,000 in 60%;
- over £50,001 in 16%.

Satisfying aspects of being a franchisee

Being own boss	37%
Franchisor support	28%
Decision-making freedom	8%
Making money	8%
Brand name of franchisor	6%
Flexibility	6%

Relationship with the franchisor

Mainly to definitely satisfactory	87%
Mainly to definitely not satisfactory	13%

Length of agreement

Sixty-three per cent of franchisees said they intended to renew their agreement, while 24% were not sure; 12% said they did not intend to renew their agreement.

The future

Seventy-nine per cent of franchisors and 62% of franchisees are optimistic that their business will improve.

Information technology

The use of IT is now widespread with:

- 91% of franchisees having a website
- 41% of franchisors having an Intranet site
- 86% of franchisees having a PC
- 90% of franchisors and 81% of franchisees have mobile phones
- 72% of franchisors and 38% of franchisees have laptop computers
- 29% of franchisors and 15% of franchisees have mobile phones with Internet

B BFA forms

Application for Membership

This Application Form has five parts:

Part 1.	Your description of the franchised business.
Part 2.	The declaration and commitments required by all prospective Members, Full and Associate.
Part 3.	The information required of all prospective members, Full and Associate, in demonstrating that they meet the Association's requirement that their businesses should be viable, franchisable, ethical and disclosed.
Part 4.	The additional information required of prospective Full members in demonstrating that their business has a proven trading and franchising record.
Part 5.	General Declaration

For the purposes of Part 2 of this application you should also have received a document setting out the codes and procedures to which you are asked to give your commitment.

Please remember that for the purpose of Part 3 and, if it applies, Part 4, the onus is on you to provide the evidence, which shows that you meet the Association's criteria. Please provide whatever information you feel is relevant.

We would like therefore to welcome you to the Association as quickly as possible but we hope you will understand that our name and our purpose depend ultimately on the strength of our standards and the accreditation procedures that support them. Your accreditation may therefore take some time and may involve more than one exchange of correspondence between us. We hope you will bear with us during the course of these essential checks.

BRIAN SMART: DIRECTOR GENERAL

Part 1: Company Information

To be completed by all applicants

1. Registered Name of Applicant Company...

2. UK Company Registration Number...

3. Date Company Established/Incorporated..

4. Name of Franchise (if different from 1 above)..

5. Date of First use of the Name (if different from 3 above)...

6. Names of Registered Directors:

Designation	Name	Date of Appointment
Chairman	....	....
Managing Director	....	....
....	....	....
....	....	....
....	....	....
....	....	....

7. Director Nominated as BFA Representative...

8. Telephone Number..Fax Number...

e-mail address..website:...

9. Address for Correspondence...

....

....

10. Name of Parent or Holding Company...

11. Names of Subsidiary Companies..

....

....

12. Nature of Franchised Business...

....

....

Part 1: Company Information

13. Do either your Parent, Holding or Subsidiary Companies act as a supplier to your business?   Yes.........................No............................

14. Do any of your Directors have an interest in any   Yes.........................No............................

15. Have any of your Directors been convicted for theft or fraud, or been declared bankrupt or been a Director of a company declared bankrupt? (If so, please enclose separately details of the convictions or declarations and any Certificates of Discharge.)   Yes.........................No............................

16. Did your company first operate through company owned outlets?   Yes.........................No............................

17. If so, from what Date?   ....

18. Have you operated a company owned outlet as an 'arms length' pilot scheme for franchising?   ....

19. If so, from what date (if different from 16)?   ....

20. If not, on what date did you open the original franchised unit?   ....

21. Number of company owned outlets operating at present   ....

22. Number of company owned outlets achieving expected standard   ....

23. Number of franchised outlets operating at present   ....

24. Number of franchised outlets achieving expected standard   ....

25. How many franchised units to you intend to open:

    in the next 12 months?...in the next five years?..

26. Please provide the following information (include name and addresses)

Bankers   ....
....

Accountants   ....
....

Auditors   ....
....

Solicitors   ....
....

Franchise Consultants (if any)   ....

Part 1: Company Information

Information is requested from the BFA for the **four** following areas. Each details where the information will be displayed and used, and may require more information from you at a later stage.

1. **BFA Website**

    This is your public information. The contact details we use here are placed on our website and should be names, contact numbers, e-mail addresses etc. that you want to be contacted on by members of the public seeking information on your Franchise. Once you become a member, login details and passwords will be sent to you to enter the members' section of the website where you can edit your details personally.

    Company Name and Address..

    ....

    ....

    ....

    Contact Name..

    Phone number..fax number..

    e-mail address..

    website address (to be accredited before added as a link)..

2. **BFA Directory**

    This is your public information too. This information is placed in our directory of members within our guides and will be provided to potential franchisees and franchisors when they purchase a guide. Once you become members you will be asked for more information to add to the directory.

    Company Name and Address..

    ....

    ....

    ....

    Contact Name..

    Phone number..fax number..

    e-mail address..

    website address..

    Business Sector (please tick)

    [   ] Building & Maintenance   [   ] Estate Agency, Property
    [   ] Cleaning & Renovation   [   ] Food, Catering & Hotels
    [   ] Commercial, Business Services   [   ] Parcel, Courier Services
    [   ] Direct Selling, Distribution   [   ] Printing, Copying, Signage
    [   ] Domestic, Personal Caring Services [   ] Retailing
    [   ] Educational Services   [   ] Vehicle Service
    [   ] Employment, Training   [   ] Other(please specify).........................

    Type of Franchise (please tick)

    [   ] Investment   [   ] Management
    [   ] Retail   [   ] Single Operator/management   [   ] Single Operator/executive

Part 1: Company Information

3. **BFA Internal Use**

This is your private information. The BFA uses this information for invitations to events, newsletters, official correspondance and contact by a member of the BFA Staff

Company Name and Address...

....

....

....

Contact Name..

Phone number...fax number...

e-mail address...

4. **BFA Financial**

This is used by the BFA Finance Manager for sending invoices, statements and any other related correspondence that would normally be directed to the accounts department.

Company Name...

....

Invoice Name (if different from above)..

Accounts Address...

....

....

....

Accounts Phone Number..

Accounts Contact...

Preferred method of payment   Cheque/BACS/Direct Debit* (*please circle one*)

please note Direct Debit option applies to Full/Associate and Affiliate only. Provisionally listed members must complete one full year before qualifying for direct debit.

PLEASE NOTE, YOU SHOULD NOT INCLUDE A CHEQUE WITH THIS APPLICATION FORM

Part 2: Declarations & Commitments

This Section invites you to give a commitment to procedures and codes, which may be amended or developed by the Association. Such procedures and codes can only be amended or developed after full consultation with Members, Full and Associate, who, if they do not wish to continue the necessary commitments, will be afforded every opportunity to withdraw from the Association without penalty or disclosure of any kind.

To be completed by all applicants

1. The information provided in and with this application is, to the best of our knowledge, an accurate, full and fair representation of our business.

2. We agree to be bound by the Association's complaints, disputes, conciliation, mediation and arbitration procedures and any amendments thereto agreed by the Association.

3. We agree to be bound by the Association's disciplinary and appeals procedures, and to comply with any notices or instructions issued under those procedures and any amendments thereto agreed by the Association.

4. We agree to comply with the Association's requirements and conditions for annual re-accreditation and any amendments thereto agreed by the Association.

5. We agree to comply with the Association's Code of Ethical Conduct and any amendments thereto agreed by the Association.

6. We agree to abide by the Advertising Standards Authority's Code of Advertising Practice.

7. We agree that we will not sell, offer for sale, or distribute any product or render any service, or promote the sale or distribution thereof, under any representation or condition (including the use of the name of a 'celebrity') which has the tendency, capacity or effect of misleading or deceiving purchasers or prospective purchasers.

8. We agree that we will not imitate the trademark, trade name, corporate identity, slogan, or other mark or identification of another franchisor in any manner or form that would have the tendency or capacity to mislead or deceive.

9. We agree to use our best endeavours to adopt best practice in franchising as agreed and published by the Association from time to time.

10. We agree to notify the Association at the earliest possible opportunity of any material change in ownership, direction, financing or operation of our business and to provide a copy of any new Franchise Agreement.

11. We agree to comply with the Association's request for copies of non-confidential information to be held by the Association, in the case of offer documents and franchise agreements, to be open to inspection by our appointed franchisees.

12. We agree to provide authorised full-time officials of the Association access to but not copies of confidential information reasonably required in accrediting or re-accrediting our company to membership but only on the basis that the conditions of employment of those full-time officials require them to maintain the confidentiality of the information to themselves alone subject on breech to their summary dismissal.

13. We agree to pass on all of our obligations as members of the Association to any Master Franchisee, Sub-Franchisee, Area Franchisee or equivalent licensee that we might appoint.

Signed...

For and on behalf of..

Position Held..

Date...
(This section must be signed by the Chairman or Managing Director of the Company making the application)

Part 3: Demonstrations

To Be Completed by all Applicants

1. **VIABILITY**

    You must enclose with this application form evidence that your business is capable of selling its products or service at a profit that will support a franchised network.

    The submission of two years' trading accounts together with your audited accounts for the same period showing a business already securing, or capable of meeting a business plan to establish, a well financed and stable operation, would ordinarily be counted as sufficient evidence.

    Please list here the documents you are enclosing to demonstrate that your business is viable:

    ....

    ....

    ....

    ....

2. **FRANCHISABLE**

    You must enclose with your application form evidence that you can successfully franchise your operation.

    The submission of the business plan for 12 months' trading and the audited accounts for either an arms length company owned pilot franchise, or a fully fledged franchise which show a trading performance at least in line with the business plan will be one part of the evidence ordinarily required here. You will also be expected to demonstrate that you have developed an operating system, which enables you to pass on your 'know-how' at arms length. You might do this by submitting details of, or providing access to, a copy of your operational manual and by setting out details of the training programme for franchisees.

    Please list here the documents (in addition to those provided in demonstrating viability) that you are submitting (or are prepared to give access to - marked 'access only') to show franchisability.

    ....

    ....

    ....

    ....

    Please also summarise the costs you incur, on average, prior to, and including opening of, a franchised outlet.

	£
Training and manual	....
Initial marketing operation including launch	....
Goods, materials and equipment, if applicable	....
Other items - please specify	....

    Please summarise your support to franchisees, i.e. management, technical and training resources:

    ....

Part 3 cont.

3. **ETHICAL**

The primary evidence required to show your business has an ethical foundation is a copy of the franchise agreement currently in use. **Please provide a copy of that agreement with this application.**

We will seek references on your business from a small sample of any franchisees you already have. **Please also include a full list of their names, trading addresses, and the date of acquiring the franchise in an electronic format ideally in an Excel Spreadsheet.**

4. **DISCLOSED**

You will need to submit with this application copies of all the documents, brochures and particularly financial projections you give to prospective franchisees in advance of their signing a franchise agreement.

Please ensure you enclose copies of your offer documents.
Please also summarise below the information presented therein:

Cost of Franchise Package to Franchisee	....
Initial Franchise Fee	....
Franchisee's total investment (including working capital)	....
Management service (or royalty) charge	....
Advertising or Marketing levy	....
Average period to establish franchise on a satisfactory basis	....
Estimated period for franchisee to recover initial investment	....

If you feel able to provide all the information requested in this part 3 (and you have completed Parts 1 and 2) your are eligible for Associate Membership. As an Associate you will be able to refer to yourself as such (in a prescribed format) on your published material. You will also be eligible for the other services and discounts the Association offers.

If you also feel able to provide the evidence required under part 4 (following) you will be eligible for Full Membership. If not, please now complete the general application and declaration (part 5) at the end of this application form.

Part 4: Full Membership

To Be Completed by Full Member Applicants

I. **A PROVEN TRADING RECORD**

You need to provide financial records to show that your franchised network is stable and profitable for you and your franchisees. Your own audited accounts showing acceptable financial trends over an extended period will be required. We will also need to agree with you a selection of your franchisees from whom we will need to obtain trading accounts. These will be treated confidentially and in the knowledge that franchisees have an obligations to 'husband' their accounts.

Please list here the series of your audited accounts enclosed with this application:

....

....

....

....

Please also provide with this application a complete list of your current franchisees (as also required under part 3) ideally in an electronic format in an Excel Spreadsheet and nominate below two franchisees from whom trading accounts can be obtained or in respect of which you are able to enclose or submit accounts (we will choose a further small selection of franchisees which we will ask you to approach for trading accounts.

(i)...

(ii)..

2. **A PROVEN FRANCHISING RECORD**

Please provide the following details, in confidence, covering at least two full reporting years:

	Current Year (Months)	Last Year	Year Before
(a) Franchise Starts	....	....	....
(b) Franchise Failures (forced)	....	....	....
(c) Franchise Withdrawals (voluntary)	....	....	....
(d) Franchises Resales from (b)	....	....	....
(e) Franchise Resales from (c)	....	....	....
(f) Franchise disputes*	....	....	....

*Only those disputes which have required intervention (through your solicitor, the franchisee's solicitor, or the Association's mediation or arbitration schemes should be recorded)

If you have been able to provide the evidence requested in this Part 4 you are eligible for Full Membership of the Association. As a Full Member you will be able to use the Association's logo on your published material. You will also be eligible to vote at the Annual and Special General Meetings, to stand for election to the Association's Council, and to receive all services and discounts which the Association offers.

Please also complete the general declaration (Part 5) at the end of this application.

Part 5: General Application **& Declaration**

To Be Completed by all Applicants

We, the applicant company declare, to the best of our knowledge and belief, that the franchise system we offer is based on sound business principles and provides a viable and ethical business opportunity for the franchise and a genuine end-product or service for the consumer. It is our belief that the systems we operate, satisfactorily protect both the franchisee and the consumer, and, accordingly, we hereby apply for membership of the British Franchise Association.

Signed...

For and on Behalf of..

Position held...

Date...

The Form shall be signed by the Chairman or Managing Director of the company making the application.

CONCLUSION

Thank you for taking the time and trouble to complete this application form. Please do not forget to enclose the documents you have listed, and we have specified, in Parts 3 and 4. We appreciate the complexity of our Membership requirements but we hope you understand that it is essential in protecting the Association's name and standing - without which you would have little reason to join us.

Criteria For Affiliate Membership

Affiliation to the British Franchise Association is available to any organisation or individual offering professional advice to the franchising community who can provide the following;

(1)   evidence of professional standing

(2)   evidence to show that staff qualified in the profession concerned are experienced in the application of that profession to franchising

(3)   a commitment by a nominated responsible officer to the maintenance of the organisation's arrangements for providing appropriately experienced advice on franchising to its clients

The requirements on prospective Affiliates to show professional standing and franchise experience will be applied as follows

Legal firms
Professional Standing   Through the Law Society
Franchise Experience   Through references

Accountants
Professional Standing   Through the Accounting regulatory bodies
Franchise Experience   Through references

Banks
Professional Standing   Through the Banking Regulatory Bodies
Franchise Experience   Through the establishment of a franchise unit

Consultants
Professional Standing   Through Examination of work done by interview or through a professional qualification in consulting
Franchise Experience   Through examination of franchising work and by interview or through FCA Membership

Other Professions
Professional Standing   Through an appropriate professional qualification or examination of work done and by interview
Franchise experience   Through examination of franchising work and by interview or by references

Interviews required under the Affiliation Criteria will be conducted by the Association's Membership Committee or by the Association's officials as appropriate. Where references are required, referees (at least two) may be drawn from Full Member Franchisors, Associate Member Franchisors and/or Affiliates in the same professional field, in any combination.

The Association reserves its rights to refuse applicants for Affiliation without declaring its reasons.

In addition Franchise Consultants will be required to adhere to the following Code of Conduct.

Code of Conduct for Franchise Consultants

A Franchise Consultant shall at all times in the conduct of his business observe the following standards:

1.   To put the interests of his clients above his own interests and to observe the highest standards of competence and integrity

2.   To adopt an independent and objective attitude towards his clients so as to ensure that advice given is based upon impartial consideration of the facts and objectives.

3.   To respect the confidentuality of all information received concerning a clients business and not to disclose or permit disclosure (to the consultants own advantage) of any such information without the clients prior permission in writing.

Criteria For Affiliate Membership

4.   To disclose to his clients or prospective clients any personal or financial interests or other material circumstances which might in any way influence his work for that client, in particular without derogating from the generality of the foregoing:

-     any directorship or significant interests in any business which competes with the client.
-     any financial interest (or other benefit) in goods and services recommended by the consultant for use by the client.
-     any personal relationship with any individual in the clients employment.
-     the existence but not the name of any other current client of the consultant whose business may compete with the clients.
-     not to advise any franchisee or potential franchisee in relation to the scheme or opportunity offered by a Franchisor for whom the consultant had acted or whose business may compete with that of a client of the consultant.

and to inform the client immediately of any change in or the coming into existence of any such circumstances as are referred to.

5.   Not to assist a franchisor with the recruitment of franchisees under arrangements which include per capita recruitment fees or other financial arrangements which could have the effect of influencing the advice given to franchisors on their recruitment decisions.

6.   To acknowledge the role and special professional skills of other advisors, and in particular franchise lawyers, advising franchisors accordingly.

AFFILIATE MEMBERSHIP

Affiliates to the British Franchise Association will be entitled to the following benefits.

1.   Use of the BFA logo on all company material.

2.   Inclusion on an Affiliate Listing which will carry the name of the Affiliated organisation, nominated officer, contact address and telephone number. An opportunity will be offered to represent additional offices (including a named contact) at an additional subscription. This listing will be circulated to all BFA Full and Associate Members and Provisionally Listed companies and will be included in the BFA Franchisee and Franchisor Information Packs.

3.   Representation on BFA Council

4.   Automatic accreditation for exhibitions sponsored by the BFA and the opportunity to contribute to the Franchisee and Franchisor seminars organised at such events by the BFA.

5.   Recognition as a sponsor for new Franchisors seeking admittance on the Provisional Listing.

6.   Access to all BFA events including the Association's Annual Convention at Members' rates.

7.   The opportunity to contribute to the Association's publications and working groups.

8.   The opportunity to enter into appropriate sponsorship and promotions arrangements.

9.   Inclusion on the BFA' s website and in the membership directory.

Application for Affiliation

Please complete all sections

Organisation name...

Address..

....

....

email address:..

Telephone...Fax...

Full name of nominated officer..

Professional Qualifications..

Description of organisation..

....

ADDITIONAL OFFICES (a supplementary fee willbe levied for each additionally listed address, see membership sunscription rates)

First additional address...

....

....

Telephone...Fax...

Contact...

e-mail address..

Second additional address..

....

....

e-mail address..

Telephone...Fax...

Contact...

Third additional address...

....

....

Telephone...Fax...

Contact...

e-mail address..

(please provide supplemenatary sheets if you have more than 3 additional offices)

Part 1: Company Information

Please give specific details of experience in the field of franchising, together with relevant dates and the names of **at least two referees** who are prepared to sponsor this application. Referees can be drawn fro the BFA Full Member Franchisors and BFA Affiliates (in the same professional discipline). A list of eligible sponsors is available from the BFA or via the website at www.british-franchise.org

APPLICANT	Company Name	Contact
SPONSOR		
1.	....	....
2.	....	....
1st Additional Office		
1.	....	....
2.	....	....
2nd Additional Office		
1.	....	....
2.	....	....
3rd Additional Office		
1.	....	....
2.	....	....

Franchising Experience

Please provide on separate sheets a brief history of your company's involvement with franchising and of the principles' of each office's involvement with franchising.

Please send this completed application form to the address shown below together with the following enclosures:

Company Literature (including short history)   [   ]

Latest published Annual Report (where available)   [   ]

DECLARATION

I hereby apply for Professional Affiliation to the British Franchise Association. I undertake to ensure the advice on franchising provided to clients is of a standard consistent with aims and objectives of the Code of Ethical Conduct of the British Franchise Association.

Signature*...

For and of behalf of...

Date...

*To be signed by the Nominated Officer making the application.

Part 1: Company Information

Information is requested from the BFA for the **four** following areas. Each details where the information will be displayed and used, and may require more information from you at a later stage.

1. **BFA Website**

   This is your public information. The contact details we use here are placed on our website and should be names, contact numbers, e-mail addresses etc. that you want to be contacted on by members of the public seeking information on your Franchise. Once you become a member, login details and passwords will be sent to you to enter the members' section of the website where you can edit your details personally.

   Company Name and Address..

   ....

   ....

   ....

   Contact Name..

   Phone number..fax number..

   e-mail address...

   website address (to be accredited before added as a link)...

2. **BFA Directory**

   This is your public information too. This information is placed in our directory of members and will be provided to potential franchisees and franchisors when they purchase a guide. Once you become members you will be asked for more information to add to the directory.

   Company Name and Address..

   ....

   ....

   ....

   Contact Name..

   Phone number..fax number..

   e-mail address...

   website address...

   Business Sector (please tick)

[ ] Bankers	[ ] Franchise Manual Publishers
[ ] Business Services	[ ] Media & Communications
[ ] Chartered Accountants	[ ] Recruitment Consultants
[ ] Development Agencies	[ ] Solicitors
[ ] Exhibition Organisers	[ ] Training Providers
[ ] Financial Services	[ ] Other(please specify)...................................
[ ] Franchise Consultants	

Part 1: Company Information

3. **BFA Internal Use**

This is your private information. The BFA uses this information for invitations to events, newsletters, official correspondance and contact by a member of the BFA Staff

Company Name and Address..

....

....

....

Contact Name...

Phone number..fax number..

e-mail address..

4. **BFA Financial**

This is used by the BFA Finance Manager for sending invoices, statements and any other related correspondence that would normally be directed to the accounts department.

Company Name......................................   ....

....

Invoice Name (if different from above)..

Accounts Address..

....

....

....

Accounts Phone Number..

Accounts Contact...

Preferred method of payment   Cheque/BACS/Direct Debit* (*please circle one*)

please note Direct Debit option applies to Full/Associate and Affiliate only. Provisionally listed members must complete one full year before qualifying for direct debit.

PLEASE NOTE, YOU SHOULD NOT INCLUDE A CHEQUE WITH THIS APPLICATION FORM

Provisional Listing

Provisional Listing, for all new Franchisors, will mean a commitment to work to achieve standards for Associate Membership within two to three years. You will also need to find one Professional Advisor, with acknowledged experience of franchising to stand as your Sponsor, together with a Bank Reference,

It is not necessary that your company be a client of your sponsors but the Association will require the Sponsors to confirm that your company is taking appropriate professional advice on the structure or funding and legal agreement for its franchise proposition and that to the best of their knowledge, the company intends to follow that advice.

IMPORTANT

PLEASE COMPLETE THE FOLLOWING

The following information must be provided with this form before this application can be considered. A list of the BFA's professional Affiliates is enclosed with this form. You should ensure that you have the agreement of the Affiliate concerned before nominating them as sponsors.

FIRST SPONSORING PROFESSIONAL ADVISOR

Firm...

Contact Name...

Address..

....

Email address..

Telephone number...

BANKERS REFERENCE

....Bank plc

Address..

....

....

Application

PLEASE COMPLETE IN FULL

1. Name of Applicant Company..

....

2. UK Company Registration Number...

3. Name of Franchise (if different from above)..

....

4. Name of Parent or Holding Company (if any)..

....

5. Parent/Holding Company Registration Number..

6. Proposed or existing method of franchising in the UK (please indicate how many if required)

   Master Licencee   [   ]   Joint Venture   [   ]

   Wholly Owned   [   ]   Subsidiary   [   ]

   Regional Master Licence   [   ]

7. Names of Registered Directors..

....

Designation	Name	Date of Appointment

8. Name of Designated representative (for purposes of correspondence).....................................

....

9. Address...

....

....

   Website..

   E-mail address..

10. Telephone Number...Fax Number..

11. Nature of Franchised Business...

Part 1: Company Information

Information is requested from the BFA for the **four** following areas. Each details where the information will be displayed and used, and may require more information from you at a later stage.

1. **BFA Website**

    This is your public information. The contact details we use here are placed on our website and should be names, contact numbers, e-mail addresses etc. that you want to be contacted on by members of the public seeking information on your Franchise. Once you become a member, login details and passwords will be sent to you to enter the members' section of the website where you can edit your details personally.

    Company Name and Address...

    ....

    ....

    ....

    Contact Name...

    Phone number...fax number..

    e-mail address...

    website address (to be accredited before added as a link)...

2. **BFA Directory**

    This is your public information too. This information is placed in our directory of members and will be provided to potential franchisees and franchisors when they purchase a guide. Once you become members you will be asked for more information to add to the directory.

    Company Name and Address...

    ....

    ....

    ....

    Contact Name...

    Phone number...fax number..

    e-mail address...

    website address...

    Business Sector (please tick)
[ ] Builidng & Maintenance	[ ] Estate Agency, Property
[ ] Cleaning & Renovation	[ ] Food, Catering & Hotels
[ ] Commercial, Business Services	[ ] Parcel, Courier Services
[ ] Direct Selling, Distribution	[ ] Printing, Copying, Signage
[ ] Domestic, Personal Caring Services	[ ] Retailing
[ ] Educational Services	[ ] Vehicle Service
[ ] Employment, Training	[ ] Other(please specify)..........................

    Type of Franchise (please tick)
    [   ] Investment   [   ] Mangement
    [   ] Retail   [   ] Single Operator/mangement   [   ] Single Operator/executive

Part 1: Company Information

3. **BFA Internal Use**

This is your private information. The BFA uses this information for invitations to events, newsletters, official correspondance and contact by a member of the BFA Staff

Company Name and Address...

....

....

....

Contact Name..

Phone number...fax number..

e-mail address...

4. **BFA Financial**

This is used by the BFA Finance Manager for sending invoices, statements and any other related correspondence that would normally be directed to the accounts department.

Company Name..

....

Invoice Name (if different from above)...

Accounts Address..

....

....

....

Accounts Phone Number...

Accounts Contact..

Preferred method of payment   Cheque/BACS/Direct Debit* (*please circle one*)

please note Direct Debit option applies to Full/Associate and Affiliate only. Provisionally listed members must complete one full year before qualifying for direct debit.

PLEASE NOTE, YOU SHOULD NOT INCLUDE A CHEQUE WITH THIS APPLICATION FORM

Declaration

I hereby apply for provisional Listing with the British Franchise Association. I have received and read the conditions which apply to Membership of the Association and in making this application agree that my company will use its best endeavours to meet these conditions.

I further agree that as and when my company engages in franchising activity, it will do so in accordance with the Association's Code of Conduct and in accordance with the Code of Advertising Practise published by the British Advertising Standards Agency.

I understand that I am not under any obligation to seek future Membership, and that the Association is under no obligation to accept any such future application. I also understand that, if I am accepted for Provisional Listing, that the listing may be withdrawn during its currency if the Association has reasonable cause to do so.

I confirm that the information provided in and with this application is a true representation of the facts and includes all information which might be reasonably regarded as pertinent to my acceptance by the British Franchise Association.

Signed..

For & on behalf of...

Position Held...

Date...

To be signed by the Chairman or Managing Director of the Company making the application.

Companies (particularly those not yet in franchising) are advised to seek pre-membership franchise agreement accreditation during the course of Provisional Listing. Please note that the assessment of your Franchise Agreement ordinarily takes up to three working weeks.

IMPORTANT

If the following information is available, please enclose it together with this completed Application Form. If the information is not available at the present time, please indicate when you will anticipate that it will be.

Franchise Agreement   [   ]

Current Audited Accounts   [   ]

(if not available, current management accounts signed by a Director together with a statement from the holding company/bank/company/auditor that there are sufficient funds to secure the franchise operation for at least the forthcoming year.)

Current Prospectus   [   ]

Financial Projections   [   ]

(Including any examples of any projection to be given to potential franchisees prior to signing an agreement)

Franchise Exhibitions

BRITISH FRANCHISE ASSOCIATION

FRANCHISE EXHIBITIONS 2004

APPLICATION TO EXHIBIT A BUSINESS FORMAT FRANCHISE BY AN ORGANISATION OR INDIVIDUAL WHO IS NOT A FULL, ASSOCIATE OR PROVISIONALLY LISTED MEMBER OF THE BRITISH FRANCHISE ASSOCIATION

BFA members are automatically eligible for entrance to BFA sponsored exhibitions as exhibitors. Enquiries about membership should be made to:

British Franchise Association
Thames View
Newtown Road
Henley-on-Thames
Oxon
RG9 1HG

Tel: 01491 578050 Fax: 01491 573517
Email: mailroom@british-franchise.org.uk

Please indicate to which exhibition this application form is applicable:

GMEX, Manchester,	30th & 31st January	[	]
Wembley, London	2nd & 3rd April	[	]
SECC, Glasgow	11th & 12th June	[	]
NEC, Birmingham	8th & 9th October	[	]

Important

Summary of Exhibition Accreditation Criteria

Established Franchises

Full or Associate membership of the BFA <u>or</u> a pilot franchised operation trading in the UK at arms length from the company's own outlet for at least a year with results in-line with the projections to be used with prospective franchisees. Established franchisors must also be using a franchise agreement in-line with the European Code of Ethics for franchising.

Major brand exclusive distributors are also eligible and should contact the organisers for details.

New Franchise

Provisional Listing with the BFA <u>or</u> businesses which have a UK operation and which are now seeking, or who will be seeking, their first pilot franchisee which can demonstrate adequate financing and arrangements for a franchise agreement in-line with the European Code of Ethics for franchising.

Overseas Master Licences

Overseas companies wishing to recruit a UK Master Licensee or joint venture partner with whom they will operate as a UK Master Licensee must be full voting members of a recognised overseas national franchise association or show that they have been operating successfully overseas for more than three years with at least ten franchised outlets. They must also demonstrate arrangements for the adoption of franchise agreements in-line with the European Code of Ethics for franchising.

NB. Overseas companies wishing to franchise directly into the UK must meet the UK requirements for either New Franchises or Established Franchises.

PLEASE RETURN THE FOLLOWING INFORMATION & DOCUMENTS WITH THIS APPLICATION FORM:

(The following information **MUST** be provided with this form before this application can be considered).

DOCUMENT REQUIREMENTS

(i)   <u>Franchise Agreement</u> or for "New Entrants" confirmation by a BFA Affiliated lawyer (or lawyer of equivalent standing) that the franchise agreement will be prepared or adapted to meet BFA criteria and confirmation from the applicant that they will adopt the agreement with the professional advice received.

(ii)   <u>Latest Audited Accounts</u> showing trading results of not less than 6 months before the date of application <u>or</u> similar management accounts signed by a Director or the company's accountants as a true representation of the company's affairs.

NB. Where the accounts as supplied show a negative net worth, significant trading losses, or a worth dependent on Director's valuation of intangible assets, the Association may seek Directors' guarantees or Auditor's opinion that the company has the financial resources/backing to support its trading and financial plans for the forthcoming year.

(iii)   <u>Franchise Prospectus</u> i.e, the brochure, explanatory literature, financial projections and other descriptive material provided or to be provided to prospective Franchisees prior to any binding undertakings.

(iv)   <u>A Completed Application Form</u> as follows, including the signed declarations contained therein, and including any additional material, information or documents as required in the application form.

Declaration & Application

PLEASE COMPLETE IN FULL

1. Name of Applicant Company..

....

2. UK Company Registration Number..

3. Brand name of Franchise (if different from above)..

....

4. Name of Parent or Holding Company...

....

5. Method of Franchising in the UK (i.e. what is the status of the UK Franchisor?)

   Master Licensee   [   ]   Joint Venture   [   ]

   Wholly Owned   {   }   Subsidiary   [   ]

6. Names of Registered Directors..

....

7. Name of designated representative (for purposes of correspondence)..

....

8. Address...

....

....

9. Telephone Number..Fax Number...

   email address..

10. Nature of Franchised Business..

....

....

....

11. Have you or any of your Directors been convicted of theft or fraud, or any other offence involving dishonesty or been declared bankrupt or been a Director of a company declared bankrupt or which went into liquidation, receivership or a voluntary arrangement?

   Yes   [   ]   No   [   ]

   (If YES please enclose separately details of any convictions or declaration and any Certificate of Discharge).

Declaration & Application cont.

12. Did your company first operate through company owned outlets?

    YES [   ]   No [   ]

13. If so from what date...

14. Have you operated a company owned outlet as an "arms length" pilot scheme for franchising?

    YES [   ]   NO [   ]

15. If so, from what date...

16. What date did you open the original franchised unit?...

17. Is this unit still in operation   YES [   ]   NO [   ]

18. If not how long did this unit operate?...

19. Number of franchised units operating in the UK at present...

20. Number of company owned units operating in the UK at present...

21. **A PROVEN FRANCHISING RECORD**

    Please provide the following details, in confidence, covering at least two full reporting years:

	Current Year (Months)	Last Year	Year Before
(a) Franchise Starts	....	....	....
(b) Franchise Failures (forced)	....	....	....
(c) Franchise Withdrawals (voluntary)	....	....	....
(d) Franchises Resales from (b)	....	....	....
(e) Franchise Resales from (c)	....	....	....
(f) Franchise disputes*	....	....	....

    *Only those disputes which have required intervention (through your solicitor, the franchisee's solicitor, or the Association's mediation or arbitration schemes should be recorded)
    Please continue on a separate page if necessary.

22. Number of franchised units overseas..

23. Number of years franchising overseas...

24. Length of franchise term...

25. Initial Franchise Fee..

26. Franchisees total investment (inc working capital)..

27. Management service (or royalty) charge..

Declaration & Application cont.

28. Advertising or Marketing Levy...

29. Any other continuing charges, (including mark up on goods/services supplied) please specify...................................

....

....

30. How many franchisees are you seeking to recruit in the next 12 months?...

31. Names and Addresses of Advisors:

Bankers:..

....

....

Accountants:..

....

....

Lawyers:..

....

....

Franchise Consultants:...

....

....

Declaration & Application cont.

I agree to the British Franchise Association seeking a Banker's reference on me/my business/the company.

In applying to exhibit at Franchise Exhibitions sponsored by the British Franchise Association, I agree to abide by the BFA Code of Ethics which accompanies this application form and declare that the franchise system offered is based on sound business principles, provides a viable and ethical business concept for the franchisee and a genuine end product for the consumer, and does not involve, nor permit the establishment of sub franchises. I agree to present to visitors to exhibitions information concerning only the franchise concept described herein and agree not to enter into any binding undertakings, nor cause any other person to enter into binding undertakings, nor take or cause any person to enter into any financial commitments nor take any deposits or any other financial considerations during the course of or on the premises of the Exhibition or Exhibitions for which this application for accreditation applies.

Signed..

For and on behalf of...

Position held...

Date..

To be signed by the Chairman, Managing Director, or owner/proprietor of the business making the application.

CODE OF PRACTICE FOR BFA SPONSORED VMG FRANCHISE EXHIBITIONS

1. Exhibitions offer a brief opportunity to meet a good quantity of prospective franchisees. Identifying quality prospects takes much longer and will ordinarily involved in-depth interview on your premises and theirs. No prospect should be asked, or even allowed, to sign any binding undertaking or to part with any money at the exhibition.

2. It is not acceptable to avoid the necessity for in-depth evaluation of a prospect and to avoid Rule 1 by taking prospects off-site to 'sign-up' or part with money within 48 hours of the exhibition's close.

3. Within the exhibition you should ensure that all your promotional messages, and your style of delivery can be reasonably described as legal, decent, honest and truthful.

4. Within the exhibition you should ensure that you and your staff, in your appearance, behaviour and language, uphold the standards of the exhibition and your business. Sobriety, cleanliness and decency are essential. Lasciviousness is not appropriate either co-incidentally or intentionally as part of a promotional stunt.

5. Courtesy both to visitors and other exhibitors - especially your competitors - is essential. Audio tracks and mechanical equipment should not be so loud as to make any one else's job difficult. Your sales activity should not encroach on any other exhibitor's space. Neither should you appear to adopt a part of the aisle as your territory. You must not station your staff near a competitor's to entice their visitors away.

Exhibitors who are seen by VMG or the BFA to have contravened any of these Rules, or are evidenced by others to have done so, will be given notice of their failure to uphold the standards of the exhibition and notice that any repetition will lead to the withdrawal of their exhibition accreditation.

BFA Code of Ethics

British Franchise Association

Code of ethical conduct

This *Code of Ethical Conduct* in franchising takes as its foundation the Code developed by the European Franchise Federation. In adopting the Code, the Federation recognized that national requirements may necessitate certain other clauses or provisions and delegated responsibility for the presentation and implementation of the Code in their own country to individual member National Franchise Associations.

The following *Extension and Interpretation* has been adopted by the British Franchise Association, and agreed by the European Franchise Federation, for the application of the *European Code of Ethics for Franchising* as presented herein by the British Franchise Association, within the United Kingdom of Great Britain and Northern Ireland.

Code of ethical conduct: extension and interpretation

This *Extension and Interpretation* forms an integral part of the *Code of Ethical Conduct* adopted by the British Franchise Association and to which its members adhere.

Application

1. This *Code of Ethical Conduct* forms part of the membership agreement between the British Franchise Association and its member companies. It does not form any part of the contractual agreement between franchisor and franchisee unless expressly stated to do so by the franchisor. Neither should anything in this Code be construed as limiting a Franchisor's right to sell or assign its interest in a franchised business.

Confidentiality

2. For the generality of this *Code of Ethical Conduct*, 'know-how' is taken as being as defined in the European Block exemption to Article 85 of the Treaty of Rome. However, for the purposes of Article 3.4 of the *European Code of Ethics* it is accepted that franchisors may impose non-competition and secrecy clauses to protect other information and systems where they may be reasonably regarded as material to the operation of the franchise.

Contract language

3. Article 5.2 of the *European Code of Ethics* reflects the requirement in certain European member states that franchise contracts be written in the language of that member state. The requirements of national and European law are pre-eminent but franchisors should seek to ensure that they offer to franchisees contracts in a language in which the franchises is competent.

Contract term

4. In suggesting in Article 5.4 of the *European Code of Ethics* that the minimum term for a franchise contract should be the period necessary to amortize a franchisee's initial investment it is recognized

    (a) that franchise contracts are ordinarily offered for a uniform term within a network;

    (b) that for a minority of the largest franchise opportunities amortizing the initial investment may not be a primary objective for the franchises. In such cases the objective should be to adopt a contract period which reasonably balances the interests of the parties to the contract.

    (c) that this section could be subject to national laws concerning the restraint of trade and may need to be met through renewal clauses.

Contract renewal

5. The basis for contract renewal should take into account the length of the original term, the extent to which the contract empowers the franchisor to require investments from the franchises for refurbishment or renovation, and the extent to which the franchisor may vary the terms of a contract on renewal. The overriding objective is to ensure that the franchises has the opportunity to recover his initial and subsequent investments and to exploit the franchised business for as long as the contract persists.

Adoption

6. This Code of Ethical Conduct comprising this *Extension and Interpretation* and the *European Code of Ethics* for Franchising was adopted by the British Franchise Association, replacing its previous *Code of Ethics* on 30th August 1990, subject to a transitional period for full compliance ending 31st December 1991. During the transitional period members of the Association are nonetheless required to comply at least with the *Code of Ethics* previously in force.

European Code of Ethics for Franchising

Preface

The European Franchise Federation, EFF, was constituted on 23rd September 1972.

Its members are national franchise associations or federations established in Europe.

The EFF also accepts affiliates, i.e. non European franchise associations or federations, and other professional persons, interested in or concerned with franchising. Affiliates have no voting rights and cannot be appointed officers of the EFF

The objects of the EFF are, among others, the ongoing unbiased and scientific study of franchising in every respect, the co-ordination of its members' actions, the promotion of the franchise industry in general and of its members' interests in particular.

The EFF also comprises a Legal Committee, composed of two lawyers from each national member association or federation and highly qualified in franchise matters.

The EFF has, furthermore, installed a Franchise Arbitration Committee which is at the disposal of parties preferring to submit their disputes to the latter's determination.

The evolution and the ever growing importance of franchising in the EC economy as well as the EC Block Exemption Regulation for franchise agreements, entered into force on 1st February 1989, prompted the EFF to revise its existing Code of Ethics.

This *Code of Ethics* is meant to be a practical ensemble of essential provisions of fair behaviour for franchise practitioners in Europe, but not to replace possibly related national or EC law.

This *Code of Ethics* is the end-product of work carried out by the European Franchise Federation and its member associations (Austria, Belgium, Denmark, Germany, France, Italy, the Netherlands, Portugal and the United Kingdom) in conjunction with the Commission of the European Community. It shall replace the previous *European Code of Ethics* as well as all national and regional Codes existing at that time in Europe.

By subscribing to the EFF, its members accept the *European Code of Ethics* and undertake not to delete or amend it in any way. It is, however, recognized that national requirements may necessitate certain other clauses or provisions and, providing these do not conflict with or detract from the Code and are attached to the Code in a separate document, permission to do this will not be withheld by the EFF.

By adhering to the EFF its members commit themselves to impose on their own members the obligation to respect and apply the provisions of this *Code of Ethics for Franchising*.

1. Definition of franchising

Franchising is a system of marketing goods and/or services and/or technology, which is based upon a close and ongoing collaboration between legally and financially separate and independent undertakings, the Franchisor and its Individual Franchisees, whereby the Franchisor grants its Individual Franchisees the right, and imposes the obligation, to conduct a business in accordance with the Franchisor's concept. The right entitles and compels the individual Franchisee, in. exchange for a direct or indirect financial consideration, to use the Franchisor's trade name, and/or trade mark and/or service mark, know-how(*), business and technical methods, procedural system, and other industrial and/or intellectual property rights, supported by continuing provision of commercial and technical assistance, within the framework and for the term of a written franchise agreement, concluded between parties for this purpose.

(*) 'Know-how' means a body of non patented practical information, resulting from experience and testing by the Franchisor, which is secret, substantial and identified;

'secret' means that the know-how, as a body or in the precise configuration and assembly of its components, is not generally known or easily accessible; it is not limited in the narrow sense that each individual component of the know-how should be totally unknown or unobtainable outside the Franchisor's business;

'substantial' means that the know-how includes information which is of importance for the sale of goods or the provision of services to end users, and in particular for the presentation of goods for sale, the processing of goods in connection with the provision of services, methods of dealing with customers, and administration and financial management; the know-how must be useful for the Franchisee by being capable, at the date of conclusion of the agreement, of improving the competitive position of the Franchisee, in particular by improving the Franchisee's performance or helping it to enter a new market.

'identified' means that the know-how must be described in a sufficiently comprehensive manner so as to make it possible to verify that it fulfils the criteria of secrecy and substantiality; the description of the know-how can either be set out in the franchise agreement or in a separate document or recorded in any other appropriate form.

2. **Guiding principles**

2.1 The Franchisor is the initiator of a franchise network, composed of itself and its Individual Franchisees, of which the Franchisor is the long-term guardian.

2.2 **The obligations of the Franchisor:**

The Franchisor shall:

- have operated a business concept with success, for a reasonable time and in at least one pilot unit before starting its franchise network;

- be the owner, or have legal rights to the use, of its network's trade name, trade mark or other distinguishing identification;

- shall provide the Individual Franchisee with initial training and continuing commercial and/or technical assistance during the entire life of the agreement.

2.3 **The obligations of the Individual Franchisee:**

The Individual Franchisee shall

- devote its best endeavours to the growth of the franchise business and to the maintenance of the common identity and reputation of the franchise network;

- supply the Franchisor with verifiable operating data to facilitate the determination of performance and the financial statements necessary for effective management guidance, and allow the Franchisor, and/or its agents, to have access to the individual Franchisee's premises and records at the Franchisor's request and at reasonable times;

- not disclose to third parties the know-how provided by the franchisor, neither during nor after termination of the agreement;

2.4 **The ongoing obligations of both parties:**

Parties shall exercise fairness in their dealings with each other. The Franchisor shall give written notice to its Individual Franchisees of any contractual breach and, where appropriate, grant reasonable time to remedy default;

Parties should resolve complaints, grievances and disputes with good faith and goodwill through fair and reasonable direct communication and negotiation;

3. **Recruitment, advertising and disclosure**

3.1 Advertising for the recruitment of Individual Franchisees shall be free of ambiguity and misleading statements;

3.2 Any recruitment, advertising and publicity material, containing direct or indirect references to future possible results, figures or earnings to be expected by Individual Franchisees, should be objective and capable of verification;

3.3 In order to allow prospective Individual Franchisees to enter into any binding document with full knowledge, they shall be given a copy of the present Code of Ethics as well as full and accurate written disclosure of all information material to the franchise relationship, within a reasonable time prior to the execution of these binding documents;

3.4 If a Franchisor imposes a Pre-contract on a candidate Individual Franchisee, the following principles should be respected:

- prior to the signing of any pre-contract, the candidate Individual Franchisee should be given written information on its purpose and on any consideration he may be required to pay to the Franchisor to cover the latter's actual expenses, incurred during and with respect to the pre-contract phase; if the Franchise agreement is executed, the said consideration should be reimbursed by the Franchisor or set off against a possible entry fee to be paid by the Individual Franchisee;

- the Pre-contract shall define its term and include a termination clause;

- the Franchisor can impose non-competition and/or secrecy clauses to protect its know-how and identity.

4. Selection of individual franchisees

A Franchisor should select and accept as Individual Franchisees only those who, upon reasonable investigation, appear possess the basic skills, education, personal qualities and financial resources sufficient to carry on the franchised business.

5. The franchise agreement

5.1 the Franchise agreement should comply with the National law, European community law and this *Code of Ethics.*

5.2 The agreement shall reflect the interests of the members of the franchised network in protecting the Franchisor's industrial and intellectual property rights and in maintaining the common identity and reputation of the franchised network. All agreements and all contractual arrangements in connection with the franchise relationship should be written in or translated by a sworn translator into the official language of the country the Individual Franchisee is established in, and signed agreements shall be given immediately to the Individual Franchisee.

5.3 The Franchise agreement shall set forth without ambiguity, the respective obligations and responsibilities of the parties and all other material terms of the relationship.

5.4 The essential minimum terms of the agreement shall be the following:

- the rights granted to the Franchisor;
- the rights granted to the Individual Franchisee;
- the goods and/or services to be provided to the Individual Franchisee;
- the obligations of the Franchisor;
- the obligations of the Individual Franchisee;
- the terms of payment by the Individual Franchisee;
- the duration of the agreement which should be long enough to allow Individual Franchisees to amortize their initial franchise investments;
- the basis for any renewal of the agreement;
- the terms upon which the Individual Franchisee may sell or transfer the franchises business and the Franchisor's possible pre-emption rights in this respect;
- provisions relevant to the use by the Individual Franchisee of the Franchisor's distinctive signs, trade name, trade mark, service mark, store sign, logo or other distinguishing identification;
- the Franchisor's right to adapt the franchise system to new or changed methods;
- provisions for termination of the agreement;
- provisions for surrendering promptly upon termination of the franchise agreement any tangible and intangible property belonging to the Franchisor or other owner thereof.

6. The Code of Ethics and the Master-Franchise system

This *Code of Ethics* shall apply to the relationship between the Franchisor and its Individual Franchisees and equally between the Master Franchisee and its Individual Franchisees. It shall not apply to the relationship between the Franchisor and its Master-Franchisees.

'A forum for franchisees'

The Franchisee Forum is a direct mail scheme to involve and represent the franchisees of British Franchise Association franchisor members, and the business interest of those franchisees, on a national scale. This British Franchise Association 'team approach' to involving and representing franchisees across the wide variety of their businesses, hallmarks franchise credibility, offers franchisees a direct input to franchising regulation as well as access to unique offers and special initiatives, and gives substantial re-enforcement to the British Franchise Association's role as the guardian of good franchising practice.

What benefits will franchising get from the Forum?

Improved representation: The British Franchise Association's voice will be considerably strengthened as full spectrum franchising involvement will enable greater authority and influence with government in the UK and in Europe.

Increased business opportunity: The British Franchise Association and the Franchisee Forum's combined promotional ability will enhance the public profile and perception of franchising, and continue to ensure that franchising attracts people and business of the highest calibre.

What benefits will franchisees get from their Forum?

Real industry input: Franchisees will be taking part in consultative research on topics of general interest in franchising – in particular the standards of good practice the British Franchise Association represents. Franchisees general views will be monitored and interpreted by the Forum's Independent Custodians to provide input to the Association on standards and procedures within the Franchise industry.

Improved business value: By enhancing the reputation of franchising and its visible success to the general public, the Forum will increase the value of all franchised units – currently 26,000 in the UK. Customers will be increasingly aware of the benefits of buying from franchisees – independent businesses which are small enough to care, but with the backing of their franchisor, big enough to cope.

Professional recognition: A Certificate of Participation for franchisees to display on their premises, day one involvement in the British Franchise Association's plans for the national professional recognition of franchising as a separate and distinguished management skill and involvement with Franchisee training and performance awards to further the recognition of the achievements of franchising.

A franchise re-sales register: To be operated solely for Forum participants reaching the stage of wanting to see their businesses and cash in on the capital value they have built up. The re-sales register will be operated through a Franchisee Forum website.

Schemes to keep franchisees on the competitive edge: A regular newsletter with updates on the franchising sector and examples of industry good practice, and special purchasing schemes which may include a Green Flag automobile insurance discount, access to a low APR credit care, and automatic cover against the cost of Inland Revenue investigations under the new self-assessment tax scheme, amongst others.

What is the history?

A Franchise Involvement Group was constituted by the British Franchise Association in 1995 to look at the potential for the inclusion of franchisees in the British Franchise Association's work as the self regulatory body for the franchise sector. It was felt that the success and capacity of any new body would be maximised, and its proper focus maintained, if it was linked with the expertise and resources of the BFA. The decisions and recommendations of the Franchisee Involvement Group were considered by a consultative meeting of British Franchise Association Members in December 1995. The Association's Policy Board subsequently agreed in the Autumn 1996 to provide pump-priming funds of up to £40,000 linked to a set of success criteria setting targets for the number of franchisees recruited to the Forum and the spread of networks represented.

Who runs the Forum?

The Forum functions as a separate arm of the British Franchise Association from its offices in Henley-on-Thames under the supervision of the BFA's Policy Board and Director General and managed on a day to day basis by a full-time Forum Manager. The objectivity and independence of consultative work with franchisee participants is guaranteed by the Forum's three external Custodians who also bring additional steering and vision to all of the Forum's activities. The current Custodians are independent franchising professionals with considerable standing and business experience – Professor David Kirby, Dean of Middlesex University Business School who is Chairman, Martin Mendelsohn, Head of National Franchising Group of Eversheds solicitors and Mark Hatcliffe, Head of Franchising with Lloyds Bank.

Who is eligible for membership?

All Franchisees who are signatory to a current franchise agreement with a BFA Member franchisor. The member will normally be the person named in the agreement, or in the case of franchises run as a company, their nominated representative.

How much will the Membership cost?

The yearly membership fee will be around £32 plus VAT per member. The cost will be set by the British Franchise Association with a view to the Forum being self-funding in the long run. All Forum income will be dedicated to pursing the objectives of the Forum. The British Franchise Association, which is a non profit making organization, is providing the initial funding.

EU Block Exemption Regulation

Commission Regulation (EC) No. 2790/1999

of 22 December 1999

on the application of Article 81(3) of the Treaty to categories of vertical agreements and concerted practices

(Text with EEA relevance)

THE COMMISSION OF THE EUROPEAN COMMUNITIES,

Having regard to the Treaty establishing the European Community,

Having regard to Council Regulation No 19/65/EEC of 2 March 1965 on the application of Article 85(3) of the Treaty to certain categories of agreements and concerted practices,[1] as last amended by Regulation (EC) No 121511999,[2] and in particular Article 1 thereof,

Having published a draft of this Regulation,[3]

Having consulted the Advisory Committee on Restrictive Practices and Dominant Positions,

Whereas:

(1) Regulation No 19/65/EEC empowers the Commission to apply Article 81(3) of the Treaty (formerly Article 85(3)) by regulation to certain categories of vertical agreements and corresponding concerted practices falling within Article 81(1).

(2) Experience acquired to date makes it possible to define a category of vertical agreements which can be regarded as normally satisfying the conditions laid down in Article 81(3).

(3) This category includes vertical agreements for the purchase or sale of goods or services where these agreements are concluded between non-competing undertakings, between certain competitors or by certain associations of retailers of goods; it also includes vertical agreements containing ancillary provisions on the assignment or use of intellectual property rights; for the purposes of this Regulation, the term 'vertical agreements' includes the corresponding concerted practices.

(4) For the application of Article 81(3) by regulation, it is not necessary to

define those vertical agreements which are capable of falling within Article 81(1); in the individual assessment of agreements under Article 81(1), account has to be taken of several factors, and in particular the market structure on the supply and purchase side.

(5) The benefit of the block exemption should be limited to vertical agreements for which it can be assumed with sufficient certainty that they satisfy the conditions of Article 81(3).

(6) Vertical agreements of the category defined in this Regulation can improve economic efficiency within a chain of production or distribution by facilitating better coordination between the participating under-takings; in particular, they can lead to a reduction in the transaction and distribution costs of the parties and to an optimisation of their sales and investment levels.

(7) The likelihood that such efficiency-enhancing effects will outweigh any anticompetitive effects due to restrictions contained in vertical agreements depends on the degree of market power of the undertakings concerned and, therefore, on the extent to which those undertakings face competition from other suppliers of goods or services regarded by the buyer as interchangeable or substitutable for one another, by reason of the products' characteristics, their prices and their intended use.

(8) It can be presumed that, where the share of the relevant market accounted for by the supplier does not exceed 30%, vertical agreements which do not contain certain types of severely anticompetitive restraints generally lead to an improvement in production or distribution and allow consumers a fair share of the resulting benefits; in the case of vertical agreements containing exclusive supply obligations, it is the market share of the buyer which is relevant in determining the overall effects of such vertical agreements on the market.

(9) Above the market share threshold of 30%, there can be no presumption that vertical agreements falling within the scope of Article 81(1) will usually give rise to objective advantages of such a character and size as to compensate for the disadvantages which they create for competition.

(10) This Regulation should not exempt vertical agreements containing restrictions which are not indispensable to the attainment of the positive effects mentioned above; in particular, vertical agreements containing certain types of severely anticompetitive restraints such as minimum and fixed resale-prices, as well as certain types of territorial protection, should be excluded from the benefit of the block exemption established by this Regulation irrespective of the market share of the undertakings concerned.

(11) In order to ensure access to or to prevent collusion on the relevant market, certain conditions are to be attached to the block exemption; to this end, the exemption of non-compete obligations should be limited to obligations which do not exceed a definite duration; for the same reasons, any direct or indirect obligation causing the members of a selective distribution system not to sell the brands of particular competing suppliers should be excluded from the benefit of this Regulation.

(12) The market-share limitation, the non-exemption of certain vertical agreements and the conditions provided for in this Regulation normally ensure that the agreements to which the block exemption applies do not enable the participating undertakings to eliminate competition in respect of a substantial part of the products in question.

(13) In particular cases in which the agreements falling under this Regulation nevertheless have effects incompatible with Article 81(3), the Commission may withdraw the benefit of the block exemption; this may occur in particular where the buyer has significant market power in the relevant market in which it resells the goods or provides the services or where parallel networks of vertical agreements have similar effects which significantly restrict access to a relevant market or competition therein; such cumulative effects may for example arise in the case of selective distribution or non-compete obligations.

(14) Regulation No 19/65/EEC empowers the competent authorities of Member States to withdraw the benefit of the block exemption in respect of vertical agreements having effects incompatible with the conditions laid down in Article 81(3), where such effects are felt in their respective territory, or in a part thereof, and where such territory has the characteristics of a distinct geographic market; Member States should ensure that the exercise of this power of withdrawal does not prejudice the uniform application throughout the common market of the Community competition rules or the full effect of the measures adopted in implementation of those rules.

(15) In order to strengthen supervision of parallel networks of vertical agreements which have similar restrictive effects and which cover more than 50% of a given market, the Commission may declare this Regulation inapplicable to vertical agreements containing specific restraints relating to the market concerned, thereby restoring the full application of Article 81 to such agreements.

(16) This Regulation is without prejudice to the application of Article 82.

(17) In accordance with the principle of the primacy of Community law, no measure taken pursuant to national laws on competition should prejudice the uniform application throughout the common market of the Community competition rules or the full effect of any measures adopted in implementation of those rules, including this Regulation.

HAS ADOPTED THIS REGULATION:

Article 1

For the purposes of this Regulation:

   (a) 'competing undertakings' means actual or potential suppliers in the same product market; the product market includes goods or services which are regarded by the buyer as interchangeable with or substitutable for the contract goods or services, by reason of the products' characteristics, their prices and their intended use;

(b) 'non-compete obligation' means any direct or indirect obligation causing the buyer not to manufacture, purchase, sell or resell goods or services which compete with the contract goods or services, or any direct or indirect obligation on the buyer to purchase from the supplier or from another undertaking designated by the supplier more than 80% of the buyer's total purchases of the contract goods or services and their substitutes on the relevant market, calculated on the basis of the value of its purchases in the preceding calendar year;

(c) 'exclusive supply obligation' means any direct or indirect obligation causing the supplier to sell the goods or services specified in the agreement only to one buyer inside the Community for the purposes of a specific use or for resale;

(d) 'Selective distribution system' means a distribution system where the supplier undertakes to sell the contract goods or services, either directly or indirectly, only to distributors selected on the basis of specified criteria and where these distributors undertake not to sell such goods or services to unauthorised distributors;

(e) 'intellectual property rights' includes industrial property rights, copyright and neighbouring rights;

(f) 'know-how' means a package of non-patented practical information, resulting from experience and testing by the supplier, which is secret, substantial and identified: in this context, 'secret' means that the know-how, as a body or in the precise configuration and assembly of its components, is not generally known or easily accessible; 'substantial' means that the know-how includes information which is indispensable to the buyer for the use, sale or resale of the contract goods or services; 'identified' means that the know-how must be described in a sufficiently comprehensive manner so as to make it possible to verify that it fulfils the criteria of secrecy and substantiality;

(g) 'buyer' includes an undertaking which, under an agreement falling within Article 81(1) of the Treaty, sells goods or services on behalf of another undertaking.

Article 2

1. Pursuant to Article 81(3) of the Treaty and subject to the provisions of this Regulation, it is hereby declared that Article 81(1) shall not apply to agreements or concerted practices entered into between two or more undertakings each of which operates, for the purposes of the agreement, at a different level of the production or distribution chain, and relating to the conditions under which the. parties may purchase, sell or resell certain goods or services ('vertical agreements').

This exemption shall apply to the extent that such agreements contain restrictions of competition falling within the scope of Article 81(1) ('vertical restraints').

2. The exemption provided for in paragraph 1 shall apply to vertical agreements entered into between an association of undertakings and its members, or between such an association and its suppliers, only if all its members are retailers of goods and if no individual member of the association, together with its connected undertakings, has a total annual turnover exceeding EUR 50 million; vertical agreements entered into by such associations shall be covered by this Regulation without prejudice to the application of Article 81 to horizontal agreements concluded between the members of the association or decisions adopted by the association.

3. The exemption provided for in paragraph 1 shall apply to vertical agreements containing provisions which relate to the assignment to the buyer or use by the buyer of intellectual property rights, provided that those provisions do not constitute the primary object of such agreements and are directly related to the use, sale or resale of goods or services by the buyer or its customers. The exemption applies on condition that, in relation to the contract goods or services, those provisions do not contain restrictions of competition having the same object or effect as vertical restraints which are not exempted under this Regulation.

4. The exemption provided for in paragraph 1 shall not apply to vertical agreements entered into between competing undertakings; however, it shall apply where competing undertakings enter into a non-reciprocal vertical agreement and:

    (a) the buyer has a total annual turnover not exceeding EUR 100 million, or

    (b) the supplier is a manufacturer and a distributor of goods, while the buyer is a distributor not manufacturing goods competing with the contract goods, or

    (c) the supplier is a provider of services at several levels of trade, while the buyer does not provide competing services at the level of trade where it purchases the contract services.

5. This Regulation shall not apply to vertical agreements the subject matter of which falls within the scope of any other block exemption regulation.

Article 3

1. Subject to paragraph 2 of this Article, the exemption provided for in Article 2 shall apply on condition that the market share held by the supplier does not exceed 30% of the relevant market on which it sells the contract goods or services.

2. In the case of vertical agreements containing exclusive supply obligations, the exemption provided for in Article 2 shall apply on condition that the market share held by the buyer does not exceed 30% of the relevant market on which it purchases the contract goods or services.

(c)

Article 4

The exemption provided for in Article 2 shall not apply to vertical agreements which, directly or indirectly, in isolation or in combination with other factors under the control of the parties, have as their object:

(a) the restriction of the buyer's ability to determine its sale price, without prejudice to the possibility of the supplier's imposing a maximum sale price or recommending a sale price, provided that they do not amount to a fixed or minimum sale price as a result of pressure from, or incentives offered by, any of the parties;

(b) the restriction of the territory into which, or of the customers to whom, the buyer may sell the contract goods or services, except:

- the restriction of active sales into the exclusive territory or to an exclusive customer group reserved to the supplier or allocated by the supplier to another buyer, where such a restriction does not limit sales by the customers of the buyer,
- the restriction of sales to end users by a buyer operating at the wholesale level of trade,
- the restriction of sales to unauthorised distributors by the members of a selective distribution system, and
- the restriction of the buyer's ability to sell components, supplied for the purposes of incorporation, to customers who would use them to manufacture the same type of goods as those produced by the supplier;

(c) the restriction of active or passive sales to end users by members of a selective distribution system operating at the retail level of trade, without prejudice to the possibility of prohibiting a member of the system from operating out of an unauthorised place of establishment;

(d) the restriction of cross-supplies between distributors within a selective distribution system, including between distributors operating at different level of trade;

(e) the restriction agreed between a supplier of components and a buyer who incorporates those components, which limits the supplier to selling the components as spare parts to end-users or to repairers or other service providers not entrusted by the buyer with the repair or servicing of its goods.

Article 5

The exemption provided for in Article 2 shall not apply to any of the following obligations contained in vertical agreements:

(a) any direct or indirect non-compete obligation, the duration of which is indefinite or exceeds five years. A non-compete obligation which is tacitly renewable beyond a period of five years is to be deemed to have been concluded for an indefinite duration. However, the time limitation of five years shall not apply where the contract goods or services are sold by the buyer from premises and land owned by the supplier or leased by the supplier from third parties not connected with the buyer, provided that the duration of the non-compete obligation does not exceed the period of occupancy of the premises and land by the buyer;

(b) any direct or indirect obligation causing the buyer, after termination of the agreement, not to manufacture, purchase, sell or resell goods or services, unless such obligation:

- relates to goods or services which compete with the contract goods or services, and

- is limited to the premises and land from which the buyer has operated during the contract period, and

- is indispensable to protect know-how transferred by the supplier to the buyer,

and provided that the duration of such non-compete obligation is limited to a period of one year after termination of the agreement; this obligation is without prejudice to the, possibility of imposing a restriction which is unlimited in time on the use and disclosure of know-how which has not entered the public domain;

(c) any direct or indirect obligation causing the members of a selective distribution system not to sell the brands of particular competing suppliers.

Article 6

The Commission may withdraw the benefit of this Regulation, pursuant to Article 7(1) of Regulation No 19/65/EEC, where it finds in any particular case that vertical agreements to which this Regulation applies nevertheless have effects which are incompatible with the conditions laid down in Article 81(3) of the Treaty, and in particular where access to the relevant market or competition therein is significantly restricted by the cumulative effect of parallel networks of similar vertical restraints implemented by competing suppliers or buyers.

Article 7

Where in any particular case vertical agreements to which the exemption provided for in Article 2 applies have effects incompatible with the conditions laid down in Article 81(3) of the Treaty in the territory of a Member State, or in a part thereof, which has all the characteristics of a distinct geographic market, the competent authority of that Member State may withdraw the benefit of application of this Regulation in respect of that territory, under the same conditions as provided in Article 6.

Article 8

1. Pursuant to Article 1 a of Regulation No 19/65/EEC, the Commission may by regulation declare that, where parallel networks of similar vertical restraints cover more than 50% of a relevant market, this Regulation shall not apply to vertical agreements containing specific restraints relating to that market.

2. A regulation pursuant to paragraph 1 shall not become applicable earlier than six months following its adoption.

Article 9

1. The market share of 30% provided for in Article 3(1) shall be calculated on the basis of the market sales value of the contract goods or services and other goods or services sold by the supplier, which are regarded as interchangeable or substitutable by the buyer, by reason of the products' characteristics, their prices and their intended use; if market sales value data are not available, estimates based on other reliable market information, including market sales volumes, may be used to establish the market share of the undertaking concerned. For the purposes of Article 3(2), it is either the market purchase value or estimates thereof which shall be used to calculate the market share.

2. For the purposes of applying the market share threshold provided for in Article 3 the following rules shall apply:

   (a) the market share shall be calculated on the basis of data relating to the preceding calendar year;

   (b) the market share shall include any goods or services supplied to integrated distributors for the purposes of sale;

   (c) if the market share is initially not more than 30% but subsequently rises above that level without exceeding 35%, the exemption provided for in Article 2 shall continue to apply for a period of two consecutive calendar years following the year in which the 30% market share threshold was first exceeded;

   (d) if the market share is initially not more than 30% but subsequently rises above 35%, the exemption provided for in Article 2 shall continue to apply for one calendar year following the year in which the level of 35% was first exceeded;

   (e) the benefit of points (c) and (d) may not be combined so as to exceed a period of two calendar years.

Article 10

1. For the purpose of calculating total annual turnover within the meaning of Article 2(2) and (4), the turnover achieved during the previous financial year by the relevant party to the vertical agreement and the turnover achieved by its connected undertakings in respect of all goods and services, excluding all taxes and other duties, shall be added

together. For this purpose, no account shall be taken of dealings between the party to the vertical agreement and its connected undertakings or between its connected undertakings.

2. The exemption provided for in Article 2 shall remain applicable where, for any period of two consecutive financial years, the total annual turnover threshold is exceeded by no more than 10%.

Article 11

1. For the purposes of this Regulation, the terms 'undertaking' , 'supplier' and 'buyer' shall include their respective connected undertakings.

2. 'Connected undertakings' are:

(a) undertakings in which a party to the agreement, directly or indirectly:

- has the power to exercise more than half the voting rights, or
- has the power to appoint more than half the members of the supervisory board, board of management or bodies legally representing the undertaking, or
- has the right to manage the undertaking's affairs;

(b) undertakings which directly or indirectly have, over a party to the agreement, the rights or powers listed in (a);

(c) undertakings in which an undertaking referred to in (b) has, directly or indirectly, the rights or powers listed in (a);

(d) undertakings in which a party to the agreement together with one or more of the undertakings referred to in (a), (b) or (c), or in which two or more of the latter undertakings, jointly have the rights or powers listed in (a);

(e) undertakings in which the rights or the powers listed in (a) are jointly held by:

- parties to the agreement or their respective connected undertakings referred to in (a) to (d), or
- one or more of the parties to the agreement or one or more of their connected undertakings referred to in (a) to (d) and one or more third parties.

3. For the purposes of Article 3, the market share held by the undertakings referred to in paragraph 2(e) of this Article shall be apportioned equally to each undertaking having the rights or the powers listed in paragraph 2(a).

Article 12

l. The exemptions provided for in Commission Regulations (EEC) No 1983/83,[4] (EEC) No 1984/83[5] and (EEC) No 4087/88[6] shall continue to apply until 31 May 2000.

2. The prohibition laid down in Article 81(1) of the EC Treaty shall not apply during the period from 1 June 2000 to 31 December 2001 in respect of agreements already in force on 31 May 2000 which do not satisfy the conditions for exemption provided for in this Regulation but which satisfy the conditions for exemption provided for in Regulations (EEC) No 1983/83, (EEC) No 1984/83 or (EEC) No 4087/88.

Article 13

This Regulation shall enter into force on 1 January 2000.

It shall apply from 1 June 2000, except for Article 12(1) which shall apply from 1 January 2000.

This Regulation shall expire on 31 May 2010.

This Regulation shall be binding in its entirety and directly applicable in all Member States.

Done at Brussels, 22 December 1999. For the Commission

Mario MONTI
Member of the Commission

Notes

1. OJ 36, 6 March 1965, p. 533/65.
2. OJ L 148, 15 June 1999, p. 1.
3. OJ C 270, 24 September 1999, p. 7.
4. OJ L 173, 30 June 1983, p. 1.
5. OJ L 173, 30 June 1983, p. 5.
6. OJ L 359, 28 December 1988, p. 46.

Index

An 'f' or 't' after a page number indicates inclusion of a figure or table respectively.